THE GULAG AFTER STALIN

THE GULAG AFTER STALIN

Redefining Punishment in Khrushchev's Soviet Union, 1953–1964

Jeffrey S. Hardy

CORNELL UNIVERSITY PRESS **ITHACA AND LONDON**

First published 2016 by Cornell University Press

Printed in the United States of America

Library of Congress Cataloging-in-Publication Data

Names: Hardy, Jeffrey S., 1978– author.
Title: The gulag after Stalin : redefining punishment in Khrushchev's Soviet Union, 1953–1964 / Jeffrey S. Hardy.
Description: Ithaca ; London : Cornell University Press, 2016. | Includes bibliographical references and index.
Identifiers: LCCN 2016013226 | ISBN 9781501702792 (cloth : alk. paper)
Subjects: LCSH: Prisons—Soviet Union—History. | Concentration camps—Soviet Union—History. | Soviet Union—Politics and government—1953–1964. | Khrushchev, Nikita Sergeevich, 1894–1971.
Classification: LCC HV8964.S65 H37 2016 | DDC 365/.4709045—dc23
LC record available at http://lccn.loc.gov/2016013226

Cornell University Press strives to use environmentally responsible suppliers and materials to the fullest extent possible in the publishing of its books. Such materials include vegetable-based, low-VOC inks and acid-free papers that are recycled, totally chlorine-free, or partly composed of nonwood fibers. For further information, visit our website at www.cornellpress.cornell.edu.

Cloth printing   10 9 8 7 6 5 4 3 2 1

Contents

Acknowledgments

This book is the culmination of many years of research and writing. My interest in studying the Soviet Gulag first developed while reading the works of Aleksandr Solzhenitsyn during high school and then living in Magadan, the "capital of the Gulag," for several months as an LDS missionary. My study of the post-Stalin Gulag then took shape while pursuing graduate degrees at Brigham Young University (BYU) and Princeton University, presenting my findings at numerous conferences, and engaging with a broad support group of mentors and colleagues. As anyone who has written a research-intensive book knows, it has been at various times exciting, challenging, stressful, humbling, and ultimately rewarding. Along the way I have incurred many debts of gratitude that I would like to now express.

The first who must be mentioned is Rodney Bohac, my adviser at BYU, who steered me in the direction of the Khrushchev era and provided fantastic advice for a budding historian. Stephen Kotkin at Princeton then guided me through my most formative years as a scholar and was in every way a remarkable adviser. My knowledge of Soviet history I owe primarily to him, and his provoking and insightful comments on my work have improved it immensely. Michael Gordin, Jan Gross, and Ekaterina Pravilova likewise were superb mentors who challenged, supported, and inspired me.

I have been fortunate over the years to converse and collaborate with scholars who specialize on the Gulag or related fields. Steven Barnes has been a mentor and friend throughout this process. Marc Elie, Alan Barenberg, Wilson Bell, Padraic Kenney, and Simon Ertz were always generous with their advice and companionship. I also benefitted immensely from my interactions with Stephen Cohen, Dan Healey, Cynthia Hooper, Jan Behrends, Peter Solomon, Stephen Norris, Maria Galmarini, Mark Vincent, Judith Pallot, Richard Wetzell, Kent Schull, Stephen Toth, Paul Garfinkel, and Volker Janssen. Other debts of gratitude for their friendship and intellectual stimulation are due to Michael Paulauskas, Emily Baran, Gleb Tsipursky, Eren Tasar, Lo Faber, Piotr Kosicki, Mayhill Fowler, Anne O'Donnell, Elidor Mehili, Pey-yi Chu, Kyrill Kunakhovich, Jeremy Friedman, Sue Naquin, Mark Beissinger, Deborah Kaple, Serguei Oushakine, Charles Townsend, Vanessa Barker, and Joy Kim. I would finally like to thank the staff at the various archives where I conducted my research. With very few exceptions they were professional, courteous, and helpful in providing access to the needed documents.

Special mention is due to Miami University's Havighurst Center, the Social Science Research Council, the George Washington University Cold War Group, and the University of Texas for providing conference-related funding that contributed to the formulation of this book. Generous funding for archival research has come from several institutions to which proper acknowledgment is due: the Fulbright-Hays Program of the United States Department of Education, the International Research and Exchanges Board, the Princeton Institute for International and Regional Studies, the Fellowship of Woodrow Wilson Scholars at Princeton University, and BYU Graduate Studies. I would also like to acknowledge Stephen Cohen and Katrina vanden Heuvel for their generous funding of the Robert C. Tucker/Stephen F. Cohen Dissertation Prize. Finally, much of chapter 4 and part of chapter 5 were previously published as "'The Camp Is Not a Resort': The Campaign against Privileges in the Soviet Gulag, 1957–61," *Kritika: Explorations in Russian and Eurasian History* 13, no. 1 (Winter 2012): 89–122. I am grateful to *Kritika* for granting permission to reproduce that work here.

The greatest debt of gratitude that I have incurred over the years is the one owed to my sweet wife, Pamela. She has endured the challenges of being an academic's spouse with admirable grace, all while raising our three beautiful children. Thank you for the joy and meaning you have brought to my life. This book is for you.

THE GULAG AFTER
STALIN

A GULAG WITHOUT STALIN

Soviet prison is one of countless manifestations of tyranny, one of the forms of total, all-embracing violence. But there is beauty even in prison life. And if you only use dark colors you won't get it right.

—Sergei Dovlatov, *The Zone*

In September 1962, nine years after the death of Joseph Vissarionovich Stalin, Aleksei Grigorevich Murzhenko was convicted of anti-Soviet agitation and propaganda for participating in a "neo-Marxist" student group. Although such a charge in the 1930s and 1940s often resulted in a decade or more behind barbed wire, Murzhenko only received a sentence of six years' imprisonment on "strict regimen." Sent to the Dubravnyi Corrective-Labor Camp (Dubravlag) in the Mordovian Autonomous Soviet Socialist Republic, his appreciation for what incarceration during the reign of Nikita Sergeevich Khrushchev meant began even on the train ride there. He encountered what appeared to be happy prisoners, with one female inmate passing him a little love note by way of a guard. He shared a large food package sent from his mother with his cellmate. And even though his new friend informed him that the golden age for prisoners of the mid-to-late 1950s was over, Murzhenko found conditions at Dubravlag more than bearable. The notorious thieves-in-law criminal gang had been eliminated; no one died of hunger, cold, or disease anymore; the workday was only eight hours; and the mostly young political prisoners exchanged their heterodox worldviews with remarkable freedom. As he concluded from his own experience and from conversations with fellow prisoners, "life generally [in the camps] was not the same as under the Mustache [a pejorative term for Stalin]."[1]

Such a proclamation stands in stark contrast to Anatoly Tikhonovich Marchenko's famous assertion in his 1969 memoir *My Testimony* that "today's Soviet camps for political prisoners are just as horrific as in Stalin's time."[2] Similar to Marchenko, Aleksandr Isaevich Solzhenitsyn declared in his landmark *Gulag*

Archipelago, "Rulers Change, the Archipelago Remains."[3] Yet Murzhenko's positive characterization of camp life under Khrushchev is far from unique; in fact, the idea of a dramatic transformation of the Soviet penal system—commonly referred to by its 1930s-era acronym, Gulag (short for Main Administration of Corrective-Labor Camps and Colonies)—is supported by other memoirs, and by many of the details in Marchenko's and Solzhenitsyn's own reminiscences. Whereas most memoirists from the Stalin-era Gulag dwell overwhelmingly on the physical and psychological destruction of the inmates, those of the Khrushchev era focus to a much greater extent on cultural and intellectual life; on the reforms that were making their existence more (though sometimes less) bearable; and on freedoms of various types, including release. As Boris Fedorovich Sporov, another Khrushchev-era memoirist confirmed, their imprisonment "was not for destruction—destruction was before our time."[4]

Surprisingly, this transition to a decidedly post-Stalin penal system has received little scholarly attention despite its importance for understanding Stalinism, de-Stalinization, and the ultimate fate of Soviet socialism. Western scholars have long been fascinated by the Soviet penal system, particularly since the appearance of *Gulag Archipelago*, which captured the Western imagination in the 1970s. The fall of the Soviet Union and availability of previously closed archives starting in the 1990s facilitated a new wave of Gulag scholarship that has greatly enriched our understanding of Soviet crime and punishment. Oleg Khlevniuk, Galina Ivanova, and Anne Applebaum have taken a comprehensive approach to studying the Gulag, focusing chiefly on the brutality and abuses of the system as experienced by its inmates.[5] Steven Barnes, Alan Barenberg, and others have provided detailed portraits of how individual camps operated, demonstrating significant tension between official policy and actual practice.[6] The Gulag was also, in their writing, the site of complex personal interactions, not just in terms of the inmates, as countless memoirs have illustrated, but among Gulag staff and leadership as well. Other scholars have focused more narrowly on particular topics such as sexuality, economics, science, and release.[7]

One commonality among these studies is that they focus heavily on the Stalin era. Those who have delved into the Khrushchev-era Gulag have focused on three main themes. First, considerable attention has been paid to the massive inmate uprisings of 1953–54.[8] Second, a number of scholars have written about the process of release and legal rehabilitation in the post-Stalin era.[9] Finally, a few scholars have investigated the process of Gulag-dominated regions transitioning to normal administrative and economic centers.[10] With the exception of a book chapter by Marc Elie, none have seriously investigated the course of Gulag reform beyond the first few years of the post-Stalin era.[11] In his last major work, renowned historian of the Soviet Union Moshe Lewin directed attention to this omission, writing, "I have not come across a reliable monograph on the post-Stalinist prison system."[12] The purpose of this book, therefore, is to provide the first major study of the transformation of the Soviet penal system under Khrushchev and to elucidate the stated goals of punishment, the policies designed to ensure such aims, and the actual practices that resulted when attempts at reform were thrust upon an entrenched bureaucracy.

The primary contention of this book is that the post-Stalin leadership, having inherited a massive, inefficient, violent, and corrupt penal system, engaged in a serious and substantive reforming effort bent on transforming the Soviet Gulag both quantitatively and qualitatively. In terms of the former, which has already been well-documented by contemporary observers and more recent scholars, mass incarceration and violence as governing principles were clearly rejected.[13] Stalin's heirs released millions of inmates through a variety of early-release programs, as well as millions more who had been sent to special settlements or sentenced to internal exile. Meanwhile, they reduced average sentences for new criminal convictions and drastically lowered the number of convictions for political offenses. These reforms, which dramatically lowered the percentage of the Soviet population directly controlled by the Soviet criminal justice apparatuses, proved to be a durable legacy of the Khrushchev era.

The more qualitative aspects of post-Stalin penal reform, which are the primary focus and contribution of this book, had a decidedly mixed result. Generally speaking, post-Stalin legal reforms aimed at restoring "socialist legality" following the abuses of the Stalin years. For the Gulag this meant condemning the brutality and economic orientation of the past, and attempting to reorient the penal system around the ideas of reeducation (perevospitanie), respect for the rights of inmates, and multiple layers of oversight. Khrushchev's commitment to reform was sincere—it was not simply a function of the post-Stalin succession struggle—and it resulted in marked improvements to the living and working conditions of prisoners. Pressure on Gulag officials to meet production plan targets, however, did not diminish; moreover, reeducation proved difficult to quantify—a serious liability in a statistics-obsessed state—and it lacked a strong institutional backer at the central decision-making level. In fact, in the late 1950s a broad coalition of interest groups, both within and without the criminal justice system, voiced staunch opposition to the amelioration of conditions for inmates, resulting in the rollback of certain of the reforms of the mid-1950s. Ultimately, however, this counterreform campaign fizzled and many of its policies were in turn reversed in the early to mid-1960s. This final round of reform solidified the legacy of the Khrushchev era as one of mostly successful de-Stalinization in the penal sphere.

By the time of Khrushchev's forced retirement in late 1964, the Gulag differed substantively from its Stalinist predecessor. Prisoners enjoyed on average more rights, less violence, and much better living and working conditions than they did under Stalin, and this is not solely attributable to rising standards in society at large. It was a conscious choice made by the top decision makers in the Soviet Union and influenced by the various criminal justice agencies and experts that advised them. Moreover, the reforms of the Khrushchev era created the penal structures and policies that remained the backbone of Soviet and to some extent post-Soviet corrections. Without question the Soviet penal system remained a penal system, with all the oppression, corruption, periodic violence, and unfreedoms inherent therein. The "pains of imprisonment," in the words of American sociologist Gresham Sykes, remained in force in the post-Stalin Soviet Union as they did in the United States and elsewhere.[14] Ultimately, however, the Gulag of Khrushchev differed substantively and deliberately from its Stalinist predecessor.

In order to make proper sense of Khrushchev-era reforms in the penal sector, this book places them within three broader narratives. First, they were just one part, albeit a very important and lasting part, of an extensive reformist program instituted by Stalin's heirs and Khrushchev in particular. Second, they were part of a global postwar penal transition toward rehabilitation and greater leniency and respect for inmates. Finally, Khrushchev's Gulag should be understood within the broader context of Soviet crime and punishment, particularly in relation to the Stalin-era Gulag.

De-Stalinization and the Reforms of the Khrushchev Era

The Khrushchev era has long been known as a period of intense reform following the long reign of Joseph Stalin; indeed, this is precisely how Khrushchev himself presented it to his countrymen and to the world.[15] Without question, Stalin's death in March 1953 was the most significant event for the people of the Soviet Union since the end of World War II. Although the subsequent era came to be known as the period of de-Stalinization, the very fact of Stalin's death was perhaps the greatest "de-Stalinization" possible.[16] None of his potential heirs could match his revolutionary pedigree, his claim to Lenin's mantle of authority, his power cemented through control of information and appointments, his attention to detail, his force of character, or his command of Marxist-Leninist(-Stalinist) theory. He was the living embodiment of the revolution and of the Soviet Union itself. He had rapidly industrialized the country and defeated Hitler in the greatest military conflict of the twentieth century. He had, the Central Committee proclaimed the day after his death, "armed the Party and the entire people with a great and clear program of building communism in the USSR."[17]

In reality, Stalin left behind a notoriously mixed legacy of social mobilization, industrialization, militarization, imperialism, and, of course, repression. Although the Soviet Union had rapidly industrialized and then triumphed in World War II, postwar recovery had proven a difficult task. Resistance movements plagued the newly acquired Western borderlands into the 1950s. Living and working conditions for the majority of the Soviet population in 1953 remained low. Homelessness and begging remained persistent problems well into the 1950s; in 1953 alone the police apprehended 182,300 beggars, 70 percent of whom were invalids.[18] The economy, though expanding, was plagued by corruption, incompetency, and low productivity. The agricultural sector was barely producing enough to feed the Soviet population. And in terms of foreign affairs, while Stalin succeeded in gaining a bloc of sorts to support the Soviet Union's global ambitions, he also faced a series of crises and setbacks that threatened the long-term viability of the socialist world order.[19]

This mixed legacy left for Stalin's heirs fruitful grounds to enact reforms.[20] So too did the fact that Stalin, like Lenin before him, failed to choose an heir from among his lieutenants. Rather, he habitually set them against each other, demoted those who incurred his displeasure, and began introducing new blood in the top leadership ranks in the years before his death.[21] This set the stage for a contentious political transition that pitted his potential successors against each other, in particular Lavrentii Pavlovich Beria, Georgii Maksimilianovich Malenkov, and Khrushchev. This transitional period lasted until Khrushchev's triumph over the so-called Anti-Party Group in 1957, and helped shape the course of reform for the duration of these four years and beyond, from foreign policy to agricultural policy.[22] Indeed, reform became the primary mechanism through which first Beria and then Khrushchev sought to distance themselves from Stalin and from their rivals.

The Gulag reforms of 1953–64 were certainly among the most significant of the post-Stalin reforms, but they were certainly not the only thing occupying the attention of the post-Stalin successors. Agricultural reform was a prominent component of Khrushchev's struggle against Malenkov and his attempt to further the country along the road of socialism. His move to improve the living conditions of Soviet subjects through dramatically increased production of consumer goods and the construction of millions of private apartments were also a key facet of Khrushchev's reforming program. In administrative and economic terms he pursued a program of decentralization, which led to massive bureaucratic restructuring. Other reforms in education and the military, not to mention the intense pressure of charting a distinctively post-Stalin vision of foreign affairs, also competed for the time of Khrushchev and his top lieutenants, on top of the limited resources the Soviet state had to offer.[23] Thus, the Gulag reforms of the 1950s and 1960s have to be understood as existing within a climate of frequent and at times contradictory reforms, combined with limited means to bring new policies and programs to fruition.

The Global Penal Context

In addition to the immediate domestic context, Khrushchev's reform of the Gulag also must be understood within the broader framework of crime and punishment, both within the Soviet Union (which will be discussed below), and within the global context.[24] Although for much of Stalin's reign and to a lesser extent thereafter the Gulag was shrouded in secrecy, the Soviet penal system nonetheless had roots in decidedly European conceptions of crime and punishment. At its root, the Gulag was a penal system that evolved out of existing institutions and philosophies combined with the ideological particularities of the Bolshevik regime. Its primary mission was crime control, which is one of the central functions of the modern state. Indeed, combating crime through new conceptions of loyalty and deviancy and through police forces and punishment systems in the eighteenth and nineteenth centuries was one of the most important elements in the rise of the modern state apparatus.[25] The conjuncture of a rise in crime associated with rapid urbanization and industrialization and a burgeoning middle class that clamored for a safe urban environment in which to live, work, and play produced societies obsessed with crime and criminals.[26] Sociologists and other scholars developed innovative conceptions of the origins and consequences of criminal behavior, such as Cesare Lombroso's biological determinism and Émile Durkheim's concept of anomie.[27]

By the 1950s and 1960s, this obsession with defining and categorizing crime and criminals had hardly diminished. Although Lombroso's ideas had been largely discredited, the concept of anomie still held much sway over international criminology. American sociologist Robert Merton, for instance, explained high levels of crime in the West as resulting from the disjuncture between lofty material aspirations held by society at large and unequal access to the means necessary for success in capitalist societies.[28] Also increasingly popular was Edwin H. Sutherland's theory of differential association, which posited that crime is not biological or structural, but is learned by association with intimate personal groups.[29] These theories, along with methods of combating crime, formed the basis of numerous international conferences organized by the United Nations (UN) from the 1950s onward at which legal experts, criminologists, penal officials, and lawmakers shared their research and proposals to reduce crime globally. Significantly, Soviet officials in the Khrushchev era began to participate in these conferences and often found common ground with their Western counterparts in defining the causes of crime and the methods of preventing it.[30] Thus, not only did the Soviet Union after Stalin's death share similar conceptions of crime and its prevention with the West, it also in the Khrushchev era engaged in high-level transnational discussions about these topics.

The same could be said on a more specific level about imprisonment. Just as every modern state defines various forms of deviance and polices society accordingly, every modern state imprisons those it considers to be criminals. Beginning in the early 1800s in Western Europe and the United States, incarceration became the dominant form of judicial punishment for felonies.[31] This form of punishment then spread to the rest of the world over the following century, often through colonial structures.[32] With roots in Christian notions of penance and enlightenment ideas of perfecting the individual, imprisonment in the modern era was designed not only to punish, but to rehabilitate. The failures of the prison to actually effect the psychological and behavioral transformations it promised to deliver have been well documented, and reforming efforts in the late 1800s and early 1900s aimed at reducing reliance on imprisonment by promoting the use of probation, parole, and other noncustodial forms of punishment.[33] These programs were intended to better use the reforming power of the community to reform convicts, yet they too met with only limited success.

Ultimately, imprisonment continued to be a widespread form of punishment in the interwar era, with penal officials becoming more concerned with administering orderly institutions than reforming their inmates. In the United States this period witnessed the rise of the Big Houses, massive penitentiaries built with the purpose of securely warehousing inmates at minimal cost.[34] In Europe, meanwhile, fascist Italy and Nazi Germany moved toward longer and harsher conditions of imprisonment in the name of state security and less emphasis on rehabilitation.[35] Even outside the fascist sphere, punishment was often retributive in nature, and limited funding ensured a lack of rehabilitational programming.[36]

Along with diminishing interest in rehabilitation and increased attention to retribution and state security, the interwar era also witnessed the rise of the camp as a place of detention. Western powers used concentration camps in colonial war settings in the late 1800s and early 1900s, most prominently during the Boer War, and both concentration camps and prisoner-of-war camps were deployed extensively during World War I.[37] These provided fascist and Soviet leaders in the interwar era with convenient and inexpensive models for how to isolate and, if desired, extract labor from large populations of potential enemies.[38] Yet the camp as a form of imprisonment also has a very different history that likewise began before World War I and then expanded in the interwar era. Often called "honor camps" or "honor farms" in the United States, these "open" institutions housed not extrajudicial detainees but inmates sentenced to deprivation of liberty. The idea was to provide well-behaved inmates with the opportunity to live in communal quarters outside the penitentiary and to perform remunerative labor. While these honor camps certainly did not always live up to their promises of better living conditions and economic salvation, they were increasingly viewed by penal officials in the West as an improvement over the oppressive and crowded penitentiaries.[39] As one American penal official declared, "camps are by no means a cure-all to our correctional problems, but are an important adjustment of a modern correctional system."[40]

World War II and the Holocaust in particular provided deep impetus for penal reform in the late 1940s and 1950s.[41] The primary focus was to revive correctionalism through expanded use of noncustodial punishment programs such as parole, open-style institutions like honor farms, and a wide variety of educational, vocational, cultural, and athletic programs. Psychological and group counseling programs were instituted, corporal punishment where it still existed was abolished, and visitation and correspondence rights were expanded. These reforms were disseminated by the UN conferences mentioned above, and ideals of rehabilitative imprisonment spread to the decolonizing world. And it was precisely in this global conjuncture that the Soviet Union after Stalin began its own penal reform program that in many ways resembled the reforms of the West. The Western and Soviet penal systems in the 1950s and 1960s therefore experienced significant convergence as they worked toward a set of common aims.[42] And this was not simply coincidence. It was the product of a common criminological heritage, a shared experience in the devastation of World War II, and a united interest in improving their own societies according to what were becoming international norms for inmate incarceration.

Soviet Criminal Justice and the Stalin-Era Gulag

In addition to understanding the Khrushchev-era penal reforms through the lens of a broad international context, it is important to situate them within the particularities of crime and punishment in the Soviet Union prior to Stalin's death in 1953. Upon taking power in 1917, the Bolsheviks promised to oversee the eventual elimination of crime, but from the beginning the Soviet system tended to multiply rather than reduce deviancy. In part this was a perceptual issue stemming from vastly increased state capacity to police the population, but heightened levels of crime also resulted from the hopes and fears of a paranoid and dictatorial regime engrossed in constructing socialist modernity amidst capitalist encirclement.[43] Until the creation of a robust welfare state in the Soviet Union in the 1960s and 1970s, crime for many was seen as necessary for survival. For others, the nature of the Soviet party-state required participation in a massive black market that paralleled and complemented the official economy.[44] Some crimes in the USSR were politically driven; the incessantly paranoid Soviet system criminalized certain behaviors such as freedom of speech and religion that were protected by law in the West. Others, such as those targeted by the notorious labor discipline laws of 1938–40, emerged from the pressures of breakneck industrialization in an agrarian state and the pressure of the anticipated war with Nazi Germany. Finally, crime in many cases was motivated by a host of social and psychological issues common to the human experience such as greed, jealousy, envy, despair, alcohol, and peer pressure.[45]

Because of the pervasiveness of crime in Soviet society alongside the ultimate hope of eradicating crime, Soviet criminologists, like their counterparts in the West, were intently interested in what caused crime, how crime could be reduced, and how to reform criminals.[46] Such academic activity was especially fruitful in the 1920s. Criminological studies were conducted, academic journals devoted to these topics appeared, conferences were held, and a variety of theories were put forward to answer these questions. These issues were of great import for the new socialist experiment. More than just about creating safer streets, stemming economic losses, or even eliminating counterrevolutionary thought, crime control in the Soviet Union was a fundamentally existential question. The Soviet Union was by definition a modernist experiment, founded on enlightenment principles of progress that envisioned the eventual creation of a utopian, crime-free society.[47] This was an ideal shared by many in the West during the nineteenth and twentieth centuries, but the Soviet Union, explicitly founded as it was on this premise, bore the nearly unbearable weight of demonstrating its possibility (in an economically and educationally underdeveloped country, no less). If man and society could not be transformed through the implementation of socialism, which Stalin proclaimed achieved in 1936, then there would be little point struggling toward the ever-vague state of communism. The struggle against crime thus constituted a vital component within the broader goal of crafting a model socialist society.

Curiously, however, the vibrant Soviet criminological establishment of the 1920s was all but shuttered in the early to mid-1930s, and remained so until Stalin's death. In Stalin's mind, it seemed, there was no need for further exploration of a social phenomenon—crime—that was supposed to be withering away. Crime was viewed as the work of traitors to the Soviet cause or the psychological "remnants of capitalism."[48] Rather than study crime, therefore, Stalin was content simply to combat it. This struggle took many forms, from education and propaganda to policing and the use of state-sponsored terror, and ultimately tough-on-crime attitudes became pervasive in the Soviet Union. Rather than engender sympathy for those suffering unjustly, Stalin's repressive regime actually succeeded in convincing the majority of Soviet subjects that harsh repression against lawbreakers was necessary. As Miriam Dobson and Brian LaPierre have shown, this psychological legacy became an important impediment to criminal justice reform in the Khrushchev era.[49]

Perhaps the most important aspect of crime control for the Soviet state, as was the case elsewhere, was the incarceration and "reeducation" of lawbreakers. From its birth amidst world war and civil war, the Soviet state relied heavily on imprisonment as a primary method of court-mandated punishment. Incarceration was seen as an appropriate way to remove harmful elements from what would eventually become a communist society. But the Soviet penal system existed not only to punish and to purify society through excision; like its counterparts in the West it was also given the fairly synonymous tasks of correction (*ispravlenie*), education (*vospitanie*, a term that implies a combination of positive socialization, character development, moral training, and cultural education), and reeducation (*perevospitanie*). In the 1930s the industrial terminology of reforging (*perekovka*) was also prominent in discussions of how to turn convicts into law-abiding socialist citizens. For the Soviet state and its criminal justice establishment, labor and the reforming power of the collective were especially prominent among ideas of how to reeducate criminals. Here the famous Soviet pedagogue Anton Semenovich Makarenko made his mark, reporting from personal experience that the power of collective life in particular could transform orphans and juvenile delinquents into conscientious Soviet citizens.[50]

This mission of reeducation was placed on prominent display for foreign visitors who toured penal facilities in the 1920s and 1930s, as well as in various propaganda efforts aimed at external and internal audiences.[51] But it was also the admonition given to penal officers by high-level criminal justice authorities such as Stalin's notorious Procurator General Andrei Ianuar'evich Vyshinskii, who in 1934 argued for a correctional program based on labor, the inmate collective, primary and secondary education, self-governance, propaganda, vocational training, and cultural and sporting programs.[52] Ultimately, this commitment to correctionalism was not constant; it waxed and waned, but it never disappeared completely, even during the height of Stalin's repression.[53] Yet in this regard the Soviet penal system was not exceptional; inherent tension between the goals of correction and punishment produced similar challenges in Western prison systems.[54]

In the Soviet Union under Stalin, the primary administrative body tasked with incarcerating and reforming criminals from 1930 onward was the Gulag.[55] With the publication of Aleksandr Solzhenitsyn's *Gulag Archipelago*, this acronym became popularized in the West and has been used in a variety of ways, including in reference to other systems of detention.[56] It has also assumed various forms of capitalization: GULAG, GULag, Gulag, and gulag. In this book, the term Gulag will be used in the two ways in which Soviet administrators used it. First, it referred in a narrow sense to the central administrative body that managed the penal system. More broadly, it was used to denote the network of corrective-labor camps and corrective-labor colonies designed to hold those found guilty by law and sentenced to deprivation of freedom.

Scholars have differed in how they interpret the role of the Gulag in Soviet society. Some authors contend that the Gulag should be viewed as an organ of political repression.[57] Others argue that it was fundamentally an economic entity created to aid in the rapid industrialization of the country.[58] These aspects under Stalin were certainly not trivial, as will be discussed below, yet they alone cannot explain the Gulag's existence or its operations. Rather, the Soviet Gulag must be understood primarily on its own terms as a penal system, a place to send dissidents and deviants, criminals and counterrevolutionaries, for the purposes of isolation, punishment, deterrence, and reeducation.[59] In other words, it shared the same basic goals found in the penal systems of the West.

Yet the Gulag bore the imprint of more than just the Western criminology from which it largely sprang. It was also shaped by the authoritarian regime that created it, by the communist ideology that regime espoused, by the economic backwardness that regime was striving to overcome, and by a society prone to violence and other crimes. As such, it constituted an integral piece of the Soviet social fabric, a place where ideology, economics, politics, social justice, education, and reeducation all combined with a measure of coercion and repression.[60] In significant ways, therefore, it differed from its foreign counterparts. It was abnormally large, its mix of prisoners was quite different from most Western regimes, and it was unusually deadly. It featured a complex organizational structure that reflected the complexity of the Soviet party-state and its ideology. It was oriented strongly toward communal facilities rather than cellular prisons, and toward economic production in the context of rapid industrialization. Finally, to a much greater extent than other penal systems, it was constantly reforming and reinventing itself.

The most distinctive feature of the Soviet Gulag under Stalin was its size. Before the opening of Soviet archives to researchers, Western observers and historians vastly overestimated the number of inmates in the Gulag, thereby creating an enduring image of the Gulag as a mass institution.[61] And a mass institution it certainly was, even if one accepts the regime's numbers now available as approximating reality. Although the Soviet state in the 1920s did not incarcerate much more than its tsarist predecessor, with the increased repression of the 1930s the number of inmates soared.[62] By 1935 over 1 million prisoners were incarcerated in Soviet penal institutions, and by 1938 that figure approached 2 million. Wartime deaths and releases brought the number of prisoners down to around 1.5 million in the mid-1940s, but the Gulag again began to expand sharply in the late 1940s due primarily to harsh antitheft laws passed in 1948.[63] On 1 January 1950 the population of the Gulag peaked at just over 2.5 million, making an incarceration rate of around 1,440 per 100,000.[64] Immediately prior to Stalin's death the Gulag had shrunk somewhat to a little under 2.5 million, but it still incarcerated a far larger percentage of the Soviet population and workforce than its Western counterparts.[65] The United States in 1950, for instance, held 166,165 inmates in state and federal prisons for an incarceration rate of just 109 per 100,000.[66] The Soviet Union's incarceration rate up to Stalin's death therefore was over ten times the comparable rate in the United States. The United Kingdom and other countries of Western and Northern Europe, meanwhile, typically had rates of imprisonment well below 100 per 100,000.[67]

In addition to size, the Soviet Gulag under Stalin was also unique due to large numbers of so-called political prisoners, a complicated term in a regime where everything was interpreted through a political lens. Most of these were convicted of "counterrevolutionary" crimes according to the infamous Article 58 of the Criminal Code, though others were convicted by an array of different statutes.[68] Without doubt some of these political prisoners were guilty of treason, espionage, conspiracy, and anti-Soviet propaganda, among various other anti-state transgressions. The vast majority of them, however, as they protested during their trials and as the case reviews of the 1950s would demonstrate, were innocent of the crimes for which they were incarcerated. Caught up in the paranoid search for enemies that characterized the Stalin era, political prisoners in the Gulag numbered nearly half a million in the early 1940s, comprising around one-third of all inmates.[69] That number then grew to 539,483 by 1 January 1953, but the relative percentage dropped: on the eve of Stalin's death political prisoners accounted for just over 20 percent of all inmates.[70] The Soviet Union was certainly not the only regime that imprisoned for antistate crimes, but none imprisoned more than the Soviet Union and none imprisoned more that later turned out to be innocent of the crime with which they had been charged.[71]

Another aspect of the Gulag that made it unique among contemporary penal systems during the 1930s and 1940s was its deadliness. The combination of primitive and communal living conditions, overcrowding, harsh environment, exhausting labor, and at times insufficient rations that characterized the Gulag produced malnutrition, disease, physical deterioration, and death. This especially held true during the famine of 1933–34, the Great Terror of 1937–38, the first years of World War II, and the famine of 1946–47. The Gulag's high mortality rate also resulted from a culture of violence that pervaded the ranks of both inmates and guards. Although violence is endemic in most penal systems, it was especially pronounced in the Gulag. Communal living quarters facilitated the formation and activity of criminal gangs, which preyed on other inmates. Gulag guards during the height of Stalinism, meanwhile, were taught that many of the inmates were "malicious enemies of the people," with the implication that abusing them would not constitute a crime.[72]

Like inmate population statistics, mortality figures were vastly overestimated before the opening of Soviet archives. Estimates of 20 million or more deaths in the Gulag alone were not uncommon.[73] Archival data, while not fully reliable, presents a picture of inmate mortality that, while far lower, was still extremely high by contemporary penal standards. In the 1930s, approximately 5 percent of Soviet inmates died each year, resulting in at least half a million deaths.[74] As many as 10 percent of prisoners were also unable to work due to illness or disability.[75] During the early 1940s, in the midst of the war, annual mortality rates in the Gulag spiked to over 20 percent, with nearly 300,000 inmates dying in 1943 alone.[76] By the early 1950s, with the chaos of rapid industrialization and the war years over, official statistics show annual mortality rates had been reduced to just under 1 percent per year.[77] Thus, whereas the number of prisoners at the time of Stalin's death was at near-record levels, the Gulag by this point had become much more survivable.

In addition to the sheer number of inmates and their high rate of mortality, another defining feature of the Gulag was its convoluted organizational structure. The structure of many Soviet institutions was quite complex, in part due to the dual reporting mechanisms inherent in the party-state, and the penal system in this regard was no different. The Gulag itself reported to the Unified State Political Organization (OGPU), which was renamed the People's Commissariat of Internal Affairs (NKVD) in 1934, which was then renamed the Ministry of Internal Affairs (MVD) in 1946. The MVD, in turn, reported to the Council of Ministers. Yet the Gulag was not the only organization administering incarceration, nor was its own administrative structure straightforward. Prisons in the Soviet Union, many of them inherited from the tsarist regime, were at times operated by the Gulag, but at other times were managed by a distinct Prison Department within the MVD. Places of forced internal exile called "special settlements" were also under the Gulag for a time but mostly fell under a separate administration within the MVD. For several years under Stalin one of the largest camp complexes in the Soviet Union—Dal'stroi—reported directly to the MVD, thus bypassing the Gulag administration. And in the 1940s many of the Gulag camps were under the control of economic administrations within the MVD, while still reporting to the Gulag as well.[78]

In terms of where the prisoners actually lived, the majority of them were housed in "corrective-labor" facilities. These belonged to one of two types of mid-level administrative structures under the Gulag: the corrective-labor camp (of which there were 105 holding over 1.5 million prisoners in 1951) and the division of corrective-labor camps and colonies (of which there were 97 with nearly 1 million prisoners in 1951).[79] The latter were organized within province- or republican-level MVD apparatuses, although they also reported to the Gulag.[80] Thus, penal facilities could literally be found all over the Soviet Union. Within each division of corrective-labor camps and colonies were several camp branches (*otdelenie*), which were sometimes broken down further into "camp points," and corrective-labor colonies; these three institutions—camp branches, camp points, and colonies—were where the prisoners were actually housed. Technically the colonies were for inmates sentenced to terms of under three years, although in practice this guideline was not always followed. Moreover, due to ever-increasing sentence lengths under Stalin—in 1951 only 300,000 out of 2.5 million inmates were sentenced to fewer than three years—the number of colonies remained small.[81] The final type of institution found in the provincial Gulag administration was transit prisons for inmates coming to or leaving the area. The Estonian Department of Corrective-Labor Camps and Colonies, to give one example of a provincial Gulag organization, on 1 March 1953 held 9,022 prisoners in 7 camp branches, 2 colonies, and 1 transit prison.[82]

Corrective-labor camps, by contrast, were not part of a provincial MVD apparatus but reported solely to the Gulag. Located near exploitable natural resources (the most common of which being gold, coal, and timber) or large construction sites (including dams, railroads, and factories), the camps tended to be in sparsely inhabited and climactically unpleasant areas of the Soviet Union: the Far East, Far North, Siberia, Kazakhstan, and the Urals. They also differed from the divisions of corrective-labor camps and colonies in size; the camps were often much larger than their provincial counterparts and their subunits were usually more dispersed geographically. Like the province-based divisions, each camp was broken down administratively into camp branches and camp points.[83] The Krasnoiarskii Corrective-Labor Camp (Kraslag) in late 1956, to give one example, had 22,583 prisoners divided into 9 camp branches and 35 camp points (one of which was a designated transit point and another was the camp hospital).[84] The word camp (*lager*) in Soviet penal lexicon referred therefore to an administrative level between the central bureaucracy in Moscow and the camp branches and camp points where the inmates were held. However, it was also commonly used in the plural, such as in the stock phrase "camps and colonies," as shorthand for all camp branches and points, whether attached to a corrective-labor camp or a division of corrective-labor camps and colonies.

The Gulag in the early 1950s operated around 3,500 camp branches, camp points, and colonies, with an average population of 715 inmates per institution.[85] In their physical appearance, the camp branches, camp points, and colonies were quite similar. Prisoners were housed in barracks, usually one-story wooden constructions, although some were built of brick, stone, or other material and they were occasionally two stories high.[86] Barracks were typically built in rows with each holding dozens if not hundreds of inmates. Each camp branch or colony was also supposed to be outfitted with a variety of other buildings: headquarters, a kitchen, dining room, club, bathhouse, locker room, drying room (for wet clothing), barber shop, laundry room, and store. These were all surrounded with watchtowers, barbed wire and lighting, with a guardhouse and gate on one side. Separated from the main zone by fencing and barbed wire stood the penalty isolator and sometimes penalty barracks, as well as the medical unit and supply depot. Some camp units and colonies also had their own production zone, which was also separated from the living quarters with barbed wire.[87] Most inmates under Stalin, however, were marched to work at a separate location from the living zone.

This method of incarcerating inmates in camps and colonies highlights another defining feature of the Soviet Gulag: its emphasis on communalism. Whereas cellular confinement with one or two inmates per cell was typical of prison systems in the West, with the exception of the honor camps already noted, the Soviet Union preferred barracks that housed dozens of prisoners in common quarters. Inmates worked together, ate together, and generally moved freely within the confines of the camps. They were also organized into communal work brigades of typically one or two dozen inmates, and these brigades defined much of the prisoner's life. Their sleeping arrangements, their work duties, and even their rations were dependent on the brigade. This communal life in the Gulag was both a function of ideology and exigency. There were simply not enough prisons inherited from the Russian empire to hold the far higher inmate populations of the Soviet era, and constructing new brick-and-mortar prisons to hold millions of prisoners would divert far too many resources away from industrialization. But philosophically, the Bolsheviks believed that communal life exerted a better rehabilitative influence than cellular confinement. It taught unselfishness and humility and allowed for the prisoner "collective" to exert a positive influence on each individual offender.

That is not to say that the Soviets did not use prisons at all. In the early 1950s several hundred prisons scattered across the country held over 150,000 prisoners.[88] Most of these prisoners were pretrial detainees, but the prisons also housed three categories of posttrial inmates: those waiting execution, those sentenced to solitary confinement for committing particularly egregious offenses, and those transferred to prison after causing too much trouble in the camps. Here punishment was administered individually rather than collectively, and few opportunities for labor or other reeducational opportunities existed.[89] Prison was viewed by the Soviet regime, therefore, as a worse punishment than the corrective-labor camp, and was used quite sparingly.

A fourth distinctive feature of the Soviet Gulag under Stalin was its heavy emphasis on labor. As already noted, labor was seen by Soviet criminologists as the primary method for rehabilitating convicts. Yet labor also served another purpose. The primary reason for creating the Main Administration of Camps (Gulag) from the fragmented penal systems of the 1920s was to engage inmates more fully in the process of rapid industrialization. The Gulag's explicit mission was to send prisoners to labor on great works projects such as the Belomor Canal or to use them to extract natural resources such as coal and gold from remote and inhospitable areas of the Soviet Union. Thus, while prisoners were not incarcerated for the express purpose of exploiting them as unpaid labor, once they were in the penal system their capacity for work was readily exploited. To the Soviets the idea of forcing prisoners to work, usually in difficult climactic conditions, did not present a contradiction. One of the founding philosophies of the Soviet Union, an avowedly workers' state, was "he who does not work shall not eat."[90] Labor was viewed in Soviet society, therefore, as both a right and an obligation. During the 1930s and 1940s, when all Soviet citizens were expected to sacrifice for the purpose of constructing socialism through rapid industrialization and collectivization, there was certainly no reason to exclude prisoners. In fact they posed a solution to the problem of recruiting free citizens to the harsh climates of places like Siberia, the Far North, and Kazakhstan.

The idea of compulsory labor for prisoners, as already noted, was not unique to the Soviets. In the Western penal systems of the nineteenth and twentieth centuries it was used as a means to partially recoup the cost of maintaining prisons, as a way to teach factory-style discipline, and as a rehabilitative tool. In fact, virtually all criminologists of the twentieth century agreed that labor was essential to rehabilitation and to the smooth operation of penal facilities.[91] Various factors mitigated against this, however. For one thing, cellular prisons were not conducive to meaningful labor, and most Western prison regimes were hesitant to allow inmates beyond prison walls for the purposes of work. Moreover, organized labor protested against competition from low-wage inmates, and in the United States successfully petitioned for laws prohibiting prison-made goods from entering the private market.[92] As a result, many prisoners in the West did not work. Therefore, while considered important, inmate labor was not an overriding ideological concern in the West, nor were policies of state-managed rapid industrialization being pursued.

In addition to its centrality in penal philosophy and in the Soviet Union's rapid industrialization, Gulag labor was unique in how it was administered. Inmates worked very long hours with few days off, pushed hard to fulfill specific production quotas. It was, without question, "the merciless exploitation of prisoners" in the name of economic development.[93] Moreover, one's labor performance fed into a range of other facets of camp life, including rations: those who failed to fulfill the norm for the day were not given their full ration that evening.[94] Indeed, it came to be practically the only indicator of an inmate's "correction," which was important for determining the possibility of early release.[95] Meanwhile, as the 1930s progressed, other aspects of reeducation receded in importance and labor itself began to lose its reeducational value.[96] For camp commanders and inmates alike, plan fulfillment trumped all other concerns. This overwhelming emphasis on labor as a vehicle of production persisted from the late 1930s to the end of Stalin's reign and rightly came to be viewed by scholars and memoirists alike as the defining Gulag experience. As Solzhenitsyn declared, "the life of the [prisoners] consists of work, work, work."[97]

The primacy of economics in the Stalin-era Gulag can also be viewed in how Gulag inmates and free workers often labored together. Although one of the purposes of penal systems generally and the Gulag specifically was to isolate criminals from the rest of society and thereby prevent them from committing further crimes, this ideal was frequently compromised in Stalin's Soviet Union. Gulag inmates often mixed openly with free workers on the jobsite; many were given special passes that allowed them to travel outside the camps without armed escort; and some prisoners were even given permission to live outside the barbed wire. All of these exceptions to the idea of strict isolation were done in the name of economic production. As Alan Barenberg has found, economic managers in charge of Gulag labor "were convinced that prisoners granted the privilege of living outside the 'zone' would be more productive than those who were not."[98] The borders of the Gulag, therefore, were rather flexible and porous. Rather than isolated from society, Gulag inmates were in many places more or less integrated into the local society and especially the local economies.[99]

A final aspect of the Soviet Gulag that contributed to some extent to its uniqueness among penal systems globally was its pervasive reforms. Reform in the enlightenment and Marxist sense of progress toward a better future was deeply embedded in the Soviet psyche, and from 1917 to 1991 incredible energy was poured into endless proposals and actual reforms aimed at transforming the state, the economy, the natural environment, Soviet society, and the Soviet citizen. With rare exception in Soviet history the status quo was considered unacceptable; progress toward communism, after all, was the Soviet Union's raison d'être. And the Soviet Union's authoritarian state structure made reforms relatively easy to initiate.[100]

Although the idea of persistent reformism, based on the periodic realization that prisons never achieved their intended aims, has been noted in Western penal systems as well, the Soviet Gulag was the site of constant experimentation.[101] Policy changes were frequent in the 1920s and 1930s as penal experts and administrators attempted to figure out what precisely incarceration should mean in the socialist context. The dramatic social upheavals combined with state-sponsored terror and the resultant rapid expansion of the Gulag in the 1930s also served to inject volatility into the system. Regulations were constantly being revised, often with the result of making imprisonment harsher. As Oleg Khlevniuk has noted, the prisoners of the early 1930s "were relatively well-off and free compared to those unfortunate enough to be imprisoned in the later period of starvation, mass shootings, and war."[102] Indeed, in the midst of the Great Terror, prisoners were subject to arrest and execution; moreover, certain stimuli for good behavior— parole and workday credits most prominently—were rescinded after nearly two decades of constant tinkering with these systems.[103] The war years also witnessed constantly changing policies and regulations in regard to labor, rations, release, and so forth.

This climate of constant reformism persisted even in the 1945–53 era of late Stalinism, which is typically known for its lack of reforming vitality.[104] Certainly some efforts at reform were stifled by Stalin, who was hesitant during these years to sanction radical restructuring in the political and economic structures of the Soviet Union. Most notable among these blocked reforms were two radical plans drafted by S. S. Mamulov (likely on the orders of Beria, patron of the Soviet security apparatus) in 1949 and 1951 to turn the majority of inmates into internal exiles.[105] Yet several significant changes to the Soviet penal system were made in the late 1940s and early 1950s. A massive amnesty freed hundreds of thousands of inmates in 1945, signifying perhaps a shift toward lower levels of incarceration.[106] But harsh antitheft laws passed in 1947, which mandated five years' imprisonment for theft and seven for embezzlement, meant a rapid expansion of the Gulag system.[107] In order to better isolate and control political prisoners, many of them from the newly acquired Western borderlands, a network of "special camps" with particularly onerous living and working conditions was created in 1948.[108] For nonpolitical prisoners, at least in certain camps, prisoner wages and workday credits aimed at increasing inmate productivity were reintroduced after being abolished in the late 1930s.[109] Finally, in the early 1950s there was a widespread campaign to enforce tighter discipline in the camps.[110] The Soviet Gulag, including in the late Stalin era, thus experienced constant experimentation in terms of policy and practice. In this respect the post-Stalin changes to the penal system, while truly transformative, were made possible in part by an existing climate of persistent reformism.[111]

RESTRUCTURING THE PENAL EMPIRE

Administration, Institutions, and Demographics

One has to feel sorry for them, too—you can imagine the oceans of paper they're floundering in! And the sea of lies!

—Evgeniia Ginzburg, *Within the Whirlwind*

On 5 March 1953, four days after suffering a massive stroke, Joseph Vissarionov-ich Stalin died. Over the radio classical music played, in the streets people wept openly. Stalin's death had great meaning for all of Soviet society. It opened up the possibility of a succession struggle among Stalin's lieutenants. As Georgii Maksi-milianovich Malenkov later remarked, "Stalin's mistake was that he had not trained anyone to fill his position."[1] Just as important as a new leader was the possibility of policy changes that would impact the daily lives of the Soviet citi-zenry. As Andrei Sakharov recalled, "It was a shattering event. Everyone under-stood that something must soon change, but no one knew in what direction."[2] Many in the various Soviet bureaucracies anticipated that the "self-perpetuating cycle of stalled reforms" that characterized the late Stalin era could be broken.[3] More broadly, people hoped for better housing and nutrition, and more con-sumer goods. And they yearned for a lessening of repression, a relaxation of the climate of fear and secrecy that had pervaded Soviet society since the early 1930s.[4] As Vera Dunham found, the burgeoning Soviet middle class after the war desired contentment, stability, and security. They were interested not in ideology or revolutionary zeal, but in cars and careers.[5] And while Stalin began the pro-cess of delivering on these desires, his death only raised the possibility of attain-ing them more quickly.[6]

Although Stalin's death was important for all of Soviet society, perhaps no-where was its potential impact felt more keenly than in the Gulag. As in the broader population, many prisoners were greatly saddened by Stalin's passing. Inmate A. P. Butkovsky later recorded that there was no rejoicing among the inmates in his labor camp on Sakhalin when the news was announced. For them and for millions of Soviet subjects, worshiping Stalin was a patriotic duty: "His name was the name of our Motherland."[7] For some inmates the announcement of Stalin's death spurred more mixed emotions. Others, especially political prisoners, took a certain pleasure in the death of him who was ultimately responsible, they felt, for their unjust imprisonment.[8] As Mikhail Rabinovich, echoing Aleksandr Hertzen when Nicholas I died, declared, "A heavy stone had fallen from our shoulders."[9] Prisoners throughout the Soviet Union expressed similar sentiments, along with hope that the new leadership would "close all the slave camps and free us all."[10] As Evgeniia Ginzburg recalled, "It was if we were all drunk. Everyone's head was spinning with the expectation of imminent change."[11]

For the guards and officials who administered the Gulag, meanwhile, Stalin's passing was met with uncertainty and trepidation. Initially, they did their best to honor the fallen leader, holding solemn assemblies and moments of silence, even granting the inmates a day off work to commemorate the life of the great leader.[12] Michael Solomon, incarcerated in Kolyma, recorded that on the day of Stalin's burial, "at the precise moment when the dictator's body was carried into the mausoleum, everybody in the camp, even the sick in hospitals, had to rise and stand at attention, facing Moscow, until camp officials considered the burial ceremony over. The officers read long eulogies to us about the great deeds of Stalin, and official mourning was imposed on the camp."[13] Beyond such ceremonies, however, Gulag officers wondered along with their inmates what would become of the vast penal "archipelago" they inhabited. As inmate Karlo Štajner recalled, "the guards, the overseers, and the other camp officials sensed that a new era was dawning."[14]

Indeed, this foreboding, this anticipation on the part of prisoners and guards alike was well founded. The Gulag in early 1953 was by no means in crisis, as a few scholars have concluded.[15] As Steven Barnes has convincingly argued, reform would not have occurred had Stalin lived.[16] Rather, Stalin's passing, the ensuing power struggle, and the existing reformist tendencies within the Gulag all contributed to the substantive reforms that would quickly and permanently alter the Soviet penal system. By 1960 the Gulag empire would be drastically reduced in size and economic importance. Its organizational structure would be decentralized to a significant degree. Reeducation as opposed to labor extraction would be proclaimed the top priority of the Gulag. The primary penal institution of the Stalin era, the corrective-labor camp, would be discredited and slated for extinction in favor of the smaller corrective-labor colony. In conjunction with this, prisoners would as a rule be kept in their home provinces rather than be convoyed to distant penal facilities. Sentences on average would be reduced and new early release mechanisms would be introduced and generously applied. Finally, the Gulag would be emptied of most of its political prisoners and became inhabited primarily by recidivists and those convicted of violent crimes. Ultimately, the reforms of 1953–60 were just as monumental in terms of transforming the Soviet penal system as those of 1930–37. In many respects, in fact, they worked to roll back the reforms of the 1930s, which in general had made the penal system larger, more economically focused, and deadlier.

Beria's Gulag

When Stalin died he left no clear successor. Like Lenin, he had a difficult time imagining any of his closest associates as capable of effectively presiding over the incredibly complex party-state structure while simultaneously serving as an ideological inspiration for the Soviet citizenry. And arguably he was correct in that assessment; while Malenkov and Lavrentii Pavlovich Beria in particular were adept at administration, few in the Soviet Union viewed any of Stalin's lieutenants as ideologically inspiring. As one Moscow professor observed (in his private diary) in 1955, "The entire Presidium consists of boring and grey personalities. When one see them, it comes to mind that the revolution had occurred long, long ago, all revolutionary cadres were exterminated, and bureaucratic nonentities triumphed. There is nothing live, spontaneous, and humane in what they say, not a word, not a single memorable gesture. Everybody looks featureless, faceless, and erased."[17] Stalin's successors therefore faced a two-pronged task. First, they had to get themselves installed in the most powerful positions of the party-state structure and then, in turn, staff the various administrative apparatuses with handpicked clients. But they also faced the distinct challenge of generating excitement for their vision of the country, of winning over a Soviet public that viewed them with considerable suspicion.

Upon Stalin's passing, his heirs quickly pronounced adherence to a policy of collective leadership and quietly moved to curtail what Malenkov already in July 1953 referred to as "Comrade Stalin's cult of personality."[18] Yet within this collective it was clear that some members were more powerful than others and that several had aspirations to inherit Stalin's mantle. Malenkov, a Civil War veteran and Stalin protégé who claimed Stalin's post as premier (chairman of the Council of Ministers), was perhaps the most logical successor. Beria, another Civil War veteran who served as head of the People's Commissariat of Internal Affairs (NKVD) from 1938 to 1945 and who then oversaw the Soviet atomic project, also had designs on Stalin's inheritance. Indeed, his power in the late Stalin era made even Stalin uncomfortable, with the latter organizing purges of Beria's networks. Upon Stalin's death Beria regained control of the Ministry of Internal

Affairs (MVD), including its intelligence wing, the Ministry of State Security (which in 1954 was reseparated and renamed the Committee of State Security [KGB]), and also served as Malenkov's deputy in the state apparatus. The final and least powerful of the three potential successors to Stalin was Nikita Sergeevich Khrushchev, another Civil War veteran who rose through the party ranks in Moscow and Ukraine in the 1920s and 1930s. Brought to Moscow for good in 1949 after overseeing the reconstruction of Ukraine after World War II, Khrushchev was underestimated by his rivals, who in March 1953 allowed him the position of first secretary of the Communist Party. As Stalin, like Lenin before him, preferred to rule through the government rather than the party, this was seen as a subordinate position to those acquired by Malenkov and Beria. Khrushchev, however, building on the momentum of the recently concluded Nineteenth Party Congress, proved capable of reversing this dynamic.

Perhaps because Malenkov seemed best poised to succeed Stalin in March 1953, Beria quickly became the most active in pressing for reform.[19] He moved to promote Georgians, Ukrainians, Belorussians, and other ethnic groups in their respective republics and to mandate greater use of local languages instead of Russian. He promised religious tolerance in the Western borderlands. More provocatively, he began working toward a policy in East Germany that could have led to the end of Soviet influence.[20] Notably for the present discussion, he also embarked on a dramatic overhaul of the penal sector. As longtime head of the security apparatuses, he certainly had the best grasp of the true state of affairs in the Gulag. Without question, therefore, he knew best what immediate action should be taken to relieve some of the pressures caused by stalled reform in the late Stalinist period.[21] Yet this observation, while perhaps necessary for explaining the speed of reform, is insufficient for explaining Beria's motive. The most frequently repeated, and likely correct, theory to explain Beria's swift reforming moves is that he initiated reform to assert his preeminence among Stalin's potential heirs.[22] The uncertainty of the succession period combined with the nature of power in the Soviet Union led Stalin's successors to pursue radical solutions to lingering problems, while casting blame for such problems on their rivals.[23] De-Stalinization was, in words of Oleg Khlevniuk, "a strong weapon in the struggle for power."[24] This was, therefore a ploy to "win popular support" and "change his own public image," a strategy that Khrushchev would eventually use to great effect.[25]

Just weeks after Stalin's death Beria launched a major package of reforms designed to reduce the inefficiency of the Gulag system and, to borrow a term from the capitalist West, rid the MVD of noncore assets. The first of these, proposed on 17 March 1953 and passed by the Council of Ministers the following day, transferred many of the Gulag's industrial enterprises to various economic ministries.[26] This shift corresponded with the simultaneous reorganization of government ministries, a project led by Malenkov that substantially reduced the total number of ministries while rearranging in part their portfolios.[27] Three days later Beria ordered that work be halted on around twenty large Gulag construction projects that he deemed unnecessarily wasteful.[28] The most infamous of these, the Salekhard-Igarka railroad line in northwestern Siberia, on which over 3.7 billion rubles had already been spent, was nowhere near completion.[29] These two decrees dramatically reduced the power of the MVD, previously among the most important economic entities in the Soviet government, and were important first steps in reorienting the penal system away from the labor extraction model that had largely guided its development since the early 1930s.[30]

Soon after the separation of these economic units from the Gulag, Beria presented to his colleagues his next major reform. On 27 March 1953, just twenty-two days after Stalin's death, the Presidium of the Supreme Soviet adopted the decree "On Amnesty," and published it on the front page of *Pravda* the following day.[31] This amnesty, thereafter referred to as "Beria's amnesty," followed a long tradition of amnesties commemorating holidays or regime changes in Russian and Soviet history.[32] Interestingly, the previous major Soviet amnesty, which freed 620,753 prisoners in 1945 to celebrate the end of World War II, was opposed by Beria on economic grounds.[33] To him, "Stalin's amnesty [of 1945] represented nothing less than a major assault on the valued labor resources of the Gulag."[34] By 1953, however, whether due to a new appreciation for the low productivity of convict labor or to the unique possibilities posed by the succession struggle, Beria quickly pushed through a similar emptying of the country's penal institutions.[35] Not for nothing, then, did a miner from Ukraine laud the amnesty as "a Stalinist idea, which his faithful comrades have brought to life."[36]

The 1953 amnesty mandated the release of convicts with terms of up to five years in length as well as special categories of prisoners such as pregnant women, women with children under ten, juveniles, men over fifty-five, and women over fifty.[37] It also cut sentences in half for most other nonpolitical prisoners, with the result that many had already served their newly reduced term and were to be set free.[38] In total, 1.2 million prisoners were released from the camps in 1953 as a result of the amnesty, mostly in the first few months following the decree, bringing the Gulag population down from 2,468,081 on 1 April 1954 to 1,273,038 on 1 July 1953.[39] In just 90 days, nearly 50 percent of Gulag inmates were released. Most of these apparently returned home quietly and without incident, but a sizable minority became infamous for terrorizing local populations after their release.[40] Already by April 1954, 84,225 of those amnestied in 1953 had been prosecuted for new crimes.[41] Compared with the previous year, registered crime increased substantially during the second and third quarters of 1953, including increases of 66.4 percent for assault, 63.4 percent for theft, 30.7 percent for murder, and 27.5 percent for rape.[42]

Among prisoners, there was mixed reaction to the amnesty. Many released or soon-to-be-released prisoners and their families expressed genuine appreciation for the 1953 amnesty by sending handwritten letters of gratitude to the Supreme Soviet, the body that formally issued the law.[43] They expressed guilt for the crimes they committed and made resolutions to live an honest life from thenceforth. One typical passage from this correspondence reads: "Beginning a new period in life, I will make every effort to justify the great trust of the party and government and will with redoubled energy give all of my knowledge and labor to the matter of further strengthening the might and the flowering of our beloved Motherland."[44] Another wrote of the amnesty, "For this great care for the Soviet man I am obligated to the end of my life to obey all the laws of our government and continually prepare myself to be a model member of the new communist society."[45] On the other hand, Beria's amnesty proved a great disappointment to the political prisoners who were excluded from its terms. As one inmate in the Far North Construction Trust (Dal'stroi) camps of Kolyma complained, "This order will free murderers, bandits, and thieves, but we, convicted by Article 58, are not amnestied."[46] Another lamented, "We have nothing to wait for, and no one to cry for us, we need to free ourselves."[47] In addition, many thought that the amnesty was initiated in preparation for war with America and that the political prisoners were left in the camps because they could not be trusted to fight. Along these lines another Dal'stroi prisoner proclaimed: "For us amnesty will come only when Eisenhower gives it to us. We have nothing else to hope for."[48]

Yet although Aleksandr Solzhenitsyn and other political prisoners became convinced by the Beria amnesty that nothing had changed, the amnesty for the Gulag apparatus meant monumental restructuring, as evidenced by the Dal'stroi camps of Kolyma.[49] Out of 146,179 prisoners held by Dal'stroi, 51,194 fell under the conditions of the amnesty and were slated for release.[50] The massive number of releases meant that a small transit town had to be established near Magadan where amnestied inmates could wait for the next available ship.[51] It also meant that production quotas, which were only belatedly adjusted to account for the reduced manpower, were difficult to fulfill.[52] Dal'stroi head Ivan Lukich Mitrakov warned about the ensuing labor shortage, ordering his camp commanders to immediately intensify all work in order to get the most out of those to be released.[53] This somewhat ambiguous order resulted in a number of commanders continuing to hold prisoners who should have been released in order to fulfill their production goals.[54] By the beginning of August 1953, however, Mitrakov commanded that the transfer of all such to Magadan be complete by 15 August, even if that meant transporting them by airplane.[55] The situation in other Gulag camps was similar, with commanders scrambling to fulfill the amnesty while still meeting their production targets.[56]

In addition to posing such challenges with logistics and manpower, the amnesty also forced the Gulag to radically downsize its operations. During and immediately following the amnesty, the Gulag drastically reduced its staff and eliminated camps and colonies that had lost most of their prisoners. Already on 29 March 1953 Gulag chief Ivan Ivanovich Dolgikh ordered all camp commanders to close dilapidated camp branches as the amnestied prisoners left, transferring the remaining inmates to camps with better facilities. He also called for a 25–30 percent reduction in staff at all camp units.[57] As a follow-up to this order, regional Gulag officials were instructed on 18 June 1953 to review their camp branches with fewer than five hundred convicts "with the goal of liquidating or strengthening them."[58] By 24 October 1954, with the amnesty complete, 104 corrective-labor camps, 1,567 camp subdivisions or colonies within the Gulag's regional networks, 11 transit prisons, 82 Gulag hospitals, and 18 adolescent work colonies had been eliminated, as had over 180,000 positions within the Gulag apparatus.[59] Yet the cuts were not made evenly across the board. Notably, the central Gulag apparatus in Moscow lost only 15.7 percent of its positions while the administrations for camps and colonies lost 48.5 percent of their staff. Similarly, the guard complement shrank by 40.3 percent with 109,206 positions eliminated, while the sanatoriums for upper Gulag leadership experienced a 2 percent increase in staff. Clearly the central Moscow administrators were protecting their own interests and clients when making these adjustments.[60]

While the Gulag was engaged in fulfilling the amnesty decree in April 1953, Beria issued his next major penal reform, transferring the Gulag to the Ministry of Justice (MIu).[61] In conjunction with the reassignment of economic concerns to other ministries, this resulted in a vastly reduced profile for the MVD. It also signaled a potential reorientation of penal affairs away from production and custodial security, the two supposed strengths of the MVD, and toward a program of correction and reeducation. This is confirmed by the fact that the ten so-called special camps for political prisoners were not handed over to the MIu but were instead moved to the MVD's prison division. The USSR's political prisoners, deemed more of a security concern and less susceptible to or worthy of reeducation, were thus retained within the police apparatus.[62]

Beyond the transfer or cancellation of many of the MVD's economic tasks, the amnesty of 27 March, and the reassignment of the Gulag itself to the MIu, other steps were taken under Beria to reform the Soviet Union's organs of repression. In the amnesty decree itself Beria called for a complete revision of the criminal codes of the Soviet Union, the implication being that they were too harsh. This stemmed from a joint report made to Beria (likely on his request) from the MIu, MVD, and

Supreme Court that found that far too many Soviet citizens were being incarcerated for minor crimes even though they presented no danger to society. The serious deleterious effects of incarceration on the prisoner and his family (and by extension all of Soviet society) were not being taken into account by the Stalinist legal system. The report therefore recommended that terms of less than three years be substituted with forced labor without deprivation of freedom, a fine, or simply with administrative disciplining. Other crimes, such as unexcused absence from work (150,000 were convicted of this in 1952) and nonfulfillment of the minimum labor quota by collective farmers (over 100,000 such cases in 1952), should be decriminalized altogether.[63] In response to these calls for sentencing reform, Minister of Justice Konstantin Petrovich Gorshenin drafted changes to the Criminal Code which, had they been implemented for 1952, would have reduced the number of convictions from 1.47 million people to around 700,000–750,000 by turning many crimes into administrative offenses and completely decriminalizing others.[64] Actually the impetus for criminal law reform predated 1953, with the MIu having worked on such a project from 1948 to 1952.[65] Now, with Stalin dead, it was time to revive the process.

Other reforms and proposed reforms followed. Noting that most Western countries did not have passport restrictions for released prisoners while the Soviet Union had 340 locations in addition to the border zone where former inmates could not live, Beria proposed to leave just Moscow, Leningrad, Vladivostok, Sevastopol, and Kronstadt as restricted areas for those formerly convicted of serious crimes.[66] In April, Beria ordered that instruments of torture be removed from Lefortovo and the Ministry of State Security (MGB)'s special prisons.[67] Also that month the "Doctors' Plot" case was swiftly reviewed and closed, with the accused physicians walking free.[68] The legality of the edicts of February and October 1948 mandating perpetual internal exile for political prisoners who fulfilled their terms of imprisonment was called into question by MVD chief Sergei Nikiforovich Kruglov, who, having investigated the matter on Beria's instructions, recommended immediate release for those exiled under these laws.[69] Finally, Beria in June 1953 proposed restricting the activity of the MVD's notorious Special Tribunal (Osoboe Soveshchanie) and freeing 1.7 million special settlers.[70]

Beyond their immediate results, the amnesty and other reforms of 1953 had great ideological significance in that they presented to the Soviet public a new interpretation of the term legality (zakonnost') or socialist legality. Rather than denoting the state's commitment to punish all lawbreakers as in the 1940s, legality came to signify a new commitment to restoring and preserving the rights of Soviet subjects, to protect them, as it were, from the state itself.[71] As declared in relation to the Doctors' Plot, "every worker, every collective farmer, every Soviet intellectual can peacefully and confidently work, knowing that his rights are under the reliable protection of the Soviet socialist law."[72] Closely associated with this was the widespread use of the term humaneness (*gumannost'*), or socialist humaneness, as an attribute of the state, suggesting compassion rather than revolutionary zeal. Designed along with collective leadership to help fill the ideological void created by the death of the great leader Stalin, this new emphasis on legality and humaneness simultaneously undercut the image of Stalin as infallible. After all, if legality was being restored, as an editorial in *Pravda* proclaimed in April 1953, that undeniably meant it had been broken during the late leader's reign.[73] If humaneness was being established, that implied that the Stalinist period was inhumane. The campaign for socialist legality and humaneness that was quickly adopted as the new party line by justice officials and procurators thus demarcated a clear shift from the recent past, even as the terms of that shift were still being negotiated.

The Gulag under Dual Control

It is debatable how far Beria would have gone toward reforming the penal system had he been allowed to continue. He had certainly been able to channel great momentum for reform in the first months following Stalin's death and one might presume that he would have continued on that path until his power was secure as first among Stalin's heirs. Indeed, the example of Khrushchev using reform and explicit de-Stalinization to separate himself from his rivals suggests as much. But Beria was not given the opportunity for further reform. Fearful of Beria's power and upset at some of his foreign policy positions, Khrushchev and his peers plotted to remove him. On 26 June 1953 they arrested him in the Kremlin, stripped him of his posts, and imprisoned him while criminal charges were prepared. In December he was found guilty of trumped-up charges of espionage, sentenced to death, and executed.[74]

Removing Beria from power, however, did not stop the reform of the Soviet criminal justice system. Indeed, Beria's actions in this regard enjoyed the support of his colleagues, who continued to explore further reforms even while rolling back some of his other initiatives. On 1 September 1953, as recommended previously by Beria, the MVD's Special Tribunal was eliminated with the injunction that all cases decided by it be reviewed.[75] As Kruglov and Roman Andreevich Rudenko, newly appointed head of the Procuracy, explained, these courts were conducted without the presence of the accused and without witnesses, thus leading to the possibility of incorrect verdicts and on occasion to "gross perversion (*izvrashcheniia*) of Soviet laws."[76] The Central Committee of the Communist

Party responded to this proposal by establishing in December 1953 a committee to review Special Tribunal cases from 1945 onward within a six-month time frame.[77]

Stalin's heirs also continued to discuss changes to the Criminal Code. Shortly after Beria's arrest, Kliment Efremovich Voroshilov sent a note to Khrushchev and Malenkov proposing the creation of a commission to review the law codes of the Soviet Union. His complaint, and that of many Soviet jurists, was that laws were contradictory, punishments often did not fit the crime (sentences for murder were capped at 10 years while group theft resulted in 10–20 years), and some acts defined as criminal should be downgraded to administrative offenses or decriminalized altogether so as to no longer "artificially raise the number of prisoners."[78] Malenkov and the Council of Ministers duly approved this proposal, instructing the MVD, Procuracy, and Supreme Court to help draft new codes.[79] Together with Beria's earlier proposal, this note set in motion a long but important process of rewriting or creating anew a host of law codes and regulatory statutes. As Harold Berman, writing in 1963, perceived, "the law reform movement which started in 1953 and gathered increasing momentum throughout the following years may prove to have been the most significant aspect of Soviet social, economic and political development in the decade after Stalin's death."[80]

While Stalin's successors continued Beria's work of revising the laws and structures that sentenced people to imprisonment, they also took a few steps toward reforming the Gulag itself. The most notable of these involved the loosening of restrictions in the MVD-administered special camps in response to mass uprisings that broke out in May in Norilsk and in Vorkuta in July 1953. Precipitated by specific cases of brutality by guards but also the product of seething discontent among political prisoners, the uprisings demonstrated the possibility of coordinated protest in the large corrective-labor camps of the Gulag. Fearing the spread of the strikes to other camps and the sustained loss of economic output, the penal authorities moved swiftly to break them, first by negotiation and concessions and then, where these failed, by brute military force. Still, during initial negotiations the strikers were able to extract significant concessions from the MVD that brought treatment of political prisoners more in line with those inhabiting the regular corrective-labor camps of the Gulag: the hated identification numbers were removed from their clothing, bars and locks were removed from the barracks, the system of workday credits (which reduced an inmate's sentence according to work performed) was granted, the workday was reduced to nine hours, and prisoners were given the right to meet with relatives, correspond with them once per month, and send money home.[81]

A final result of the uprisings of 1953 came on 30 September 1953, when the MVD, MIu, and Procuracy issued a joint order calling for the transfer of all prisoners out of the special camps except for those convicted of the most serious

counterrevolutionary crimes: traitors, spies, diversionists, terrorists, Trotsky-
ists, rightists, Mensheviks, and Socialist Revolutionaries. To this end special
commissions were formed to review the file of every prisoner in the special
camps and given six weeks to complete their task.[82] This order highlights a
constant problem for the Gulag, both under Stalin and at least for the first several years under Khrushchev. Soviet penology consistently called for the classification and separation of inmates by a variety of factors that changed over
time, including gender, sentence type and length, number of convictions, health,
age, and behavior while in places of confinement.[83] And this was not just a
Soviet impulse, but the recommendation of penal reformers globally.[84] Due to
insufficient resources, overcrowding, a lax attitude toward such restrictions,
and constant "production concerns," however, classification in practice was
regarded by most within the Stalinist Gulag apparatus as a suggestion rather
than a mandate. Indeed, these 1953 commissions were the first of several in the
Khrushchev era tasked with sorting Gulag inmates according to new or existing regulations. Nonetheless, prisoners continued to be improperly mixed on
a mass scale until 1962–63 when, after a final Gulag-wide sorting and the creation of new institutional controls, such mixing became a minor phenomenon.

As the new caretaker of the Gulag, the MIu was supposed to be a more natural
institutional home for the country's correctional facilities, allowing the same
agency that sentenced the criminal to imprisonment and correction to then administer that sentence. Yet a few factors worked against this new arrangement.
Although the MIu had administered a portion of Soviet places of confinement
through the early 1930s, it was by 1953 some twenty years removed from such
experience. The leadership simply did not know how to run a prison system.
Moreover, the MIu was overwhelmed by the sheer size of the penal system, not to
mention its entrenched problems. It already presided over several layers of courts
in addition to various educational institutes and programs, lawyers, and notaries,
and it had responsibility, along with the Supreme Court and other bodies, for the
codification and systematization of laws.[85] And whereas the entire central apparatus of the MIu in 1953 had only 519 employees, the Gulag apparatus had over
1,000.[86] These factors resulted in a distinct lack of interest in the Gulag on the
part of MIu leadership, including Deputy Minister of Justice P. I. Kudriavtsev, to
whom direct responsibility for the Gulag was given.[87] The MIu's lengthy plan for
top-level ministerial leadership in the third quarter of 1953, for instance, called
only for a review of the Gulag's personnel department and the fourth-quarter
plan ignored the newly acquired penal system completely. This lack of interest in
the Gulag was duly replicated at the republican level; the Ukrainian Ministry of
Justice's third-quarter plan contained not a single item related to the Gulag and

the only Gulag-related plan for the fourth quarter was a review of the guard contingent.[88]

On 21 January 1954 the Council of Ministers ordered the return of the Gulag from the MIu to the MVD.[89] Whereas the original transfer of the Gulag to the MIu was designed to break the power of the MVD, this reversal represented a realization that after decades of experience the MVD was simply more capable of running the labor-camp system. A letter from Gulag inspector V. C. Liamin to Malenkov on 30 December 1953 explicitly made the claim that the MIu was unsuitable as the Gulag's parent organization.[90] Liamin found that the MIu was never prepared to take on the responsibility of running the camps, and "does not engage this work which is new for them."[91] He further contended that the relationship between the Gulag/MIu leadership in Moscow and the local camp units had "in essence, a symbolic, but not practical character."[92] This viewpoint is, not surprisingly, confirmed by an MVD report from May 1954, which blamed the MIu for allowing a serious degeneration of control over the camps.[93]

Yet the removal of the Gulag from the MIu also stemmed directly from the power struggle occurring in the top ranks of the Soviet Union. Whereas Malenkov and Beria took steps toward consolidating ministries and increasing the centralization of power, a process that included the transfer of the Gulag to the MIu, Khrushchev positioned himself against Malenkov at the end of 1953 and the beginning of 1954 as an advocate of decentralization. The transfer of the Gulag back to the MVD was part of a new proliferation of ministries in early 1954 that resulted from this stance. It also constituted the beginning of a gradual campaign to emasculate and, in 1956, eliminate the All-Union MIu, which had become for Khrushchev a poster child for overcentralization and unnecessary bureaucracy.[94] Thus, relieving the MIu of the Gulag was not only about efficiency and inexperience; it was also part of the post-Stalin power struggle between Khrushchev and Malenkov.

Associated with the return of the Gulag to the MVD was the transfer of the special camps from the prison division of the MVD back to the Gulag administration. This occurred on 8 February 1954 and gave the Gulag responsibility for ten additional camps populated by 208,537 political prisoners and 31,387 guards.[95] Over the next few months, however, the special camps gradually lost their special status. On 26 March 1954, for instance, the MVD ordered that cultural-educational work in the special camps would no longer be governed by the special decree of 21 August 1949 but by the regular decree governing all camps of 26 February 1954.[96] This process culminated in the spring and summer of 1954 when the special camps were formally turned into regular camps. Already in May, for instance, Special Camp No. 6 was liquidated, its camp units turned over to the Vorkutinskii Camp (Vorkutlag).[97]

With the Gulag transferred from the MIu back to the MVD and the soon-to-be-eliminated special camps reintegrated into the system, the Gulag empire in May 1954 consisted of 65 corrective-labor camps and another 798 camp subdivisions or colonies in the 90 administrations (or departments, depending on size) of corrective-labor camps and colonies attached to republican, provincial, and territorial MVD apparatuses.[98] Together they held 1,360,303 prisoners on 1 April 1954, with 897,051 of them being held in the camps.[99] In addition, the Gulag apparatus included 1,986 ambulatory stations and 1,167 hospitals for its inmates, which together featured 71,641 beds. Thus, although a significant reduction in the size of the Gulag had taken place during 1953 as a result of the Beria amnesty, the penal empire remained enormous. To administer this empire a total of 205,574 people worked for the Gulag, including 872 central administrators in Moscow, 17,997 local administrators, 116,040 guards, and 70,665 other personnel.[100] The Gulag staff at this point thereby equaled almost one-fifth the inmate population of the camps and colonies. During the remainder of the decade this proportion would only grow.

The Reforms of 1954

The transfer of the Gulag back to the MVD and of the special camps to the Gulag in early 1954 set the stage for a new cycle of reform. After the spate of reforms during the spring and summer of 1953, Stalin's heirs paused in their reform of the penal system. This was no doubt due to a number of factors: the matter of substantive reform needed to be studied and analyzed, there were other pressing affairs to attend to, and there was likely some hesitancy caused by the uncertain political climate. None wished to be seen as a second Beria eager to enact far-reaching reform in order to gain the upper hand in the succession struggle. There was likely also some anticipation, unfounded as it turns out, that the MIu would take the lead in continuing the process of Gulag reform. The return of the Gulag to the MVD in early 1954, however, brought renewed determination to decisively transform the Soviet penal system.

This determination is evident in a meeting of the Central Committee Presidium held on 8 February 1954 to address the creation of the KGB and the reappointment of Kruglov to the position of minister of internal affairs. Kruglov had made a name for himself in the Soviet security apparatus while purging Nikolai Ezhov's clients from the NKVD in 1938, and was then promoted to deputy people's commissar of internal affairs to Beria in 1941. When Stalin removed Beria from that post, Kruglov was promoted to MVD chief, where he remained throughout the late Stalin era, and he was part of the plot to depose Beria in

1953.[101] Kruglov was thus a remnant of the Stalinist justice apparatus who survived the initial purges of 1953 through his useful opposition to Beria.

The transcript of this February 1954 meeting to reappoint Kruglov, though abbreviated and incomplete, is quite valuable as it provides one of the few glimpses, outside of official reports and orders, into how Stalin's successors viewed the MVD and its penal system. As the discussion turned to the issue of the MVD, Khrushchev and his fellow Presidium member Lazar Moiseevich Kaganovich began by criticizing Kruglov for the "passive" attitude his ministry had displayed since the arrest of Beria. It appears they were primarily referring to the process of eliminating Beria's former allies from the security organs, but the general critique was that Kruglov was too set in his past ways. He was unwilling to fight to change the old attitudes prevalent in his ministry.

The discussion then turned to the Gulag and here Stalin's heirs leveled three primary criticisms at Soviet penal institutions. First, echoing the broader critique of untrustworthy personnel in the MVD, Presidium member and minister of defense Nikolai Aleksandrovich Bulganin charged that the camps were poorly staffed. Specifically, he criticized the informal procedure of "sending [recently disciplined] officers to serve as camp commanders as a penalty assignment." Because the Gulag was viewed as the lowest rung in the MVD hierarchy, this was a long-standing practice.[102] Second, Stalin's heirs criticized the Gulag for being too focused on economic affairs. While Kaganovich remarked that Kruglov had a developed a good record with construction, Voroshilov retorted that he should "pay primary attention not to construction, but to the correction of people."[103] Khrushchev agreed, arguing with a hint of sarcasm that Kruglov "doesn't understand his task—as head of the camps he's saying, 'I am building.'" It is clear that Stalin's heirs were trying to distance themselves from the Stalin-era policy of treating the camps primarily as, in the words of Maksim Zakharovich Saburov, head of the State Planning Agency (Gosplan), "a source of labor power."[104]

The final criticism leveled at the Gulag, which echoed to a great extent the inordinate focus on economics, was the very reliance on corrective-labor camps themselves. According to Presidium member and Khrushchev ally Anastas Ivanovich Mikoian, who lamented the incarceration of people convicted of minor crimes such as petty theft, "the camps ruin" their inmates rather than correct them. Khrushchev continued this line of attack by proposing that the penal system should "return to Dzerzhinskii's system of factories and workshops." In other words, it should be based on much smaller institutions that kept inmates close to home, taught them valuable vocational skills, and cultivated the power of the prisoner collective. This model, supposedly rooted in Leninism rather than Stalinism, would restore to the penal system its intended function of reeducation rather than repression. Finally, Malenkov summarized the sentiment of the Presidium by simply stating: "The camps are not our ideal. [The penal system] must be rebuilt anew."[105] This, then, was the task set forth by Stalin's heirs in early 1954: replace the large camps with a different type of penal institution, diminish the economic focus in favor of reeducation, and provide better cadres to staff the Gulag.

It is notable that even in this time of political uncertainty and power struggle, Stalin's heirs agreed that the process of transforming the Gulag was far from complete. With the partial exception of Khrushchev's vague proposal of replacing the camps with a system of workshops, however, there was no clear vision of how to transform the Gulag into a reeducational apparatus. Moreover, with the rivalry between Malenkov and Khrushchev growing, neither was able to place a protégé at the head of the MVD who might have pursued Gulag reform more aggressively. In fact, while criticizing Kruglov for his attention to economic affairs, they nonetheless retained him as the man primarily responsible for the planned transformation. Later that year Dolgikh was replaced as head of the Gulag, but his successor, Sergei Egorovich Egorov, had served since 1939 as a top-level economic manager within the MVD.[106] Thus, the personnel decisions of 1954 reflect not a change in direction but rather the continuation of Stalinist policies.

A series of decrees passed between March and July 1954, however, did set forth the new mission of turning the Soviet penal system into a place of reeducation rather than labor extraction. The first, "On the Primary Tasks of the MVD," passed by the Presidium of the Central Committee on 12 March 1954, declared the utmost importance of "improving the operation of corrective-labor camps in regard to reeducating inmates." It called for better and more qualified personnel and admonished the Gulag to improve the use of labor, education, and political work in preparing inmates to return "to an honest working life." Finally, it mandated that a new statute governing corrective-labor camps and colonies be presented in short order to the Council of Ministers.[107] In the wake of this decree the MVD created commissions to inspect a number of Gulag institutions. The information they gathered then informed a summary report sent on 26 May 1954 by Kruglov to the Central Committee on the state of the Gulag, which contained a draft of the Central Committee decree that was subsequently passed on 10 July 1954.[108]

This decree, "On measures for improving the work of the corrective-labor camps and colonies of the MVD," provided a more detailed outline for revamping the penal system. In line with the conclusions repeated by the Presidium months earlier, it began by stating that the "primary attention in the corrective-labor camps and colonies is devoted to economic activity to the detriment of fulfilling the important state tasks of educating and correcting convicts, teaching

[them] labor professions, and returning them after serving their sentences to an honest working life."[109] From poor living conditions to unqualified political workers, the correctional aspect of the Gulag's correctional-labor facilities had too long been neglected. The lax attitude toward crime perpetrated by prisoners in the penal facilities was also heavily criticized. Attached to this edict was the new "Statute on the Corrective-Labor Camps and Colonies of the Ministry of Internal Affairs of the USSR," which essentially replaced the old corrective-labor code of 1933 as the document governing Gulag affairs.[110] In order to facilitate the reeducation of prisoners, it called for sending a greater number of inmates to the colonies rather than the camps. Amending the previous code, which sent only those with sentences of up to three years to colonies, the new statute added two more categories of prisoners who should be incarcerated in colonies rather than camps: all first-time convicts, excepting political and otherwise dangerous prisoners; and those entering the system from a juvenile correctional facility upon turning eighteen years of age.[111] This desire to send increasingly more prisoners to the smaller, local colonies instead of the large and distant camps endured throughout the Khrushchev era and may be considered a crucial element of the post-Stalin reform of the Soviet penal system.

In practice, one would expect new regulations requiring a higher proportion of convicts to be sent to colonies rather than camps to result in an increase in the number of prisoners in colonies and a simultaneous decrease in the number of prisoners in camps. Due to the various release programs to be discussed below, however, both categories of prisoners declined. What is surprising is that the percentage of prisoners in provincial Gulag corrective-labor divisions, which administered the colonies, actually decreased, from 35.8 percent on 1 July 1954 to 29.9 percent on 1 January 1956. A year and a half after the 1954 statute was passed, contrary to its intentions, a greater percentage of prisoners were being held in the large camps. Much of this can be explained by the nature of release programs, which tended to free a disproportionate number of short-term inmates, those that would have been held in the colonies. Yet other evidence from regional corrective-labor networks suggests that this decline in the percentage of inmates being held in colonies was also due to other factors. The Lithuanian Department of Corrective-Labor Colonies, in response to the 10 July document, dutifully transformed one of its camp subdivisions into a colony in September 1954.[112] The Estonian Department of Corrective-Labor Colonies, however, actually turned its only corrective-labor colony into a camp subdivision after the 10 July decree.[113] Such paradoxes evident in the push to favor colonies over camps suggest at minimum a lack of oversight but also a half-hearted commitment to structural reform.

Reducing the Inmate Population:
The Releases of 1954–1955

In addition to admonishing the MVD to keep inmates in smaller and more correctional facilities in their home provinces and reorient its operations around reeducation, which will be discussed in greater detail in chapter 2, the Soviet leadership also took steps in 1954–55 to reduce the rate of incarceration. The process of law code reform ultimately stalled, with the Central Committee rejecting in both 1955 and 1956 the Criminal Code and Criminal Procedure Code drafted by the legislative commission established in December 1953.[114] Thanks in part to Khrushchev's insistence on decentralizing these codes to the republican level, and thus involve fifteen additional commissions in the process, new codes would not be issued until 1958–61. In the meantime, however, some laws were passed to mitigate the worst provisions of the Stalinist legal framework. A Supreme Court explanation in May 1954 followed by a retroactively applied petty theft law of 1955 that mandated up to only three months imprisonment or twelve months corrective labor without incarceration allowed small-scale thieves to escape the draconian antitheft laws of 1947.[115] The last of the notorious Stalin-era labor laws was rescinded in April 1956, which freed those incarcerated for quitting their jobs without permission.[116] And in 1956–57 new categories of petty speculation and petty hooliganism greatly reduced punishments for minor crimes.[117]

While reform of the Criminal Code continued in piecemeal fashion, still-existing harsh sentencing guidelines continued to put upward pressure on the inmate population. Despite the Beria amnesty of 1953, as early as 24 October 1953 Dolgikh warned that a dramatic rise in sentencing was rapidly refilling the camps.[118] This was not wholly accurate; whereas the total number of convictions by all courts in the early 1950s was around 1.6 million per year, from 1953 to 1956 the number hovered between 1.1 and 1.23 million.[119] Still, these numbers were significant and until the legal framework could be fully amended, stopgap measures were necessary to prevent the shrunken Gulag from being expanded back to its Stalinist dimensions. Thus, the amnesty of 1953, while important, was certainly not the only mass release of the 1950s. More limited amnesties along with other release mechanisms were put into effect in 1954 and 1955, freeing hundreds of thousands of prisoners. At the same time, work was begun on reviewing the individual cases of political prisoners, whom the government still deemed too dangerous to be simply covered by an amnesty.

The first of the early release programs of 1954–55 was an amnesty announced on 24 April 1954 that provided for the release of those who had committed crimes under the age of eighteen, providing they had they served at least one-third their term (and a minimum of six months) and exhibited good behavior and a positive attitude toward work.[120] This freed a total of 22,670 Gulag inmates.[121] Another step taken to reduce the inmate population in 1954 was greatly increased use of Article 457 of the Russian Criminal Procedure Code (and its corollaries in the law codes of other union republics), which provided for early release for those suffering from incurable diseases. This resulted in the release of 44,136 inmates during 1954–55; indeed, almost 10 percent of all releases in 1954 were made according to this article.[122] Heavy use of this statute allowed the Gulag to jettison those who cost too much to maintain and who provided little economic benefit, but it also created an easy avenue for corruption: well-connected prisoners could buy their freedom through Article 457 by working out a deal with their camp commander and a local doctor.[123] After 1955, however, Article 457 was used much less frequently, falling to under 1 percent of releases by 1958.[124]

The final early release mechanisms instituted in 1954 were parole (*uslovno-dosrochnoe osvobozhdenie*) and workday credits. Although it had featured prominently in the early Soviet penal system, parole had been rescinded on 15 July 1939.[125] Passed by the Supreme Soviet on 14 July 1954, the new parole act called for the early release of those who had served two-thirds of their sentences and were not perceived as further threats to Soviet society. In fact, the 1954 decree was almost an exact copy of the 1926 Russian Criminal Code; the lone exception was that according to the 1926 Criminal Code and the 1933 Corrective-Labor Code, prisoners could be released having served only half their term on good behavior.[126] The reinstatement of parole was a significant step both in reducing the Gulag population and in providing a stimulus for reeducation. For Khrushchev and the reforming wing of the Soviet criminological establishement it signified a return to Leninist ideals of socialist legality and a turn away from the legal distortions of Stalin's reign. It also placed Soviet penal practices more in line with international norms; indeed, the post-World War II era globally witnessed a dramatic rise in parole and similar release mechanisms as part of a broader push toward the deinstitutionalization of punishment.[127]

Workday credits, which granted sentence reductions of one or two days for every day plan targets were met, provided a different opportunity to earn early release. Similar to parole, it had played a prominent role in the early Soviet penal system, but was rescinded in 1939. In the late 1940s, however, a few camp bosses lobbied successfully to have it partially restored, citing its ability to motivate inmates to work hard. It was then gradually extended to more and more inmates until 1954, when it was made available to all. This system was appealing to both Gulag officials, who had full control over the system and who appreciated its ability to prompt plan fulfillment, and to prisoners, who received tangible benefits in exchange for their labor. Parole, meanwhile, was administered by the courts and for the inmates was far less certain. Moreover, workday credits for most inmates offered a quicker path to release.[128]

Not surprisingly, therefore, many camp commanders in the 1950s were reluctant to use parole. The task of gathering the necessary materials and sending them to the local court (together with the prisoner) was tedious, and the courts were often overloaded with cases and had little time for parole requests.[129] There was also confusion about whether workday credits should be counted toward the amount of sentence served when calculating parole eligibility until May 1955, when the Supreme Soviet decreed that the two systems could not be combined.[130] Fortunately for Gulag officials disinclined to use it, parole was easy to deny based on the vague wording of the law, which sanctioned parole only for inmates "firmly on the path to correction." Sparing use of the new parole statute prompted a multitude of complaints by prisoners who claimed that they had fulfilled the requirements of the law but were not being freed, or that only those who were close to the administration or who paid bribes were granted parole.[131] But little was done to compel camp commanders to make broader use of parole. As one official reportedly told his prisoners after they lobbied for parole, "If we want to, we'll release [you], but if we don't want to, we won't."[132] Although in 1955 parolees accounted for 5.3 percent of all prisoners—with 12.7 percent of all releases in 1955 coming through parole—by 1958 those figures had plummeted to 0.2 percent and 0.7 percent respectively.[133] Still, a total of 117,570 prisoners in 1954–55 gained their freedom as a result of the parole decree.[134] Workday credits, meanwhile, became a well-established path for obtaining early release.

Additional amnesties in 1955 aided the process of maintaining a reduced Gulag population. The first, passed on 24 May 1955, was designed to free those convicted of minor theft either of personal or government property before 1 January 1955. This only resulted in the release of 2,128 inmates, however, as sentences for "minor" theft were generally very short and few theft convictions were categorized as minor.[135] The next amnesty of 1955, passed on 3 September, released 77,333 invalids, seniors, those suffering from incurable diseases, pregnant women, and women with small children. Although these categories had already been covered in the amnesty of 1953, such economically undesirable inmates had again populated the Gulag.[136] This time, though, the amnesty was heavily criticized not only because it emphasized the economic orientation of the Gulag, but it also released inmates convicted for dangerous crimes on the sole basis that they could not be used in the Gulag as productive laborers.[137] Among the prisoners freed under the 3 September 1955 decree were 3,954 counterrevolutionary prisoners, 2,721 murderers, and around 10,000 recidivists. Upon receiving this information on 6 February 1956 the Supreme Soviet instructed Rudenko of the Procuracy, Ivan Aleksandrovich Serov of the KGB, Gorshenin of the MIu, and Semen Nikiforovich Perevertkin of the MVD to review these cases individually to determine which of these ex-cons should be returned to the camps.[138] It also issued an order disallowing the future amnesty of such prisoners and halted the application of the amnesty to those convicted of grand theft of socialist property.[139]

The last amnesty of 1955, passed on 17 September, was the first and only to cover specific political crimes. Point one of this decree provided for the immediate release of Soviet citizens who assisted the German invaders during World War II and who received a sentence of up to ten years according to Article 58 of the Criminal Code. Of course, as this decree was passed approximately ten years after the end of the war, the actual benefit was minimal. More importantly, point two reduced longer sentences by one half, and points three and seven freed citizens convicted of serving in the German army or police corps or of being captured by the Germans. All prisoners freed by this amnesty were to have their convictions overturned and their citizen rights restored in full.[140] Initially this amnesty did not apply to former soldiers convicted of surrendering to the enemy, but on 18 September 1956 they too became subject to release.[141] In total, 59,610 Gulag inmates were released as a result of this measure.[142]

Because the Soviets perceived political prisoners on average as potentially more destructive to society than common criminals, the vast majority of them were not covered by the above-mentioned amnesties. Yet Khrushchev and his peers knew intimately that many of those incarcerated for political crimes were, in fact, innocent. After all, all of Stalin's lieutenants had been involved in purging perceived or potential enemies, notably during the Great Terror of 1937–38. Beginning already in 1953, therefore, they began a secretive process of reviewing individual files on a case-by-case basis to determine who was innocent and who was properly convicted of anti-Soviet activity. Almost immediately after Stalin's death, reviews of the most noteworthy political cases from the postwar era began, resulting in the release and rehabilitation (often posthumously) of those convicted in the Doctors' Plot, the Leningrad Affair, the Mingrelian Affair, and many others.[143] Initially, however, these reviews did not extend to crimes committed during the 1930s and were not conducted on a mass basis. Once begun, however, the process of reviewing the past could not easily be stopped. This is apparent in a 19 March 1954 letter from MVD head Kruglov, Procurator General Rudenko, KGB chief Serov, and Minister of Justice Gorshenin and others to Khrushchev and Malenkov, in which they encouraged a review of cases for every political prisoner being held in camps, colonies, prisons, or exile.[144] As a basis for this request they cited the uncovering of improper criminal investigative techniques and wholesale falsification of cases perpetrated by the MVD against honest and devoted Soviet citizens.

In response to this letter, the Presidium on 4 May 1954 passed a decree providing for the review of political cases. It created a central commission to investigate the cases of prisoners or exiles convicted by the Special Tribunal of the NKVD-MGB-MVD and Unified State Political Organization (OGPU) Collegium (*kollegiia*). It also ordered the establishment of local commissions to review cases of the NKVD troikas. Due to the overwhelming number of cases requiring review, work proceeded slowly at first. But by 29 April 1955 a total of 237,412 cases had been reviewed, resulting in freedom or a reduced sentence for 107,114 prisoners and exiles.[145] By March 1956 these numbers had grown to 337,183 and 153,502, respectively.[146] Largely as a result of these case reviews, the number of political prisoners plummeted from 448,344 on 1 April 1954 to just 91,833 on 1 April 1956.[147]

Despite this drop, one cannot ignore the fact that nearly 100,000 prisoners remained incarcerated for political crimes after their files had been reviewed. As Nanci Adler notes, many of the commission members, "who loudly proclaimed the need for reform, were exhibiting a very different attitude when they rejected the overturning of so many sentences."[148] One prominent prisoner not freed was Lev Nikolaevich Gumilev, son of renowned poet Anna Akhmatova. On 8 February 1954 she wrote of his innocence and her immeasurable suffering on his account, concluding, "The only thing that could restore my strength is the return of my son who is suffering, I am convinced, free from guilt." In June, however, the Procuracy denied her appeal in a report signed by Rudenko himself, claiming that Gumilev was properly charged for slandering the Soviet state (for saying, among other things, that there was no freedom of the press).[149] Most of these remaining inmates, as discussed below, would soon be covered by the second round of case reviews during 1956.

Partially due to the 1953 crime wave but also because of the public's longstanding mistrust of criminals, those returning from the camps in the post-Stalin years faced numerous difficulties readjusting to society. Arranging for housing and employment was difficult, as was adjusting to social and family life. And difficulties readjusting were not solely the product of discrimination imposed by state and society. As Małgorzata Gizejewska so eloquently writes regarding Polish inmates released from the Dal'stroi camps, "none of them could entirely fill the gap between their lives and the lost possibilities."[150] More bluntly, in the words of Orlando Figes, "people returned from the labour camps physically and mentally broken."[151] The difficulty of returning to society after years in prison, however, is not unique to the Soviet case but is a problem common to all societies. Part of this has to do with social dynamics and perhaps even human nature, but the absence of formal release proceedings may also play a role. As Kai Erikson writes, the criminal "is ushered into the deviant position by a decisive and often dramatic ceremony, yet is retired from it with scarcely a word or public notice. . . . Nothing has happened to cancel out the stigmas imposed upon him by earlier commitment ceremonies. . . . It should not be surprising, then, that the people of the community are apt to greet the returning deviant with a considerable degree of apprehension and distrust, for in a very real sense they are not at all sure who he is."[152] Indeed, as will be discussed later, this apprehension and distrust in the Soviet case would by the late 1950s play a role in reversing the trend toward reeducation as the primary aim of the Gulag.

The early release of hundreds of thousands of inmates in 1954–55 led to a second round of downsizing of the Gulag, both in terms of staff and penal institutions. Not only was there no need to maintain the same sprawling apparatus, the costs of doing so constantly threatened to undermine Gulag budgets. Whereas in early 1954 there were still 65 corrective-labor camps, by early 1956 only 45 remained.[153] Correspondingly, the administrative and guard staffs of the Gulag declined dramatically. In January 1954, following the deep personnel cuts of 1953, there were a total of 205,574 people employed by the Gulag, including 116,356 guards; just two years later those numbers had been cut to 169,832 and 96,653 respectively.[154] Yet several factors mitigated against an orderly cutback of excess administrators, guards, camps, and prisons. First, after the initial amnesty of 1953, the camp population was in a state of constant flux, with the various mass releases countered by a constant inflow of new inmates. Not knowing the level at which the inmate population would stabilize made planning difficult. Understandably, in such a climate, local camp bureaucracies often attempted to minimize cutbacks in their domains. Moreover, economic concerns sometimes dictated that some camps remained open despite a lack of inmates, and a limited number of new camps were even created to service important construction projects.[155] In a few cases the resistance to personnel cuts resulted in gross inefficiencies. By mid-1954, for example, the Gulag colonies in Pskov Province employed 238 administrators but held only 420 prisoners. Similarly the 848 inmates remaining in the Penza Province colonies were managed by 406 administrators.[156] Yet despite these pressures to resist the closure of camps, a marked reduction in the size of the Gulag did occur.

The downsizing of the Gulag from 1953–56 was important not only for the Gulag but for the local state and party organs where the Gulag operated. Citing the need for prisoner labor, a few provinces lobbied for the MVD to retain their camp subdivisions.[157] For the most part, however, local economic agencies and provincial party organizations were eager to acquire abandoned camp property. In Vorkuta, local agencies turned former inmate barracks into dormitories for newly recruited free workers, although predictable complaints from the workers quickly forced the construction of new housing.[158] The Stavropol' party and government petitioned to turn one depopulated corrective-labor colony into a summer resort due to its proximity to a picturesque lake.[159] Even more desirable for provincial administrations than the camps and colonies were the MVD's prisons, which were often located in the center of town. Arguing they presented an offending spectacle to passersby and that the valuable urban space and buildings could be better used for housing, offices, schools, factories, or hospitals, local party and state bodies lobbied (often successfully) in the mid-1950s to take possession of these local prisons.[160]

Nikolai Dudorov and the Reforms of 1956

The reforms and releases of 1953–55 signaled a significant break with the late Stalinist Gulag. Characterized as too large, too unwieldy, and too focused on economic production at the expense of other goals, notably the reeducation of prisoners, the penal system was tasked with a wholesale reinvention of what it should look like and what deprivation of freedom should mean to its inhabitants. Yet changing the size, structure, and orientation of the Gulag proved a monumental task. Significant reforms had been accomplished by the end of 1955, most notably a substantial drop in the inmate population and a new statute that unambiguously declared the reeducation of prisoners as the top priority of the penal system, but much remained unchanged.

The year 1956 marked a reinvigoration of Gulag reform, prompted by Khrushchev's famous "secret speech" at the Twentieth Party Congress and his appointment of Nikolai Pavlovich Dudorov, who had never worked in the security apparatuses, as head of the MVD. That year the vast majority of political prisoners that still remained incarcerated after the 1954–55 reviews were released, and a new plan for transforming the Gulag was drafted and approved. During the following years additional reforms and a new statute governing the Gulag were instituted and two mass releases were carried out, bringing the inmate population down to levels not witnessed since the 1920s. Simultaneously, the Gulag administration was decentralized until at last, with the liquidation of the All-Union MVD in January 1960, the formal structure of the Soviet Union's penal system split along republican lines into fifteen pieces.

Khrushchev by 1956 had emerged triumphant in the post-Stalin succession struggle, having replaced his chief rival, Malenkov, as head of the Council of Ministers with his ally Bulganin the previous year. His next target was Kruglov, head of the MVD. Although Kruglov had presided over the reforms of 1954 and had convened an unusually large convention of Gulag workers to emphasize the importance of reeducation, he remained at heart an economic manager and a symbol of the Stalinist regime. And he was certainly not one of Khrushchev's trusted clients; as Khrushchev later recalled, "I hardly knew Kruglov."[161] In late 1955 the Presidium of the Central Committee formally condemned Kruglov as an "indifferent Minister of Internal Affairs" and ordered him replaced.[162] During the transfer of power in early 1956 Kruglov was criticized by the Central Committee for not bringing to pass the reeducational reforms contained in the decrees of 12 March and 10 July 1954.[163] It is likely that Procurator General Rudenko, Khrushchev's ally and an advocate of sweeping reform in the security apparatuses, also had a hand in Kruglov's final undoing. Procuracy reports detailed a host of problems, most notably unreformed attitudes toward prisoners, in the country's correctional facilities. The Procuracy was also building a criminal case against Kruglov for crimes perpetrated under Stalin, notably the Chechen-Ingush internal deportations of 1944. This case ended not in conviction, however, but only demotion and ultimately, in 1960, expulsion from the party.[164]

In advancing the outsider Dudorov to minister of internal affairs in early 1956, Khrushchev sought to break the entrenched patron-client system in the upper ranks of the MVD. Born in 1906 in Vladimir Province, Dudorov joined the Communist Party in 1927 and quickly became an upwardly mobile student (*vydvizhenets*) of the first five-year plan. He studied at the Mendeleev Institute in Moscow from 1929 to 1934, becoming a factory shop manager upon completion. Then in 1937 Dudorov began ascending the industrial bureaucracies of the party-state, a process that culminated when Khrushchev promoted him to head the construction department of the Central Committee in December 1954. One wonders if Khrushchev and his colleagues felt any irony in giving the reigns of the MVD to a lifelong economic manager, after criticizing Kruglov and the Gulag in general for being excessively production-oriented. But as Dudorov was a trusted outsider not tainted by the crimes of Stalin's security apparatus, the Presidium on 30 January 1956 confirmed him minister of internal affairs.[165]

A party man himself, Dudorov sought to reform the culture of the MVD and Gulag by infusing its leadership and bureaucracy with trusted party cadres. On 29 February 1956 he asked the Central Committee for 20–25 good communists to serve in high-ranking positions within the MVD leadership, including as new commanders and deputies for the Gulag, police force, and department of juvenile colonies.[166] The same day he also asked for 1,000 lower-level party members for the Gulag's corrective-labor institutions, 450 of which would be made commanders or deputies of colonies or camp points.[167] In response to the first request he was given fourteen leading cadres from party or state organs, including his deputy M. N. Kholodkov (recently from the Moscow party apparatus), who would oversee the Gulag, Gulag commander Pavel Nikolaevich Bakin, and Gulag deputy commander P. N. Kolesnikov.[168] Like Dudorov, Kholodkov and Bakin were not members of the security services but rather Khrushchev's protégés from the party and government organs of Moscow. Beyond creating a break with the previous leadership, Bakin's appointment to head the Gulag also had symbolic importance that spoke to the stature of the penal system within the Soviet state. Whereas the previous two Gulag commanders, Dolgikh and Egorov, had been respectively a lieutenant general and major general, Bakin upon appointment to head the Gulag was made only a colonel in the MVD ranks.

In addition to replacing Kruglov with Dudorov and installing new cadres to lead the Gulag itself, Khrushchev continued the process of reviewing the cases of political prisoners. In early 1956, as his biographer William Taubman asserts, "Khrushchev took the lead in gathering information, pressing for reconsideration of cases, and releasing prisoners."[169] As Khrushchev himself recalled, "for three years we were unable to break with the past, unable to muster the courage and the determination to lift the curtain and see what had been hidden from us about the arrests, the trials, the arbitrary rule, the executions, and everything else that had happened during Stalin's reign."[170] Unsatisfied with the end results of the 1954–55 case reviews of political prisoners, Khrushchev pressed for a second round. On the same day Dudorov was appointed, 30 January 1956, the idea to send party commissions to the camps to review the files of political prisoners and determine releases was proposed by Khrushchev and approved by the Presidium, despite certain unrecorded objections by Voroshilov.[171] As he prepared for his momentous secret speech, therefore, Khrushchev was already taking proactive measures to partially correct the perversions of justice that characterized Stalin's reign.

Delivered on 24 February 1956, Khrushchev's secret speech at the Twentieth Congress of the Communist Party, officially titled "On the Cult of Personality and Its Consequences," was a watershed moment in Khrushchev's de-Stalinization effort. With the succession struggle won, Khrushchev was only partially motivated by a desire to raise his stature in the eyes of party members. More pressing, it seems, was a genuine desire to break with the crimes of the Stalin era, while famously placing all blame on Stalin and Beria, and to unify the party around the banner of Leninism.[172] As Taubman concluded, the speech was "an act of repentance, a way of reclaiming his identity as a decent man by telling the truth."[173] Notable for the criminal justice apparatus reforms of the mid-1950s, Khrushchev accused Stalin of inventing the concept "enemy of the people," of needlessly waging a repressive struggle against the Soviet people and Communist Party, of subverting the mechanisms of justice, and of abandoning the Leninist principles of "persuasion, explanation, and patient cooperation with people." He uncovered to the audience how specific charges, such as those against popular party leader Robert Indrikovich Eikhe, were wholly fabricated. He explained how torture was used to extract confessions.[174] The message could not be clearer: justice under Stalin had been perverted, but it was now being restored. Those falsely accused of being "enemies of the people" would now be rehabilitated.

With Stalin's crimes semipublicly denounced, Khrushchev continued to push for a second round of case reviews of political prisoners. On 12 March, the order to create the commissions tasked with reviewing the files of those convicted under Article 58 was approved in principle, with only minor details to be worked out.[175] The Presidium passed the final version on 19 March 1956 and it became law on 24 March.[176] In contrast to the commissions of 1954–55, the 96 new commissions, staffed by 375 workers, had the authority to release inmates without approval from a central commission in Moscow, although a central commission for coordinating their work was created.[177] In a progress report from 1 August 1956, over 60 percent of cases reviewed ended in a complete overturning of the case and over 20 percent resulted in reduced sentences.[178] These percentages exceeded those of the commissions operating in 1954 and 1955, despite the fact that by 1956 the majority of the most obviously fabricated cases had already been overturned. The work proceeded quickly and in October 1956 the commissions concluded their review.[179] The results were unmistakable: by 1 January 1957 only 18,187 political prisoners remained in the Gulag.[180] Thus, in just a matter of months, the mass contingent of political prisoners that had so long characterized the Soviet Gulag had almost completely disappeared. As memoirist Alla Tumanova later rehearsed: "The period of the Stalinist camps was coming to an end; indeed, they were later exchanged for Khrushchev camps and after that for Brezhnev camps, but those were other camps, with other prisoners."[181] In the following years political cases continued to be overturned by central authorities, but after 1956 this occurred sporadically. Sometimes, as with the previous reviews, the reversal came too late. V. I. Gutianskii died in the Usol'skii Corrective-Labor Camp in 1956 after his appeal to overturn his and his wife's 1950 conviction had been twice denied. In November 1957, however, it was finally reversed by the Supreme Court.[182]

As the Gulag population continued to decline due to the release of political prisoners, its leadership under Dudorov began to devise a plan for a complete reorganization of the penal system. Having received the appropriate signal from Khrushchev, MVD administrators could recommend a substantially altered camp system that rejected the Stalinist model. On 5 April 1956 Dudorov sent the first draft of his proposed overhaul to the Central Committee for review.[183] Setting the tone for the document, the opening paragraph charged that "the state of affairs in the corrective-labor camps and colonies of the MVD USSR has over the course of many years remained poor. The Ministry of Internal Affairs does not provide for the fulfillment of the important state task of reeducating prisoners and returning them to an honest working life in Soviet society." The problem, Dudorov found, was twofold: the Gulag still oriented operations around "economic interests" rather than reeducation, and it took a lax attitude toward isolating dangerous criminals and gangsters from first-time offenders.

The most significant section of the ensuing proposal called for the complete elimination of the corrective-labor camps by the end of 1958 and the establishment of corrective-labor colonies in each republic, province, and territory. The vast majority of criminals were thus to serve their terms in their home regions instead of being sent to faraway camps. This reform would greatly reduce the financial burden associated with transferring inmates to their place of detention and would promote reeducation by providing opportunities for convicts to be visited by their families and former work collectives. In addition, colony inmates, after a lengthy period of good behavior in which a desire to reform was displayed, were to be given the opportunity to live with their families outside the colony.

To further promote the reeducation of prisoners in the colonies, the MVD reorganization plan called for colonies to orient their operations around teaching prisoners new work skills, educating them, and indoctrinating them politically in order to prepare them for life outside the colony after the expiration of their sentence. To this end, inmates were not to be used, as a rule, as construction workers, miners, loggers, or as manual laborers in unskilled positions, but they were to continue to receive workday credits for good performance on the job. Every prisoner was to leave the camp better qualified professionally than when he entered and the colony was to help him find work upon release. Moreover, the MVD harshly criticized the previous system that based camp location on economic needs rather than prisoner needs, forced camp administrators to constantly worry about productivity and output, and ignored the reeducational aspects of camp life. To this end, one proposal in the plan called for colony managers to be released from trying to operate on the funds earned from prisoner labor, placing colony operations on the general state budget rather than having them operate on the principle of self-financing (which was never achieved anyway).[184] To Dudorov this issue of financing was key to reorienting operations away from economics.

In order to further the reeducational mission of the Gulag, the plan also called for increased order in places of detention. The smaller colonies would allow administrators and guards to keep a closer watch on individual prisoners than was the case in the camps. Further, political and otherwise dangerous inmates were to be kept not in colonies or camps, but in "corrective-labor prisons" under heightened security. Dudorov proposed that two such prisons be built in the area of the Salekhard-Igarka railroad, itself "in essence a natural prison," which would provide complete isolation of these dangerous prisoners from other inmates and from Soviet society outside the barbed wire. In case the "natural" elements were insufficient, a guard limit of 20 percent of the inmate count was to be granted, instead of the 12 percent used for corrective-labor camps and colonies. A provision for the eventual transfer of these dangerous prisoners to a colony based on good behavior, however, was made, signifying continued faith in the ultimate reformability of all. Finally, regimen regulations, which separated prisoners into different colonies based on gender, type of crime committed, and length of criminal record, were to be much more strictly maintained. This categorization was to ensure full isolation of the dangerous "criminal-bandit element" from first-time offenders and others viewed as more reformable, thus protecting inmates from the traditional choice of either joining criminal gangs or being harassed by them. In sum, this was a radical reform plan for the structure and mission of the Gulag that aimed at bringing the Soviet penal system out of the lawless and exploitative Stalinist system into a smaller, orderly, and "progressive" (in the sense of moving inmates from stricter to more lenient correctional facilities as they demonstrated that reeducation was taking place) correctional model.

Dudorov's proposal, however, was not well received by other state agencies. In a letter to Presidium member Leonid Brezhnev, who headed the Central Committee commission charged with overseeing the restructuring of the Gulag in 1956, KGB chief and Khrushchev ally Ivan Serov detailed several objections to this new plan.[185] First, he thought the number of prisoners slated to be sent to prisons far too high, resulting in excessive spending on new prisons. He also noted that these prisoners would not be able to work; thus, "the most important factor of reeducating prisoners, labor, would not be used." On the creation of new colonies, Serov considered the plan unnecessarily expensive and thought that a multitude of new institutions would create the impression that the Soviet Union had massive numbers of prisoners. He also criticized the proposal to not allow inmates to work in heavy, unqualified positions, maintaining rather that such work, when properly organized, was in fact reeducational. The KGB chief further vehemently objected to the idea of allowing prisoners to live outside the colonies with their families, arguing that this would lead to a general weakening of the regimen structure. Serov leveled a final criticism at the practice of workday credits by which, according to him, the physically strong got off early without regard to their attitude and the weaker prisoners obtained no benefit. In other words, Serov, while paying lip service to the idea of reeducation, advocated a continuation of the Stalinist camp model.

Serov's objections were certainly influential, but they did not stand alone. A joint letter to Brezhnev from Gosplan and the State Economic Commission also lobbied against much of Dudorov's plan. Massive new prisons in the Salekhard-

Igarka region would be prohibitively expensive (the proposal called for 70 million rubles) and since they were not provided for in the sixth five-year plan there was no available funding for such a project. More importantly, the economic agencies rejected Dudorov's plea to place the correctional system on the state budget, arguing that "this would lower the responsibility for organizing production and the use of prisoner labor."[186]

Taking these objections into account, on 10 October 1956 the Presidium approved a revised version of the MVD plan that differed somewhat from the April draft, and on 25 October 1956 the Council of Ministers and Central Committee formally passed the reorganization plan. Much of the text was taken directly from Dudorov's original proposal, including the dictate that "the primary task of corrective-labor institutions is the reeducation of prisoners" through labor, vocational training, cultural activities, and increased political and social consciousness. The camp system was condemned as insufficiently reeducational and the MVD and Gosplan were obligated to prepare within three months a detailed plan for the organization of a new web of corrective-labor colonies in each republic, territory, and province so that prisoners could serve time in their home region.[187] A new set of guidelines governing the operation of the colonies and prisons was also ordered to replace the 10 July 1954 statute. This planned creation of colonies to replace the camps was a huge victory for Dudorov and his sponsor, Khrushchev. In order to reflect this new direction of penal policy, the MVD on 27 October 1956 changed the official title of the Gulag from the Main Administration of Corrective-Labor Camps and Colonies to the Main Administration of the Corrective-Labor Colonies.[188] The word "camp" (lager), tainted with the stain of Stalinism, was thus eliminated from the official name of the Soviet penal system.

But not all of Dudorov's proposals were accepted. The construction of large prisons on the abandoned Salekhard-Igarka railway was dropped, although the decree did admonish the Gulag to hold dangerous prisoners (which it restricted to gangsters and dangerous recidivists who refused to work in the colonies) in prisons or strict-regimen colonies. But most importantly, the Presidium refused to place the Gulag on the state budget; rather, it was still directed to fund its own operations through inmate labor (although in practice this had never been accomplished, resulting in ad hoc yearly "subsidies"). This was a significant defeat for Dudorov's vision of the new correctional system; without freedom from overriding economic concerns, camp managers would not be free to devote their primary attention to reeducation. Indeed, as the next chapter illustrates, this was precisely the result of keeping the Gulag off direct budgetary support.

As the colony-based reorganization plan was being discussed and ultimately approved, a simultaneous move to decentralize the powerful Gulag administration was proceeding apace. In general, Khrushchev in the 1950s was a staunch advocate of decentralizing the enormous state administration. This was done ostensibly to reduce bureaucratic waste, but, as already noted, it had roots in the succession struggle as well. As head of the party, Khrushchev had an explicit interest in weakening the state, which would, in turn, enhance the power of party structures. The most significant moves in this campaign in the mid-1950s were the elimination of the All-Union MIu in 1956 and the creation of the regional Eeconomic councils (*sovnarkhozy*) in 1957. The MVD and Gulag were not immune from this impulse either. Already on 19 June 1954 a proposal from the Gulag's organizational department recommended that the Gulag be decentralized.[189] At the time the MVD took no action, but the following year the significant step of creating an MVD for the Russian Republic was taken, a move that foreshadowed the eventual liquidation of the All-Union MVD in 1960.

Coming from Khrushchev's party apparatus, Dudorov was on board with this decentralization process within the MVD. A conference for top MVD and Gulag administrators on 14 April 1956 determined to pursue a course of weakening the All-Union MVD. Five days later, on 19 April 1956, three of these officials composed a letter to Dudorov, formally recommending a review of the relationship between the All-Union Gulag and its Russian counterpart, with the goal of strengthening the latter. In fact, they encouraged the transfer of 34 camps with their 443,840 prisoners from All-Union to Russian control and a subsequent downsizing of the All-Union Gulag administration.[190] That same day a meeting of the Presidium of the Central Committee confirmed the decision "to move toward decentralizing the MVD."[191] In response to these proposals, the MVD Collegium on 9 May 1956 instructed newly appointed Gulag chief Bakin and two deputy ministers from the MVD to work out a plan with the ministers of internal affairs from each of the fifteen republics for transferring the Gulag's camps from the Soviet MVD to the MVDs of each republic. The purpose of this transfer, according to this order, was to increase "the responsibility of the MVDs of the Union-Republics for the reeducation and correction of prisoners being held in corrective-labor camps."[192] By eliminating one layer of management, it also aimed at fostering a greater sense of responsibility for Gulag institutions among lower management ranks. These efforts resulted in the MVD decree of 13 August 1956, which ordered all camps and colonies transferred to the MVDs of their respective republics.[193] In fact, all but two republics (Russia and Kazakhstan) already administered all of their penal facilities. And in the case of labor camps within the Russian Federation, this order was not immediately applied. Due to the size and complexity of these camps, the MVD delayed their transfer until the following year in order to give the Russian MVD more time to prepare to receive them.

The final substantive Gulag reform of 1956 that affected the penal system's structure involved the transfer of the MVD's remaining economic functions to other ministries. Much of this had been accomplished by Beria in the spring of 1953, but the MVD in 1954–55 remained a powerful economic agency. In fact, under Malenkov's direction, it maintained and even began to increase its economic portfolio. Upon accession to the head of the MVD, Dudorov moved immediately to finish the work of divesting the MVD of its economic ownership. Already on 9 February 1956 he sent such a proposal to the Central Committee, arguing that this change would "give the ministry the opportunity to concentrate its attention on fulfilling its primary assignments," among which is listed the reeducation of prisoners.[194] This sentiment may also be found in a multitude of inspection reports from the mid-1950s. One inspector, while reporting on the abysmal living conditions and rampant gang activity at one of the Gulag's forestry camps, for instance, noted that "as long as the camp is concerned only with the fulfillment of the industrial plan the current situation will continue."[195]

Significantly, this plan faced opposition from the Ministry of Forestry, the ministry that would be most heavily affected by such a transfer. Under Stalin, the Ministry of Forestry experienced significant difficulties with forced labor in the logging industry and did not want to become responsible for overseeing the economic aspects of the Gulag's logging camps. Certain members of the Gulag bureaucracy also complained that in transferring away its economic units, the Gulag "in essence disassociated itself from the management of and responsibility for the productive activity of the corrective-labor colonies."[196] This ostensibly made it more difficult to ensure that each prisoner was provided with meaningful labor. Nevertheless, these pleas went unheeded and on 4 June 1956 the Council of Ministers transferred the remainder of the MVD's major economic functions to other ministries.[197]

These four reforms of 1956—the release of the political prisoners, the plan to exchange camps for colonies, the decentralization of the Gulag administration, and the loss of the MVD's expansive economic profile—coupled with a new leadership brought from the party apparatus, signified a substantive break with the past. These were serious reforms brought about not only by the succession struggle, but by a genuine desire to create a system wherein criminals were transformed into good Soviet citizens. Certainly much of this was motivated by the drive to create a stronger and more efficient state populated by productive workers, but humanitarian concerns and the renewed devotion to "socialist legality" played a significant role in the releases and the restructuring of the entire system.[198] Although, as will be seen, the subsequent implementation of the new reformist agenda was imperfect at best, there can be no question that the reforms of 1956 left the purpose, structure, and demographics of the Gulag substantively and permanently altered.

Implementing the Reform Program, 1957–1959

The structural reforms of the Gulag from 1957 to 1959 consisted of further administrative decentralization, the construction of new colonies, and gradual depopulation of the remaining camps. Following the decentralization push of 1956, the actual power of the All-Union Gulag administration declined significantly during its final three years. On 12 October 1957, in fulfillment of the decree of 13 August 1956, the MVD ordered that all remaining camps in the Russian Federation be transferred to provincial MVD administrations, which in turn reported to the Russian MVD.[199] This left the All-Union Gulag without direct responsibility for the operation of its camps and colonies; each of the fifteen republics now managed its own system with increasingly less supervision from above. This is evident in the number of orders issued by the head of the Gulag, which fell from 328 in 1954 to a mere 20 in 1958 and 1959 combined.[200] A close reading of these directives reveals that the Gulag by this point acted as an occasional inspection committee, a court of arbitration, and a facilitator of information sharing, but it no longer functioned as the day-to-day manager of camp and colony affairs.

In fulfillment of the 25 October 1956 decree, the MVD and Gosplan worked out a colony construction plan by January 1957 that called for 276 new corrective-labor colonies and the expansion of 215 existing colonies over the next four years at a cost of 2.7 billion rubles.[201] According to this plan, every republic or province would have at least one colony each for light, standard, and strict regimes. In addition, male and female prisoners were to be separated, thus creating the need for six separate colonies in every administrative region. This proved burdensome for the many smaller republics and provinces that did not have sufficient prisoners in each category to warrant the construction and administration of so many colonies. In order to mitigate this hardship, the MVD proposed that neighboring republics, such as the Baltics, should share women's colonies and strict-regimen colonies. Although a seemingly good idea, the republics in question often could not agree on how to implement this plan. Moreover, a general lack of funding for colony construction and a shortage of guards made the fulfillment of the conversion from camps to colonies difficult.[202]

Despite these difficulties, a total of 301 new colonies were constructed in 1957–58, nearly doubling the total number of colonies in the Soviet penal system to 610 by 1 January 1959.[203] These new colonies, in addition to expansions to existing colonies, provided space for 181,385 inmates.[204] Another 72 colonies were added in the first nine months of 1959, bringing the total to 682.[205] This allowed the number of camps to be reduced somewhat during 1957 and 1958 from 31, housing 492,095 inmates, to 28, with a population of 371,157.[206] Significantly, three of the largest and most notorious of the Stalinist camps, the Severo-Vostochnyi Corrective-Labor Camp (Sevvostlag) that served Dal'stroi, the Karagansinskii Corrective-Labor Camp (Karlag), and the Noril'sksii Corrective-Labor Camp (Noril'lag), were liquidated in 1957–59.[207] And starting in mid-1958, the Gulag held more convicts in colonies than camps, making clear that substantial progress had been made toward the elimination of the camp system and the retention of prisoners in colonies in their home provinces. As Kholodkov triumphantly reported in 1959, "From year to year the number of prisoners held in the corrective-labor camps of the MVD is declining."[208] But impressive as this building campaign was, it was still insufficient to fulfill the original plan; at this rate, accomplishing the goal of completely eliminating the camps in favor of colonies still seemed far off. Indeed, with these facts in mind, the Council of Ministers on 14 November 1958 ordered that the camps could be temporarily retained for four to five years. In early 1959 one Gulag administrator forecasted 1962 as the earliest possible date for the realization of the final elimination of the camps and estimated that another 5.6 billion rubles were needed to meet even that deadline.[209] Despite the costs of the colony-building campaign, the goal of housing all inmates in colonies rather than camps was maintained; as one Gulag report in 1959 reaffirmed, "the existence of camps as a place of confinement may only be allowed under extraordinary circumstances in the country, in normal times the camp, as an institution for isolating convicts and rehabilitating them is without question inexpedient (*netselesoobrazen*). Our experience of working with [corrective-labor camps] convincingly affirms this conclusion."[210]

The creation of hundreds of new colonies throughout the Soviet Union meant that the lengthy and costly prisoner transfers that were a prominent feature of the economically oriented Stalinist Gulag could be dramatically reduced. In 1955, while some economic agencies were still requesting prisoner labor, more than 350,000 inmates were transferred from one camp to another.[211] In 1956, however, camp and colony commanders became much more vocal in resisting in-transfers of inmates, especially those on strict regimen and those with work restrictions stemming from disability or sickness. Due to the somewhat slow pace of colony construction in 1957–58, however, the Gulag was forced to continue transferring inmates to the remaining camps, which were better able to handle large influxes of prisoners than the smaller colony networks. At a large conference for Gulag leadership, held in Moscow in May 1957, this issue came to a head when one commander of a logging camp complained vocally about being sent excessive numbers of prisoners. Dudorov, his patience already thin over this and other complaints, sarcastically retorted, "We can't send them to logging camps, we can't send them somewhere else, what, are we supposed to send them to Iran?"[212]

This struggle over inmate transfers was fought not only at the camp level, but at the republican level as well. With the decentralization of the administrative structure of the Gulag, the Russian and Kazakh Republics, net receivers of inmates from the other republics due to the location of the large corrective-labor camps within their borders, began to complain about the smaller union republics sending them their unwanted prisoners.[213] But smaller republics complained of in-transfers as well. The Estonian MVD in 1956, for instance, blamed an increase in regimen violations by prisoners that year on recidivists brought in from Latvia and Lithuania and requested that all transfers of prisoners to Estonia be halted. During 1957–58, however, it received a large contingent of dangerous prisoners from several prisons in Russia, including Vladimir, Orlov, Novocherkask, and Vologda. This group of prisoners, the Estonian MVD complained, "is systematically violating the prison regimen."[214]

By 1959, however, with a large number of colonies constructed in the preceding years, substantive improvements were made with respect to keeping newly convicted prisoners in their home republics, provinces, and territories. Whereas 209,074 inmates in 1956 and 129,243 in 1958 were sent to camps and colonies outside their native administrative districts, that number for 1959 fell to just 48,940.[215] Crucially, this focus on eliminating transfers was supported by the Central Committee, even as state economic agencies sought to maintain them. In late 1959 the Russian Council of Ministers requested the transfer of at least 65,000 inmates to the logging camps, including some 8,000–10,000 from the other union republics, without which the logging plan for 1960 would go unfulfilled. Citing decrees ordering the MVD to keep prisoners as much as possible in their home provinces, to cut down as much as possible on costly transfers, and to eliminate the logging camps altogether, the Central Committee denied this request.[216]

In addition to these structural reforms, the Gulag continued its program of mass releases in 1957–59. Although the number of prisoners decreased dramatically in the first years following Stalin's death due to amnesties and case reviews, reaching a nadir of 781,630 on 1 January 1956, unfinished revisions to the criminal codes coupled with continued high levels of crime and policing in the country threatened to quickly increase the inmate population once such extraordinary releases ceased. Indeed, despite the release of nearly 100,000 political prisoners in 1956, the total number of inmates actually increased that year to 807,977 on

1 January 1957 because of over 500,000 newly admitted inmates. This surge continued during the first several months of 1957, with relatively few releases being more than offset by the number of new convicts sentenced to deprivation of freedom.

With the aim of relieving overcrowding in the prisons and corrective-labor establishments of the Gulag, an amnesty commemorating the fortieth anniversary of the October Revolution took effect on 1 November 1957.[217] This amnesty was prepared by Rudenko and Dudorov, who sent a draft to the Presidium on 21 October 1957. Similar to the previous amnesties earlier in the decade, it called for the release of those with sentences under 3 years, men over 60, women over 55, pregnant women and those with children under the age of 8, and adolescents under the age of 17. Additionally, those with sentences of three years or longer were to have their sentences halved. The amnesty did not apply, however, to those convicted of banditry, premeditated murder, robbery, assault, malicious hooliganism, rape, or large-scale embezzlement; those with more than two convictions; those previously released under the various early release programs and amnesties of the 1950s; and inmates who had caused trouble while incarcerated. In order to ensure the execution of this amnesty went according to plan, the Gulag convened conferences for central and local MVD and Gulag administrators in September and October 1957.[218] There they discussed such matters as how to find work for amnestied prisoners, which penal institutions to liquidate after the prisoners left, how to ensure that former inmates arrived home without committing further crimes, and who should be on the amnesty commissions that decided which prisoners to release. Following the announcement of the amnesty, 511 commissions were dispatched to ensure its fulfillment and it was mostly complete by the end of the year.[219] In total, 151,030 prisoners were released from the Gulag as a result of the 1957 amnesty.[220]

The Gulag population in 1958, however, once again began to rise. By 1 July 1959 over a million convicts populated Gulag institutions, an increase of 348,406 since the beginning of 1958.[221] This growth and the problems it created in constructing sufficient housing and finding work for additional prisoners resulted in the increased use of parole, which had flagged during 1956–58. It also spurred the final mass release of the 1950s and of the Khrushchev era as a whole, passed by the Presidium on 14 August 1959.[222] This was not strictly an amnesty, but called for commissions sent by the Supreme Soviet to review the files of first-time offenders and those convicted of minor crimes to determine their suitability for early release. In Russia alone, 188 review commissions were created out of local party, government, Communist Youth League (Komsomol), Procuracy, MVD, court, and labor unions personnel to review prisoner files.[223] Provincial party organizations were to ensure that prisoners released by the 1959 commissions received employment and housing and the Central Committee also tasked them with providing for the ex-cons' "further reeducation and correction."[224] By the end of 1959, a total of 325,681 prisoners obtained release due to this amnesty and as a result the Russian MVD alone liquidated 184 colonies that could accommodate 106,900 prisoners.[225] By the time the commissions finished their task on 1 April 1960, 615,000 files had been reviewed with 471,858 inmates freed. Roughly half of those released had been convicted of theft and embezzlement, while 29 percent had been serving time for hooliganism, and the remainder were serving time for other minor crimes.[226]

Memoirist Valerii Rodos describes the work of one commission at Dubravlag, which summoned twenty-six young political prisoners for case reviews on account of their age. After interviewing each one, the commission freed fourteen of them. Rodos, aided by an excellent character statement from the camp administration, was released after a brief five-minute conversation with the commission in which he apparently admitted his guilt and promised to become a worker in order to care for his widowed mother.[227] Although one must read Rodos's memoir with caution, as he was the son of a high-ranking secret police investigator who was attacked in Khrushchev's secret speech and subsequently executed, the speed and ease of his 1959 release appears to have been representative. One even more prominent inmate whose release by the 1959 amnesty was not as quick was Stalin's son, Vasilii, who had been sentenced in 1955 to eight years imprisonment for anti-Soviet agitation and abuse of office. His case required special permission from the Presidium, but on recommendation from KGB head Aleksandr Nikolaevich Shelepin and Procurator General Rudenko, on 8 January he was granted early release. Just months later, however, he fled to the Chinese embassy to request residency in China. Upon hearing this, the Presidium ordered him returned to prison to serve out the remainder of his term.[228]

Gulag Demographics, 1953–1960

The policies of the mid-to-late 1950s, particularly the mass releases of that era, had a great effect on Gulag demographics. The prisoner population of the Soviet Gulag had never been stable. Since 1917, successive waves of prisoners came and went, constantly changing the quantitative and qualitative makeup of the overall contingent. In its volatility, therefore, the 1953–60 era differed little from the preceding decades. The nature of the demographic transformation, however, was significant. Beyond the drastic reduction in prisoner transfers already noted, three trends in particular stand out: the overall reduction of inmates; the release of most political prisoners; and an increase in repeat offenders as a percentage of the total inmate population.

On 1 January 1953 the Gulag held 2,472,247 inmates in its camps and colonies. After the amnesty of 1953 reduced the number of prisoners to 1,273,038, by 1 July 1953 the Gulag population hovered around the 1.2–1.3 million mark until early 1955, when it dipped below 1 million. It continued to decline to under 800,000 by the start of 1956 and rose only slightly that year. After a more significant rise in 1957, the amnesty of that same year cut the number of prisoners back down to 721,899. This number rose again to over 1 million by mid-1959, but the case reviews of 1959 slashed the total figure to just 582,717 by 1 January 1960. This reduced number of inmates proved to be fleeting, however, as the Gulag population in the 1960s rose again to the 700,000–800,000 level.[229] Yet even if one takes 700,000–800,000 as the final settling point of the Khrushchev reforms, it cannot be denied that this represented a monumental shift in the social control mechanisms used by the Soviet Union. Three-quarters of a million people was still a massive number compared with other countries at the time. Yet the incarceration rate of roughly 370 per 100,000 population in the early 1960s was dramatically below the 1,440 per 100,000 population experienced at the end of Stalin's reign.[230] Mass incarceration it may still have been, but it was mass incarceration of a much smaller magnitude.[231]

The decline in the number of political prisoners was even more dramatic than that of the overall prisoner population. On 1 January 1953 the Gulag held 539,483 inmates convicted of counterrevolutionary crimes, who made up 21.8 percent of the total inmate population. By 1 January 1954 the percentage of prisoners incarcerated for counterrevolutionary crimes had jumped dramatically to 34.8 percent, the result of many ordinary criminals being freed in the 1953 amnesty, despite the absolute number of political prisoners declining to 460,557. The case reviews of 1954–56, however, ended the period of mass incarceration for political offenses. On 1 January 1957, 18,187 political prisoners remained, comprising just 2.3 percent of the total Gulag population. By 1 January 1960 those figures had fallen to 9,596 and 1.6 percent, and in early 1962 only 6,466 remained incarcerated for state crimes.[232] The Gulag by the end of the 1950s, and really already by the end of 1956, was populated almost exclusively by common criminals. People convicted of counterrevolutionary crimes, redefined during this period as state crimes, continued to inhabit the Soviet Gulag until its fall in 1991 (and they took justified offense when Khrushchev publicly declared there were no political prisoners in the Soviet Union).[233] Never again, however, would they constitute a significant percentage of the total number of inmates.

With the political prisoners mostly released, the Soviet Gulag witnessed a dramatic jump in the relative weight of inmates convicted of violent crime. Those in for premeditated murder rose from just 1.8 percent of the total population in early 1953 to 7.1 percent by January 1960; the corresponding numbers for banditry rose from 1.9 percent to 3.4 percent and for robbery from 5.8 percent to 16.1 percent. Rapists increased from 0.5 percent to 6.0 percent. Other categories of criminals also saw their percentages rise, even as their numbers declined. The percentage of prisoners convicted of theft (of either private or state property) in early 1953 was 42.3 percent. During the next several years that figure fluctuated from 36.7 percent to 47.4 percent as amnesties for minor criminals only temporarily mitigated the inflow of small-time criminals. One final category of crime tracked by the MVD was hooliganism, which stood at just 5.6 percent of the total inmate population in early 1953 but, with Khrushchev's antihooligan campaign, rose to 18.2 percent by January 1959 before falling to 12.9 percent by 1 January 1960 in the wake of the 1959 case reviews.[234]

Another important demographic shift that occurred within the Gulag after Stalin's death was a gradual decrease in sentence length. This resulted from the release of the political prisoners, who were usually given very long sentences, and also from the push to lower criminal sanctions for a range of crimes, notably theft. On 1 January 1953 only 20 percent of inmates had sentences of less than 5 years, 49.3 percent had sentences of 5–10 years, 16.9 percent were in for 10–15 years, and the remaining 13.9 percent had long sentences of 15–25 years. By 1959, however, the percentage of prisoners sentenced to short terms of less than 5 years had increased to 45.8 percent, with the remaining three categories falling respectively to 33.5 percent, 11.2 percent, and 9.5 percent.[235] This trend was reversed somewhat by the 1959 case reviews, but only temporarily. In 1960, the average sentence length given by regular courts to those sentenced to deprivation of freedom was only 3.3 years, as opposed to 5.6 years in 1950.[236]

A final trend in inmate demographics that must be noted is the significant increase in the number and percentage of recidivists inhabiting the Gulag. The term recidivist was used in two ways in official documents. Usually employed pejoratively in the Stalin and early post-Stalin era as a synonym for gangster, it also often meant, as in the West, simply a person with two or more convictions. This figure was not consistently tracked by Gulag authorities under Stalin, but with the newfound emphasis on reeducation, it became a primary indicator of success (or failure) under Khrushchev. The first significant attempt to quantify the problem of recidivism is found in Dudorov's 5 April 1956 reorganization plan, which reported that 25 percent of all inmates had previously been incarcerated.[237] A more detailed report clarified that at the beginning of 1956, 206,552 prisoners (26.4 percent) were serving time for at least their second conviction.

By 1 April 1958 over 45 percent of all Gulag inmates were repeat offenders, and on 1 January 1960 that number reached 52.6 percent.[238] Thus, even as the number of inmates fell in the 1950s, those who remained in the Gulag by 1960 were more likely to have multiple convictions and convictions for violent crimes.

The Dissolution of the All-Union Gulag Apparatus

In January 1960 Khrushchev disbanded the All-Union MVD and with it the All-Union Gulag. Although most remaining administrators in the central apparatus were put to work in the Russian MVD, Dudorov was released from the security apparatus and assigned to other tasks.[239] The Soviet Gulag, since 1930 the primary bureaucratic agency charged with administering deprivation of freedom, had been decapitated, with each republic becoming independently responsible for organizing, maintaining, and inspecting their own system of camps, colonies, and prisons under the direction of the Central Committee. This final act of decentralization represented Khrushchev's program of promoting local and party control over many aspects of Soviet life, but it also demonstrated Khrushchev's desire to de-Stalinize the repressive organs of the state.

If the Stalin-era Gulag was emblematic of the 1930s and 1940s—decades of mass upheaval, rapid industrialization, terror, and death—then the Gulag of the 1950s reflected a new vision of state and society that Stalin's heirs and Khrushchev in particular tried to forge. In part this new vision meant greatly decreased reliance on terror as a governing strategy and a new culture of "socialist legality." It meant more stability and better living standards to reflect a maturing of the socialist experiment. Likewise, it meant increased autonomy for local government and economic agencies, and a new commitment to "rationalize" (i.e., downsize) bloated administrative structures. These reforms are well reflected in the Gulag of 1960. It was much smaller, much less important economically, and much more decentralized. It no longer served as a major repository for the politically suspect, nor did it house masses of people convicted of minor crimes. This does not mean, however, that penal transformation had been wholly successful. Indeed, as the next chapter will demonstrate, the renewed focus on reeducation was much more difficult to achieve than a permanent reduction in the size of the Gulag.

REORIENTING THE AIMS OF IMPRISONMENT

Production, Reeducation, and Control

'Nowadays it's fun being locked up,' Švejk continued with relish. 'There's no quartering, no Spanish boots. We've got bunks, a table, a bench. We're not all squashed together like sardines: we get soup; they give us bread and bring us a jug of water. We've got our latrines right under our snouts. You can see progress in everything.'

—Jaroslav Hašek, *The Good Soldier Švejk*

On 5 May 1955 the leadership of the Estonian Ministry of Internal Affairs (MVD) met with administrators of Camp Branch No. 2 to discuss the progress of that correctional facility in fulfilling the decrees and statute of 12 March and 10 July 1954. Problems and deficiencies abounded, the twenty-page investigatory report made abundantly clear, but the primary criticism leveled was insufficient attention to the reeducation of prisoners. During the discussion, none other than the deputy director of production for the branch gave this interpretation of their poor performance: "Devoting the majority of our attention to production, we did not notice the mistakes allowed in the reeducation of prisoners. We received the MVD orders and directives corresponding to this work, but we did not understand them, we did not understand how to put these decisions into practice. We have not been told how to do this."[1]

Confusion over Gulag reform was also evident in how the legacy of violence inherited from the Stalinist Gulag was confronted. As an internal memorandum from the Procuracy in 1955 makes clear, camp commanders were struggling with how to deal with the criminal gangs that flourished in the 1940s and early 1950s. "The activity of these groups has become especially enlivened recently," the note reads, "as somewhat of a relaxing of the regimen, intended to stimulate [good] behavior and labor from the majority of prisoners, is being used by the criminal bandit element for their own ends."[2] From theft and extortion to riots and grisly murders, crime perpetrated by the criminal gangs posed a serious challenge to the intended reorientation of the penal system toward a more humane correctional model. Clearly, it was one thing to proclaim an end to the Stalinist camp system, but another thing altogether to define what precisely that meant at the remaining penal facilities. Whereas the previous chapter provided a chronological summary of the major Gulag reforms and restructurings from 1953 to 1960, the present chapter delves deeper into how these reorganizational plans shaped specific policies within the Gulag bureaucracy, and how these polices were interpreted and implemented by penal workers who interacted directly with inmates.

The Gulag in the mid-to-late 1950s was tasked with three basic functions: production (and its corollary of fiscal restraint); reeducation; and custodial control. Perhaps not surprisingly, these three aims of Khrushchev's Gulag remained unchanged from the Stalin era.[3] In fact, the Soviet penal system from its inception held to similar internal aims; thus, it was not even Stalin or his penal officers who created this framework for penal operations.[4] Indeed, the emphasis on economics, control, and reeducation was not a Soviet phenomenon, but rather a set of aims common among prison administrations globally; most prison systems in the twentieth century proclaimed (or at least privately acknowledged) the exact same goals. Regardless of ideology or level of development, they strove toward or paid lip service toward reducing the costs of prisoner maintenance, preparing inmates to return to society, and ensuring that prisoners did not escape, riot, commit new crimes, or otherwise disrupt the prison order while incarcerated. Such was the nature of modern penal institutions, aimed as they were at controlling the mind and body of their inmates while minimizing the burden to the state.[5]

Similarities in broad goals do not mean, of course, that twentieth-century penal systems were indistinguishable. Differences resulted from a number of factors, the most important of which was the relative weight assigned by prison administrators to the three goals. The aims of fiscal discipline, correction, and control were not harmonious, and the extent to which one or two of the three prevailed over the other(s) in large measure (along with other factors such as specific historical and cultural factors) determined the nature of the prison system and its policies. During the 1940s and early 1950s in the Soviet Union, economic aims clearly trumped the other two, with control lagging far behind and correction placing a distant third. After Stalin's death, as will be discussed, the relative weight assigned to these priorities underwent a drastic revision that permanently altered the nature of the Gulag.

Those familiar with criminological literature may be surprised by the omission of two traditional functions of imprisonment, namely deterrence and retribution.[6] Soviet criminology held that incarceration was mandated for certain crimes in part to deter others, and this seems to have been the motivating factor behind the draconian labor and antitheft laws of the 1930s and 1940s.[7] As noted in the previous chapter, however, Soviet legal officials in the mid-1950s recognized that long prison terms did not, in fact, have an appreciable deterrent effect on the population. Moreover, deterrence as a concept, while important to issues such as determining the type of punishment or sentence length for particular crimes, did not inform internal Gulag policy. Retribution, interpreted through the prism of class enemies, wreckers, Trotskyites, and other such categories, also played a significant role in the Stalinist repressive apparatus. Yet with the rejection of Stalinism in the mid-1950s, retribution was officially discarded as a theory and significant efforts were made to excise it from penal practice as well. Retribution was not completely dead, however. In the late 1950s and early 1960s (as will be seen in chapter 4), retribution came to be frankly admitted as an aim of imprisonment and specific, though limited, policies stemmed from this reversal.

Before proceeding to a detailed discussion of how the aims of economics, reeducation, and control were restructured in the post-Stalin era a word of caution is in order. Although it is vital to understand the aims of the Gulag and the policies and practices that resulted from these aims, as David Garland reminds, "institutions are never fully explicable purely in terms of their 'purposes.'"[8] The Gulag had a particular history, a unique culture, and specific interactions with other institutions (especially those that funded it) that defined its existence, sometimes in conjunction with its various internal and externally ascribed aims (of which repression is most common), but other times at odds with or irrelevant to them. One cannot adequately describe the endemic corruption within the Gulag, to mention just one example, strictly through the lens of economics, reeducation, and control. Nor can one hope to understand inmate society and culture within the framework of the Gulag's primary goals. Moreover, one must bear in mind that just as the internal goals of the Gulag were never harmonious, the Gulag administration was also fractured, especially in the first decade following Stalin's death. Different sections within the bureaucracy favored one goal over the others; meanwhile, local camp officials had their own ideas about which aim was paramount and their actions did not necessarily coincide with evolving Gulag policy. Finally, many policies enacted in the post-Stalin era can be attributed to furthering more than one of the three primary goals, making interpretation of motive particularly difficult. The revision of the relative weight assigned to the three primary goals of the Gulag was a messy, nonlinear process. This is a story, therefore, not just about changing goals and policies, but about the at times fierce debates that surrounded such reforms.

Production and Self-Sufficiency

In the late Stalinist Gulag, production reigned supreme; not for nothing was it labeled a system of slavery by its critics.[9] The forced tempos of the five-year plans, pressing wartime and postwar reconstruction demands, an ideology grounded in the working class, and the availability of a massive and mobile workforce in the form of incarcerated prisoners assured an important place for labor in the penal system of the Soviet Union under Stalin. Moreover, a low level of economic development combined with the physical geography of the natural resources needed to industrialize virtually guaranteed that most labor performed by inmates would be hard, manual labor. Mining coal and metal, constructing railroads and dams, felling trees, and performing agricultural work were therefore the standard work assignments for Gulag prisoners under Stalin, although prisoners could be found engaged in virtually all sectors of the Soviet economy. As Aleksandr Solzhenitsyn wryly remarked, "it is indeed much easier to enumerate the occupations the prisoners never did have: the manufacture of sausages and confectionary goods."[10] Hours were long, days off were few, and various systems of reward and punishment were devised to increase productivity, from distributing rations based on output to providing piece-rate wages and workday credits. The entire rhythm of the camps and colonies of the Gulag revolved around compulsory labor.[11] One cannot solely attribute the use of prisoner labor to the drive for factory inputs and infrastructure, however. Soviet penology since its inception espoused labor, as will be discussed in greater detail below, as a reeducational device. Nonetheless, from the 1930s to the early 1950s it is clear that production concerns rather than the idea of "reforging" prisoners through labor ruled the camps of the Gulag.[12]

Closely connected to the drive for maximum output during the 1930s and 1940s were efforts to keep expenses at Gulag institutions to a minimum. There was an impetus within Soviet penology from the very beginning to create self-sufficient penal institutions that would not prove a burden to the state budget.[13] In a country where all were asked to sacrifice for the greater good, and more specifically for the better future that communism promised, convicts were certainly not exempt from the tendency to provide the majority of Soviet subjects with only what was necessary for survival or, in times of war or drought, substantially less. This is the Gulag presented to us by Evgeniia Ginzburg, Varlam Shalamov, Solzhenitsyn, and countless others. From poor accommodations and insufficient rations to an undersized and underpaid staff, the Gulag faced endless shortages and underfunding. Part of this can be attributed to the shortages and difficult financial situation that faced most Soviet enterprises during the Stalin years, which stemmed not only from economic underdevelopment but from the growing pains and inherent contradictions associated with centralized economic planning.[14] But another contributing factor was the idea of class warfare pushed so forcefully under Stalin; if those sent to the camps were class enemies, there was little incentive to spend money on them when workers and peasants were going hungry. The drive for economic self-sufficiency also translated into the widespread practice of hiring prisoners not engaged in projects assigned directly to the MVD out to other ministries.[15]

At times the push for economic production and self-sufficiency conflicted with the other goal of maximum output and institutional control in Stalin's Gulag. The special camps for political prisoners in some ways emphasized control over production, even as inmates were required to perform hard labor.[16] The system of tying rations to productivity at times worked against production; hungry prisoners, after all, are less productive than well-fed ones. Even the practice of low compensation for administrators and guards could damage production goals, as poorly paid employees tended to embezzle output and supplies to supplement their income.[17] The Gulag under Stalin, with conflicting goals and a lack of resources, was certainly rife with contradictions, and these did not disappear under Khrushchev. Speaking in general terms, however, it is clear that production and "profitability" were the most important of the three conflicting aims of the Gulag.

The twin goals of production and institutional self-sufficiency were not unique to the Soviet system. Penologists and penal administrators worldwide broadly shared the view that prisoners should help recoup the costs of their incarceration through work, and that said work simultaneously aided in their path back to full citizenship. Moreover, there was widespread interest in the particular form of imprisonment employed by the Soviets: the labor camp. As Negley Teeters explained in 1944, "Any plan to keep men out of the unhealthy atmosphere of a large prison should be studiously considered. Penal institutions with their fetid air, inside cellblocks, lack of open recreation space and monotonous routine are inimical to reform so that their renovation, if not elimination, is of significance in ushering in a new day in penal treatment. Work camps represent such a plan."[18] Such enthusiasm for the camp model continued in Western penological circles through the 1950s and 1960s. Both labor and the labor camp were considered ideal correctional tools by penal experts globally.[19]

After Stalin's death, production concerns still occupied a central place in Soviet penal practice, although the overwhelming focus on output to some extent diminished. As noted in the previous chapter, Lavrentii Pavlovich Beria took several steps to reduce the economic profile of the MVD, yet ultimately the MVD retained economic control over various special construction projects as well as the Gulag's lumber camps, agricultural units, and various other small-scale production facilities. Indeed, by mid-1954, over 56 percent of Gulag prisoners still labored directly for the MVD.[20] More strikingly, even as wasteful construction projects were being closed down, other sites were being opened or expanded. Already in June 1953 the MVD organized a new subdivision of the Kamyshevnyi Corrective-Labor Camp (Kamyshlag) at the construction site of an Omsk oil refinery. With an anticipated population of 30,000 inmates, it was to be stocked initially with prisoners from the liquidated Dal'nyi Corrective-Labor Camp (Dal'lag).[21] Later that year the Council of Ministers ordered that the number of prisoners constructing the Kuibyshev Hydroelectric Power Plant should be raised to 58,000 in the coming months and that tents could be used to house the additional prisoners as a temporary measure.[22] In other words, Stalin's heirs did not initially have in mind a wholesale turn away from using prisoners on massive construction sites; they just had different ideas about which projects were important and which, notably the Salekhard-Igarka railroad, were a waste of resources.

Even the short-lived transfer of the Gulag to the Ministry of Justice (MIu) in 1953 did not diminish the push to fulfill economic targets. Many of the first decrees issued by the MIu upon receiving the Gulag concerned production and construction and this tendency to address primarily economic concerns continued largely unabated throughout the year.[23] In late May 1953, for instance, the MIu castigated those who were not fulfilling their yearly plan targets, which contributed to the quarterly economic plan for the Gulag being fulfilled by only 95.2 percent.[24] In October the MIu admonished its camps and colonies to rein in production costs (while still meeting plan targets, of course).[25] Yet despite such concern, a primary reason why the Gulag was transferred back from the MIu to the MVD in early 1954 was the experience of the latter in ensuring the fulfillment of production targets.[26]

Indeed, the desire to maintain a high level of production using forced labor still existed at the highest levels of government. The state could not disassociate itself immediately from the massive use of forced labor that had for so long been, in the words of Oleg Khlevniuk, a "narcotic for the economy."[27] A look at the types of projects in which prisoners were engaged in is revealing. On 1 April 1954, of 1.3 million inmates in the Gulag system, almost 900,000 were located in large camps in the Urals, Siberia, the Far East, the Far North, and Kazakhstan.[28] By work assignment this latter number was broken down as follows: 230,000 prisoners were engaged at logging camps; 277,000 at mining camps; 96,000 in oil production; 204,000 in building railroads, power plants, and other economic facilities; 45,000 in agriculture; and 46,000 in camps assigned to "other" jobs.[29] Not all of these inmates were engaged in the primary economic activity of their assigned camp; many were employed in camp service or performed other ancillary tasks. Yet this does not diminish the fact that the majority of Gulag prisoners continued to labor on the same primary tasks—mining, construction, logging, and agriculture—that they had under Stalin.

The desire to maintain high industrial output using forced labor is evident in a number of practices in the early post-Stalin Gulag. The Council of Ministers ensured a steady flow of prisoners to the gold-producing region of Kolyma, for instance, approving a plan to send an additional 4,500 prisoners to Dal'stroi and several thousand more to other projects considered important to the state.[30] This corresponded with another 1954 Council of Ministers directive to the MVD to only assign physically healthy prisoners to Dal'stroi, demanding that the number of inmates there be kept constant at least through 1955.[31] Accordingly, an additional 13,000 prisoners were slated to be sent to Dal'stroi in 1955 to replace those whose terms were expiring.[32] Camp commanders throughout the Gulag sought to eliminate their chronically sick and invalid prisoners through early release, and in this they were supported, as noted in the previous chapter, by MVD boss Sergei Nikiforovich Kruglov.[33] After the official workday was reduced to eight or nine hours for inmates, prisoners frequently complained to higher authorities that they were still being forced to work twelve-hour days.[34] For at least the first few years after Stalin's death, therefore, the work norm in at least some camps remained, in the words of Solzhenitsyn, "senior in rank to the length of the workday."[35] Finally, in recommending Mikhail Nikolaevich Kholodkov as his new deputy minister of internal affairs who would oversee the Gulag, Nikolai Pavlovich Dudorov noted to Khrushchev that "he knows production well," a trait seen as important to the plan to expand the network of colonies and provide each with a production facility.[36]

Heavy emphasis on production in the mid-1950s is also evident in the massive expansion of the workday credit system, cited in the previous chapter as a method of early release. This system, inherited from the Stalin era, had a clear re-educational design, but in practice it was seen by Gulag administrators principally as a method to increased production.[37] When the Council of Ministers asked the Gulag to increase its production of furniture and instructed the State Planning Agency (Gosplan) to allocate 30 million rubles for capital construction, for instance, Kruglov agreed with this request, but asked in exchange that prisoners working in furniture shops receive workday credits as a labor incentive to help meet the new targets.[38] As emphasis shifted away from production in the late 1950s, however, workday credits came under harsh attack. The "Fundamentals of Criminal Law," passed by the Supreme Soviet in 1958 as a guide for republican criminal codes, omitted any reference to workday credits and a decree of 6 January 1959 halted early release by this mechanism.[39]

Other indicators also point to somewhat reduced emphasis on production in the late 1950s. Certainly the plan to abolish the large labor camps in favor of colonies that was discussed in the previous chapter is significant here, as these camps were explicitly founded in the 1930s and 1940s to exploit inmate labor for rapid industrialization. The colonies, with their small-scale and local economic profile, had an inherently less productive mission. Moreover, in those institutions that continued to hire out their prisoners to other agencies in the late 1950s one begins to find in the archives complaints from the production sites that camp commanders no longer cared about output. In Kolyma after the elimination of Dal'stroi and its massive camp complex, for instance, the roughly 11,000 inmates that remained in 1959 labored for the newly established council of the national economy (*sovnarkhoz*). The deputy *sovnarkhoz* manager, however, quickly complained that camp officials often failed to bring prisoners to the work site, or brought them home before the work was finished. Whereas under Dal'stroi "the entire work of the camp administration was directed toward fulfilling the interests of production, of fulfilling the plan," he continued, "now the situation has completely changed. The administration of the camp practically doesn't pay any attention to [production] or to the maximum utilization of the prisoners."[40] Even memoirists noted the reduced pressure to fulfill the plan. As I. V. Ovchinnikov noted, his camp in 1959 had its own production zone but it was so small that many prisoners did not work.[41] Thus, while it would be incorrect to say that pressure for plan fulfillment disappeared in the late 1950—the anti-subsidy drive about to be discussed ensured continued discussion of output—the importance of production was clearly reduced as Dudorov reoriented operations more around reeducation and control.

Despite this reduced profile for production, fiscal concerns in the Gulag remained important. The goal of reducing the cost of maintaining the Gulag was certainly not new, having been alternately emphasized and forgotten since the 1920s, but the inevitable outcome of each campaign was failure.[42] As Solzhenitsyn remarked, "not only does the Archipelago not pay its own way, but the nation has to pay dearly for the additional satisfaction of having it."[43] Hard numbers on the level of state subsidy are difficult to find (or trust) due to the convoluted nature of Soviet accounting practices and the extensive nature of the system itself, but one internal source gives a figure of 4 billion rubles for the year 1953.[44] The Soviet Gulag was hardly the only prison system with self-sufficiency as a goal. Indeed, this had been and continued to be the dream of many penal reformers and government budget-makers since the rise of incarceration as the dominant form of judicial punishment in the nineteenth century.[45] With the overwhelming emphasis on labor in the Soviet Union, especially under Stalinism, one might think this goal could have been attainable. But decisions on where to locate prisoners and what labor to have them perform seem to have been made primarily out of output concerns, with much less emphasis on making individual units or the system as a whole self-sustaining. After all, one of the primary rationales for the camp model was to exploit resources in distant regions to which free laborers were unwilling to move. The distances involved, combined with harsh geologic and climactic conditions, necessarily drove up the expenses involved. Other factors, such as the inherently low productivity of forced labor, also played a significant role.

As noted in the previous chapter, the MVD under Kruglov and especially under Dudorov attempted to remove self-sufficiency as an operating principle for the Gulag by financing its operations directly out of the state budget. But with the powerful Gosplan and Ministry of Finance blocking these moves, themselves under considerable pressure to fund Khrushchev's various other reform programs, the Gulag was forced to continue striving toward financial independence.[46] Indeed, in the wake of Dudorov's failed proposal to move the Gulag onto the state budget and with the financial hardship of creating hundreds of new colonies to fulfill the 1956 reorganizational plan, the MVD launched a new campaign to eliminate the state subsidy and make the Gulag financially self-sufficient. Like other campaigns in Soviet history, it was presented as a grassroots initiative. In early 1957 one Comrade Matveev, head of Colony No. 14 in the Kazakh division of corrective-labor colonies, pledged to operate his colony without subsidy so that valuable state resources could be devoted to more pressing concerns.[47] The MVD swiftly gave its approval to this scheme and helped disseminate it to the entire Gulag structure. At a conference in 1958, the peak year for the subsidy reduction campaign, Dudorov expressed a goal of reducing the subsidy in 1959 by 60 percent and of becoming completely subsidy-free in 1960.[48]

From 1957 onward, each camp and colony was expected to establish goals and make progress toward becoming subsidy-free. In Estonia, for instance, the head accountant of the Estonian department of corrective-labor colonies dutifully outlined an initial goal of reducing its subsidy by one-third, which was later followed by more ambitious targets of eliminating the subsidy altogether.[49] Then at central Gulag conferences, which were particularly plentiful in 1957–58 as Dudorov aimed to restructure the system, each administrator was expected to report the degree to which the corrective-labor institutions under his domain had achieved self-sufficiency. In 1957, the deputy minister of the Russian MVD reported that 80 colonies, 6 provinces, and 3 camps in the Russian Republic operated without subsidy and in 1959 he announced with some pride that 219 colonies in Russia had achieved this goal.[50]

In order to lessen their dependence on government funds, the Gulag attempted to cut unnecessary expenses by a variety of means. It advocated colonies consisting of between 500 and 700 inmates, as opposed to the smaller ones found especially in the smaller republics of the Soviet Union, aiming to reduce administrative overhead and raise the prisoner-to-guard ratio.[51] One Gulag bureaucrat in 1958, caught up in the spirit of saving, even proposed slashing the amount of money paid to prisoners for the work they performed to an average of 100 rubles per month (the average wage per prisoner per day in 1958 was 26 rubles and 26 kopeks), which would provide, according to his estimates, savings of 535 million rubles.[52] At the local level, many suggestions were made for reducing expenditures including switching barrack heating from a stove-based system to a centralized water-based system.[53]

In addition to efforts at eliminating unneeded expenses, by far the simplest method of reducing government subsidies was providing each inmate with paid work. One paradox of the Gulag was that despite its orientation around production it was often unable to use its prisoners efficiently. This was true under Stalin, especially when the Gulag system was overwhelmed in the early 1930s and then again during the Great Terror by huge numbers of new prisoners.[54] In the 1950s, the problems were similarly caused in large measure by the various restructuring efforts and by the constantly changing demographics of Gulag inmates. In 1955, for instance, the Gulag was only able to gainfully employ an average of 69.4 percent of its prisoners, far short of its goal of 77.7 percent. Some of the remaining inmates were engaged in servicing the camps and colonies, others were invalids, but many did not work for other reasons: they refused to work; they were locked up in penalty isolators and deprived of the "right" to labor; or, most commonly, they were simply not able to work due to an absence of work or convoy guards.[55] The theme of increasing the percentage of prisoners on productive labor became a topic of incessant discussion during the conferences of 1957 and 1958; indeed, the MVD held a special conference for colony commanders and their deputies on 2 January 1958 devoted solely to this. In the introductory statement of that meeting, Gulag leadership divulged that only 66 percent of prisoners on average during 1957 were provided with paid work, compared with 69 percent in 1955 and 1956, and a full 12.5 percent did not work at all, as opposed to 10.7 percent in 1956.[56]

This state of affairs was unacceptable for a number of reasons, not least of which was the financial difficulty it created. Whether employing prisoners in colony-run workshops or hiring them out to other agencies, labor was virtually the only source of income for penal institutions outside of subsidies. As Kholodkov in 1958 remarked, giving prisoners work "is considered of utmost importance."[57] Even prison inmates, previously denied the "right to labor," were put to work in order to make prisons less dependent on state funding.[58] Invalids and prisoners on strict regimen posed the most significant problem with arranging work for prisoners. Camp commanders frequently complained that economic enterprises would not take the former because of their limited ability nor the latter due to their reputation as troublemakers.[59] After all, economic managers outside the Gulag structure were rewarded for their fulfillment of their own piece of the government plan, not for their contribution to the financial self-sufficiency of the Gulag. They did not want to be hindered by or pay wages to laborers perceived as unfit for work. In order to correct this, Kholodkov and other administrators admonished their subordinates to go personally to the local *sovnarkhoz* and ensure that each prisoner was given a job.[60] Many *sovnarkhoz* officials, however, continued to treat convicts with suspicion and thwarted the Gulag's goal of providing each inmate with paid work.

Whether through accounting tricks or actual progress made toward reducing expenses and increasing income through prisoner labor, the campaign to reduce the state subsidy quickly boasted of substantial achievements. According to official statistics, Gulag expenses outpaced revenue by 1.38 billion rubles in 1956 just prior to the campaign, then 1.16 billion in 1957, and 0.92 billion in 1958. Per prisoner this amounted to 1,717 rubles, 1,396 rubles, and 1,180 rubles per year respectively.[61] As more colonies became self-sufficient, some even began realizing profits that they, with much fanfare, sent to Moscow for use elsewhere.[62] In response, Gulag administrators sought to temper their enthusiasm, warning against placing too great an emphasis on eliminating subsidies and generating profit. Dudorov, for example, explicitly stated that "profit is not our goal and we should not think about it. . . . The mission of our corrective-labor establishments is to educate and reeducate people and to put them on the correct path."[63] But despite such cautions, the emphasis on reducing government subsidies continued unabated.

The Estonian department of corrective-labor colonies is a good example of such enthusiasm. After a timid beginning in 1957, it made rapid progress toward eliminating its subsidy, reducing it from 440 rubles per prisoner in the first quarter of 1958 to 85 rubles in the second quarter, and finishing the year with a total subsidy of only 629 rubles per prisoner.[64] By contrast, in the first five months of 1955 it had an annualized per capita subsidy of around 1,100 rubles, and in 1957 it received a subsidy of 1,050 rubles per prisoner.[65] Then, in the first nine months of 1959, the Estonian penal system reported even better statistics, a profit of 195,000 rubles (58 rubles per prisoner) and for the first nine months of 1960 it claimed a profit of 1,992,000 (1,660 rubles per prisoner).[66]

By 1960, however, the campaign to reduce state support had run its course as attention turned first to administering the case reviews of 1959 and then to the campaign to eliminate privileges (which will be discussed in chapters 4 and 5). The elimination of the All-Union MVD contributed to the demise of the subsidy reduction drive as well, as it had been the agency promoting this socialist competition in the first case. And there was no doubt a growing realization that while certain pieces of the Gulag could eliminate their subsidy and even make a profit, the system as a whole was not economically self-supporting. The final figures for 1959 confirm this: a subsidy of 1,047,082 rubles, or 1,163 rubles per prisoner, represented complete stagnation compared with the previous year. Finally, it appears that the Central Committee itself had a hand in ending the anti-subsidy campaign. After receiving numerous complaints from local party officials and investigating the matter itself, the Central Committee in its 1960 report on the state of the MVD criticized the ministry harshly because it was interested primarily in "fulfilling the plans, receiving profits, and striving to achieve a high percentage of prisoners on paid work," all aspects of the drive to eliminate the subsidy.[67] The more important task of correcting and reeducating inmates, meanwhile, was suffering.

Reeducation

In Vladimir Voinovich's futuristic satirical novel *Moscow 2042,* the character Edison Xenofontovich, who presents a sort of insider's guide to everything wrong with communism, waxes eloquent on the reeducational aims of twentieth-century Soviet society: "In a word, I am speaking here of the creation of communist man. That was a task that had been posed in your time as well, but back then the stress was put on education and reeducation. But as time showed, that was a pernicious practice and a pernicious theory. In the process of education many people grew worse and not better. This was as stupid as trying to educate a donkey to become a horse."[68] Solzhenitsyn had a slightly different, though no less condemnatory, take on the correctional work of the Gulag and the camps' cultural-educational sections (KVChs) that were given the primary task of reeducation: "But if anybody should ever try to tell you with shining eyes that someone was reeducated by government means through the KVCh—the Cultural and Educational Section—you can reply with total conviction: Nonsense! Everyone in Gulag was reeducated—reeducated under one another's influence and by circumstances, reeducated in various directions. But not even one juvenile, let alone any adult, was reeducated by means of the KVCh."[69] The dominant narrative of political prisoners and dissidents, therefore, is that reeducation not only failed to achieve the desired result, it often had the opposite effect of reinforcing anti-Soviet views and habits.

Since its inception, the Soviet penal system held reeducation as one, if not the most important, of its tasks. Although at different periods in the first decades of Soviet existence some groups of people were cast as uncorrectable, Soviet criminology in general held that, in Khrushchev's famous dictate, "there are no uncorrectable people." Crime was seen as the product of exploitative relationships and mind-sets created by capitalism; in the socialist Soviet Union, therefore, crime occurred due to the "remnants" of the capitalist worldview and social order, and to the pernicious work of traitors and foreign agents bent on destroying Soviet socialism. The point of reeducation, therefore, was to excise these "remnants" and put in their place new socialist habits and a Soviet worldview. The emphasis on correctionalism in the first decades of Soviet rule reached a distinct apex during the Stalin revolution of the early 1930s, when books, films, plays, poems, songs, and other media proclaimed the successes of creating new Soviet men out of criminals both within and without the penal apparatus. Emblematic of this era is the famous *Belomor,* coedited by Maxim Gorky, which proclaimed the simultaneous transformation of man and nature by the reforging power of the Gulag.[70]

From the time of the Great Terror until Stalin's death in 1953, relatively little practical emphasis was placed on reeducation. That is not to say, however, that it disappeared completely. Each camp had its KVCh, local administrators on occasion delivered politically themed lectures, and labor according to Soviet ideology was promoted heavily as the most important reeducational device. Yet the Gulag from the mid-1930s to the end of Stalin's life consistently prioritized labor as a means of production over labor as reeducation; moreover, it devoted sparse resources to the cultural, educational, and political reprogramming of prisoners.[71] Months after Stalin's death the head of the political department of the Gulag informed Minister of Justice Konstantin Petrovich Gorshenin of the state of the KVChs. Positions were unfilled for years at a time, turnover was high, and new recruits were generally inexperienced and often "morally weak." Much of this was due to poor living conditions, the difficult nature of the work, and the exceedingly low pay. Earning only 550–700 rubles per month, the cultural staff of Gulag camps made less than even the guards. The best cultural workers, therefore, were doing everything they could to be transferred to different positions.[72]

Gorshenin might have added in his report that the KVChs were simply not tasked in the late Stalin period with the business of preparing inmates to return successfully to Soviet society. As deputy chief of the Gulag expressed in a 1941 report on reeducational work, "a fundamental restructuring" was needed to bring cultural-education work in line with the production process and to ensure maximum "mobilization of inmates for the fulfilling and overfulfilling of production plans." Camps whose reeducational work was not oriented around production often failed to meet production targets, the deputy continued, without any mention of the supposedly transformative power of labor on the inmates themselves. This attitude was quickly disseminated throughout the Gulag and persisted until Stalin's death.[73] As the Estonian MVD reported in the second quarter of 1952, "cultural-correctional work among the prisoners was concentrated on strengthening the regimen among the prisoners and improving the use of their labor."[74] In other words, the goal of reeducation, even reeducation through labor, was subordinated to the goals of control and economic production. Instead of preparing convicts to succeed as new Soviet men after release, penal officials were concerned primarily with maintaining a population of controllable prison laborers.

Reeducation, including reeducation through labor, was by no means a Soviet invention. Preparing inmates to return to society by adjusting their worldview, habits, and values had long been the aim of most prison systems globally and although relatively deemphasized in Western prison practices in the interwar era, rehabilitation (as it was known in the West) after the war made a strong comeback. Loudly proclaimed as the top aim of incarceration by criminologists and other penal experts, it was enshrined in the 1955 United Nations (UN) Standard Minimum Rules for the Treatment of Prisoners: "The treatment of persons sentenced to imprisonment or a similar measure shall have as its purpose, so far as the length of the sentence permits, to establish in them the will to lead law-abiding and self-supporting lives after their release and to fit them to do so."[75] And this renewed emphasis resulted in tangible changes to penal practices around the globe. In the Netherlands, to mention just one example, solitary confinement and corporal punishment were abolished, rations and living conditions improved, prisoners were provided social workers and psychologists, wardens were instructed to treat the prisoners as "brothers," and the state mandated that penal facilities "give a convict back to society as a less socially disruptive element and, where possible, a better person."[76] Thus, we must be careful to place Soviet efforts to reeducate within a larger framework of penal programs that have, since the early nineteenth century to the present day attempted to transform their prisoners into law-abiding and productive citizens. In conjunction with this, failure by Soviet penal officials in their reeducational efforts as they attempted to prioritize this goal in the post-Stalin era should be heavily qualified with the knowledge that prison systems universally have been notoriously bad at rehabilitating inmates.[77] Thus, while Solzhenitsyn and Voinovich may be to some extent correct in their assessment of Soviet reeducational efforts in the Stalin or post-Stalin periods, it must be remembered that in failure the Gulag stood in good company.

The post-Stalin reemphasis on reeducation did not emerge during the Beria reforms, although, as already noted, Beria advocated far less reliance on incarceration in part because of the realization that the camps were not serving as places of correction. As early as September 1953, however, the Procuracy in its official reports to the Central Committee and Council of Ministers began to criticize the Gulag heavily for its failures in reeducating convicts.[78] Rather than preparing inmates to return to society as productive citizens, the Procuracy charged, the Gulag was allowing them to become recruited into or terrorized by criminal gangs. This emphasis on reeducation in preparation for the inmate's future life outside the barbed wire is what distinguishes such calls for reform from late Stalinist critiques of reeducation as achieving too little toward increasing productivity. By early 1954, this vision of turning the penal system into a place of correction rather than production had taken hold among the top leadership. As Kliment Efremovich Voroshilov noted at the 8 February 1954 Presidium meeting, the Gulag must "pay attention not to construction but to the correction (*ispravlenie*) of people."[79] Numerous reports on the state of the Gulag during 1954 reflected this idea, especially the 12 March and 10 July decrees and statute that unambiguously declared reeducation as the primary mission of the Soviet penal apparatus.

Although Kruglov, as feared by the Presidium when they reappointed him as minister of internal affairs in February 1954, remained at heart an economic manager, he was able at times to convey an attitude of serious reform. Immediately following publication of the new statute governing corrective-labor institutions, Kruglov mandated that local meetings be held to discuss the revamped mission of the Gulag. The proper tone for such meetings was captured in Estonia: "All administrative and economic activity should be subordinated to the primary task of reeducating prisoners."[80] The seriousness of reform was then exhibited at an extensive union-wide conference held by the Gulag for its local administrators from 27 September to 1 October 1954. Devoted to improving camp operations generally and reeducational work in particular in accordance with the new statute of 10 July 1954, this convention allowed central and local officials to discuss old and new methods for reeducating convicts. In his lengthy opening remarks at this conference, Kruglov declared, "We're talked about a fundamental restructuring (*perestroika*) and a fundamental improvement in camp and colony work. This can only be accomplished if our entire staff understands the complete responsibility of the tasks which lie before them."[81] In this manner the MVD tried to convey to its workers the magnitude of the change that was supposed to be occurring in every aspect of the Gulag.

More important than proclamations and conferences, however, Khrushchev instituted structural reforms to ensure that reeducation would be more than a passing campaign. In part this took the form of outside oversight, as will be discussed in chapter 3. But more importantly, the Gulag's own political department, the wing of the Communist Party within the penal system, was tasked with the responsibility for reeducating prisoners. Prior to 1954, the political department had a host of responsibilities, including production, discipline, and the political and educational development of Gulag personnel. Beginning in 1954, however, it was instructed to become concerned primarily with the correction and reeducation of prisoners.[82] Whereas the cultural-educational department of the Stalin period was a weak advocate for reeducation within the Gulag bureaucracy, the political department, especially with the rise of party structures generally in the wake of the Nineteenth Party Congress and with the successful maneuvering of Khrushchev after Stalin's death, was potentially a powerful organization to which most Gulag administrators, by virtue of their party membership, belonged. This structural shift in how reeducation was administered was a crucial component to weakening the deeply entrenched culture of production within the Gulag.

Within the eighteen months following Stalin's death, his heirs had laid the groundwork for turning the production-oriented Gulag into a correctional system concerned with preparing inmates to return to "an honest working life." Decrees, conferences, and a new statute were paired with the delegation of reeducation to the party's own apparatus within the Gulag. But how was reeducation to actually occur? What specific processes would be used to transform criminals infected with the "remnants of capitalism" into model Soviet citizens? In fact, much of the reeducational program from 1954 onward only amplified and reoriented what was already taking place during the 1940s and early 1950s, or else restored programs that were active in the 1930s. This was not a complete break from the past, then, but primarily a period of renewal and reinvigoration. The reorientation of Gulag reeducational efforts may be broken down into three components that will now be discussed in turn: attitudes, living conditions, and programs.

One of the first and primary targets for reform was the attitude of guards and administrators toward the prisoners. Convicts were no longer to be viewed and treated as labor power at best or enemies of the people at worst, but as wayward citizens in need of encouragement, support, trust, training, and education. As Dudorov at a conference in April 1958 so eloquently remarked, "What could be more humane, [or] important, than the labor that we put into the work of reforming a person (*chelovek*). A person committed a crime, he was convicted by a people's court, but he is a Soviet person. Our task is to return this person to an honest working life. . . . It is a noble and humane labor."[83] For many this was a serious mental leap. Guards especially under Stalin had been trained to view prisoners as class enemies or violent beasts just waiting for the opportunity to kill and escape. As former guard Petr Dmitriev recalled, this was not wholly unfounded—the camps were violent places and he suffered from constant paranoia and frequent nightmares as a result.[84] Then, all of a sudden after the death of Stalin, came the new slogans: "obey revolutionary legality," and "respect the individual dignity of the prisoners."[85] Such a change in attitude would not occur overnight, especially as the better-behaved prisoners were released through amnesties, case reviews, and parole, leaving the more violent inmates behind.

Beatings and other forms of physical abuse perpetrated by guards and administrators against prisoners were the most glaring indicators of an improper attitude toward inmates and serious efforts were taken to curtail this seemingly habitual breach of "socialist legality." Whereas physical abuse of prisoners under Stalin was largely ignored, beginning already in 1953 accounts of beatings filled inspection reports and conference proceedings, and those guilty were shamed, punished, and brought to criminal prosecution.[86] In an order distributed to all camp commanders as a warning in September 1953, for instance, the MIu announced criminal charges against three administrators in the Kargopol'skii Corrective-Labor Camp (Kargopol'lag) for beating prisoners themselves or allowing others to do their dirty work for them. Moreover, the camp commander, who had recently been promoted to assistant deputy minister, was to be demoted to frontline Gulag work.[87] Another order from the ministry detailed how two guards, seeking only to make the prisoners miserable, forced them to lie down in the mud multiple times while returning from the worksite. For this the pair received sentences of one and seven years respectively, while their commander was demoted.[88] Over the next several years this campaign against the physical abuse of prisoners continued. Much of the decline in physical abuse of inmates by guards and other personnel can be attributed directly to renewed procuratorial oversight, which will be discussed in chapter 3, and is evident in Khrushchev-era memoirs. Beatings and other forms of physical abuse never disappeared from the Gulag (or from any prison system for that matter), but forceful examples of justice meted out against those who continued to treat inmates improperly helped to turn beatings into isolated exceptions.

Physical abuse was not the only indicator that Gulag personnel lacked a reeducational approach toward convicts. The files of the Gulag are full of complaints about guards and administrators being unnecessarily rude to prisoners or otherwise "denigrating their human dignity."[89] In response to this problem the Gulag issued various decrees admonishing its personnel to be respectful toward prisoners. The Ukrainian minister of justice already in July 1953 declared that "foul language (*matershchina*) should be quickly rooted out of the lexicon of our workers."[90] Similarly, a high-ranking official in the Russian Procuracy in early 1956 reminded his subordinates that Gulag administrators and wardens should be "a model of restraint, tactfulness, and courtesy when addressing prisoners. Every act, action, and word should develop in the prisoner respect for the warden staff as his educators."[91] In support of this the political department wrote articles detailing the proper behavior toward prisoners, and in rare cases punishments were even meted out. A guard in Altai, for example, was placed under arrest for five days for nothing more than being rude to his prisoners.[92] Changed attitudes of guards and administrators toward prisoners were noted by many memoirists. "It was as if something human (*chto-to chelovecheskoe*) had suddenly been awakened," recalled Rygor Klimovich, speaking of the Krasnoiarsk Prison in 1953. The guards still used rough language, but they refrained from swearing at the prisoners and even let them converse between cells, even though this was forbidden. "All of this for us was a pleasant surprise," Klimovich concluded.[93] A. E. Kropochkin at the Sibirskii Corrective-Labor Camp (Siblag) also noticed that the guards in 1954 became noticeably kinder to the inmates.[94] And Mark Goldman, incarcerated in Dubravlag in 1957, remembered that the guards were well-behaved and never used foul language.[95]

Using only anecdotal evidence it is impossible to determine exactly how much effect these measures had; while physically abusive treatment of prisoners clearly declined over the Khrushchev years, rudeness toward prisoners likely decreased but it certainly never disappeared. Yet this problem was certainly not unique to the Soviet context, nor was it solely about the prisoner-guard relationship.[96] As one colony administrator in Ukraine noted, Gulag personnel were incessantly rude *to each other*, cursing for no good reason.[97] Likewise, a procurator complained of incessant swearing by the administrators of a colony in Kharkov both among themselves and with the prisoners.[98] And such attitudes and habits were prevalent outside the Gulag as well; a Central Committee decree on the state of the police force noted that policemen were too often being rude to citizens and otherwise trampling on their rights without cause.[99] It proved difficult to cultivate respect for inmates among administrators and guards when they were themselves steeped in a broader culture that tolerated and even cultivated rudeness and disrespect for all but superiors.

In addition to working to change attitudes toward prisoners, the Gulag also pushed consistently during the 1950s to improve the living conditions of its inmates. If inmates were considered no longer enemies but citizens preparing for release back into society, then their physical habitation should reflect this. As P. M. Losev of the Higher School of the MVD made clear, for proper reeducation to take place, prisoners' dormitories (not barracks!) should not differ from workers' dormitories, nor should amenities of daily life.[100] In conjunction with this admonition for penal institutions to replicate life outside the barbed wire, prisoners were allowed to wear their own clothes and grow their hair long.[101] For many long hair was a particularly important concession after enduring the humiliation of shaved heads under Stalin; as Małgorzata Giżejewska explains, "it was for them a symbol of freedom and return to normal life."[102] Decent living conditions, moreover, came to be considered a prerequisite for the various correctional programs that were put in place or strengthened in the post-Stalin era. Initial reports of living conditions in the post-Stalin era document a wide variety of conditions in the camps and colonies of the Gulag, but most corrective-labor institutions were found deficient in this area. Dilapidated and overcrowded barracks, rotten or insufficient rations, the absence of outbuildings, threadbare clothing, missing bedding and eating utensils, dirt and lice, and a host of other problems litter Gulag reports for the 1953–56 period.[103]

A series of orders aimed at ameliorating living conditions for prisoners together with increased inspections and punishments for those who failed to provide minimum standards resulted in rapid and marked improvements. Rations were improved and portions were enlarged; bread was distributed at meal times in unlimited quantities. As Margaret Werner recalled, all the prisoners began to gain weight. "Our daily menu suddenly became varied, an exciting alternative to the dull sameness," she noted. "We began to see bits of meat and fat in our daily servings, a wonderful new thing."[104] Well-stocked stores for prisoner use, commercial dining halls that provided better food than the regular mess halls, and kitchen facilities where prisoners could cook their own meals appeared, as did self-tended vegetable gardens.[105] An MVD order from 22 April 1954 called for camp points to organize mushroom and berry-picking parties, using prisoners incapable of regular labor.[106] Starting 19 May 1954 the MVD allowed most prisoners to buy tea, even though it was often used to brew the narcotic *chifir*.[107] Better focus on hygiene and improved medical care led to a decline in sickness in the camps and colonies; it also contributed to a more than halving of the reported mortality rate, from 0.84 percent in 1952 to 0.37 percent in 1959.[108]

Closely related to the matter of living conditions was the expansion of rights in the post-Stalin era. The statute of 1954 included a section explicitly devoted to spelling out prisoners' rights, which was to be posted in all prison cells and camp barracks as a reminder to both inmate and guard that they were not mere chattel. The number of hours prisoners were forced to labor was reduced to eight or nine and they were given more days off work. Correspondence rights were increased markedly, culminating in the announcement of unlimited correspondence with relatives on 10 June 1954.[109] Visitation rights were introduced or expanded. In stark contrast to the Stalin era when photography in the camp was forbidden, under Khrushchev prisoners were able to have their portrait taken to send home to their families.[110] The 1954 statute introduced new light-regimen facilities for well-behaved prisoners that further increased their rights and privileges; some light-regimen inmates were allowed to live outside the camp zone with their families, thus officially sanctioning and vastly expanding a long-standing but legally ambiguous practice. In Vorkutlag, for instance, the percentage of prisoners living outside the zone rose from just over 3 percent to 29 percent over the course of 1955.[111] The MVD even ordered that prisoners should no longer be searched when leaving for and returning from work, arguing that this only wasted the prisoners' valuable time for relaxation and cultural activities.[112]

Memoirists overwhelmingly agree that the mid-to-late 1950s was a period of rapidly improving living conditions.[113] One memoirist at the Vorkutlag recalled that "by 1955 we had already stuffed ourselves with bread! And sheets even appeared. Made from calico."[114] Karlo Štajner, incarcerated at the Ozernyi Corrective-Labor Camp (Ozerlag), recalled that "there was a big increase in our days of rest—four a month now—and instead of four letters a year, prisoners could now write two a month."[115] Tsvi Preigerzon enjoyed the benefits of lightened regimen, wandering in and out of the camp as he pleased before being given the privilege of living outside the zone, when he only had to check in with the camp once per week.[116] A woman who served in a Kazakh colony from 1959 to 1963 reported that during her first years she lived outside the zone, worked as a nanny, received actual money as wages, wore her own clothing, enjoyed a well-stocked colony store, and visited freely with male prisoners.[117] As Jerzy Różanowski, recounting the many improvements in camp life, declared, "Every day the wind of freedom was reaching us."[118]

Like the process of changing attitudes toward convicts among administrators and guards, the process of improving living conditions was neither uniform nor linear. Similar to Soviet society at large, living and working conditions for some (notably in the logging camps and other isolated institutions) remained miserable, and complaints about food and medical care persisted. A review of correctional facilities in Magadan Province in 1958, for instance, found that around one-fifth of all barracks were in dire need of replacement; many were not sufficiently outfitted with furniture; bathhouses and lockers for inmates' belonging were missing in some subdivisions; there were no commercial dining halls or kitchens for self-preparation; and some prisoners were still living in tents.[119] Overall, however, there can be no question that life for the average prisoner by the late 1950s was much easier than it had been a decade previously.

Changed attitudes and improved living conditions were considered vital for reeducation in the 1950s, but for Gulag policymakers and criminologists they only set the stage for the actual reeducational programs that would change the mind-sets and habits of the prisoners themselves. The most important program, if it can be called that, remained labor. Since its inception, Soviet criminology had lauded labor as the foremost reeducational instrument in the correctional officer's toolbox. This was, after all, a workers' state founded in part on the ideology that "he who does not work, neither shall he eat." But labor was more than an obligation to society; it was the primary method for creating the new Soviet man. Tales of shock workers, Stakhanovites, labor competitions, and rapid industrialization filled the presses of the Soviet Union, lauding the unique nature of socialist labor and its ability to transform human nature and the physical environment and to craft a more just and prosperous society. Upholding labor as the primary means to reeducate convicts, therefore, was the natural and unassailable theoretical position.

But prison labor as a reeducational device is not unique to the Soviet case and in this vein it seems odd that some commentators and historians of the Gulag have taken such a negative view of compulsory prison labor for convicts, comparing it directly to slavery.[120] Galina M. Ivanova in particular points to 23 June 1956, the date when the Soviet Union ratified the 1930 Forced Labor Convention of the International Labour Organization (No. 29) as a symbolic end point to the Gulag, even though this convention was directed at the use of compulsory labor in the colonial setting and explicitly excluded prison labor from its list of prohibited activities.[121] Contrary to their presuppositions, prison labor throughout the nineteenth and twentieth centuries has been viewed by most penologists as requisite for reeducation and the maintenance of order. Even the 1955 UN Standard Minimum Rules for the Treatment of Prisoners admonished not only that prisoners should be able to work, but that "all prisoners under sentence shall be *required* to work, subject to their physical and mental fitness as determined by the medical officer."[122] Such an emphatic statement leaves little doubt that the Soviet Union in this regard was in harmony with mainstream penological theory. One can certainly take issue with the abuse of forced labor under Stalin, but not the premise of compulsory labor as an internationally accepted form of convict rehabilitation.

Under Khrushchev, labor for the most part retained its dominant position as the crux of reeducation in the Gulag. The effect work was supposed to have on inmates is found in a letter reportedly from prisoner Ovchinnikova from Perm Province that was published in *Pravda* in 1959. Ovchinnikova, a recidivist with eight convictions, declared her newfound love of labor: "I was formerly a thief. But now I understand and realize how uselessly we lived our lives. I fell in love with work for real, only work will give me freedom."[123] Similarly, a complaint from a prisoner from Vorkutlag reaffirmed the Soviet belief in the value of labor; because his commanders were not providing him and his fellow prisoners with work, the petitioner lamented, the inmates in his camp, instead of being reeducated, were only getting stupider.[124] The extent to which these letters, which may have been written for ulterior motives or simply invented in the *Pravda* case, reflected the genuine feelings of these prisoners is not at issue here; the point is that labor as the primary reeducational device of the Gulag was the known and accepted frame of reference for administrators and prisoners alike.

Two innovations, or rather rediscoveries, as they were borrowed from the 1920s and early 1930s, distinguished prisoner labor under Khrushchev from its use under Stalin. First, hard, manual labor, typified by Solzhenitsyn's firsthand account of mining clay with his bare hands because using spades in the rain was fruitless, came to be dismissed as having little reeducational value.[125] Specialized work, by contrast, was considered far superior in that it engaged the mental faculties and prepared inmates for higher-paying work upon release. Yet the vast majority of prisoners in the early post-Stalin period continued to be engaged in hard, manual labor. As the MVD in 1956 lamented, "the majority of prisoners are used as general laborers, without accounting for their professional specialties."[126] The expansion of the corrective-labor colony network in the late 1950s to replace the camps was to a large measure informed by this conviction that skilled labor for prisoners was needed, for each colony under the 1956 restructuring plan was to have its own workshops where prisoners could use their existing skills or be trained to a new profession.

As a corollary to this revamped view on labor, the Gulag greatly expanded its existing program of vocational training, eventually creating the goal of ensuring every prisoner had a vocational specialty upon release. The training usually involved theoretical courses held in the evening after the conclusion of the working today along with a certain amount of practical experience. To illustrate the range of professions taught, in Estonia inmates obtained credentials as excavator operators, chauffeurs, mechanics, textile workers, masons, and a host of others.[127] Although progress was halting in the first post-Stalin years, by the late 1950s some success could be heralded. Official statistics for 1957 and 1958, for example, claimed that 246,409 and 263,259 prisoners respectively received a vocational specialty, far more than the number of convicts trained in the early to mid-1950s. Similarly, the Gulag in 1958 released only 18,635 persons from its camps and colonies without a specialty, compared with 48,000 in 1956.[128] As far as providing qualified work while incarcerated, one Gulag administrator in early 1959 noted that "the overwhelming majority of prisoners in camps and colonies work according to a given specialty."[129] Such statistics must be questioned as they could easily be falsified at numerous levels. Indeed, other reports from the late 1950s found that many jobs at which prisoners worked could be characterized as unqualified work with few prospects for acquiring a specialty.[130] A study group commissioned by the Russian Bureau of the Central Committee found in 1960, for instance, that prisoner labor was often oriented not around reeducation, but the maximization of output.[131] This "obviously incorrect practice" held especially true of the logging camps where in 1960 around half of the Gulag's prisoners were located: "Prisoners in these camps in most cases are used as muscle power on unqualified work, which does not provide them any specialty."[132] Still, this does not mean that progress toward the goal of providing specialized work and vocational training was not being made; the authors of these reports, after all, had their own motives for framing the issue differently. In an important counterpoint to the official reports, memoirist Maiia Ulanovskaia recalled that whereas many of the reeducational programs were met with suspicion, the new vocational courses at Ozerlag in the mid-1950s were genuinely appreciated by the prisoners.[133]

As hinted at in the Central Committee report just mentioned, some within the penal apparatus did not wholly accept the shift toward specialized labor and vocational training. Committee of State Security (KGB) chief Ivan Aleksandrovich Serov, in his response to Dudorov's reorganization plan, rejected the need for skilled labor, and he was not alone. One deputy minister of internal affairs for Estonia likewise opposed Gulag policy concerning vocational training, contending that the reeducational difference between skilled and unskilled labor was not great and that the latter, in fact, was more beneficial for recidivists, many of whom had never worked before.[134] This justified the continued use of prisoners in manual-labor jobs, in particular logging, gravel mining, and construction. And, as will be discussed in chapter 5, these arguments fed into the broader counterreform movement aimed at creating harder living conditions for inmates. Lack of funding also contributed to slow progress in establishing vocational training. In 1956 Dudorov submitted a plan to create a formalized network of vocational training centers within the Gulag, asking the Council of Ministers to compel other organizations to provide without compensation unneeded tools, machinery, and materials. While the Ministry of Finance approved, the State Economic Commission prevailed in allowing such a program only for juvenile colonies.[135]

In addition to the shift to specialized work, the second novelty of the Khrushchev era in regard to inmate labor was the partial resurrection of a controversial tenet taught by Anton Makarenko, who in the late 1950s and 1960s was canonized as the patron saint of Soviet pedagogy and whose ideas informed other reeducational programs of Khrushchev's Gulag. For Makarenko, labor by itself was not naturally reeducational. As the deputy minister of internal affairs for Ukraine, citing Makarenko, made clear, work is a "neutral process" that must be accompanied by a wide range of reeducational programs.[136] A softer version of this point was also made in the 23 March 1956 inspection report that accompanied Dudorov's ascension to the head of the MVD. The report's authors noted that "as a result of the poor organization of labor many honest working prisoners do not fulfill their production norms, receive very low wages, and do not receive their workday credits, which leads to worse discipline in the camp, work refusals, and disobedience toward the camp administration."[137] In other words, labor, when properly organized and rewarded, was reeducational; when poorly organized and thus underappreciated it had the obverse effect of corrupting the prisoners. Thus, it was not the labor itself that influenced prisoners for good; it was the entire culture surrounding labor.

In order to accompany labor and make it reeducational, therefore, the Gulag expanded or newly implemented a number of other programs designed to prepare its inmates to return to an "honest working life." The political departments of each corrective-labor facility, now charged with spearheading the reeducational effort, recruited agitators and lecturers from among administrators and guards to conduct political exercises and discussions with the prisoners. Political departments expanded the production of newspapers, wallpapers, and various other forms of propaganda oriented toward prisoners.[138] Efforts were made to install radios for propaganda purposes in all barracks and cells, televisions were installed in barracks and clubs, and films were shown on a regular basis.[139] Emblematic of this drive to teach prisoners how to properly interpret the world around them through Marxism-Leninism was a quote hung above the door of M. M. Molostov's barrack in Dubravlag: "The absence of proper political convictions is equal to the absence of a soul."[140] But political work in the camp was often subjected to mockery from the prisoners, especially from political prisoners who were on average far more educated than the administrators and guards trying to teach them. Others simply refused to attend political discussions or else sat quietly trying not to listen.[141] N. I. Krivoshein and his fellow prisoners at Dubravlag referred to the camp newspaper not by its official title of *Za otlichnyi trud* (*For Excellent Labor*), but instead as *Za otlichnyi trup* (*For an Excellent Corpse*).[142]

But not all reeducational measures were so politicized; after all, the new Soviet man was not only to be conversant in Marxist theory and world political events, he was to be cultured, physically fit, and well educated. During the last several years of Stalin's life there had been a slight resurgence in cultural activities in at least some camps after a barren period during the Great Terror and World War II, but under Khrushchev this drive was greatly expanded and extended.[143] Libraries were replenished and readers' conferences convened; clubs with stages for performances were constructed; orchestras, choirs, dramatic troupes, and other performing arts groups were organized; and artistic workshops and competitions were held.[144] In 1958 the political department began publishing an occasional pamphlet for prisoners called *Literaturnyi sbornik* (*Literary Digest*), with stories and poems written by and for inmates. It also featured a yearly literary competition for the best stories, poems, and short plays written by prisoners.[145] Nikita Krivoshein remembered biweekly choir concerts as part of the reeducational program at Dubravlag in the late 1950s.[146] The Gulag also brought in outside speakers, including party and industry leaders, to speak with the prisoners. The most popular speakers, however, proved to be actors from the local theaters.[147]

Sporting activities, also employed to a limited extent under the conditions of late Stalinism, experienced a dramatic resurgence after 1953.[148] With the workday reduced to just eight or nine hours, there was suddenly time and energy for sport. Mark Goldman recalled playing many sports and games at Dubravlag in the late 1950s, including hockey, soccer, basketball (which the Balts dominated), volleyball (where the Russians got their revenge), table tennis, weightlifting, and chess.[149] Preigerzon's camp played a lot of soccer and beginning in 1953 camp commanders even arranged intercamp matches.[150] For many inmates this recreational activity was quite meaningful. As Juozas Butrimas recalled, "to be able to play basketball [in] the Gulag allowed us to feel human again, not only like a slave, and to survive the captivity."[151] Finally, the Gulag vastly expanded its existing educational programs for prisoners, focusing first on providing basic reading and writing skills to those considered illiterate and eventually offering a full primary educational system.[152] By 1 January 1959, 72,744 inmates were enrolled in school, a large increase over the 57,628 enrolled in classes the year previously.[153]

In order to facilitate the implementation of these various programs and to demonstrate its new humane attitude toward inmates, the Gulag greatly expanded its set of self-governing institutions at each camp and colony. Before Stalin's death prisoner "activists" participated in organizing certain aspects of camp life through the KVChs. Starting in 1954, beyond expanding this system of "sections" organized around particular areas of camp life, such as security, sanitation, and culture, the Gulag reintroduced prisoner-run comrades' courts and established activist councils (*sovety aktiva*) to run the "sections" and otherwise help manage the corrective-labor institution. These various "self-organized" groups were elected by the prisoners themselves, although, as might be suspected, such elections were prone to manipulation by camp authorities.[154]

The dramatic expansion of self-governing institutions within the Gulag in the 1950s was part of a broader movement within Khrushchev's Soviet Union to place more policing power into the hands of ordinary citizens. Comrades' courts and voluntary people's militia were tasked with educating the Soviet public on proper behavior and were also given limited policing and sentencing functions. As Khrushchev confidently declared in 1959, "the Soviet public can cope with the violators of socialist legal order."[155] Notably, Soviet self-governing organizations were also in line with international criminological thought, with various prison agencies in the 1950s and 1960s experimenting with similar inmate groups.[156] Yet because of their ideological commitment to communal reeducation, Gulag officials after Stalin's death were prepared to more fully develop inmate self-governance, even as they also ensured control over these groups.

Comrades' courts, which existed in corrective-labor colonies in the early Soviet period up to the early 1930s before being disbanded, were restored in 1954 in lightened- and standard-regimen penal institutions and given authority to try their fellow inmates for various disciplinary infractions in public shaming rituals. Comprised of seven to nine inmates elected by their peers (and approved by the administration, of course), they had power to issue formal reprimands that stayed on the inmates' records for at least three months and could also recommend to the camp administration that extra measures of punishment be taken.[157] As it turned out, however, this model of self-organization proved to be largely ineffective. Prisoners elected to serve on the courts were often loath to perform their functions, likely in part due to threats of violence.[158] But the courts also suffered from the fact that the activist councils too were charged with dealing with regimen violators. In the end, comrades' courts within the Gulag proved underused and ineffective and were abolished in the early 1960s.

The activist councils, however, proved to be much more active and durable institutions. According to the new Statute on the Council of the Prisoner Collective, the councils were to be made up of nine to fifteen persons openly elected by their fellow prisoners (although the statute stipulated they could only include prisoners "firmly set on the path of correction") and they functioned under the direction of the camp or colony administration.[159] The goal of the councils was to administer much of camp life, encourage their fellow prisoners to work, teach them the importance of following Soviet laws, and arouse in them an active economic and cultural consciousness. This was to be done through the organization of reeducational programs and through individualized discussions about and with troublemaking prisoners. In Estonia in 1955, for example, the councils at the various camp subdivisions reported holding formal discussions on 297 prisoners who had committed regimen violations or who were not meeting their production norms. Crucially, in making parole decisions, the camp administration was supposed to consult with the activist council to verify the potential parolee's level of reeducation.[160]

For inmates, one perk of being elected to the activist council (though this did not hold for comrades' courts or the "sections") was being freed from regular production obligations.[161] That they were to devote their entire workday to managing the camp and reeducating their fellow prisoners indicates how serious the Gulag was about transitioning from a productive to a corrective mode of operations. Already by the end of 1954, roughly one-quarter of all prisoners in Estonia were members of the activist councils, comrades' courts, and self-organized sections, suggesting some success in reorganizing its camps around the prisoners themselves in order to attain reeducational results.[162] That the prisoners involved in these groups had their own motives for participating (including personal satisfaction, greater chance of early release, possible liberation from labor duties, potential perks from the administration, and opportunities for corruption) does not diminish the fact that they played the role designed for them by the Gulag.

Elsewhere, there was less success with self-governing institutions. In many places inmates involved were loathed by the other prisoners, and on occasion they were beaten or even killed for collaborating with the administration. Solzhenitsyn recalled that after a few heads of the activist council were murdered or beaten up, no one would willingly volunteer for the position.[163] The violence sometimes went the other way, though. An activist council member and a cultural organizer, along with an accomplice at Colony No. 2 in Estonia, for instance, beat up two other prisoners while in a drunken state, and were subsequently removed from their posts.[164]

The issue of inmate self-organization was a serious matter to Gulag academics and bureaucrats, who in the Khrushchev era were constantly searching for new ways to influence inmates. A methodological conference was held in November 1960 for camp administrators in which social scientists instructed them on how to create healthy collectives among prisoners.[165] Most prominently, Makarenko's ideas on crafting productive collectives out of delinquents were studied and restudied, and various conferences devoted to this topic were held within Gulag structures. As one such meeting held in Ukraine in 1960 made clear, reeducation was a product of myriad factors, but in order for these to have effect prisoners must be given trust and responsibility, thereby turning the inmate into the subject rather than the object of reeducation. Most important, however, was Makarenko's primary idea that reeducation was to take place "in a collective, by means of the collective, and for the collective."[166]

In addition to being led by capable inmates, Makarenko and his Khrushchev-era admirers stressed, inmate collectives must be directed by devoted and competent correctional officers who can motivate the prisoners to improve themselves and who are not tied down to the mundane operational of the facility. Dudorov therefore determined to organize inmate collectives as detachments (*otriady*).[167] This specific idea appears to have originated in the early 1930s, with Ida Leonidovna Averbakh's seminal 1936 work *From Crime to Labor* noting the experimental formation of large detachments of 500–600 inmates to replace smaller labor collectives, with each having a full complement of self-organizational structures to aid in the prisoners' reeducation.[168] A revised version of this idea then appeared in a prisoner complaint from 1955, which suggested the creation of much smaller detachments of 50–60 inmates (2 brigades) in each.[169] In its adopted post-

Stalin form, detachments were to be comprised of between 75 and 200 prisoners, meaning that each colony or camp point would have multiple detachments and each detachment would have several work brigades.[170] The Gulag made detachment leaders, selected from the ranks of lower-level Gulag employees in each camp and colony, the primary point of contact between prisoners and the administration. As such, they were supposed to accompany their detachment to the work site, attend and participate in cultural activities, and engage in one-on-one reeducational work. They were also instructed to keep in touch with prisoners after their release to encourage and support them as they started life anew.[171] In short, as pronounced at a regional Gulag conference held in Kemerovo Province, the detachment head "should be a good educator (*vospitatel*), a good administrator, and a good father among the prisoners."[172]

In order to foster the reeducational goals of the detachment system, the Gulag devoted an entire conference in January 1958 to sharing experiences associated with the successes of this reform.[173] At this event MVD chief Dudorov admonished detachment heads to visit detachments in other colonies in order to learn from them. In a new training manual entitled *What the Head of the Detachment Needs to Know,* the Gulag reminded its detachment heads that the main goal of Soviet corrective-labor institutions was the reeducation of prisoners.[174] Further, the Gulag created awards for "model detachments" and encouraged friendly competitions between detachments based on indicators such as productivity or based on sporting or cultural events.[175] In some places this new structure no doubt had the desired effect. Comrade Lillepea, head of the first detachment in Colony No. 1 in Estonia, for instance, reported that the detachment system created a better atmosphere for reeducation, noting that none of her prisoners missed production norms or avoided attending the colony school anymore.[176] In other places, however, the detachments were not as successful in facilitating the reeducation of their inmates. Nikita Krivoshein, for instance, reported that his detachment commander in the spring of 1959 was a pensioner who rarely appeared.[177] And, despite the emphasis on reeducation in the detachment system, Dudorov in April 1958 complained that detachment heads in many cases had become primarily economic rather than reeducational figures.[178] More concerned with ensuring high production among their prisoners, they neglected to carry out the important work of one-on-one counseling.

Control

The final of the three primary aims of central Gulag administrators and local officials alike was that of control, or, as they termed it, maintaining the regimen (*rezhim*). This meant, above all, enforcing a strict daily regimen along with preventing disciplinary infractions and more serious incidents such as escapes, murders, violence against guards or fellow prisoners, and mass uprisings. Control over the prisoners was important for multiple reasons, the most important of which in the decades prior to Stalin's death was ensuring "the most effective use of the labor of prisoners."[179] Rioting prisoners, escapees, and those who refused to work only prevented the successful fulfillment of the economic plan, after all. This focus on discipline and control was, of course, not unique to the Gulag but rather a feature of all prison regimes. A British criminologist in 1960 found that in the British penal system "the senior uniformed officers pay only lip service to all but the disciplinary aspects of the job."[180] Similar attitudes dominated the U.S. prison system in the first half of the twentieth century and proved resilient even during the height of the correctional movement of the postwar era. As noted by Gresham Sykes in the late 1950s, custody and maintaining the internal order, rather than reeducation or economic aims, were the top priorities of officials in the New Jersey State Penitentiary.[181] And the UN Standard Minimum Rules for the Treatment of Prisoners made clear that "discipline and order shall be maintained with firmness."[182]

Stalin's heirs inherited a penal system that, while stressing the importance of internal order and discipline, was notoriously bad at attaining this goal. Despite a partially successful campaign to impose order on the camps in the early 1950s, violence by prisoners was pervasive, corruption was endemic, escapes were common, uprisings and strikes were on the rise, and regular disciplinary infractions were literally numberless.[183] The massive size of the camps, the use of communal barracks rather than cells, the mass nature of production, the dearth of qualified personnel, and the general attitude of disregard toward convicts contributed to this situation which, in the uncertain atmosphere of the first post-Stalin years, erupted into an unprecedented number of mass disturbances. Whereas much has been written about the three uprisings in the special camps during 1953–54, the Gulag also faced hundreds of other large-scale disturbances in the regular camps.[184] A little-known but sizable uprising in Chukotka, for instance, resulted in scores of deaths and a months-long interruption of tin production.[185] This lack of control is also evident in the numbers of prisoner-on-prisoner murders and incidents of banditry, which in 1954 stood at 515 and 410 respectively.[186]

Contributing to the persistently high rate of violence in the early post-Stalin Gulag was the continuation of rampant gang activity, including the so-called bitches' wars. These gangs—thieves-in-law, the "departed" (*otoshedshie*—known more commonly as "bitches"), Polish thieves, red-caps, and so forth—were notorious for robbing other prisoners, conducting brutal warfare among themselves, killing stool pigeons, and leading strikes and riots. The late Stalinist

Gulag, focused on maximizing production, attempted to manage rather than eliminate the gangs by employing gang members in positions of responsibility, designating certain camps as the domain of one gang or the other in order to prevent violence, and in some instances supporting one gang's fight against another.[187]

Although the Gulag began to emphasize in 1954 the necessity of destroying the criminal gangs, entrenched coping strategies continued for years. As the Gulag acknowledged in internal reports and conference, gruesome murders and other crimes were being carried out, especially when the gang members in a camp split into rival groups. In one typical example noted by a memoirist held at Ozerlag, a thief-in-law in 1954 threw a bomb into a cell containing several of the "departed," killing ten of them.[188] Although some camps had ostensibly by this point eliminated the influence of the thieves, many continued the practice of legitimizing them by working with them and by assigning prisoners to camp points based on gang affiliation, not according to sentence or conduct while in captivity.[189] As late as 1957 Deputy Minister of Internal Affairs Kholodkov complained that "often in the camp points it is not the administration but the recidivists who are in command."[190] Some commanders took steps toward eliminating the gangs, but did so by granting them early release on account of disease or because they had ostensibly "stood on the path of correction" (often through bribery), or simply by transferring them to another camp or to prison.[191]

The continued violence and uprisings of 1953–55 were due in no small part to the uncertain situation surrounding the death of Stalin and arrest and execution of Beria. As Stalin's heirs proclaimed renewed devotion to socialist legality, and began to seriously punish guards and administrators who abused the prisoners, a certain hesitancy in regard to discipline began to pervade the camps. Oleg Borisovich Borovskii, a prisoner who worked in the medical section of Vorkutlag, remembered the lax regimen of 1953. "Everything held to the principle: it is useless to vex the prisoners," he recalled. "Do they work? Does the mine fulfill the plan? What else do you need?"[192] Beginning in 1954, the new stress on cultivating an attitude of reeducation through encouragement rather than discipline no doubt contributed to the reduced emphasis on strict control. Leniency, it was thought, would help change the prisoners' attitude toward the administration, production, and the communist project in general.[193] This changed attitude was certainly felt by the inmates. As Štajner recalled of the early post-Stalin years, "there was, above all, a relaxation of discipline. Until then, no prisoner had dared to protest against the daily bullying and harassment, since even the slightest objections would be brutally punished. Now you could see people quite openly refusing to perform the most strenuous work, and no one thought of punishing them for it."[194] This is certainly confirmed by Gulag statistics, which noted a large increase in the number of prisoners refusing to work, and in other memoir sources. Danylo Shumuk and a friend in Ozerlag in the late-1950s, for instance, took eager advantage of the hesitancy of Gulag officials to force prisoners to work, a decision that gave them "ample free time." "I occupied myself," Shumuk related, "by growing onions, radishes, cucumbers and potatoes in a small garden."[195] As will be seen in chapter 5, this attitude among some prisoners and the reticence of officials to punish them contributed to a movement to create a much stricter set of guidelines governing inmate life in the early 1960s.

Despite this relaxation of discipline, the rhetoric of maintaining control continued unabated. Indeed, many saw strict internal order as a precondition for reeducation. As one inmate complaint in 1955 made clear, new prisoners and especially the youth were subjected to the pernicious influence of the gangs, starting in the transit prisons that were all ruled by hardened criminals. And this continued in the camps, where newcomers were not separated from the recidivists, a situation that prevented the policies of reeducation from taking hold. The camp administration was aware of this situation, but tolerated it as long as production plans were fulfilled. In the same spirit they showed great leniency toward the many prisoners who committed crimes or regimen infractions.[196]

This oft-repeated complaint found voice not just among prisoners, but among criminologists and penal officials as well. In 1955 even Voroshilov began to press Kruglov on this issue. He responded in a letter dated 12 April 1955, detailing various measures taken since the 10 July 1954 statute to restore "strict order" in the camps. He also justified the situation with the fact that after the 1953 amnesty only the hardest criminals were left in the Gulag.[197] In fact, efforts to control the gangs and other sources of disorder began to pay off. Official reports of murder, banditry, and mass disturbances all declined significantly from 1954–56: the number of murders fell from 515 in 1954 to 181 in 1956; figures for banditry in the same period declined from 410 to 130; and there were only 60 mass disturbances in 1956 compared with 130 in 1954.[198] This decline can only be partly explained by the reduction of prisoners overall, which fell from around 1.3 million in 1954 to 800,000 in 1956. At the same time, however, the numbers of escapes remained high, increasing from 1,662 in 1954 to 2,424 in 1955 before declining to 1,796 in 1956.[199]

One issue that played prominently in the mid-1950s debate over control was the deconvoying of prisoners. This long-standing practice, which allowed inmates to labor or perform errands outside the camp without the supervision of guards, became pervasive in the early post-Stalin years.[200] Although seen as necessary by camp commanders and production personnel, those concerned with reeducation and control began to criticize the mass use of deconvoying. In the 23 March 1956 MVD inspection report, for instance, Kruglov was castigated for allowing "in the sole interest of economic activity" far too many prisoners (around 70,000 out of a total population of 781,630, or approximately 9 percent) to be deconvoyed. Among those were inmates convicted of especially dangerous crimes, who by regulation were not supposed to be deconvoyed. Indeed, many deconvoyed prisoners abused their privilege by committing crimes while outside the camps, including murder, rape, and escape.[201] Another report on deconvoyed prisoners at Sevvostlag noted that camp commanders were deconvoying inmates known to be dangerous recidivists and that, as a result, deconvoyed inmates were responsible for nearly every case of embezzlement at Dal'stroi in 1955, plus half of the incidents of theft of private property.[202]

The 1956 reorganization of the structure of the Gulag and the continued re-orientation of its mission toward correctionalism were accompanied in the second half of the 1950s by increased calls to bring order to the camps and colonies. The September 1956 reorganization plan made clear from the start that reeducation was to take place "in the spirit of strict obedience to Soviet laws and the rules of socialist society." The MVD was further admonished to "bring strict order to the regimen and guarding of prisoners."[203] As part of this effort to heighten control during the 1957–60 period, the Gulag in April 1957 decided to concentrate in four corrective-labor camps all political prisoners whose convictions were upheld during the 1954–56 review process.[204] The MVD had proposed in 1956 to isolate such inmates in special prisons, but this idea had not been accepted as part of the reorganizational plan; isolating political prisoners in just a few camps was the next best alternative. By October 1957 the number of institutions housing politicals had been cut from thirty-eight to ten, and by 1959 the work of isolating them into four camps had been completed.[205] This process of consolidation continued in the early 1960s, when nearly all political (including religious) prisoners were concentrated at Dubravlag.[206]

More important than isolating political prisoners, however, was a major push to combat criminal activity and eliminate the gangs. In 1957 alone the MVD of the USSR and the MVD of the Russian Republic issued eight major directives on fighting crime in the camps.[207] Evidence of this campaign is also located in the files of the guard department, where over a thousand pages on this subject were written from October 1957 to July 1958.[208] Here too one finds a seventy-eight-page unpublished monograph entitled "Groups of Recidivist Thieves" by MVD academic Vadim Ivanovich Monakhov, which outlines the main traits of the gangs and several suggestions for combating them.[209] The campaign to suppress the Gulag's gangs in the late 1950s featured death sentences for the worst gangsters and special camp points with strict, disciplinary regimens for others. During 1957 and 1958, 71,853 inmates were transferred to strict-regimen camps and colonies and another 16,341 were sent to prison.[210]

Additionally, the number of deconvoyed prisoners was reduced by over 12,000 in 1958.[211]

Another method of fighting crime and the gangs in the camps was the (attempted) elimination of money inside all places of confinement through the implementation of cash-free accounting (*beznalichnyi raschet*). This program, which maintained an account ledger for each inmate, was used at times under Stalin, most notably in the special camps, but the dominant practice before and after his death was the distribution of wages and money transfers to prisoners in rubles.[212] The infusion of large amounts of cash into the camp led to monthly spikes in criminal activity; indeed, the day of the month when prisoners received their wages was termed the "nightmare day" (*koshmarnyi den'*) by one camp official because of the gambling, theft, and murder that reigned on that and the following days.[213] To fix this problem, Procurator General Roman Andreevich Rudenko in early 1956 proposed to the Central Committee that cash-free accounting be established for all inmates, and the program was implemented the following year.[214]

Not surprisingly, Gulag administrators both in Moscow and in the camps and colonies attributed this reform with reducing incidents of disorder as it eliminated the primary object of theft in places of incarceration.[215] It also created a situation where prisoners, devoid of the chance to gamble or drink their money away, began to send significant money transfers home to their families.[216] This reversed the trend of prisoners receiving more money than they sent. Inmates also, at least in Sergei Dovlatov's semifictionalized memoir (which was based on his time as a guard in a Khrushchev-era correctional facility), joked that the absence of money signaled that "true Communism" had been achieved in the camps.[217] Persistent problems with drinking and gambling during the following years, however, call into question the long-term effectiveness of this system. Prisoners continued to receive cash illicitly from their families and other contacts outside the barbed wire, and a lively barter system, which by this point included an increasing amount of narcotics, ensured that alcohol abuse and gambling persisted.[218]

In addition to repression and the establishment of cash-free accounting, the Gulag attempted to persuade gang members to "abandon their former ways." The defining moment in this effort was a letter written by Valentin I. Kozhevnikov, a prominent thief-in-law who in 1956 arrived at Prison No. 4 in Latvia. After a few months of making trouble, however, Kozhevnikov turned from his life of crime, began working in the prison workshop and participating in the cultural activities of the prison, and started writing for the prison newspaper. Then in February 1957 he wrote a lengthy letter in which he forcefully renounced his former gang and called on his colleagues to follow suit.[219] "Your mothers wait for you," he poignantly reminded them after exposing the dead-end life of the thief: "Only through an honest attitude toward life can you save yourselves and bring joy to your mother, who knows no peace, neither day nor night."[220] Kholodkov seized on this opportunity to emasculate the gangs, ordering the letter along with a picture of Kozhevnikov to be placed on display in every prison and correctional facility and calling for a public reading and discussion of the letter.[221]

Kozhevnikov's letter had a predictably polarizing effect on embattled gangsters: many rejected his call, accusing him of betrayal and threatening violence against him; others suspected that his letter was simply fabricated by the MVD.[222] But many wrote apparently sincere responses to his letter, pledging to likewise abandon their criminal traditions and begin to repair their crime-ridden lives. As one former gangster wrote, "I am no longer the same [man]. I want to live honestly like all Soviet people. . . . I ask only the right to work and be a member of Soviet society."[223] Dozens of these letters, along with a few poems (including one by Kozhevnikov himself entitled "Forward"), were then published in a two-volume pamphlet issued by the political department of the Gulag under the name for use in the camps.[224] And according to a former editor in the political department, these letters were faithfully reproduced with a minimal amount of editing. In the interests of preserving their authenticity, the editors wanted to ensure that the thieves' argot was not altered. Ultimately, however, the campaign fizzled after it became clear that Kozhevnikov was using his newfound publicity to gain special favors while privately mocking the MVD.[225] In the end, using gangsters to combat the gang problem had at best mixed results.

Yet despite the problems with Kozhevnikov, the Gulag's struggle against crime and gangs in the late 1950s had tangible effects. Although Kholodkov to some extent exaggerated in mid-1958 when he reported to the Central Committee that "the criminal gangs are for the most part liquidated, they don't exist as an organized force," by 1960–61 this had largely become a reality.[226] Official documentation, including procurators' reports, in the early 1960s is essentially devoid of any talk of the gangs, with the occasional exception of small groups of prisoners trying to restore the gangs' traditions. Memoirists likewise noted this significant change in Gulag society.[227] Although camp administrators would continue to use select inmates as trusties, and prisoner groups in localized units would at times band together to terrorize the other inmates, the mass phenomenon of organized criminal gangs within the Gulag largely disappeared.

Increased control over the Gulag population also had an effect on at least certain categories of crime perpetrated within the penal system. Incidents of banditry in the Gulag's camps and colonies decreased from 130 in 1956 to only 28 in 1959; the number of mass disturbances fell to just 16 from 60 in 1956;

murders declined from 181 in 1956 to 115 in 1959; and only 1,067 escapes were registered in 1959 against 1,796 in 1956.[228] However, although overall crime figures for the Gulag recorded a 10 percent decrease in 1957 compared to 1956, the total for 1958 came in just above those of 1957. In 1957 there were 7,783 crimes committed by 11,086 prisoners compared with 7,723 crimes committed by 11,865 prisoners in 1958. Alongside the declines in violent crime stood a rise (at least on paper) in theft, hooliganism, and homosexual relations.[229] Whereas these precise numbers cannot be taken at face value, Procuracy reports and memoirs tend to support this reduction in crime in the late 1950s.[230] Thus, although the anticrime campaign of the late 1950s was not wholly successful, the elimination of the gangs together with dramatically reduced numbers of uprisings, murders, escapes, and acts of banditry indicates a much higher level of control.

Measuring Success

The three aims of the Gulag—economics, reeducation, and control—were debated heavily during the 1950s at multiple levels within the penal apparatus. The orientation of change in this period was decidedly toward reeducation, with a smaller but growing movement toward increased control, but in the end a lasting commitment toward reeducation was only partially realized. One of the primary challenges faced by the political department of the Gulag and others interested in reorienting the penal apparatus around reeducation was the matter of quantifying progress and success. The aims of production and cost control had very tangible indicators by which to measure the operation of a particular camp or the Gulag as a whole. Although such numbers were easily and often manipulated, production (by output and value), productivity, cost of production, and the difference between expenses and production-related income created an easily quantifiable and comparable metric of success or failure. Likewise, certain indicators within the rubric of control, most notably the number of escapes, murders, acts of banditry, and mass disturbances, presented an equally satisfying numerical value by which to judge operational success.

Reeducation, by contrast, was a much fuzzier category. The authorities could and did keep track of multiple indicators related to political, cultural, and educational work: the number of lectures delivered, the number books in the library and journals subscribed to, the number of cultural events held, the number of prisoners serving in self-organizational groups and attending school, the number of inmates released on parole, and so forth.[231] But how could one tell if the prisoners were actually being reformed by all these programs? As noted by one

Gulag administrator, "the fulfillment of the production plan is controlled sys-tematically, but no one in sufficient measure asks the colony commander about the results of reeducation, which are in any case not that easy to determine."[232] During the 1950s few efforts were made to calculate recidivism rates, except in relation to specific amnesties. Thus, even as new attention was being focused on corrections, the reeducated soul proved much more difficult to quantify than a kilogram of coal or a bushel of barley. And in a society that placed such a high premium on statistics, this proved a major obstacle.

In order to cope with the lack of reliable indicators of correction, Gulag offi-cials simply modified the existing strategy of interpreting existing hard catego-ries of analysis within the spheres of control and production. Infractions of the camp regimen were attributed to poor reeducational work, as properly indoctri-nated prisoners should naturally obey camp regulations.[233] Similarly, if prisoners were not meeting and overfulfilling their production norms or if they refused to work, this pointed to shortcomings in their reeducation.[234] In the late Stalinist period such analogies were standard practice for judging the work of the KVCh, oriented as it was on improving discipline and raising productivity.[235] But under Khrushchev, when reeducation was placed above production and control in sig-nificance, these indicators continued to be used as a measuring stick for how committed camp commanders were to the correctional mission of the Gulag. If a camp fulfilled its norm and had a low level of disciplinary infractions, the logic went, the commander must be correctly implementing the reeducational pro-grams. In other words, although the interpretation and application had been slightly altered, in the end the same figures used under Stalin were employed under Khrushchev to judge camp operations. As may be imagined, rather than facilitate a turn toward correctionalism, this only served to keep heavy emphasis at the camp or colony level on production and control.

In the end, whether for lack of alternative indicators of reeducation or because of the continued emphasis on plan fulfillment, the MVD in 1958 and 1960 reaffirmed the principle of rewarding its Gulag officials according to production figures alone. This policy was criticized by Russian Procuracy chief I. F. Osipenko in a December 1960 report to the Central Committee.[236] And the Central Committee agreed with his assessment, finding that "the matter of reeducation is often judged only according to the results of fulfilling the pro-duction plans, without account for the prisoner's level of correction and his preparation for life and work in freedom."[237] In contrast to this, the Central Com-mittee proposed that corrective-labor institutions be evaluated on "the prison-ers' level of correction and their preparation for life and work in freedom."[238] Yet the specific manner in which such evaluations should be conducted and the numbers on which they should be based were left to the imagination.

Beyond the problem of quantifiable indicators of success, the turn toward reeducation also suffered because it lacked powerful institutional (and therefore financial) backing. True, charging the political department of the Gulag with responsibility for reeducation created strong institutional support within the penal bureaucracy itself. And this, along with the institutions of oversight that will be discussed in the next chapter, went a long way toward ensuring changed attitudes, improved living conditions, and a much stronger commitment for reeducational programs. But whereas production and financial interests within the Gulag had the backing of the Council of Ministers, various economic ministries, Gosplan, and the Ministry of Finance, no important governing body, other than perhaps the Procuracy, played the same role for reeducation. The Central Committee, to which the MVD party apparatus reported, at times displayed strong support for reeducation. But this support appears to have been periodic, coming at crucial moments in 1954, 1956, and 1960, but flagging in the intervening years. The Communist Party of the Soviet Union, after all, was responsible for economic production along with various ideological aims such as inmate reeducation. And once Khrushchev was securely in power he no longer needed the party to operate as a voice of opposition against a state apparatus dominated by Beria and Georgii Maksimilianovich Malenkov. In the end, the vast majority of reports flowing from the MVD to Khrushchev in regard to the Gulag during the 1950s were concerned with matters other than reeducation, primarily staffing, emergency situations, the implementation and effects of amnesties and case reviews, and the visits by foreigners to penal institutions.

The difficulty of quantifying reeducational success and the lack of a consistent, high-profile institutional patron for the correctional agenda acted as brakes on the turn toward correctionalism in the penal apparatus. No less important, however, was the universal bureaucratic impulse to resist rapid and substantive change. As Richard McCleery, writing on changes in the U.S. penal system in the postwar era, remarked, "A fundamental principle that seems to guide much penal administration, and which is generally confirmed by our study, is the notion that any significant change is dangerous and disorganizing."[239] The same conclusions have been reached in regard to Khrushchev's Gulag and this book to some degree confirms that view. As I. D. Batsaev notes, "the power of inertia was far too great" for any great change to happen immediately.[240]

Despite these liabilities, the reeducational program of the 1950s to a great extent succeeded. Prisoners witnessed changed attitudes on the part of guards and administrators, improved treatment, better living and working conditions, a clearer and expanded set of rights, greater opportunities for education and vocational training, more time for cultural activities and sports, shorter sentences, and increased chances for early release. They came to be held, for the most part, in small correctional facilities close to home, rather than sent to the sprawling camps of Central Asia, the Far North, or Siberia. In addition, thanks to greater attention paid toward exerting control over the inmates, the criminal gangs largely disappeared from the Gulag, as did much of the prisoner-on-prisoner violence that characterized the Stalinist camps. These successes were tangible and beneficial to the prisoners of Khrushchev's Gulag. Yet these were only partial victories for Khrushchev and the reforming elements within the penal apparatus. The demands of production and fiscal plans remained strong, if not as all-consuming as before 1953, and the growing trend toward heightened control began to flow (as will be discussed in chapter 5) into a movement aimed at reversing to some extent at least the improved conditions of the mid-to-late 1950s.

OVERSIGHT AND ASSISTANCE

The Role of the Procuracy and Other Outside Agencies in Penal Operations

> **How should one evaluate the behavior of people condemned to live in a world where coercion and degradation were the norm? Should we condemn all those who chose to compromise, who sought a normal way of living in an abnormal world? Or should we try to understand the context of this abnormal world? And what form should this reckoning take—a procuratorial indictment or an attempt to understand other people and their mistakes, as well as their motives, which were not necessarily dishonorable?**
>
> —Adam Michnik, "Scenes from the Polish Hell"

On 10 September 1956 three young Lithuanian prisoners escaped from the Gulag. Taking advantage of lax guarding in the fields where they worked, Algirdas Petrosevichus, Napoleonas Iursho, and Algirlas Liorentas quietly disappeared into the forest. The following day, with guards in hot pursuit, they separated. Iursho and Petrosevichus were each apprehended by lone guards who shot them in the woods; Iursho quickly died of his wounds, but Petrosevichus, who was shot in the right arm and the chest and then beaten, somehow survived and was taken back to the camp. Liorentas, meanwhile, was found hiding in a tree by a group of guards who shot at him until he fell mortally wounded from gunshot wounds. The inspection subsequently conducted by Dubravlag's guard division concluded that firearms in each case were used properly and recommended disciplinary punishment only for the guards who allowed the escape in the first place. Under Stalin, the matter almost certainly would have rested at that; the prisoners were, after all, guilty of escape. Unfortunately for those involved in the shootings, however, Khrushchev's campaigns for both legality and humaneness in the camps were beginning to bear fruit. As soon as the other prisoners in the camp found out what happened, they fired off an impassioned petition to Moscow for justice to be served, ending their letter with the accusation (and standard prisoner petition line): "Only enemies of the

Soviet peoples act in such a way."[1] A second review was initiated, but this too was conducted by the camp's regimen department together with guard officers; hopelessly biased, it recommended disciplinary reprimands for a few officers involved in the disorganized pursuit but proposed commendations for bravery for the guards who had shot Iursho and Petrosevichus. Again, the matter at this point may have been dropped, but the prisoners' petition by this point had reached the recently reactivated Procuracy, which immediately launched its own inspection. Armed with testimony from Petrosevichus (who had not even been questioned by the camp investigators!) and the doctor who attended to his wounds, a criminal investigation into the shooting of all three prisoners was opened.[2] The age of murdering escaped prisoners without consequence had ended.

When we think of the Stalinist Gulag, among the last things that come to mind is the presence of institutions apart from the Ministry of Internal Affairs (MVD) that were responsible for overseeing the legality and ensuring the proper functioning of the Soviet Union's corrective-labor camps and colonies. True, the Soviet Union as a hyperbureaucratized (and paranoid) state had a long history of organs of control (*kontrol*).[3] But did they extend to the Gulag? After all, the picture that emerges of the Stalinist penal system both from memoirs and official documentation is one of unrestrained power (*proizvol*), corruption, and lawlessness uninhibited by external interference. Yet just as in the rest of Soviet state and society, the Gulag, too, was subject to oversight from a variety of institutions and mechanisms, most notably the Procuracy. Crucially, such control was very weak under Stalin compared with the power of the MVD and its local camp bosses, but it never completely disappeared.[4]

As detailed in chapter 1, Stalin's heirs upon his death in 1953 proclaimed a return to socialist legality aimed at removing the excesses and what they termed "legal nihilism" of the preceding two decades. While never resolving the fundamental tension between the rule of law and the extralegal nature of the Communist Party, this campaign resulted in a host of new legal codes, a better-educated corps of judges and lawyers, renewed academic study into the nature of crime and punishment, and the many reforms in the penal sector detailed in the first two chapters. Yet Khrushchev and his peers faced a fundamental problem in reforming the penal system: the Gulag and the MVD could not be trusted to bring about the significant institutional and cultural transformations required by the new focus on reeducation and order. The MVD, after all, had presided over the lawless, production-obsessed penal system that Stalin's heirs inherited. As already discussed, the unreliable nature of the MVD was powerfully acknowledged soon after Stalin's death when the Gulag was (temporarily it turned out) transferred to the Ministry of Justice (MIu).

Largely due to this lack of trust in the Gulag's ability to reform itself and as part of the socialist legality campaign more broadly, Stalin's heirs enacted a series of reforms that strengthened, reestablished, or created from scratch organizations outside MVD control that were devoted to overseeing legality in the Gulag and assisting in camp operations. Whereas oversight over the Gulag under Stalin had been limited and weak, resulting in a high level of abuse and corruption, Khrushchev's penal system by the mid-1960s was enmeshed in a multifaceted and robust network of oversight and assistance that helped curb violence and other illegalities, promoted the reeducation of prisoners, and even supported the economic responsibilities of the individual penal facilities. In this manner the corrective-labor institutions of the MVD were integrated more fully into the party-state apparatus and their surrounding communities, thereby reducing the conditions of isolation that led to abuse. Never again would the Soviet Gulag function as an autonomous empire within the empire.

Activation of the Procuracy

The most powerful and important institution in the Gulag's new network of oversight and assistance was the Procuracy.[5] Tasked with a multitude of functions including authorizing arrests, investigating and prosecuting crimes, appealing verdicts, monitoring the work of the MVD and the Committee of State Security (KGB), and inspecting the legality of orders issued by governing institutions, the Procuracy was a very powerful body within the Soviet criminal justice establishment. In addition to these responsibilities, it also had charge to oversee the legality of operations in the Soviet Union, including, from 1922 onward, its various places of confinement.[6] This oversight up to 1953 took the form of procurators assigned to particular corrective-labor camps, who then reported to a central administration for oversight over places of confinement within the Procuracy.[7] The power of these camp procurators, however, was weak, and procurators' activities were largely limited to investigating crimes committed by prisoners as well as a few more obvious crimes perpetrated by guards and administrators. Many camp procurators formed cozy relationships with the camp officials they were supposed to be monitoring, leaving the latter basically free from external oversight.[8] It surely did not help that procurators were included in the camp, rather than regional, party organizations, where they could be bullied when necessary by camp administrators looking to disregard the law in defense of their own "narrow institutional interests."[9] Nor did a stark lack of training for procurators facilitate independent thought or action on their part. Indeed, Soviet law schools only adopted a course on procuratorial supervision in 1954 after Roman Andreevich Rudenko found that law school graduates hired by the Procuracy had "no idea of how the duties of the Procuracy in the field of supervision over the strict execution of the laws are carried out in practice."[10] Clearly, Moshe Lewin's conclusion that the presence of procurators "made no difference to what went on in the camps" is not much of an overstatement.[11]

Near the end of Stalin's life, as noted previously, the Gulag embarked on a law-and-order campaign aimed primarily at reducing gang violence that had increased dramatically starting in the late 1940s and at increasing the economic productivity of prisoners. Charged with overseeing the legality of both prisoners and administrators, the Procuracy issued an order on 6 August 1952 instructing its local procurators to become more active in their responsibilities.[12] It appears to be the case that most procurators continued to operate as before. A deputy camp procurator from Sverdlovsk, for example, was issued a reprimand in February 1953 because, instead of ensuring the laws were followed, he himself had hired a prisoner to make a table for him on the side, and then failed to pay him for it.[13] At least some procurators charged with monitoring the Gulag, however, took such instructions to heart; in January 1953, for instance, the procurator for the camps of the Yenisei Construction Trust brought criminal charges against thirteen prisoners for using their low-level administrative positions and tacit approval from the camp administration to abuse and rob other prisoners. After a review of the case the Gulag handed over a few members of the camp leadership for prosecution as well.[14] Thus, just as the Nineteenth Party Congress served to invigorate the party on the eve of Stalin's death, the law-and-order campaign in the Gulag in the early 1950s created at least some momentum going into 1953 for increased oversight over the unruly camps.

Soon after Stalin's death, as part of the more general campaign to restore socialist legality, Khrushchev and his peers took a series of steps to strengthen the Procuracy in general and its role of overseeing the Gulag in particular. This stands in stark contrast to the All-Union MIu, which was weakened and then finally eliminated in 1956, and the All-Union MVD, which was weakened and then liquidated in 1960. While these law-and-order organs were targeted precisely for their "hypercentralization," not to mention their complicity in Stalin's crimes, the Procuracy escaped this fate.[15] In order to reform the organs of justice, Stalin's heirs and Khrushchev in particular understood that they needed one centralized agency to help them in this task. The Procuracy, with its mission of oversight complementing the oversight mission of the party, appeared a natural fit. Thus, despite Khrushchev's penchant for decentralizing the Soviet bureaucracy, the centralized Procuracy emerged strengthened rather than weakened after Stalin's death. And Procuracy leaders on their own accord no doubt saw in

Stalin's death and the ensuing push for legality an opportunity to increase their own power and prestige.

From March through June 1953, under Stalin's last procurator general, Grigorii Safonov, the Procuracy continued the law-and-order campaign of the early 1950s even as it became heavily involved in enacting the mass amnesty of 1953. Upon Lavrentii Pavlovich Beria's arrest in late June, Safonov was forced into retirement and Khrushchev succeeded in getting his client Rudenko confirmed as the next procurator general.[16] Rudenko, who had worked previously in the Procuracy in his native Ukraine and had also served as the Soviet Union's lead procurator at the Nuremberg Trials, was initially very busy heading the prosecution of Beria. But he also conducted a massive housecleaning campaign designed to root out Beria's perceived allies in the Procuracy and to inculcate new allegiances. Most importantly, a number of high-ranking provincial and republican procurators were purged and replaced.[17] But this process extended into the camp oversight bureaucracy as well, where a number of camp procurators were sacked. Officially they were fired for dereliction of duty: one was released for rarely visiting the camps and overlooking serious crimes committed by camp administrators, another for allowing wretched living conditions for prisoners and improper disciplinary practices, and a third for drunkenness and for illegally freeing a prisoner (whose husband was the procurator's drinking companion).[18] Perceived loyalty to Beria and Safonov, however, no doubt played a significant role in many of these replacements.

This housecleaning campaign was complemented by a series of orders issued by the central Procuracy instructing its local procurators to become more active in their responsibilities, signaling that a lax attitude toward Gulag oversight would no longer be tolerated. The most detailed of such decrees, "On Strengthening Procuratorial Oversight over Obedience to the Law in the Corrective-Labor Camps and Colonies of the MVD USSR," issued 28 July 1954, outlined a number of long-standing problems with Gulag oversight: procurators rarely visited the penal institutions to which they were assigned; they were not familiar with the work of camp commanders; they seldom conversed with prisoners; they did not conduct a principled fight against illegalities; they rarely brought guilty parties to justice; and they did not pay attention to the reeducation of prisoners or the legality of their living conditions. To combat these entrenched practices, Rudenko admonished his procurators to systematically visit the places of confinement and receive prisoners for private interviews; "react sharply to every incident of arbitrary rule (*proizvol*) from the camp and colony workers in regard to the prisoners—beatings of prisoners, illegal use of firearms, and so forth"; ensure proper and sanitary living and working conditions; monitor the legality of disciplinary measures meted to prisoners who violated the camp regimen; and in general ensure the 1954 statute governing the MVD's places of confinement was meticulously followed.[19] Indeed, Rudenko took seriously the responsibility to oversee the MVD and restore "socialist legality" to the repressive apparatus of the Soviet Union. This spirit of Leninist renewal is captured by his deputy, who in 1954 remarked at an MVD conference that "camp workers to this day continue to work in the old fashion and still do not feel all that is new and progressive, which our party and government have brought to the work of the corrective-labor institutions of our state."[20]

Rudenko's 28 July 1954 order to his procurators to become more active guardians of socialist legality in the camps was quickly followed by detailed instructions for local procurators on how to thoroughly inspect a camp and compose the appropriate inspection reports.[21] During inspections, procurators were to identify situations, practices, or events that broke the existing laws and statutes governing penal operations. Those that required immediate attention and could be readily fixed—such as prisoners being held in the penalty isolator without due cause—were to be corrected during the inspection. At the conclusion of an inspection procurators were to leave a formal report with the camp commander, detailing the results of the inspection and recommending specific actions to bring camp operations in full compliance with the law. If the inspecting procurator found an especially egregious offense or encountered intransigence on the part of camp commanders, he had the recourse of sending a protest to local or regional party, state, court, or MVD officials. Such low-level machinations did not always have the desired effect, however, and in such an event the procurator could petition his superiors in Moscow for assistance in resolving the matter at higher levels. In addition to such protests, the other recourse available to procurators was to launch a criminal investigation against the offending party and possibly bring the matter to court. As Gavriil Stepanovich Tsvyrko, head of the Procuracy's department for oversight over places of confinement, admonished in a November 1956 meeting for Komi Autonomous Soviet Socialist Republic procurators, if prisoners are being forced to endure poor living conditions, a criminal investigation should be opened against the camp leadership. Even if such an investigation does not have "judicial perspectives," it will still yield practical results.[22]

In addition to purging old cadres, criticizing past practices, and clarifying the duties of local procurators, Rudenko and his patron Khrushchev enacted more concrete reforms to strengthen procuratorial oversight in the camps. The first of these, proposed by Rudenko in December 1953 and issued in February 1954, made chief procurators of the province, territory, or republic directly responsible for legality in corrective-labor institutions.[23] In conjunction with this order, a whole new layer of bureaucracy, the provincial department for oversight over places of confinement, was created. This restructuring increased the power and responsibility of regional procurators, making them personally answerable for the work of camp procurators, and mitigated the isolated conditions that had led camp procurators under Stalin to become, in essence, beholden to the camp commanders. The new structure also gave camp procurators a higher authority that could lobby for them at the regional level. Bolstering the chain of command and demanding increased scrutiny of camp operations (along with firing a number of existing procurators) required additional cadres in the camp and provincial Procuracy networks. Indeed, a large number of new procurators were recruited and sent out to the provinces to help monitor the extensive network of corrective-labor camps and colonies. Ivan Vasil'evich Pantiukhin, for instance, records how he was summoned to Moscow in January 1954 by Deputy Procurator General Aleksandr Nikolaevich Mishutin, who told him of the arrest of many procurators who had been loyal to Beria. Mishutin then offered Pantiukhin a substantial pay raise to relocate to Magadan Province and serve as a camp procurator under Dmitrii Artemov, who had himself been transferred there from Iakutiia. Many others were recruited in similar fashion.[24]

The increase in Procuracy staffing in the provinces is difficult to quantify precisely, but it certainly occurred, despite a large decrease in the number of prisoners after Stalin's death. Already in 1954 the Procuracy of Leningrad Province, with only six colonies and one camp point, had three procurators and investigators in its department for oversight over places of confinement.[25] The Mineral'nyi Corrective-Labor Camp (Minlag) in Komi, with just over 8,000 prisoners in 1956, was monitored by four procurators while the larger Kizelovskii Corrective-Labor Camp (Kizellag) with nearly 15,000 inmates also had four and the massive Vorkutlag with over 50,000 prisoners had nine.[26] In 1956 the department for oversight over places of confinement in the Irkutsk Province had four procurators plus a secretary who were in charge of inspecting seven camp points and one colony and overseeing the camp procurators at the Kitoiskii Corrective-Labor Camp (Kitoilag), Angarskii Corrective-Labor Camp (Angarlag), and Ozerlag. The procurator's office at Kitoilag, with over 16,000 inmates, had six operational workers plus four clerical and janitorial staffers. Angarlag, with nearly as many prisoners, also had ten in the procurator's office, but only three were staff; the smaller Ozerlag, with 9,000 inmates, had four procurators and two others.[27] Such staffing levels seem fairly standard, although there was considerable variation. Turkmenistan that same year had only two colonies so one procurator was more than sufficient and Uzbekistan in 1958 had three operational workers in the Procuracy's oversight department to cover fourteen small colonies.[28] On average therefore, each procurator in the mid-1950s was responsible for monitoring several colonies or camp points holding a few or even several thousand prisoners, and many had charge over one or two prisons as well.

A second notable reform that facilitated increased oversight of the Gulag was a new statute to govern the Procuracy's operations. Already in August 1953, echoing similar calls from the late Stalinist period, Rudenko insisted on the need for such a document.[29] The previous statute, from 1933, was out of date, he argued, and only covered the central apparatus. Drafts for a new statute had been prepared in 1950 and 1951 but, similar to many reforming projects in the late Stalinist period, they were shelved without enactment.[30] Rudenko's request was granted and on 24 May 1955 the Presidium of the Supreme Soviet passed the new statute, which listed oversight over penal operations among the six primary responsibilities tasked to the Procuracy.[31] Section 5 of this document clarified that proper oversight entailed immediately freeing inmates being held illegally; "systematically" inspecting places of confinement (this was eventually defined as quarterly for corrective-labor institutions and monthly for prisons); becoming familiar with their administration; protesting illegal or contradictory orders; and prosecuting those guilty of lawbreaking.[32] Accordingly, procurators were given the right to inspect all areas of corrective-labor institutions and prisons at any time; access all documents relating to the prisoners; conduct private discussions with inmates; receive without delay their written complaints addressed to the Procuracy; and demand explanations for any uncovered illegalities. As explained by D. I. Mashin, head of the Russian Procuracy's department for oversight over places of confinement, procurators were responsible not just for ensuring laws were obeyed, but also for protecting "the rights of the convict, his life, health, and human dignity."[33] Camp administrators, in turn, were obliged to fulfill the suggestions of procurators.[34] With such a document in hand, Khrushchev could with some confidence announce at the Twentieth Party Congress in 1956 that "the supervisory powers of the Procurator's Office have been completely re-established and strengthened."[35]

The Challenges of Increased Oversight

A new structure and statute, however, did not immediately translate into effective oversight over the Gulag. Indeed, a host of challenges worked against the Procuracy's efforts to hold Gulag officials accountable to their own regulations. The most basic obstacle, common to any reforming drive, which inhibited enhanced oversight was the simple inertia of old habits and ideas. Although a number of procurators were fired in the aftermath of Stalin's death and a substantial cohort of new cadres was recruited, most procurators of the Stalin era were retained.[36] Not surprisingly, procurators in a number of localities, at first at least, continued the Stalinist practice of working closely with camp administrators. When convoy guards on 20 March 1953 shot and killed four prisoners at Vorkutlag, alleging that they tried to escape, for instance, the camp procurator was content to accept the results of the superficial investigation performed by the regimen department of the camp which found the use of firearms justified.[37] In 1954 procurators from Noril'lag were found to be drinking with their counterparts in the camp administration.[38] Such relationships resulted in procurators continuing to actively shield administrators from prosecution.[39] Senior investigator Iakovtsev of the Kizellag procurator's office, for instance, was found in 1956 to be habitually getting drunk with camp administrators (once to such a point of intoxication that he accidentally shot himself in the leg) and had on multiple occasions closed criminal cases opened against them without just cause.[40] Until an investigation uncovered these practices, however, Iakovtsev was protected by his superiors. Indeed, it is not surprising that many procurators, despite their charge to be impartial defenders of the law, had an easier time sympathizing and siding with camp officials—roughly their equivalent in rank and stature—than with prisoners. Facilitating this attitude in many remote locations was the simple fact that procurators had few other options outside the Gulag bureaucracy when it came to socialization. In 1956 the procurator of the Minlag was labeled a "pocket procurator" and fired because "he was practically in the service of the camp administration."[41] Such laxness led the head of the Procuracy's department for oversight over the Gulag to criticize procurators for confronting problems in the camps "in a familial manner" with the camp commander instead of being "merciless toward breakers of Soviet legality."[42] These attitudes were not lost on the prisoners; one from Moscow Province in 1955, for example, informed the Supreme Soviet that when they complained to their procurator that camp officials were ignoring the decree restoring parole, the procurator simply replied, "I do not have the right to resolve these issues, your commander is your law!"[43]

Even procurators not inclined to cooperate directly with Gulag officials, however, were often timid in their approach to correcting illegalities. A common complaint by central procurators from Moscow who periodically inspected their regional appendages was that local procurators in charge of places of confinement had reconciled themselves to the lawlessness of the camps and colonies.[44] This meant they conducted infrequent inspections of their own, their inspections tended to be superficial, and they raised few legal protests against camp administrators.[45] The procurators at Kizellag, for instance, conducted only forty-four inspections in 1955 and the first half of 1956, many of which were conducted very quickly and superficially (six of those so-called inspections occurred in the same month and covered the same camp point while four of the thirty camp subdivisions were never inspected). During the year and a half only sixteen protests of lawlessness were raised, despite a multitude of known violations.[46] This tendency toward rare and often perfunctory visits is confirmed by former prisoner Iu. E. Ivanov, who received only the most cursory visit from the local procurator while on hunger strike in Vladimir Prison (although it likely did not help that Ivanov responded sarcastically to the procurator's initial inquiry into his well-being).[47] Another procurator drew the ire of prisoners by conducting his inspection of their camp through binoculars instead of actually meeting with them; upon noticing him, a few prisoners registered their displeasure by exposing their bared buttocks to him.[48]

Local procurators were frequently reminded that they should take immediate action in regard to many of the issues they noted in their reports, which seems to suggest that most preferred to simply identify problems rather than fix them personally.[49] Many were hesitant to launch criminal investigations into camp officials, preferring to limit their recommendations to administrative reprimands or, at worst, dismissal. Anatoly Marchenko noted this in his memoir, as did prisoner G. F. Oskin from Angarsk, who wrote to higher authorities that the local procurator took no action after he complained of a vicious beating by a warden.[50] As Tsvyrko warned his subordinates in November 1956, "You are still working in the old style; in much you give ground to the administration." Rather, Tsvyrko continued, Gulag officials must fear their local procurators and the prisoners should respect them.[51] And Tsvyrko's words had teeth: in November 1956 the chief procurator for Vorkutlag Ia. S. Melashenko was fired in large part for not pressing for the prosecution of camp administrators who beat their prisoners, and many others received reprimands for not being firm in their opposition to lawbreaking by investigating and prosecuting specific individuals.[52]

Beyond inertia and complacency, the nature of procurators' work also posed a challenge to effective camp oversight. Sent to the distant camps of the Soviet Union to enforce legality, procurators were often thrust into very difficult living and working conditions. Pantiukhin, upon arrival in Magadan, for instance, was forced to lodge along with his wife in one small room, using a table for a bed. Others slept in their offices. Only after a month and a half was he fortunate enough to get an apartment, but it was located 5 kilometers outside the city.[53] Moreover, procurators were easily overwhelmed, not to mention disturbed, both by the quantity and the character of crimes and infractions perpetrated by officials and prisoners alike. From relatively minor violations such as insufficient furniture in barracks or the use of convicted embezzlers as bookkeepers to shocking stories of abuse and neglect, including vicious beatings and cold-blooded murder, procurators' reports chronicled a complex and interwoven fabric of lawlessness in the camps. Inmate gangs were warring among themselves (often with the administration's approval, if not direct participation); murders and escapes were rampant; camp workers were selling prisoners narcotics; guards were beating and punishing prisoners for little or no reason and their superiors (in collusion with the camp medical staff) were often covering the tracks of their crimes. In short, every imaginable crime could be and was being committed in the Gulag in the early and mid-1950s. To cite just one specific example, a procurator in Molotov Province in late 1954 discovered that male prisoners were working alongside female free workers, breaking both the regulation regarding separation of the sexes and prisoners from nonprisoners, and this had led to the women illicitly bringing the men vodka and the men on occasion raping the women on threat of murder.[54] That the procurator's protests initially yielded little change in camp operations must have no doubt been demoralizing.

Another serious burden on procurators was the requirement to review prisoners' complaints, which could be submitted directly to the procurators, thus bypassing the camp administration. Although the possibility of complaint was technically available before Stalin's death, the Procuracy under Khrushchev began to more actively solicit and respond to inmate concerns. Given the entrenched nature of Gulag practices and the torrid pace of reforms in the 1950s, not to mention a newfound realization by the inmate contingent that at least some petitions were being acted upon, the flow of complaints could at times be overwhelming. This is perhaps not surprising when one reads from memoir accounts that some prisoners wrote continually to procurators to appeal for case reviews or simply to complain about problems in their place of confinement. A fellow inmate of A. N. Kuzin, for instance, wrote the same complaint every day and left it in the box for the procurator.[55] It is not surprising, therefore, that procurators such as A. K. Pakhomov from Sverdlovsk Province complained that they were overloaded with work, especially with reading and investigating letters from prisoners.[56]

Beyond their regular responsibilities, camp procurators also performed other periodic duties related to the Gulag in the Khrushchev era. In 1953 they helped review the files of all prisoners held in the special camps of the MVD to find which were being held there in violation of statute; as a result of their work, 87,290 prisoners were slated for transfer to regular Gulag facilities.[57] On a similar note, following the passage of new statutes governing the Gulag in 1958 and 1961, procurators helped the MVD re-sort its prisoners according to revamped regimen determinations.[58] Procurators also participated directly in the amnesties and releases of political prisoners of the 1950s by serving on case review commissions. This not only added to their workload, it also meant they had to cope with the crimes of the past.[59] Pantiukhin later noted how shocking it was to review to the work of the infamous troikas and how difficult it was psychologically to simply tell former political prisoners, "You're rehabilitated; sorry that our scoundrel colleagues sent you here without any cause."[60]

Although inertia and the nature of the work took their toll, the most serious challenge to effective procuratorial oversight was the response of Gulag officials. Bureaucrats as a rule are at best uncomfortable with the constant presence of supervisory agents in their institutions and Gulag officials, accustomed to ruling their own fiefdoms with only minimal oversight, certainly did not appreciate the increased power and activity of camp procurators.[61] Not surprisingly, camp commanders openly encouraged close cooperation between themselves and procurators in joint meetings of the two agencies.[62] In this they hoped to defuse contentious issues before they reached the level of procuratorial protest or prosecution. When the camp commander of Ozerlag, Sergei Kuzmich Evstigneev, argued at a 1955 conference for more cooperation between camp officials and procurators, Tsvyrko interjected that this was not possible. When Evstigneev pushed further, saying that they shared common goals, Tsvyrko replied that their "difference in methods" precluded close collaboration.[63] This sentiment was echoed in 1958 by MVD officials in Magadan, who asked not just for inspections from procurators, but also "practical assistance."[64] But the chairman of the administrative department of the Magadan party apparatus responded, "Some [camp workers] think that the Procuracy is a helpmate (*pomoshnitsa*). No, it's not a helpmate, it's oversight and it needs to be obeyed."[65] This sentiment was repeated by a procurator in Iakutiia, who accused the local Gulag chief of thinking the procurators worked for him.[66] At higher levels as well MVD officials pressed the Procuracy to have its local procurators offer assistance of a more practical nature to the camps. Gulag chief Mikhail Nikolaevich Kholodkov, for example, in 1958 asked procurators to help the MVD find employment opportunities for prisoners, explaining that "the local authorities listen to them more."[67] Thus, whereas other institutions in the Khrushchev era were called on to provide concrete assistance to corrective-labor institutions, procurators, in order to preserve their impartiality, were to remain more aloof.

When procurators refused to cooperate with camp officials, various methods of resistance to increased oversight occurred, especially in the early post-Stalin years. The most common form of such resistance was to simply ignore procurators' inspection reports. Accounts of this practice litter the Procuracy archives, evidence that most camp commanders were prone to resist not only oversight, but other reforms the MVD was attempting to institute. In December 1954, for instance, a procurator at Sevvostlag inspected one camp point, found a number of violations of the statute governing the camps, and left a formal inspection report. After three months, having received no reply from the camp administration regarding the report, the procurator conducted a follow-up visit and found that none of the offenses had been corrected.[68] The same occurred with more prominent inspections. A Procuracy inspection that investigated Du-bravlag in December 1956, to cite one example, found that none of the problems noted in an October 1956 inspection by the Russian Procuracy had been addressed.[69] Perhaps not surprisingly, this practice was also common regarding reports by MVD inspection teams. Thus, perhaps the agency did not matter so much as the idea of outside interference in local affairs.

Other forms of resistance were more active in nature. At first, some camp officials attempted to withhold information from procurators. When procurator Alekseev, charged with overseeing Karlag, attempted to review orders issued by the camp for their legality (along with various demographic data including mortality rates) in September and November 1953, he was denied access by Z. P. Volkov, the camp commander. In January 1954 he finally complained to his superiors in Moscow that he could still not review camp directives; he was not being informed regarding the opening and closing of camp points; he did not even know how many prisoners there were in the camp; and all this was being done "under the banner of maintaining secrecy." How was he supposed to oversee the camp, Alekseev asked, without this information and without access to camp documents?[70] The paper trail on this case ends with a letter from Volkov to his superiors stating his case for denying access but asking for clearer instructions on the matter; one can only assume that Alekseev eventually gained access to the camp archive.[71] In another case a procurator in Ukraine discovered in 1955 that a healthy prisoner had been categorized—for a bribe, no doubt—as having an incurable disease and was about to be released according to Article 457 of the Criminal Code. The procurator ordered the prisoner transferred out of the colony, but the commander refused to comply. Instead, he secretly appealed for pardon to the Ukrainian Supreme Soviet, and when the latter body reduced the prisoner's sentence to five years, the commander freed him by applying unearned workday credits.[72] A similar situation existed at the Vostochno-Ural'skii Corrective-Labor Camp (Vosturallag), where camp commanders withheld as much information as possible from their local procurators. When an invalid prisoner who had been held illegally in a strict-regimen camp point for two years was put in the penalty isolator without sufficient cause and then raped multiple times by other prisoners, he committed suicide. Yet the local procurator found out only when a fellow prisoner wrote a complaint to the Procuracy, which then mobilized a criminal investigation.[73]

Resistance was especially staunch in areas where few, if any, party or state institutions existed outside the camp sphere—places such as Dal'stroi-run Kolyma. Dal'stroi commanders, accustomed to no oversight except by the occasional Gulag inspection committee, had a difficult time adjusting to the presence of procurators starting in 1954.[74] One chief engineer of a mine, claiming to be

too busy, refused when summoned to come to the local Procuracy for questioning after an explosion left a few people dead. He was eventually taken by force and
convicted.[75] Geography clearly played a role here, with camp officials embedded
deep in the taiga more prone to resist oversight (and procurators far less able to
exert control). As a commander of distant camp point in Krasnoiarsk Territory
told his prisoners in 1954 (at least according to a prisoner complaint), "we're
100 kilometers from Soviet power; here the taiga is the law and the bear is the
procurator."[76] Camp officials, especially in such distant locales, often protested
against procurators who, not knowing the specific challenges or dynamics of a
particular camp, would write up a very unflattering report based on a day or two
on site. Furthermore, administrators complained of the tendency of procurators
to judge everything based on the letter of the law. In regard to a procurator's
complaint that Ozerlag was deconvoying prisoners improperly, the camp commander Evstigneev accused the procurator of formalism, replying that "we, the
camp workers, study our prisoners, know our prisoners, every day converse with
them, and the procurator sees them maybe once a year. Therefore we must be
trusted."[77] In another exchange between Evstigneev and Procuracy official Tsvyrko,
the former suggested that instead of simply listing all the problems in the camps,
procurators at such conferences should focus on camps and colonies that are
doing well, with the goal of explicating why they are performing well. To this
Tsvyrko curtly replied, "unfortunately, I don't know any such examples."[78]

Opposition to increased procuratorial oversight was not confined to local penal officials. Even central Gulag administrators at times resisted the oversight of
procurators, primarily in the interest of ensuring plan fulfillment. When procurators at Kraslag reported a number of illegalities to a team of Gulag inspectors
from Moscow, a high-ranking Gulag official simply issued a decree to legalize
those practices.[79] After a high-level protest was lodged in 1956 regarding the illegal
practice of recidivists working and living together with first-time offenders in logging camps, the MVD simply responded that "to avoid thwarting the state plan
for logging, a part of the prisoners with multiple convictions and specialists convicted of anti-Soviet crimes . . . are being temporarily held together with first-
time convicts and convicts for less dangerous crimes."[80] It is clear from this and
the MVD's many terse responses to Procuracy protests saying that all issues had
already been or would soon be corrected that even high-level lobbying could be
and frequently was ignored by the MVD.[81]

In more poignant examples where Gulag officials committed serious crimes,
procurators often faced difficulties bringing the offending parties to trial. The
MVD, which had a well-known history of "defend[ing] the honor of the uniform,"
had authority to prevent the opening of a criminal investigation or ensure that
the investigation was closed without charges.[82] A guard at Vorkutlag beat up a

number of prisoners in February 1956 but the administration refused to fire him as the procurator requested.[83] In another case a prison official responsible through both negligence and direct abuse for the suicide of a mentally ill prisoner received a demotion and a party reprimand, but avoided the prosecution called for by local procurators and the Procuracy because he was, according to the MVD, a good worker and the sole breadwinner for a family of seven.[84] In fact, the MVD was not alone in infringing on the law to defend the interests of the state economy or in "defending the honor of the uniform." The party also intervened in criminal cases against prominent officials, most commonly to protect those who committed crimes in the interest of plan fulfillment and those "whose prosecution seemed to discredit the party or the state."[85] This parallel was no consolation, of course, to prisoners who suffered abuse at the hands of unpunished Gulag officials. Although procurators had significant rights when it came to inspecting places of confinement and even launching criminal investigations, they lacked independent authority to enforce the law in all places and at all times.

Results of Procuratorial Control

Despite the myriad obstacles that complicated the Procuracy's task of overseeing legality in the Soviet Union's correctional-labor facilities, particularly in the early post-Stalin years, the revitalized system of procuratorial control could rightly boast of tangible results. Spurred on by the Procuracy to become more active in their responsibilities, and no doubt fearful of being removed from their positions, local procurators assigned to oversee penal institutions quickly began to assert their authority after Stalin's death; already in mid-1953 procurators began submitting a deluge of reports detailing an endless stream of infractions and abuses perpetrated by Gulag administrators and guards.[86] These and similar reports were then compiled into a summary statement and delivered from the head of the department for oversight over places of confinement to Rudenko on 31 December 1953, who sent the report on in slightly revised form to Minister of Justice Konstantin Petrovich Gorshenin, who then presided over the Gulag.[87] Many of the more egregious of the offenses noted in these reports were quickly corrected. Illegally created penalty camp points in Sevvostlag, where prisoners were kept in small, dark cells for years at a time without even the right to work, were shuttered.[88] The practice of holding public trials of prisoners in the camps after the workday had ended, established to set an example to other prisoners but called "stupid and savage [dikii]" by one local procurator, was ended.[89] In the Chaun-Chukotskii Corrective-Labor Camp (Chaunchukotlag) the gruesome practice of guards killing escaped prisoners in the tundra and returning with just a severed hand as evidence was uncovered and stopped by procurators.[90] On a less violent note, when a procurator visited a large colony near Verkhoiansk in 1954, the inmates there were astonished to see a procurator who actually cared about their existence, asked them for complaints, and ensured they were properly fed.[91] Another notable effect from increased scrutiny from procurators was an increase in arrests of guards, wardens, and low-level administrators for mistreating prisoners.[92] Although hard statistics on the exact numbers are difficult to locate in the Procuracy archive, in the first three quarters of 1955, seventy-seven guards and administrators were prosecuted for crimes, mostly for beating or killing prisoners.[93] The Procuracy even managed to orchestrate the removal of a few powerful camp commanders, such as P. I. Kuznetsov of Noril'lag.[94]

These initial results of 1953–54 were important, and they led to increased convictions of Gulag personnel in the mid-1950s.[95] Indeed, as the 1950s progressed, procuratorial control strengthened as camp officials and procurators alike became more accustomed to their restructured relationship and much of the active resistance to oversight illuminated above ceased. An important tool toward combating lawlessness in the camps came on 14 May 1957, when local procurators were given the authority to initiate criminal investigations against Gulag officials without the approval of the MVD.[96] This order eliminated a serious roadblock to independent oversight, giving Gulag officers less protection from their superiors. Although the MVD ultimately retained power to stop investigations from proceeding to trial, this veto could only be used selectively, and guards and local Gulag officers quickly realized that beating prisoners or committing other serious crimes could easily result in serious punishment, including dismissal and even criminal prosecution.[97] The MVD inspectorate for Kemerovo Province, for instance, citing the "pettiness of the crime," refused in 1956 to prosecute a guard at the Severo-Kuzbaskii Corrective-Labor Camp (Sevkuzbaslag) for beating and whipping while in a drunken state two deconvoyed prisoners in town and then, after bringing them back to camp, viciously beating one of them again when he tried to hide to avoid being put in the penalty isolator. But when the Procuracy got involved, the guard was tried and punished for his crime.[98] In another example, a group of prisoners in Colony No. 4 in Bashkiria were playing soccer on 9 July 1959 when the ball ended up in the forbidden zone adjacent to the outer fence. A prisoner went to retrieve the ball and was shot dead from the watchtower. Local procurators investigated the shooting, pronounced it illegal, and prosecuted the guard who opened fire.[99] Although official statistics on abuse in the Gulag are unreliable, memoirists and procurators alike by the early 1960s noted that beatings and other serious abuses (including the nonviolent humiliation of prisoners) had become rare occurrences that often brought administrative punishment or prosecution.[100]

Procurators were also instrumental in the 1950s in combating the "gang element" that had long plagued the Gulag. Restoring socialist legality, after all, applied not only to Gulag guards and officers, but to the prisoners as well. At one camp point of the Kuneevskii Corrective-Labor Camp, for instance, procurators found a gang leader more powerful than the commander. He personally authorized the deconvoying of prisoners, dictated which prisoners would be admitted to the camp and which would not when a convoy of inmates would arrive, and committed other abuses, all while paying large bribes to various officers. This was quickly brought to a halt, with the local procurators convicting him of ordering a murder.[101] This case was certainly not unique. Already in 1954, 5,737 prisoners were charged with crimes and convicted, and that figure jumped to 6,880 for just the first nine months of 1955.[102] For the first nine months of 1956 the number of inmate convictions rose again to 7,574, with most of the increase coming from violent crime and hooliganism.[103] And procurators became more active in prosecuting administrators who allowed gang activity in their camps and colonies. The commander and his deputy at Colony No. 10 in Azerbaijan were sentenced to deprivation of freedom themselves in 1958 for allowing thieves to rob and terrorize the other inmates and then take a cut of the profits from this operation.[104] Even after the gangs had been virtually eliminated in the early 1960s, procurators were quick to isolate and bring new charges against those who tried to revive the "thieves' traditions."[105]

Beyond the most egregious cases of violence and abuse, procurators also launched investigations into lesser infractions of socialist legality, recommending administrative punishment and even opening criminal cases against those who flaunted the laws and regulations governing the Soviet Union's places of confinement. A procurator in Ukraine launched a criminal investigation against a colony commander simply for ignoring his protests, a tactic that apparently had the desired effect.[106] When a procurator in 1958 complained about poor living conditions for prisoners at a few of the camp points he oversaw, Deputy Procurator General Aleksandr Novikov recommended that he open a criminal investigation to help bring the camp authorities into compliance.[107] Acting on such instructions, procurators at the Nyrobskii Camp opened criminal investigations against camp officers who improperly deconvoyed dangerous prisoners out of production concerns.[108] Corruption by Gulag officers was also targeted by procurators. N. A. Labazin and his assistant B. F. Selznev, procurators over the Unzhenskii Corrective-Labor Camp (Unzhlag), uncovered a workday credit bribery racket and successfully got two MVD officers sentenced to deprivation of freedom for their involvement.[109] Similar such instances of procurators convicting Gulag workers for corruption involving workday credits occurred at Kraslag, Vostur-allag, and the Severo-Ural'skii Corrective-Labor Camp (Sevurallag).[110]

Indeed, as more egregious offenses became sufficiently rare, procurators devoted increasing attention to the minutia of regulations that governed the camps.[111] A representative inspection report by Deputy Procurator General Mishutin of Colony No. 25 in Kharkov Province demonstrates the type of ille-galities a careful procurator could uncover in the late Khrushchev period. Issued in 1962, the report found that the colony was seriously underreporting regimen infractions committed by prisoners; moreover, most of these unreported infrac-tions had gone unpunished. Healthy prisoners refusing to work, for example, were not always being put on reduced rations, as called for in the statute governing colony operations. Production targets were being artificially lowered and even then colony administrators were forced to fudge production figures to show plan fulfillment (as a result of which forty-six colony workers illegally received mon-etary bonuses). Colony officials were ignoring legitimate complaints brought forward by prisoners, then punishing those who complained too much. But most critically, in Mishutin's eyes, administrators did not concern themselves with in-dividualized work among the inmates, leaving the majority of them categorized as "unstudied." As a result of this carelessness, most prisoners were not being re-educated during their time in the colony and many were committing crimes soon after release.[112] With these findings in mind, Mishutin recommended that the colony commander be replaced.[113] In addition to the complaints enumerated by Mishutin, procurators frequently criticized camp administrators for such infrac-tions as overcrowding, not providing enough work for prisoners, deconvoying too many prisoners, including those convicted of violent crime, and attempting to parole prisoners not worthy of such a privilege. A procurator at the Iuzhno-Kuzbasskii Corrective-Labor Camp (Iuzhkuzbasslag) succeeded in getting the camp commander fired due to numerous infractions, including the existence of camp points that had no armed guards.[114] Throughout the Khrushchev era procurators such as Mishutin also complained that camp commanders remained obsessed with economic matters and "forget about the people" they were sup-posed to be reeducating. During inspections these officials could readily report production figures, but often displayed ignorance of prisoner behavior and re-cidivism rates and a lack of enthusiasm for reeducational efforts.[115]

A final development associated with the activation of the Procuracy in rela-tion to the Gulag concerned prisoner petitions. Although the substantial rise in petitions from prisoners to procurators in the post-Stalin era certainly increased the workload of procurators, this outlet for complaint provided an important counterweight to the authority of camp officials. While inmates had no legal recourse to ensure procurators fulfilled their duty correctly, still, as Leon Boim persuasively argues, "in a one-party state, lacking a free market, free press, an independent judiciary and other means to help the citizen in his contacts with the government, the very possibility to complain, especially before the [Procuracy], is of great importance; the injured citizen believes that if [it] . . . investigates his complaint, not only will injustice be remedied, but also the person guilty of violating his civil rights will be punished."[116] Indeed, as the inmates of Dubravlag proved in the case of the Lithuanian escapees mentioned at the beginning of this chapter, complaining to procurators or even threatening to complain provided prisoners with a structured and sometimes effective recourse to stem abuse by Gulag officials and fellow prisoners. In a less brutal case, a camp commander commissioned ten prisoners to perform labor for the personal profit of camp officials in exchange for 250 rubles per prisoner. After the work was completed and the commander tried to renege on his promise of payment, the prisoners took the matter to the procurator, whereupon they were paid in full.[117]

The desired result of procuratorial oversight is described well by R. K. M. Khalidov, deputy minister of internal affairs for Dagestan, at an April 1964 meeting held to discuss the results of an inspection of the republic's places of confinement. Addressing the visiting inspector from the Russian Procuracy, he noted that Comrade Medzhidov, the local procurator in charge of oversight over places of confinement, was often to be found in the colonies, "and we feel this."[118] The clear implication here was that Gulag officials adhered to the law because of the procurator's constant monitoring. Seemingly omnipresent, the procurator affected behavior even when absent. Indeed, despite the plethora of minor violations discovered by Mishutin and other procurators from the late 1950s onward, the nature and extent of crime in the Gulag changed substantially for the better under Khrushchev, and much credit for this improvement must be given to the Procuracy. Oversight was by no means perfect by the mid-1960s, but after the freeing of innocent prisoners through case reviews, strengthening the oversight role of procurators over places of confinement appears to have been the most important step in Khrushchev's campaign to restore "socialist legality" in the Gulag.

Oversight Commissions and Sponsoring Organizations

Although the Procuracy was clearly the most important part of the Gulag's network of oversight and assistance under Khrushchev, other institutions, most notably oversight commissions (*nabliudatel'nye komissii*) and sponsoring organizations (*shefskie organizatsiia*), also played a significant role in ensuring legality in the camps and promoting the reeducation of inmates. In some respects connected with the campaign to restore "socialist legality," oversight commissions and sponsoring organizations were more fully tied to Khrushchev's campaign to activate society in the building of communism. This movement, loudly trumpeted at the Twenty-First Party Congress in 1959 and supported in the press in the late 1950s and early 1960s, emphasized the transformative potential of society in general and various social groups in particular.[119] It resulted in strengthened trade unions and the creation or restoration of various citizens' groups such as party-state control groups, housing committees and women's councils.[120] Social committees for assisting local procurators were also formed, which performed such functions as responding to complaints and questions and monitoring shop comment books for potential illegalities.[121] In the legal sphere, the clearest examples of this campaign were the resurrection of comrades' courts, the formation of people's volunteer squads (*druzhiny*) to help police city streets, the campaign against parasites, and the ability of judges to turn convicts over to the care of family members or social collectives instead of incarcerating them.[122] Newspaper articles from this period often featured stories of minor criminals who had been reformed by such mechanisms, thus promoting the power of the collective in the imagination of Soviet subjects. Indeed, Harold Berman and others have posited that it was precisely this campaign that replaced Stalin's use of terror: "one is free from arbitrary arrest by the secret police, but one is not free from the social pressure of the 'collective.'"[123]

For the Gulag, the campaign to activate society in part implied greater activity by the prisoners' re-created self-governing organizations, designed to mimic social and party organizations on the outside of the barbed wire. But more significantly for the present discussion, it also meant closer connections with local nonpenal institutions and better use of "the power of society" in reeducating prisoners.[124] Procurators, devoted to ensuring legality, were expected to some extent to exert a reeducational influence on the prisoners they oversaw, but this was not their primary mission. For this other institutions outside the legal sphere were needed. Like other penal reforms of the Khrushchev era, there was precedent for such arrangements; the Soviet penal system in the 1920s featured oversight commissions—boards of local officials outside the criminal justice system—that helped make parole decisions, met with prisoners to aid in their reeducation, and otherwise assisted penal officials. In these early years, however, the oversight commissions were never very influential, and, like many other reeducational projects of the 1920s, they disappeared in the 1930s.[125]

The idea to resurrect oversight commissions in the post-Stalin era began with a desire to involve local party and government workers in the affairs of Gulag institutions. Already in 1954 and then in Nikolai Pavlovich Dudorov's 1956 reforming project the MVD had called for local government and party leaders to "strengthen control and oversight" over places of confinement by periodically visiting them, listening to reports by Gulag officials, and offering help where necessary.[126] Subsequently, and somewhat more specifically, a report commissioned by the Supreme Soviet in August 1956 on the state of Unzhlag noted that whereas in the 1920s and 1930s law codes mandated the inclusion of society in the operation of places of confinement, primarily though not exclusively through oversight commissions, the contemporary statutes governing such penal institutions largely excluded such possibilities. The report authors therefore called for prisoners to be kept in their home provinces and for local organs to become much more involved in the correctional work of local places of confinement.[127] Such suggestions culminated in the 25 October 1956 decree on improving the work of the MVD, which ordered republican Councils of Ministers to ensure the creation of oversight commissions.[128] The following year new statutes governing their operation were passed in the fifteen union republics and oversight commissions were formally reintroduced into the penal affairs of the Soviet Union.[129]

Led by the deputy director of the executive committee (*ispolkom*) of the local municipal council and comprised of five to seven government, party, Komsomol, labor union, and industry representatives from the surrounding community, oversight commissions bore responsibility for overseeing corrective-labor institutions, assisting in reeducating prisoners, and facilitating their reintroduction back into society.[130] More specifically, this translated into visiting the camps and colonies with or without prior warning, checking the workday credit system for irregularities, meeting with prisoners, addressing their written complaints, helping camp commanders find work for their inmates, inviting lecturers into the camps, recommending prisoners for pardon or parole (or transfer to prison for poor behavior), and, perhaps most importantly, helping released prisoners find employment and housing.[131] The potential importance of the commissions is highlighted in the December 1958 Statute on Corrective-Labor Colonies and Prisoners of the MVD where Article 5 states that colony and prison operations were "under the control" of local oversight commissions.[132] And theoretically, at least, in the event of a disagreement between the oversight commission and the camp commander, the matter was to be settled by the chairman of the executive committee, thus cementing the role of local government in penal operations.[133]

When the oversight commissions were first created in 1957, they existed only in those regions that had corrective-labor institutions or prisons. Starting in late 1959, however, in order to help released prisoners transition smoothly to life outside the Gulag, oversight commissions in some republics were established in all regions and city districts. In conjunction with this, they were given the additional responsibility of organizing reeducational activities for ex-convicts living in their areas.[134] Additionally, some republics, notably Ukraine and Kazakhstan, mandated the creation of one oversight commission for every penal institution to prevent commissions in localities with several institutions from being overburdened.[135]

Not surprisingly, many executive committees were slow to convene oversight commissions and most commissions at first showed little initiative in their work.[136] Each member served on his commission on a volunteer basis in addition to his other responsibilities, a situation that made inaction in essence the default position. Tellingly, when the chairman of the Lithuanian Council of Ministers in 1958 asked a camp commander if a local oversight commission existed, he responded with the ambiguous, "There seems to be."[137] In other places, however, oversight commissions were quickly formed and began to take initiative in their new responsibilities. Already in 1958 the six commissions in Voronezh Province were found visiting the colonies, talking with prisoners, and addressing their complaints.[138] Select commission members in Ukraine attended a republic-wide conference devoted to oversight commissions in late November 1958 and all attended regional seminars in January and February 1959 devoted to sharing their successes and failures.[139]

Gulag officials, for their part, were often not enthusiastic about inviting local government and party leaders into their domain. At a meeting of Estonian penal workers in 1959, the MVD for the republic had to rebuke several colony administrators who doubted the value of social organizations such as oversight commissions in penal affairs.[140] Some like-minded Gulag officials in the late 1950s and early 1960s attempted to circumvent oversight commissions by sending parole requests straight to the courts, even though they were supposed to first be approved by the commissions.[141] At MVD headquarters, the attitude of senior Gulag officials is visible in comprehensive reports on the state of the Gulag from the late 1950s, which mention oversight commissions last and only in cursory fashion. A twenty-seven-page report delivered to the Central Committee by the MVD in April 1959, for instance, contained a mere three sentences on oversight commissions, which said little more than the Soviet reporting boilerplate that matters were improving but challenges still remained.[142]

Yet in 1960–62, with the campaign to activate society in full swing, the place of oversight commissions in the Soviet Gulag solidified. Whereas Ukraine in 1959 had only 65 oversight commissions with 479 members for its 86 corrective-labor colonies, by 1962 there were 105 commissions with some 800 members serving 113 colonies.[143] In Russia by 1964 there were some 435 oversight commissions with over 3,500 members.[144] And these commissions did not exist solely on paper. In Briansk Province, an inspecting procurator lauded the local oversight committee for lobbying the provincial court for sentence reductions for twenty-one prisoners deemed reeducated.[145] Oversight commission members in Vorkuta began reading lectures to the prisoners, conducting question-and-answer sessions with them, and meeting with them individually.[146] The oversight commission assigned to Colony No. 7 in Altai was praised by an inspecting procurator for organizing numerous visits with Civil War veterans and other local dignitaries (and inviting family members of prisoners to attend as well), and assigning one member to each detachment in the colony to facilitate one-on-one interaction with the inmates.[147] Although other oversight commissions in Estonia continued to demonstrate little initiative in early 1960, the commission in Tallinn was reportedly meeting with prisoners, organizing visits by notable citizens of the republic, and inspecting the medical section, reeducational programs, comrades' court, and school curriculum.[148] The oversight commission over Colony No. 5 in Belorussia helped organize a conference for prisoners on "what a prisoner should become before he is released."[149] The oversight commission of Colony No. 159 in Zaparozhskaia Province helped arrange many of the 172 visits by social representatives, including the secretary of the city party committee, who came to the colony to talk with its prisoners in 1960.[150] And by 1962, according to MVD documentation, they had made significant strides in helping released prisoners find work.[151]

At a July 1964 conference devoted to discussing the work of oversight commissions in Ukraine, the oversight commission of the Komintern district of the city of Kharkov was brought forward as a model commission. Its membership had been stable for five years, allowing the commission members to become experts at their job. The commission met every month to discuss employment of prisoners, the "to freedom with a clean conscience" campaign (more on this in chapter 5), the work of providing legal advice to prisoners, the working and living conditions of those recently release, the educational and vocational programs in the colony, and other matters. Commission members regularly visited the colonies, conducting individual discussions with prisoners, listening to their complaints, and conducting political work among them. They helped engage local enterprises as sponsoring organizations and worked to keep them active in colony affairs. And they also ensured that the regional executive committee was informed about the state and needs of the colonies. Partly as a result of their efforts, the Ukrainian Gulag bestowed on all colonies attached to this commission the award of Colony of Highly Productive Labor and Model Behavior.[152]

Yet even in the 1960s the work of oversight commissions was inconsistent, with many providing assistance to the camps while at least as many simply ignored their obligations.[153] Although oversight commissions were to be monitored not just by the executive committee but also the local party committee, these bodies had insufficient vested interest in ensuring the success of this program.[154] Moreover, not all oversight commission members were convinced of the reeducational mission of the Gulag. As will be demonstrated in chapter 4, much of Soviet society, including its local leadership, remained convinced that penal facilities should be places of punishment rather than reeducation. These factors led many commissions to be far less active than those mentioned above; some rarely visited the colonies to meet with prisoners or did not respond to prisoner complaints in a timely fashion.[155] The Estonian Council of Ministers in early 1961 criticized many of the republic's commissions for not helping released prisoners trying to find work and a place to live.[156] At Kargopol'lag in Arkhangelsk Province some oversight commissions were found to be staffed primarily by camp workers, which directly contradicted the statute governing the commissions and the spirit of independent oversight.[157] Another violation was reported in Sverdlovsk Province in 1964, where many oversight committees did not have as their head a member of the local municipal executive committee. Moreover, one oversight committee was found to be serving nine different colonies, clearly an impossible amount of work.[158] A review in late 1962 of the Viatskii Corrective-Labor Camp (Viatlag) found that oversight commissions there were barely functional.[159] In part this was no doubt due to the distances involved; with oversight commissions located in large towns and cities and camps such as Viatlag strung over enormous territories, actively monitoring the many camp points was a serious burden.[160] The oversight commission assigned to Dubravlag, to take another example, was in Saransk, some 200 kilometers away from camp headquarters.[161]

As they shared similar goals in relation to corrective-labor institutions and their inmates, procurators and oversight commissions were supposed to be in constant contact with each other and inspect places of confinement together.[162] In practice, however, they usually preferred to work independently of one another, which naturally created some confusion. On the issue of parole, for instance, procurators variously accused oversight commissions of approving prisoners for parole who should have been denied and denying parole to those who should have been approved.[163] Gulag officials for their part, although some doubted the value of oversight commissions, exhibited far less overt frustration with oversight commissions than with procurators. For one thing, commission members were better able and indeed were supposed to offer practical assistance to the camps; perhaps more importantly, they did not possess the same power to launch criminal investigations. Moreover, as noted above, the default position for oversight commissions was relative inactivity while rubber-stamping administrators' parole and other requests.[164]

Tension between oversight commissions and the camps only flared when the former habitually denied the administration's requests for parole and pardon.

When one oversight commission member, with support from the camp procurator of Viatlag, denied a number of prisoners put up for pardon by the camp administration in 1962 because of the seriousness of their crimes, they were brusquely told by a camp official there was a secret order allowing this action. After the procurator retorted that no such order existed, another administrator from the political department asked the commission member if he was a party member. Upon receiving an affirmative response the official then said, in the words of the commission member, that "because I hold in my pocket a party card, I am obliged to sign everything that is signed by the political department and the camp administration."[165] In the end, however, the oversight commission and procurator prevailed in denying pardon to those deemed unworthy. This example, though illustrative, appears to be not particularly representative. Due to their tendency to assist or ignore rather than confront camp officials, relations between oversight commissions and Gulag administrators were usually cordial if not fully harmonious.

In addition to their primary tasks of assisting in the reeducation of prisoners and facilitating their return to society, oversight commissions were obligated to enlist local factories, mines, farms, and educational institutes as sponsoring organizations for their local camps and colonies. Like many reforms of the Khrushchev era, this was not a new idea. As voiced by Andrei Vyshinskii in 1934, "every colony should be attached to some sort of factory, collective farm or state farm," and there should be close relations between the free workers and the inmates.[166] Designed to serve next to oversight commissions as a second key point of contact between incarceration and freedom, sponsoring organizations in the Khrushchev era were tasked with offering a wide range of services to corrective-labor institutions and their prisoners. They were to provide equipment to colony workshops and vocational training to prisoners; participate in cultural events and award ceremonies for well-behaved and highly productive inmates; deliver lectures to and hold one-on-one discussions with the convicts; and even offer employment to released prisoners. Sponsoring organizations in the Gulag were modeled on similar institutions in the broader Soviet economy. Factories assigned as sponsors to state and collective farms, for example, helped fix machinery, aided in capital construction, served as consultants for workflow processes, and increased levels of mechanization. This was all done without compensation from the state or the farms they assisted.[167]

As with the oversight commissions, the creation of sponsoring organizations in the penal system got off to a slow start. An internal Gulag report from April 1958 devoted primarily to propagating methods for employing the maximum number of prisoners mentioned the assistance of sponsoring organizations only once, briefly noting that Sverdlovsk Province sponsors had provided the equipment and expertise needed to set up a number of new workshops in the local colonies.[168] More strikingly, in his lengthy 22 April 1959 report on Gulag operations to the Central Committee, Minister of Internal Affairs Dudorov completely omitted any reference to the sponsoring organizations, even when detailing difficulties providing each prisoner with labor.[169] Indeed, only during 1959 were sponsoring organizations established for Vorkuta-area colonies and in Ukraine, where the sponsoring program had a quicker start, some colonies in 1960 were still without sponsors.[170] In Estonia the sponsoring system was established for the main prison for the republic and its women's colony, but the factories assigned as sponsors to two other colonies were refusing to participate in the program.[171]

The Central Committee's closed letter of 5 November 1959 on raising the role of society in fighting crime spurred the Gulag to expand the sponsoring program. Drawing on the positive example of the work of sponsoring organizations in Cheliabinsk Province, which was even featured in *Izvestiia,* local Gulag officials were admonished to appeal to government and party leaders to assist in enrolling local economic, social, and educational organizations as sponsors of corrective-labor colonies, camps, and prisons, so that each penal institution "in its practical work relied broadly on the assistance of Soviet society."[172] Representatives from sponsoring organizations were to inspect Gulag worksites for inefficient use of labor and be invited to sit on newly formed technical councils, devoted to perfecting production methods.[173] The Gulag also instructed its political department to start highlighting the best practices of sponsors in its monthly instructional journal for administrators and guards, *K novoi zhizni* (*Toward a New Life*), and in brochures such as the 1964 "Social Control and Assistance."[174]

More important than central directives in fostering sponsoring relationships with the camps and colonies, however, was the gradual awareness on the part of MVD commanders that sponsoring organizations could provide significant assistance with minimal interference in colony operations. Unlike procurators and oversight commission members, representatives from sponsoring organizations were not tasked with inspecting orders or living conditions for legality, nor did they deal with prisoner complaints. Rather, they provided free-of-charge reeducational and production assistance. Already in 1960, a number of sponsors in Ukraine were providing significant aid by donating equipment for the colonies' production zones, training inmates in production techniques, and meeting with the prisoners to deliver lectures and conduct discussions on a variety of topics.[175] The two sponsoring organizations for Colony No. 159 in Zaporozhskaia Province, for instance, provided sufficient funds to organize two workshops and had donated some two hundred tools and pieces of equipment to outfit them. They also sent a constant stream of engineers, leading producers, members of communist labor brigades, and heroes of socialist labor to the colony to meet with the prisoners, show them how to organize their work better, and in general talk about political and labor-related themes.[176] Sponsoring organizations in Ukraine also actively participated in colony meetings held to honor prisoners who attained the title of leader (*peredovik*) of production and model behavior, sending as representatives and speakers such notables as old Bolsheviks, factory Komsomol chiefs, and even former inmates who had become good workers in their new crime-free life.[177]

Many other examples of sponsoring organizations providing material or reeducational support to their assigned penal institutions can be found. A tractor factory in 1960 sent production leaders to Colony No.1 in Belorussia to meet to the prisoners and the "Motherland" furniture factory provided ongoing technical assistance and training to the same colony's furniture workshop.[178] The furniture factory sponsoring Colony No. 5 in Estonia was sending workers to meet with prisoners and inspire them to work better; one related his own five years in a corrective-labor camp, emphasizing that upon release he was able to get an education, find a spouse, and secure a good job.[179] The boiler factory sponsoring a colony in Altai helped repair the production zone in the colony while another sponsoring organization, a sewing factory, provided drapes, games, tablecloths, and other things.[180] Similarly, a sponsoring factory in Chita turned over a production site to its local colony when the latter was in need of employment for its inmates.[181] Many sponsoring organizations went a step further by assigning individual workers to help reeducate particularly intransigent prisoners in one-on-one fashion.[182] Others staffed colony schools and enlisted Old Bolsheviks to talk with the prisoners.[183] And assistance often continued when prisoners were released; sponsoring organizations of the colonies of Dnepropetrovsk city in the early 1960s provided employment for 116 prisoners after their terms had ended.[184] The Magadan MVD, recognizing that reeducational assistance from sponsors took pressure off their own administrators, requested that the regional party apparatus make local Komsomol organizations sponsors for colonies that housed large numbers of youth.[185] And one colony in Kharkov had four sponsoring organizations that sent representatives to lecture the inmates on such topics as "revolutionary Cuba" and "religion and its harm."[186]

Because of such unremunerated support, Gulag officials were willing to rapidly increase the number of sponsoring organizations in the early 1960s. Whereas Ukraine in mid-1959 had only 115 sponsoring organizations for its 86 colonies, by October 1962 there were 356 sponsors for the expanded network of 113 colonies.[187] In 1964 the 771 camp subdivisions and colonies of the Russian MVD had over 1,300 sponsoring organizations.[188] Starting in 1962, sponsoring organizations were frequently assigned to individual detachments of prisoners with the goal of creating closer relations with individual prisoners.[189] By 1964, as a result of this policy, Colony No. 80 in Krivoi Rog alone had sixteen sponsoring organizations and when colony officials found themselves unable to provide work for each prisoner, they appealed to their sponsors and received enough orders for products from the colony workshops to employ every inmate.[190] The successes noted above combined with increased number of sponsoring organizations were balanced out, of course, by organizations that provided very little assistance to their colonies—after all, they had their own plans to fulfill. And some, such as those attached to Viatlag, were also inhibited by large distances between them and the corrective-labor institutions.[191] Yet the sponsoring organizations, because of their ability to provide tangible assistance without direct interference in colony operations, were welcomed by camp commanders to a much greater extent than procurators or oversight commissions.[192]

Other Institutions of Oversight and Assistance

In addition to procurators, oversight commissions, and sponsoring organizations, a few other bodies were given charge to oversee and assist in penal operations in the Khrushchev era. Among the most important of these were the provincial and republican courts, especially after the abolition of the camp courts in 1954.[193] Like members of the abovementioned organizations, court justices were encouraged to visit the colonies and assist in reeducational work, primarily through delivering lectures or holding question-and-answer sessions.[194] But more importantly, although courts had always been involved in the Gulag by providing corrective-labor institutions with a steady (or at times not so steady) flow of new inmates, under Khrushchev they became critical gatekeepers to other important decisions that helped regulate Gulag operations. On 17 August 1957 the Supreme Soviet, on advice from the Supreme Court, ordered that inmates sentenced to prison could be transferred to a corrective-labor institution after serving one-third of their sentence and demonstrating suitable progress toward reeducation. Critically, such transfers had to be approved by provincial court.[195]

Another important gatekeeper function gained by local courts in the Khrushchev era, as noted in chapter 1, was to pass final judgment on parole requests. Gulag administrators at times chafed under this regulation, arguing that the already overworked courts produced a bottleneck in the parole process. They also complained, not surprisingly, that the courts too often denied the prisoners they had nominated for parole. A complaint in 1959, for instance, noted that parole requests often took three months for courts to process and 15,674 requests had been denied in the first five months of the year, comprising 16.8 percent of the total requests for that period. Of that number, 5,059 prisoners were denied parole for reasons not permissible by law such as the serious nature of their crime, multiple crimes on their record, or even the shortness of their sentence.[196] Procurators too criticized courts for at times denying parole to prisoners worthy of such, although when paroled prisoners quickly committed new crimes, procurators were equally quick to wonder why the court had granted the parole request.[197]

Similar to the ability to approve or deny parole was the courts' function in implementing a 1958 change in sentencing guidelines, which saw the maximum sentence for any crime reduced from twenty-five years to fifteen. For those already serving twenty-five-year terms, this raised hope in a sentence reduction. Ultimately, however, the decision was made to reduce terms not automatically but on a case-by-case basis. And significantly, the power of review was given not to camp authorities but to the courts. Thus, on 25 April 1960 the Supreme Soviet decreed that local courts should review the files of those sentenced to longer than fifteen years who had already served at least half their terms and to take into account several factors when deciding whether to grant a reduction or not. These included the danger posed to society by the criminal; the character and level of his participation in the crime; his age at the moment of the crime; his attitude toward labor and behavior while incarcerated; and other circumstances that reflected on the character (*lichnost'*) of the convict. In this manner the courts were given the mandate to protect society by deciding which potentially dangerous criminals had placed themselves firmly on "the path to correction."[198]

Another important gatekeeper function gained by the courts during the Khrushchev period was the power and obligation to assign prisoners to a particular type of colony. During the 1950s and leading into the early 1960s, regimen determination was made by a prison commission at the facility where the inmate was held during investigation and trial. Its decision was to be based on the sentence, number, and character of prior convictions, and the prisoner's behavior in the prison before his transfer to a colony. With the new corrective-labor regulations of 1961, however, the authority to assign a particular regimen type was turned over to the court issuing the sentence. Such determinations were to be made, with rare exception, based purely on the crime committed and number of prior convictions, taking behavior while in prison out of the equation. Not all justices adjusted well to this new practice; a common complaint voiced by the MVD but more vociferously by procurators in the early 1960s was that courts often assigned prisoners to the wrong regimen, thus inhibiting the work of reeducation.[199] Courts also became responsible for approving all transfers among the various regimens, including to prisons and to the minimum-security colony-settlements that were established in 1963.[200]

Local party and Komsomol organizations, apart from their involvement in oversight commissions, also played a role in regulating and assisting corrective-labor institutions. Camps and colonies each had party and Komsomol cells comprised of wardens, guards, production personnel, and MVD administrators, and these, as in other nonpenal institutions of the Soviet Union, were expected both to agitate in support of the current goals of the organization and in general raise the political awareness of both members and nonmembers alike. Critically, however, these local cells reported up an internal party hierarchy that culminated not in provincial party leadership but in the head of the political department for the All-Union (and after January 1960, the republican) Gulag. Thus, Gulag party organizations were in essence departments within the state structure. They were admonished in August 1958 to maintain constant communication with the local non-MVD party organizations, but they were separate from them.[201]

The local party organizations, for their part, were also tasked in the Khrushchev era with monitoring local places of confinement. For the most part this took place through party representatives on the oversight commissions, but the local party was also supposed to monitor the work of the oversight commissions. As the MVD of Ukraine in 1961 reminded, local party committees should always have the prisons and colonies "in their field of vision."[202] The provincial party committee in Briansk took this advice to heart, helping its penal facilities sort prisoners by number of convictions and publicizing stories of inmates who had become reformed.[203] Others helped colonies find sponsoring organizations.[204] In reality, however, the local party hierarchies were inundated with other concerns and had little contact with local penal facilities. An exception to this (as will be detailed in chapter 5) came in September 1960 when provincial party committees were tasked with inspecting places of confinement and reporting their findings and suggestions for improvement to the Central Committee.

The Komsomol had somewhat of a closer relationship with the Gulag than the party, primarily through factory and other Komsomol cells that functioned as sponsoring organizations.[205] But that was not the extent of their involvement. Some Komsomol groups attempted to maintain contact with former members who had been incarcerated. A prisoner in 1959, for instance, reported receiving a letter from the Komsomol committee from the factory where he used to work, noting that it restored his faith in Soviet society and in his ability to "redeem [his] guilt before the Motherland."[206] In other cases, the local or regional Komsomol organizations worked more directly with local corrective-labor institutions. Even the head of the provincial Komsomol in Briansk visited the local colonies to meet with young prisoners.[207]

To encourage such activity, the Central Committee of the Komsomol on 5 November 1959 sent a letter entitled "On Furthering the Role of Society in the Struggle with Crime and Infractions of the Social Order" to its regional organizations, admonishing them to get local Komsomol cells involved in reeducating young prisoners.[208] L. D. Lukoianov, head of the Gulag political department, reminded his subordinates of this letter in a conference report from the same year, admonishing them to "actively use the assistance of local Komsomol organizations in working with the youth."[209] Indeed, such attention stemmed not just from the campaign to activate society, but also from the regime's newfound concern with youth.[210] After the amnesties and other releases of the 1950s, youth comprised a large percentage of Gulag inmates; by October 1962, 40 percent of prisoners in Ukraine were under the age of twenty-six.[211] And the Ukrainian Komsomol in response issued multiple decrees in the 1960s admonishing its local cells to aid in the reeducation of troubled youths both in the colonies and after their release.[212] Efforts to involve local Komsomol organizations in penal affairs, however, met with only mixed success. A review of Vinnitsia Province colonies in August 1960, for example, showed that the head of the Komsomol cell at Colony No. 59 was not even aware of the Central Committee letter and had no contact with outside Komsomol cells.[213]

Labor unions played a fairly minor role in Khrushchev's Gulag, but they were not completely absent. As part of the broader drive under Khrushchev to strengthen the unions, union committees were organized in the 1960s among non-MVD production personnel that staffed colony factories and workshops. And in addition to serving the needs of these free workers, they were also instructed to serve the needs of the inmates. In many ways they duplicated the work of sponsoring organizations, but they operated from within the colony rather than without. The committee at Colony No. 14 in Odessa reported in 1964 that they pursued reeducational work among prisoners by finding out where the inmates worked prior to incarceration and then inviting former colleagues to visit the colony. The prisoners were particularly impressed by one such visitor who had served time himself but who was now secretary of his factory's Komsomol organization.[214] Labor union committees also assigned individual members to work as correctional officers (*vospitateli*) in specific detachments, to conduct political exercises, and to help produce radio programming for prisoners.[215] They staffed vocational training programs and schools. As the head of the correctional unions in Sverdlovsk Province declared, every union member had the responsibility to be "a teacher, a mentor (*vospitatel'*), and a tutor (*nastavnik*)." Yet many union members felt no such responsibility to the prisoners and at times even penal administrators warned against interfering with the inmates.[216]

A final institution that merits discussion in conjunction with oversight and assistance is that of the Soviet family. The Gulag during the Khrushchev period increasingly instructed its local officials to involve parents and wives in the process of reeducating their children and spouses.[217] Part of this was simply allowing visits by family members, a privilege facilitated by the push to keep inmates in corrective-labor colonies in their home provinces, and extending correspondence rights. As one correctional official in Ukraine explained, mothers should be brought into the colonies to tell their husbands how hard it was to raise their children alone.[218] But other steps were taken as well. Detachment commanders were encouraged to maintain written contact with their young inmates' parents both to encourage the parents to write encouraging letters to their (primarily) sons and to get personalized suggestions on how to help the prisoners "stand on the path to correction."[219] Special cultural or political evenings to which parents were invited were occasionally put on by corrective-labor colonies.[220] When the Supreme Soviet in 1958 passed the new "Fundamentals of Criminal Law," which provided the basis for new republican criminal codes, for instance, many camps and colonies held question-and-answer sessions not just for inmates but for their families as well.[221]

In a few provinces, contact with parents became more structured with actual parents' committees being formed to aid in reeducational work among their incarcerated children and help support other parents whose children had run afoul of the law.[222] In Bashkiria such a council of some twenty parents was attached to the colony school and assisted its operations by interviewing prisoners who refused to study or who disrupted the classroom.[223] In Armenia a similar group of parents put on a conference for the inmates of Colony No. 5, on "what a prisoner should become before he is released." According to official reports this resulted in increased productivity, improved discipline, and the confession by two prisoners of unsolved crimes.[224] At the same time, it was recognized that many prisoners' families could exert a pernicious influence by supplying inmates (often at worksites) with alcohol, drugs, and money. A cartoon from the November 1961 issue of *K novoi zhizni* depicts an "Open Doors Day" for family members to come visit their inmates, but instead of running toward their parents, the prisoners are depicted running toward vodka, beer, and playing cards.[225] Gulag officials therefore attempted to keep contact with family members within the controlled environment of censored letters, monitored visits, and officially sanctioned events.[226] Perhaps for this reason the political department of the Russian Gulag announced in early 1962 that it had rejected the idea of a formal family members' council at the detachment level.[227]

Beyond the standing bodies discussed to this point, the Gulag's network of oversight also included intermittent inspections dispatched most prominently by the Central Committee and the Supreme Soviet to report on the state of the camps. Such inspection teams were usually comprised of procurators, legal advisers, supreme court associates, and sometimes party and Komsomol officials, and often had the additional responsibility of reviewing prisoners' case files.[228] The case review commissions of 1956, for instance, were tasked in addition to their primary duties to conduct a thorough inspection of each camp and colony visited and report back to central authorities.[229] This information was then used to develop the 1956 restructuring plan and the 1958 statute. In 1960, as will be discussed in greater detail in chapter 5, inspection teams were tasked with investigating places of confinement and making suggestions on how penal operations could be improved. In this manner the supreme organs of governance in the Soviet Union exerted direct, though periodic, oversight over Gulag operations.

Soviet Oversight in a Global Context

Together with the mass releases of the 1950s and the renewed orientation toward correctionalism, the network of oversight and assistance comprised a key component of the transformation of the Soviet penal system which implied a frank assessment that the MVD could not be trusted with, nor was it able to cope with its renewed mission to turn convicts into useful members of society. This creation of an enhanced system of oversight and assistance, by eliminating the conditions of isolation and autonomy that defined the late Stalinist Gulag, made important (though ultimately insufficient) strides toward reviving the correctional orientation of the Gulag and ensured that the systematic and largely tolerated abuses of the Stalinist system were vastly curtailed by the early 1960s. Yes, due to tensions inherent in the nature of penal systems and the development level of many Soviet provinces, instances of violence and privation in Khrushchev's penal system persisted.[230] Crucially, however, because of the influence of procurators, oversight commissions, sponsoring organizations, and other outside groups tasked with monitoring and assisting the Gulag, such cases became isolated rather than systemic.

Among penal systems globally, the creation of such an extensive network of oversight and assistance is unique. As in the Soviet case, there were attempts in the West in the 1950s and early 1960s to enroll society in the rehabilitation of criminals. With noted exceptions, however, these efforts largely failed; the commitment of community groups was often weak while the resentment of these organizations by prison officials was high. More importantly, the role of the Soviet Procuracy was much stronger than that of the various prison inspectors in the West and the Soviet oversight commissions wielded more power than Western parole boards.

Curiously, there was little to no discussion of oversight among penologists and policymakers in the United States, to take one prominent example, even as they documented and decried instances of administrative abuse and pressed for greater concern for the individual convict. The American Correctional Association, a professional society that trumpeted the cause of rehabilitation, completely neglected this issue in its otherwise comprehensive blueprint for prison operations, the multi-edition *Manual of Correctional Standards*.[231] And it was only in the mid-1960s that American courts began to act on prisoner complaints, to intercede in the operation of correctional facilities.

Yet perhaps it is not surprising that while both Western and Soviet systems were reorienting their penal operations toward the "rehabilitative ideal" in the postwar era, only the Soviet side implemented such an extensive network of oversight and assistance. To some extent the presence of an independent media in the West compensated for this absence. Press coverage of prisons was certainly not constant but episodic, focusing mostly on emergency situations such as prison riots, but it could in such cases result in serious reforms.[232] The Soviet press, though more able to investigate and report on penal affairs after Stalin's death, was still not free to report on the worst excesses and illegalities of the system. What the Soviet Union lacked in an independent press, therefore, it made up for with multiple layers of inspection and oversight. More important than the presence or absence of a free press was the Soviet Union's long history of organs of oversight and control and the absence of such institutions in the free-market democracies of the West. This was, in other words, the natural Soviet administrative response to problems. Finally, Western prison systems, though by no means ideal, had never experienced to such a degree the lawlessness and abuse of the Stalinist Gulag. Abuses in the former were uncovered and dealt with sporadically, and therefore never called for the creation of extensive oversight bodies.

UNDOING THE REFORMS

The Campaign against "Liberalism" in the Gulag

> What we have been saying in large measure explains the fact that
> for Russia at its various historical epochs it is not conservatism
> that is typical, but on the contrary both reactionary and progressive
> tendencies.
>
> —Iurii Lotman and Boris Uspenskii, *The Semiotics of Russian Culture*

In 1959 Vladimir Mikhailovich Gridin arrived at the 11th Camp Division of Dubravlag to serve a "child's term" (*detskii srok*) of three years for anti-Soviet writings. His lenient sentence, compared with the typical twenty-five year terms of the Stalin era, was a pleasant surprise, but the camp itself was even more astonishing. Guards and administrators were courteous and efficient in fulfilling their duties. The prisoners, with their "unforced smiles," friendly questions, and willingness to carry the suitcases of the new arrivals, did not seem like prisoners at all. They were dressed well and seemed to be enjoying themselves— some were even playing billiards. Indeed, they made Gridin feel "as if he had turned up at his own home." And the camp itself hardly resembled a penal facility. There were "straight paths with gravel and white bricks, to the right and left there were wooden buildings with clean entryways and little windows with bright curtains, all around there were many flowers and posters." The barracks were "clean, cool, and spacious." Rather than a prison, Gridin concluded, "it looked just like a resort."[1]

Gridin's initial impressions and experiences at Dubravlag confirm the genuineness and the impact of the post-Stalin reforms detailed in the previous chapters. Although the Soviet Union at this time was taking pains to invite foreigners to a few specially prepared penal institutions to demonstrate their humaneness, Dubravlag was not one of these institutions.[2] Its conditions were not produced for show, but for the benefit and reeducation of its inmates. True, the reforms did not touch all corners of the Gulag equally; living conditions in corrective-labor institutions in the less developed regions of the Soviet Union, and especially in the logging camps, generally lagged behind those of, for example, Ukraine or the Baltics. Overall, however, there can be no question that life for the average prisoner by the late 1950s was much easier than it had been a decade previously. And this was precisely the intent of the reforms; living conditions similar to those of nonprisoners were considered a requisite part of the Gulag's new aim: preparing inmates to return to "an honest working life."

Yet not all were satisfied with the post-Stalin reform to Soviet criminal justice, with its emphasis on leniency, humaneness, and reeducation. As Stephen Cohen reminds, "reform from above everywhere is always limited in substance and duration, and it usually followed by a conservative backlash."[3] Indeed, just as the judicial reforms of the mid-1950s were beginning to bear fruit, a potent counterreform movement coalesced in the late 1950s and early 1960s and ultimately succeeded in reintroducing overt elements of punitiveness into the Soviet system of criminal justice. This "conservative shift," as Marc Elie terms it, manifested itself in a barrage of petitions from Soviet citizens asking for more protection from criminals, newspaper articles detailing soft punishments meted out for terrible crimes, legislation mandating harsher sentences for some types of crime, and antiparasite legislation aimed at banishing nonproductive members of local communities' penal system.[4] Thus, whereas Khrushchev and his top allies in the 1950s tried to move the country away from the punitive justice of the Stalin era, Stalin's rule left behind a powerful tough-on-crime psychology among Soviet society and Soviet officialdom that ultimately proved resistant to change. As Miriam Dobson argues, the reforms of the mid-1950s ultimately "failed to resonate" with the Soviet public and that as a result Khrushchev and his peers in the late 1950s turned instead to optimism for the future as a ruling technique, a trope that was inseparably coupled with intolerance for those unwilling to move forward toward communism.[5] In the end, therefore, even Khrushchev and most top justice officials turned against the "soft line" of justice and became caught up in a renewed campaign against various enemies of socialism.[6]

In addition to pushing for harsher sentences and increased protection from criminals in society, the counterreform movement of the late 1950s and early 1960s also took aim at altering the conditions found by Gridin in 1959. Pressing for harsher living conditions and increased restrictions on those already incarcerated, justice officials, penologists, the press, the general public, and the country's senior leadership looked to restore a measure of punitive retribution to a penal system that had gone soft. And although their justifications for opposing the reforms of the mid-1950s were not uniform, they were united linguistically both among themselves and with prisoners such as Gridin in their depiction of post-Stalin correctional facilities as resorts (usually *kurorty*, but sometimes *sanatoria* or other synonyms), that is, places of relaxation, light treatment, relative freedom, and the enjoyment of fresh air in a temperate climate. Such "liberalism," another favored term of the counterreform campaign, was seen as undeserved, dangerous, and ultimately a stumbling block in Soviet society's march toward communism.

"The Camp Is Not a Resort" in the Criminal Justice Establishment

It is unclear who first began referring to Soviet penal facilities as resorts, but this terminology seems to have already been in currency by the late 1930s. As one of Evgeniia Ginzburg's guards in Kolyma yelled, "This isn't a seaside resort! You've got your norm to fulfill, and you'll be fed according to output. For sabotage you'll go to the punishment cell."[7] But with the reforms of the 1950s, the prisoners themselves began to use the term in the positive sense. Like Gridin, inmate N. F. Odolinskaia upon her arrival at Dubravlag in 1955 noted that "in the camp everything was like a resort—full of flowers and beautiful trees."[8] Michael Solomon recorded the words of a fellow inmate serving in Kolyma: "the camps now look like health spas in comparison to what they used to be in Stalin's time."[9] Even the French socialist Henri Dusart, after visiting a corrective-labor colony in Tula as part of a guided tour in 1956, referred to it as a "country house (*maison de campagne*)."[10] Perhaps Dusart thought of this analogy on his own, but it is quite possible he encountered it while talking with the prisoners or the colony staff.

The imagery of a resort, if not the term itself, is also evident in a pamphlet published by the Georgian Ministry of Internal Affairs (MVD) and distributed to penal facilities across the USSR. This fascinating document illustrates through prose and photographs the transformation of one of its corrective-labor colonies from a decrepit institution to a beautiful and well-maintained colony. New whitewashed barracks intersected by attractive tree-lined avenues feature prominently in the pictures, as does an almost ornate dining room complete with tablecloths, chandeliers, and large windows and a well-stocked library. A new club building and school building, new production machinery housed in new workshops, and new metal beds instead of wooden bunks complete the picture. The effect of this physical transformation of the colony, according to the narratives presented by both staff and inmates, was a psychological transformation of its prisoners. Populated once by lazy regimen violators, the colony now housed a vibrant, hardworking, and repentant prisoner collective.[11] Such were the supposed effects of the camp-turned-resort in the Gulag's internal instruction manuals.

Yet throughout the reforming efforts of the mid-1950s some questioned whether camp life was not simply turning into a vacation for unworthy law-breakers. This questioning only intensified as the decade wore on and as the level of criminality in the Soviet Union as a whole remained persistently high. By the late 1950s, even as Minister of Internal Affairs Nikolai Pavlovich Dudorov began to redouble the effort to turn the Gulag into a humane correctional system, the backlash against such reforms began to gain a critical mass. Some of this counter-reformist rhetoric came from within Dudorov's own ministry, but it mostly stemmed from outside groups united by the goal of eliminating "liberalism" in the penal sphere. They were also brought together by the reductionist imagery of the resort, most prominently through the slogan "The camp is not a resort." In just these few words the opponents of de-Stalinization in the penal sphere were able to quickly dismiss most correctional measures as excessive leniency. The camp-as-resort thus became a powerful trope in the post-Stalin negotiation of values and priorities when it came to law and order.[12]

Aleksandr Solzhenitsyn and other Gulag memoirists have laid the blame for this counterreform campaign on the Gulag administration itself. This is natural considering their perspective as inmates of the system, and certainly some of the counterreforming impulse came from within it. Yet Solzhenitsyn's idea that it resulted from the job security fears of "the whole cast of practical workers" that staffed the Gulag is not correct.[13] Indeed, Gulag and prison officials under Khrushchev frequently complained about overcrowding and lobbied for minor of-fenders to be diverted from the camp system, suggesting impetus for a stable if not reduced number of inmates, not a new expansion of the penal apparatus.[14]

Rather, for the MVD and other agencies associated with the Gulag, the "camp is not a resort" campaign was closely associated with the campaign to liquidate the criminal gangs in the Gulag. Although the gang phenomenon certainly predated the period of liberalization in the camps, it became possible after years of "liber-alism" to argue that leniency toward prisoners only facilitated the persistence of the gangs. As noted in chapter 2, prisoners in this period were often not forced to work and the criminal gangs, especially the thieves-in-law, took full advantage of this. Instead of being reformed by it, prisoners were taking advantage of the lightened regimen to commit new crimes and live off the labor of others. Because Soviet penology had long held, and continued to hold under Khrush-chev, that labor was an indispensable part of reeducation, relaxed attitudes toward prisoners appeased the gangs and their "parasitic way of life," undermin-ing reeducation (not to mention production, which remained a serious concern even after the obsession with production of the late Stalinist period was de-nounced) in the process. The war against the criminal gangs therefore featured measures to implement a much harsher regimen for those deemed worthy of such punishment, thus preparing the ground for the broader movement to eliminate excessive privileges for all inmates.

A related process that led many MVD officials, procurators, and others involved with the penal system to call for a harsher regimen was changing Gulag demographics. As described in chapter 1, with every mass release of prisoners the percentage of prisoners convicted of dangerous or multiple crimes increased. By 1 January 1960, more than half of Gulag inmates had a prior conviction on their record.[15] Crucially, as political prisoners and those convicted of minor crimes were freed in the various release programs of the mid-1950s, the Gulag by the late 1950s became increasingly populated by murderers, rapists, bandits, and robbers. Such criminals were not necessarily gang members, but they were perceived by Gulag workers as more prone to crime and regimen infractions and less worthy of lenient treatment in the name of reeducation. These sentiments were on display already in a series of Gulag conferences convened by Dudorov in 1957 and 1958. One camp commander voiced the need to create "harsh conditions" for professional criminals.[16] Another complained that those sent from the camps to prison for repeated regimen violations enjoyed too light of a regimen: "They're vacationing there!"[17]

After these conferences certain Gulag officials continued to call for revisions to regimen policies to make life harder for dangerous criminals and recidivists. But notably, the lines between such hardened criminals and Gulag inmates as a whole often became blurred or disappeared completely. For many, the lightened regimen instituted in the wake of Stalin's death was a structural problem that had the tendency to create new recidivists rather than reform existing ones. As S. P. Strelenko from Cheliabinsk Province explained at a 1961 conference in Saratov, some prisoners were intentionally committing crimes to return to the camps where life was good, saying, "We'll just spend the winter with you, fulfill half our sentence, work a little, and toward summer we'll be free again."[18] A. P. Kuznetsov, deputy head of the Saratov penal apparatus, agreed, noting that recent experience had demonstrated that a weak regimen only creates disciplinary problems.[19] Likewise, V. V. Andreev, director of the Saratov Prison, lashed out against "resort-like conditions," arguing that things were better back in 1953 when the regimen was harsh and prisoners could feel "the weight of punishment."[20] According to an MVD officer with whom Solzhenitsyn conversed in 1962, "things were completely out of hand [in the late 1950s]! Those who didn't want to didn't even go to work. They bought television sets with their own money."[21]

Similar attitudes could be found throughout the Gulag apparatus, including the Baltic republics. Comrade Burov, head of Colony No. 2 in Estonia, complained at a March 1958 conference for Estonian Gulag workers that the regimen was too "liberal" and proposed that camp commanders be given more power to punish disobedient prisoners.[22] The first deputy of the Estonian MVD struck a similar tone, arguing that that the regimen should be strengthened and that hard labor, rather than specialized work, was particularly beneficial for recidivists.[23] Another conference for Estonian penal officials held in December 1958 came to similar conclusions, with the head of the guard division for Estonia noting that in the wake of the 1954 reforms the regimen in the camps had become far too relaxed and the procurator general of Estonia reminding participants that prisons and colonies were "not resorts."[24] Likewise, the Lithuanian MVD in early 1960 criticized its penal officials for replacing reeducational work with recreational (*razvlekatel'nye*) activities and for paroling prisoners who had not demonstrated correction.[25] And in Ukraine, a colony commander, reacting against a proposal to move prisoners to a seven-hour workday, argued that criminals "should atone for their guilt and return to the path of an honest life by way of long and strenuous labor."[26] In this he was supported by the Ukrainian minister of justice, who complained of a relaxation of the penal regimen and of a wage system that saw prisoners "get[ting] rich at the expense of the government."[27]

On the other side of the Soviet Union, a 1958 MVD inspection of corrective-labor institutions in Magadan Province revealed a host of improper practices associated with excessive leniency: too many prisoners, including murderers, recidivists, and regimen violators were being deconvoyed, put on lightened regimen, and allowed to live outside the zone; many were being freed early on improperly awarded workday credits; male and female prisoners were not properly separated resulting in a rash of pregnancies; and regimen infractions were only rarely being punished.[28] As a result, violent criminals were taking advantage of these permissive conditions to commit new crimes; most distressingly, a hardened recidivist with six convictions (including two for escape from correctional-labor institutions), placed on lightened regimen in 1958, used his unwarranted privilege of free movement to rape a ten-year-old girl and kill both her and her younger brother.[29] Similar cases of deconvoyed prisoners and inmates living outside the zone—often in violation of regulations—committing crimes (although few were so heinous) were not uncommon.

MVD officials who advocated the elimination of various privileges enjoyed by inmates were strongly supported in such sentiments by the Procuracy and many of its local camp procurators. As noted in chapter 3, the Procuracy was instrumental in the reform of the Gulag by providing constant oversight over penal operations, leading especially to decreased violence by guards and administrators. Yet as guardians of "socialist legality," they also had charge to ensure that prisoners were following the laws and regulations governing them and that court sentences were respected. Such responsibilities by the late 1950s led the Procuracy to begin advocating a more restrictive, even punitive environment for prisoners. Already in 1956 Procurator General Roman Andreevich Rudenko had complained of excessive privileges—most notably deconvoying and lightened regimen—being distributed too readily. Many camp procurators, when asked for comments on a draft version of a new statute governing the Gulag, criticized it heavily for allowing too many privileges.[30] As voiced by one of these local procurators, when describing proposed new restrictions for strict-regimen prisoners, "this harshness of regimen will facilitate the quickest reeducation of prisoners."[31]

Two years later this conviction was even stronger. In 1960 the procurator general of Ukraine, listing the many privileges enjoyed by inmates, complained that "the regimen and holding conditions of prisoners in the colonies and prison of the republic are so light that many criminals stopped being afraid of places and confinement and after release commit further crimes."[32] Adding to this criticism, Rudenko accused certain members of the Gulag establishment of misunderstanding the term "socialist humaneness." Immediately after Stalin's death, as noted in chapter 1, "socialist humaneness" and "socialist legality" were often used to describe the same policies, such as amnesties or the release of inmates imprisoned on trumped-up charges. Rudenko in 1958, however, demarcated a clear difference between the two, reminding Gulag officials that in restoring socialist humaneness "we never said that we are turning away from punishment."[33] Thus, socialist legality demanded punishment for crimes committed, which could not be superseded by an appeal to humaneness.

This theme continued at an All-Union meeting for procurators in 1960 where Rudenko lamented: "When the criminal is given privileges, then it is not correction and reeducation of the convicted, but a mockery of the sentence."[34] This attitude was also propagated by Rudenko's deputy, Aleksandr Nikolaevich Mishutin, who faulted local procurators for spending too much time caring about prisoners' living conditions, while neglecting such things as ensuring prisoners were strictly following regulations and preventing too many prisoners from obtaining parole.[35] Not all procurators needed such a reminder, however. In Magadan a procurator was incensed to learn that a number of female prisoners had become Orthodox nuns and had thereby succeeded in avoiding work for two years. Announcing that they had been sentenced to labor, not to a "resort-like life" (*kurortnaia zhizn'*), the procurator confiscated their religious material and forced them back to work. The women commenced a hunger strike, but the threat of forced feeding convinced them to end their protest.[36]

Curiously, however, a number of MVD officials disagreed with the growing movement to roll back the reforms of the mid-1950s. Many low-level Gulag officials were unenthusiastic about creating harsher conditions for all prisoners, often out of concern for fulfilling their economic plan. In response to Burov's complaint about the liberal regimen cited above, for instance, a detachment commander from a different colony in Estonia retorted that Burov "obviously does not understand those tasks that the party and government have placed before the MVD organs."[37] Also in Estonia, a competition was held in Colony No. 3 to see which detachment could create the best living conditions, with the winners receiving a television for their dormitory.[38] As late as 1960, the Lithuanian MVD created a lightened-regimen colony literally out of a summer camp and stocked it with films, billiards, table tennis, musical instruments, and volleyball equipment.[39]

The MVD political department, although it began to push in the late 1950s to make strict-regimen institutions much harsher, complete with hard physical labor and special uniforms, continued to advocate trust in and better treatment of most prisoners.[40] In 1960, while the chorus of voices opposing lenient treatment of inmates was growing in other circles, the political department began publication of its internal instructional journal *K novoi zhizni* (*Toward a New Life*), and focused its content on reeducation rather than retribution.[41] As voiced by the editors in the first issue, "To correct, reeducate [prisoners], raise them up to a new life—that is the goal! In fulfilling it, the soviet state helps these people make amends for their guilt and return to the ranks of the honest workers—the builders of communism."[42] In the pages of this journal, which was not available to inmates or those outside the correctional apparatus, readers were instructed on how to organize effective sponsoring relationships with local enterprises, how to properly organize labor competitions and political indoctrination sessions, and ultimately how to persuade inmates to change their lives for the better. In fact, shortly before the peak of the "camp is not a resort" campaign, camp workers were instructed by *K novoi zhizni* to not pursue a "harsh course" of disciplinary practices. In the view of the political department, the conversation about liberal excesses was "not well thought through."[43]

The most important supporter of the more lenient approach toward inmates in the MVD, however, was Dudorov himself. Like the political department, he advocated a differentiated program of harsher conditions for the gangs and other intransigent inmates combined with continued leniency toward the remaining prisoners.[44] Under his direction the MVD in mid-1959 protested proposals for prison uniforms for inmates, arguing that "this is not compatible with the tasks of corrective-labor policies and contradicts the laws that disallow the debasement of human dignity."[45] Also in 1959 he lobbied for an increase in funds for improving living conditions in places of confinement.[46] When the All-Union MVD was liquidated in January 1960 and Dudorov was reassigned to other work, however, this crucial voice of moderation was lost.

Still, academics serving with the MVD educational system were largely aligned with Dudorov and expressed concern with the movement to make camp life harsher. Boris Samoilovich Utevskii, then head professor at the Higher School of the MVD, voiced his approval of continued leniency toward prisoners who demonstrated good behavior and a strong work ethic. Citing Lenin, he argued that the Gulag should continue to move "from the prison to correctional (*vospitatel'nye*) institutions," calling for the "progressive system," which moved prisoners to increasingly lighter regimens inasmuch as they approached release, should be enshrined in law.[47] The support of Utevskii is significant because in many ways he was the dean of Soviet criminology, serving as a living link between the lively debates of the 1920s and the reemergence of the discipline in the 1950s. It also helped that he was the son-in-law of Andrei Vyshinskii, the famous procurator of the 1930s show trials and foreign minister of the USSR from 1949 to 1953. Under his influence other scholars associated with the MVD maintained that deprivation of freedom was already a very serious punishment and did not need the additional weight of difficult living conditions, not to mention outright abuse or privation.[48] Thus, many within the MVD, not only in its top-level administration but in its academic institutions as well, adhered even in the late 1950s to the idea that widespread privileges and rewards for good behavior aided the goal of reeducation, even while acknowledging the necessity of punishment and harsher regimens for uncooperative prisoners.

Among academics and other prominent legal authorities outside the MVD, who were only in the late 1950s able to reopen the fields of criminology and penology after their repression in the mid-1930s, Utevskii's view found some support.[49] Chairman Aleksandr Fedorovich Gorkin of the Supreme Court protested to the Central Committee against "turning away from humane principles of correcting and reeducating prisoners in places of confinement."[50] Similarly, Iosef Solomonovich Noi, professor at the Saratov Law Institute and somewhat of a rebel against the criminological establishment, warned that the push for harsher living conditions in the camps played "on feelings of revenge against criminals." Indeed, he even suggested a further loosening of the regimen by removing all restrictions on visits and correspondence, allowing reprimands to fall off a prisoner's record after a year of good behavior, and permitting vacations outside the colony.[51] Noi's close associate L. G. Krakhmal'nik concurred with this proposal, and N. N. Pashe-Ozerskii from Voronezh State University proposed restoring the possibility of parole to even the most hardened recidivists, a right that was removed in 1958.[52]

Other criminologists, however, disagreed. At a conference held at Tomsk in February 1959, a number of participants spoke out in favor of creating stricter regimen conditions for all prisoners. As voiced by A. L. Remenson, the view that the camps existed to correct prisoners was one-sided; they also existed to deter and this was realized through the harshness of their regimen. Drawing on Lenin's famous dichotomy of persuasion (*ubezhdenie*) and coercion (*prinuzhdenie*), he argued that coercion should exist in equal measure with persuasion in the camps.[53] F. P. Miliutin, in turn, criticized the practice of keeping even the worst criminals in their home provinces, including the southern regions of Ukraine, Belorussia, the Caucasus and other places with pleasant climates. Instead, he argued, they should be shipped off to the east and "the climate itself will assist in hastening reeducation."[54]

By the time the campaign peaked in 1961, academics had almost wholly abandoned the positions of Noi and Utevskii. This is epitomized in a 1961 conference that rejected the progressive system as a bourgeois invention that promoted individualism, slyness, envy, and other faults.[55] Arguing (disingenuously) that only recidivists remained in the camps, I. I. Bakov of the MVD Institute in Lvov insisted on a strengthening of the regimen, including the elimination of conjugal visits, mandatory uniforms, shaved heads for male prisoners, limiting inmates' right to complain, and extending sentences for those who refused to work.[56] Iu. A. Frolov from Kiev State University agreed, declaring that while reeducation was necessary, "places of confinement should be for [prisoners] a harsh school."[57] Indeed, law professor I. S. Samoshchenko went so far as to claim that "the more serious [punitive sanctions] are and the greater the associated suffering . . . the greater its correctional influence."[58] In a similar vein, N. Struchkov revisited the Leninist equation of coercion and persuasion, instructing Gulag workers that coercive reeducational measures should take precedence over persuasive ones within penal institutions, because criminals had already rejected persuasion in committing a crime.[59] Even Utevskii by 1960 began teaching the necessity of retributive punishment, reminding participants at a conference devoted to the penal philosophy and practice of Anton Semenovich Makarenko that the reeducation of prisoners takes place in institutions of coercion and punishment.[60]

Noi, Krakhmal'nik, and others were also criticized by MVD academic P. Ganin in *K novoi zhizni*, which after 1960 began to adopt the harsh new tone of the counterreform campaign, for rejecting the goal of punishment through the regimen and advocating for increased wages and other privileges for inmates. Rather, according to Ganin, we should heed the words of Lenin and be unmerciful to lawbreakers.[61] Thus, by the early 1960s, most penologists had rejected the theory that leniency and the extension of myriad privileges to prisoners should stand alongside labor and various educational programs as a vital component of reeducation; rather, they postulated, a strict disciplinary regimen and relatively harsh living conditions should accompany labor and other programs to achieve the reeducation of inmates.[62] Moreover, harsh living conditions were necessary in order to create the proper deterrent effect for both the inmates themselves and potential criminals in broader society.

Calls for Retribution by the Public and the Press

The same intolerance toward bestowing lenient conditions on criminals found voice among the broader Soviet population, which in the Khrushchev era was encouraged to participate more freely in public debates. As George Breslauer perceived, Khrushchev relied on the public for both input and for the energy needed to carry out his reforms.[63] Yet, as noted by Dobson, Soviet inhabitants, raised with a sharp sense of social justice, had never looked on criminals with compassion, and wave after wave of releases from the Gulag (and the temporary spikes in crime that often resulted) under Khrushchev only reaffirmed the general view that criminals should be dealt with harshly.[64] The highest levels of party and government, along with newspapers and lower-level officials, received a constant barrage of letters from concerned citizens regarding the level of crime during the Khrushchev era. Afraid to walk around town at night or even in parks on the weekend for fear of murder, rape, robbery, and harassment from criminal gangs or hooligans, people complained that the police were ineffective, amnesties were applied too broadly, and criminal punishments were too lenient to deter criminals.[65] Petr E. Shelest, then secretary of the Kiev party organization, captured this mood in his memoir when he recalled feeling "offended" by unceasing instances of violent crime in Ukraine in the 1950s.[66] Popular anger against criminals during this period pervaded the USSR-wide discussions on antiparasite legislation that proposed internal exile and mandatory labor for those perceived to be living off the labor of others. Many people came forward at meetings held to discuss the draft decree with specific names of people who should be prosecuted and exiled as parasites. Some wanted to expand the list of those who could be considered parasites, others wanted to expand the maximum sentence from five to ten years.[67] As one petition from a Novocherkassk pensioner stated, "The people aren't happy with such mild measures against parasites, and I think that a bandit and anyone who kills a man are class enemies. We need to wipe them from our earth."[68]

Notably for the present discussion, ordinary Soviet subjects also denounced the "soft regimen of holding prisoners and the practice of releasing them on parole," a viewpoint surely fueled not only by anger over criminal deeds, but by persistent miserable living conditions for many Soviet subjects outside the barbed wire.[69] An illustrative letter from Saratov Province stated that all criminals know "that in places of confinement one can live without care: there are movie theaters there, and schools, and the living conditions are not bad." "No," the petitioner continued, "for them not humaneness is needed, but repressive measures and harsh conditions in the camp."[70] Another lengthy letter by A. M. Dorodnitsin, a former prisoner from Chukotka, made wide-ranging suggestions on how to reform the Gulag, including the restoration of corporal punishment, labeling people as thieves or hooligans in their passports, and placing numbers on prisoner uniforms.[71] Many petitioners complained that prisoners were being released early, before correction could take place. Others doubted the correction of criminals could occur at all, calling for them to be strictly isolated in prison or in the Far North for the rest of their lives.[72] Some even called for public executions for murderers and recidivists.[73]

While it is impossible to gauge precisely how widespread among the Soviet populace these calls to get tough on crime through increased sanctions and harsher conditions in the camps were, what is important is that Soviet policymakers in the mid-to-late 1950s, in an era where Khrushchev actively courted public opinion, felt besieged by an increase both in crime and popular anger toward criminals.[74] Crucially, whereas many MVD and Gulag administrators took a differentiated approach toward prisoners, advocating strict conditions for some and continued leniency for others, the public more frequently called for a harsh regimen for all prisoners. Although this conclusion that the Soviet public exhibited greater punitiveness than the security organs themselves may seem counterintuitive, this phenomenon is not unique to the Soviet case. As early as 1918 George H. Mead noted that American society was "almost helpless in the grip of the hostile attitude it has taken toward [lawbreakers]," which inevitably led to "attitudes of retribution, repression, and exclusion" and drowned out discussion on lowering the crime rate through rehabilitating delinquents. Indeed, Meade concluded, "it is quite impossible psychologically to hate the sin and love the sinner."[75] Similar to this central tenet of Christianity, the post-Stalin trumpeting of socialist humaneness in the form of leniency toward lawbreakers proved difficult to maintain in the face of continued criminality that affected ordinary citizens.

The attitude of intolerance toward criminals that pervaded the Soviet public was found not only in public meetings and in letters to officials; it was also on prominent display in the press in late 1950s and early 1960s. A prominent example of this came in late 1958 after the Supreme Soviet passed the new "Fundamentals of Criminal Law," the foundational document for the post-Stalin criminal codes in the fifteen union republics . Press reports covering these "Fundamentals," which made many violent criminals and recidivists ineligible for parole and virtually ended the system of workday credits, made clear the reason for enacting such changes.[76] As related in *Pravda*, the chairman of the legislative proposals committee of the Council of the Union D. S. Polianskii declared, "'No leniency or indulgence for dangerous criminals!' is the people's demand. And it is our duty to fulfill it."[77] Echoing this remark, *Izvestiia* published a speech by a Supreme Soviet deputy from Armenia which proclaimed that "excessive leniency, a false humaneness displayed toward the criminal, merely weakens our struggle against crime."[78] Notable here is the definition of leniency toward lawbreakers as a "false humaneness" rather than "socialist humaneness." Even more damningly, B. I. Samsonov reported his inspection of the corrective-labor colonies in Moscow Province, noting that "many convicts speak favorably of places of detention. Some of them state outright that they are quite satisfied with life in the colonies. In their letters they write of the good food, entertainment and good treatment accorded them. Has not too good a life been established in places of detention for those who violate the law and who spoil the life of honest Soviet people? Should we not establish a stricter regimen in the corrective-labor colonies and educate prisoners in the conditions of more arduous labor . . . ?"[79] Clearly, both questions were to be answered in the affirmative.

At the same time, however, the press occasionally reported on criminals being reformed, whether through the influence of society or in corrective-labor institutions. The most important of these was Khrushchev's speech to the Third Writers' Congress in 1959, published on the front page of *Pravda* on 24 May 1959. In this rambling monologue on the duties of the Soviet writer, Khrushchev emphasized the importance of giving people second chances, of believing that "there are no uncorrectable people." "In our conditions we must approach people sympathetically, believe in people, and see our end goal—the struggle for communism," he stated. Khrushchev continued his lecture on the perfectability of man by introducing a former thief-in-law who had repented of his crimes and wanted to live a normal life, but who faced universal distrust and therefore could not make ends meet. Frustrated, he left his job and his family and wrote an appeal to Khrushchev for help, with the implication that he would have to return to a life of crime if none were proffered. In response, Khrushchev met with him, ensured he was given a good-paying job plus a loan with which to build a house, and later learned that he had indeed turned his life around. Simply putting him in prison again would not have solved anything, Khrushchev instructed his audience. "In order to place this person on the correct path," he continued, "it is necessary to believe in man, in his better qualities."[80] Although this story did not deal directly with conditions in corrective-labor institutions, its implications were clear: even the vilest criminal, when he demonstrates a desire to change, should be trusted and treated like a Soviet citizen.[81]

In response to Khrushchev's speech, *Pravda* reported an overwhelmingly positive reader response, publishing several letters praising the first secretary for vision. One, anticipating protest from those who advocated harsher penalties for dangerous criminals, wrote, "This is not liberalism, but rather your unparalleled concern and supreme humaneness for the individual."[82] Echoing Khrushchev's remarks, two *Izvestiia* articles from late 1959 reported that corrective-labor colonies were successfully rehabilitating convicts. The first described the experience of an inmate who, when first admitted to the corrective-labor colony, refused to work. His fellow prisoners challenged him, asking, "Does this mean you've decided to sun yourself as if you were at a resort?" To this he reportedly responded, laughing, "Well, isn't this a resort? It is warm and light, the air is pure and there's food." Notably, the author of the article does nothing to dispel the notion that the colony bore resort-like conditions. Indeed, the protagonist eventually became reformed by the colony school, his ability to serve in the public order section, and by gentle persuasion rather than coercion. The article concludes with a statement from the local oversight commission, who declares, "The procurator, the colony administration, and our commissions are working toward a common goal.... We are correcting and reeducating persons who have committed crimes."[83]

In the second article from the national press in 1959 which portrayed the Gulag in a positive light, the authors noted that deprivation of freedom itself was a harsh punishment reserved for only the worst offenders, but it was geared toward reform, not revenge. According to a letter reportedly sent in by an inmate, "Where once I dreamed of stealing millions, now I dream of something big but completely realistic: becoming a man." Moreover, the authors criticized others in the press who described prison "as some sort of resort."[84] In response to these articles, *Izvestiia* received hundreds of letters from Soviet inhabitants on both sides of the barbed wire, affirming their belief in the reformability of man and their support for reeducating convicts. The article summarizing these letters even mocked those who insisted on harsh punishment for criminals, likening them to gossiping housewives who "talk nonsense whenever they hear about crime reports." Among these, the author continued, were educated yet ignorant men, who howled that "one must not pity the criminals" and that "the chief thing was to put them behind bars and keep them there."[85]

The next article in this series came in March 1960, when *Izvestiia* published excerpts from a series of letters allegedly sent from a prisoner, Irina Papina, to her father. Irina wrote about her difficult life in the colony and the unjustness of her long sentence, but also her newfound penitence and determination to reform. In a particularly poignant moment after her request for pardon had been denied, she wrote, "I am a new person. I want to work and to march in step with the whole people, but they do not trust me." Months later, however, she continued to demonstrate her changed attitude: "I am making a large pillow case. It is turning out quite well. Life will be wonderful. I feel good at work—I am sewing. Work brings me moral satisfaction." In the end, the author of the article concluded, "the strength of our socialist society and its true humaneness lies in the fact that even the punishment inflicted on the criminal helps him to emerge cleansed, to look people straight in the eye and to return to a joyful and honest life where there can be no place for filth and idleness."[86] The authenticity of these letters cannot be verified (even if they were authentic, the prisoner certainly wrote with the knowledge her letters were subject to censorship by the colony administration). Yet the argument here is not that Papina (if such a person even existed) discovered a new, honest life in the colony, but that *Izvestiia* saw fit to publish such a narrative of redemption. It is clear from these stories, very reminiscent of those contained in Maxim Gorky's famous volume on the Belomor Canal, that some belief in the reformability of man through trust and leniency endured in the public consciousness.[87]

The final article to appear in the national press that lauded the possibility of correction through trust, leniency, and the full range of reeducational measures was "The Criminal and Society" by Vadim Monakhov, which appeared in the August 1960 issue of the literary journal *Novyi Mir* (*New World*). Monakhov's article tells the story of Valentin Korsakov, a longtime thief-in-law with numerous convictions. True to his gang, Korsakov refused to work while imprisoned, but eventually a foreman, who was widely respected by the inmates, began to take an interest in Korsakov; he treated Korsakov like a peer rather than a criminal and in time invited him to help out in the workshop. This trust and respect reportedly made a huge impression on the gangster, who turned from his parasitic ways, began working and reading, joined the council of the collective, and eventually returned to an honest working life. Those that continue in crime despite time in the camps, the author concluded, had been "deprived of the one thing that could save them—the trust of society and perspectives for returning to [society] with full rights and as a full-fledged worker."[88] And, echoing Khrushchev, Monakhov proclaimed that "the example of Korsakov and many other former criminals whom I know confirm that, yes, in our current Soviet conditions everyone can be corrected."[89]

Such articles lauding the power of humaneness and leniency in reforming deviants, which blossomed in 1959, represent the apex of the post-Stalin correctional drive. These were soon overtaken, however, by a simultaneous wave of articles calling for strict, even harsh punishments for lawbreakers that began in earnest in 1958 with the aforementioned press reports on the "Fundamentals of Soviet Law." As noted by Thomas Wolfe and as illustrated by the articles just discussed, the press in the Khrushchev era was unleashed to some extent to locate the new Soviet man and investigate how he was formed. By the late 1950s, however, reporters increasingly turned to negative examples highlighting antitheses of the new Soviet man and the means of their degeneration.[90] In this they served not to promote examples of the model citizen, but rather to police the "normative outlines of society." This tendency to demarcate the acceptable margins of behavior was certainly not new to Soviet culture, nor is it a distinctly Soviet or socialist phenomenon. As Kai Erikson notes in his discussion of punishment in early American society, "deviant forms of behavior, by marking the outer edges of group life, give the inner structure its special character and thus supply the framework within which the people of the group develop an orderly sense of their own cultural identity."[91] Seeking to promote this sense of "cultural identity," newspaper reporters in the USSR in the late 1950s began to increasingly define socialist society not by reporting on what it should be, but by reporting on what it was not.

An article from *Izvestiia* in mid-1958 exemplifies well this growing trend of demarcating the boundaries of acceptable society. In it the author reported on a former Gestapo agent whom "the Soviet state, guided by humane principles," amnestied, expecting that he had been reformed. But instead, he soon thereafter committed a vicious murder and was sentenced to death, leading the newspaper to editorialize: "He was a degenerate, a man without honor or conscious, and he did not change."[92] In other words, some people were simply beyond help; for them, reeducation in a corrective-labor facility was without purpose. A similar article from the 23 July 1960 edition of *Literaturnaia Gazeta* (Literary Gazette), a prominent weekly newspaper issued by the Union of Soviet Writers, highlighted the court case of rival gang members in Orel who had been involved in a vicious fight. The author complained that instead of meting out the appropriate punishment, all involved in the case "had been seized by a Christian all-forgiveness. Not humaneness, not a desire to help people who had strayed for the first time, but an all-forgiveness that can lead to nothing but harm in the fight against crime."[93] Notable in both articles is the use of the term humane or humaneness, which is clearly no longer associated with socialist legality. Although humaneness is still lauded to some extent as an admirable trait, it is also criticized as excessively naïve and insufficient. The humaneness of the Soviet state, in other words, must be tempered by a rational evaluation of internal threats and not descend to the level of "liberalism."

This trend of highlighting the ineffectiveness of leniency in rehabilitating criminals in the press culminated with the appearance of "Man behind Bars" in the 27 August 1960 edition of *Sovetskaia Rossiia* (*Soviet Russia*). The authors of this article—well-known reporter Natal'ia Il'inichna Monchadskaia and the unknown I. Kasiukov—introduced to their readers the supposedly comfortable life of unrepentant recidivists in a strict-regimen corrective-labor colony who were merely biding time until their release. Seven-hour workdays, excellent wages, clean sheets, curtains, radios, games, grass lawns, flowerbeds, volleyball, soccer matches, daily films, guitars, conjugal visits, unlimited and "appetizing" food, and a well-stocked hospital led the authors to exclaim in indignation that this was "not a prison, but home with all the comforts!" Calling for a much harsher regimen, including hard manual labor instead of sewing, wooden planks instead of mattresses, and prison uniforms in place of civilian clothes, Monchadskaia and Kasiukov concluded: "We visited the places of confinement and saw 'the men behind bars.' But there were no bars. Is this humaneness or indulgent pity? Is it not because of such soft-heartedness that these people give society so much trouble and themselves remain adrift from life?"[94] In response to these questions, the newspaper reported receiving one thousand letters in support of harsher treatment of inmates and only one hundred (mostly from criminals themselves, the editor assured his readers) that disagreed. Selected as representative of the majority, a letter from a Leningrad metalworker (who better to set policy in a workers' state?) declared: "What the recidivist needs is a hard plank-bed without mattress, bars, a harsh schedule, iron-clad discipline and a ten- or twelve-hour day of heavy manual labor. Let the bandit feel that no one means to coddle him."[95]

The newspaper that published "Man behind Bars," *Sovetskaia Rossiia,* was relatively new. Launched in 1956 and operated by the Russian Bureau of the Central Committee of the Communist Party, it quickly gained traction as a venue for conservative thought within the Russian Republic (later becoming a leading publisher of the village prose movement) and eventually boasted a circulation that exceeded that of *Izvestiia* and rivaled that of *Pravda.* But significantly, "Man behind Bars" had not been approved by the Central Committee. Although this was certainly not the first article to treat conditions in the Gulag since Stalin's death, the topic was still considered highly sensitive. As high-ranking Central Committee bureaucrats Vasilii Petrovich Moskovskii and Vladimir Iosifovich Tishchenko pointed out in a note dated 20 September 1960, the editor of *Sovetskaia Rossiia,* Ivan Stepanovich Pustovalov, should not have broached such a theme in the national press without explicit permission. Worse, Moskovskii and Tishchenko charged, the article directly opposed Soviet policy in penal affairs by attacking recent reforms and calling for harsher conditions in the country's corrective-labor facilities.[96] On 28 September 1960 the Central Committee approved the stance taken by Moskovskii and Tishchenko, but Pustovalov remained defiant, claiming that penal affairs should be opened to broader public scrutiny and that the article was in fact in line with Khrushchev's address to the Writers' Congress. Those who worked hard to redeem themselves in the colonies should be treated with humaneness, he charged, but the point of "Man behind Bars" was to make clear that those who continued to lead lives of crime and dependency while incarcerated should not be spoiled by "rotten liberalism."[97] In the end, the Central Committee decided against Pustovalov, agreeing with a subsequent note by Moskovskii that claimed the article failed to place its criticisms within the framework of the existing (and recently passed) legislation governing crime and punishment.[98] Notably, however, *Sovetskaia Rossiia* never published a retraction of the article or a follow-up article to mitigate the harsh conclusion of "Man behind Bars." Thus, although the tough stance toward prisoners taken in the article was condemned by the Central Committee, it was allowed to stand as the new party line in penal affairs.

Months later the same theme of excessive leniency in the Gulag was repeated in *Komsomolskaia Pravda,* the newspaper of the Communist Youth League, which published a letter from a woman whose son was murdered but the murderer had been paroled after serving only four years of his ten-year sentence. Worse still, the murderer himself admitted to the author of the article: "I was kept under guard only for the first two years. The rest of the time I lived in the colony's free zone. I earned 1,500 rubles to 1,700 rubles a month loading lumber. I lived excellently. At home I have lost a great deal of weight. There I looked much better."[99] In one final example of the wave of press attacks on excessive leniency in the camps and colonies of the Gulag, *Izvestiia* in mid-1961 chronicled the exploits of a recidivist in Armenia by the name of Mnatsakan Manukian. He had been imprisoned three times but had been released early each time, whether by amnesty, pardon, or through workday credits. Convicted a fourth time and sentenced to one and half years deprivation of freedom, after only two months he was deconvoyed by the local corrective-labor colony, made a chauffeur, and allowed to drive all over Yerevan. Such unjustified "liberalism" swiftly resulted in the vicious beating and attempted murder of an invalid doctor.[100] Finally, with a new fifteen-year conviction, the author concluded, justice had been served. But the matter did not end there. A month later *Izvestiia* reported to its readers that the colony commander, his deputy, and the head of the Armenian penal system had all received reprimands.[101] By 1961 the point had clearly been made. While petitions for harsher treatment of criminals continued to flow to Moscow, the national press, though still clamoring for harsher sentences, remained virtually silent until late 1962 on the treatment of inmates.[102]

The Campaign in the Corridors of Power

The evidence on Khrushchev and his colleagues concerning this counterreform shift in criminal justice policy is scant and somewhat contradictory. Elie argues that a high-level power struggle between "conservatives" and "reformists" erupted in the late 1950s, with the conservatives by 1961 convincing Khrushchev that "liberalism" in the Gulag had gone too far.[103] This is certainly true to some extent, yet as Dobson rightly notes many of the "conservatives" of the late 1950s were actually "reformists" that Khrushchev himself had appointed, and even among the top leadership there is remarkable fluidity in terms of penal policy orientation.[104] To a great extent they were reacting to events as they unfolded amidst the rapid reforms of the 1950s and to the expressions of harsh justice from the public described above. The actual decision-making process that shifted criminal and penal policy from a soft line to a hard line, therefore, is often difficult to discern. As opposed to his firm policy decisions of 1954–56, Khrushchev ultimately was reactive rather than proactive in 1959–61.

Whatever the nature of the actual decision making, by 1961 the top leadership in the Soviet Union mostly supported the "camp is not a resort" campaign. The Committee of State Security (KGB) chief Ivan Serov had always been a staunch opponent of granting privileges to inmates, even those who demonstrated a desire to reform. In his 1956 commentary to Dudorov's proposed reorganization of the Gulag system, for instance, he noted that allowing well-behaved inmates to live outside the zone only weakened the regimen and spoiled the reeducational significance of the colonies.[105] Others began to adopt a similar line of reasoning in the late 1950s. Kliment Voroshilov in 1959, for instance, complained that criminals were getting sentences of fifteen years but were freed after only serving five, often by abusing the workday credit system. As evidenced by the subsequent crimes committed by many of these released prisoners, Voroshilov concluded that such privileges were clearly not having the desired effect.[106] Also that year he recommended the death penalty for a Nazi collaborator against Rudenko's recommendation of a lengthy prison term. "You want to reeducate him," Voroshilov charged, "but this person deserves punishment. I don't understand why the Procuracy has become weak."[107]

Yet Voroshilov is a prime example of top officials not always falling neatly into "reformers" or "conservatives." On 26 December 1959, while discussing the ramifications of the "Fundamentals of Criminal Law," Voroshilov showed continued devotion to "liberalism," reminding his colleagues that although he supported harsh penalties for violent offenders, "if there is hope for their correction, we should move in that direction."[108] Leonid Brezhnev too, as late as 1960, can be found expressing his faith in the correctional power of leniency toward lawbreakers. After hearing a report on the 1959 commissions that released hundreds of thousands of minor offenders from the Gulag, the very sort of unwarranted "liberalism" that the "camp is not a resort" campaign focused on, Brezhnev remarked that "the Central Committee with its decision provided the opportunity to perform a great reeducational work. The very fact of freeing these people is truly a big reeducational measure that has a huge meaning."[109]

Ultimately, though, even Khrushchev's hope in correctionalism, most prominently exhibited in the reforms of the 1950s together with his speech to the Third Writers' Congress already discussed, was not unconditional. Soon after the conclusions of the releases of 1956, which he personally pushed through, Khrushchev lamented in a 6 December 1956 Presidium meeting: "On releases from prison and exile—some of them do not deserve it."[110] And even at the same time that his speech to the Writers' Congress was being published, Khrushchev's lack of tolerance for deviants is hinted at in a speech reprinted in both *Pravda* and *Izvestiia*. Responding to W. Averell Harriman's request to see the construction of the Bratsk Hydroelectric Plant, Khrushchev declared: "There has been and still is much clamor in the bourgeois press to the effect that construction in our country is carried out by persons serving time in camps for crimes. Of course the USSR still has people in prison for criminal acts, or for stealing. But . . . [y]ou won't build the Bratsk Hydroelectric Station with such people. This requires the great labor and ebullient energy of indefatigable patriots."[111] Although this is not an unambiguous rejection of policies of leniency toward inmates, Khrushchev is clearly exhibiting frustration with the penal system. And by distinguishing "such people" sharply from "patriots" of the Soviet Union, he casts inmates not as reformable citizens but as an underclass of ungrateful parasites.

The publication of "Man behind Bars" in 1960 appears to have been a turning point for Khrushchev and others who wavered between harsher and more lenient penal policies. Whether because they feared the implications of an about-face in the public press after so many letters to the editor expressing support for "Man behind Bars" had been published, or because they had become convinced by growing evidence of recidivism following the mass release of 1959 that the "liberal" policies of the mid-1950s were failing, Khrushchev and other Soviet leaders from this point forward moved swiftly in the direction of harsher measures of punishment for convicts. Although the article had not been approved by the Central Committee, it officially sanctioned the growing trend toward public impatience with thieves and hooligans, rapists and murderers. Rather than fight against this sentiment, Khrushchev decided to embrace it. As Viacheslav Mikhailovich Molotov late in life cynically remarked about Khrushchev, he was easily swayed by public opinion.[112]

Behind closed doors Khrushchev's new attitude of harshness toward lawbreakers was on prominent display in 1961. At a Presidium meeting held on 17 June that year, Khrushchev expressed outrage at a criminal who was released after serving only five years out of a fifteen-year sentence. "I'm ashamed to look the people (*narod*) in their eyes," he exclaimed, after cursing out the "liberal" Rudenko for allowing this to happen. Khrushchev also lashed out at chairman of the Supreme Court Gorkin for his hesitancy to apply the death penalty: "You are afraid, afraid of hooligans, and afraid that we have barbarian laws. I am for barbarian laws; when there aren't any murderers, then we won't need barbarian laws, but for now we do." And, demonstrating his continued selective use of even the repressive aspects of Stalin's reign, Khrushchev announced that "Stalin took the correct position in such matters. . . . One must beat his enemies accurately and without mercy. . . . We need to fight, and we will fight vigorously (*zhestko*), and the more vigorously we will fight, the more influence we will have on reeducation," he concluded. Thus, reeducation was to take place not just in the camps but through the supposed deterrence of capital punishment. In relation to large-scale currency speculators, for instance, Khrushchev called for death: "Why pay to feed and guard him for fifteen years?"[113]

This rapid about-face from his 1959 speech to the Third Writers' Congress was expressed not just to Khrushchev's inner circle. Although toned down somewhat for public consumption, Khrushchev made similar statements at the Twenty-Second Party Congress later in 1961. Calling for a fiercer struggle against crime and parasitism, Khrushchev labeled criminals and drunkards society's "weeds."[114] The policy of retribution against lawbreakers and the idea that harsh punishment actually facilitated the reeducation of inmates thus received official sanction. If the campaign to eliminate privileges in the camps did not originate with Khrushchev and his colleagues (and there is no direct evidence that it did), by 1960–61 it had received their full blessing. Khrushchev at the time was searching for a populist policy stance that would help bolster his standing among the general population and the state apparatus after a series of perceived blunders.[115] This rapid swing to harsh justice after just having proclaimed leniency toward and trust in lawbreakers, however, likely only reinforced the idea that he was inconsistent and unpredictable.

The Reports of 1960

In late 1960, with the public, press, academics, the Procuracy, and many MVD officials clamoring for harsher treatment of criminals, the Central Committee issued a damning assessment of the state of the Gulag and commissioned two sets of reports to provide detailed recommendations on how to reform the Gulag system. The first came from inspectors—largely from the Procuracy, Supreme Court, and Ministry of Justice—dispatched to various penal institutions while the second set was composed by provincial party organizations tasked with meeting with their party counterparts within the Gulag and inspecting their local camps and colonies.[116] Fueled by the press, the public, and their own indignation at the real or perceived "privileges" enjoyed by prisoners and the Gulag's lack of control over their behavior, the central inspectors and local party personnel were equally condemnatory in their appraisal of the state of the corrective-labor institutions.[117] Crime and regimen infractions were rampant, there was no strict separation between recidivists and first-timers, prisoners enjoyed numerous rights and privileges but had seemingly few obligations, and, in the end, the inmates were not being consistently reformed. As two inspectors from the Russian Procuracy noted, the Novosibirsk MVD had recently ordered that colony stores could sell unlimited quantities of bread, meat, milk, sugar, tea, and other products and prisoners were receiving money transfers and numerous packages to supplement their earnings. One inmate convicted of embezzling a million rubles was receiving 300–500 rubles per month through transfers plus 1–2 packages stuffed with 8–10 kilograms of food products each per month. Another reportedly remarked to inspectors that the only thing lacking was the ability to go home on Saturday and return Monday morning.[118] In short, as procurators inspecting the Novosibirsk colonies concluded, prisoners did not feel as though they were being punished; living conditions were so good that inmates were not being corrected but learning how to be parasites.[119]

As a result of these findings, the majority of suggestions made in the reports of late 1960 centered on creating harsher living conditions for prisoners. Some proposed eliminating the camp stores; most at least wanted them to offer only a small selection of necessary products. Others wanted to limit or take away visitation rights, especially conjugal visits, noting that prisoners were choosing to visit not with their wives but with lovers. Proposals were made to severely curtail the number of care packages, abolish money transfers to prisoners, eliminate the commercial dining halls and self-service kitchens, and institute penalty rations for regimen violators. Some spoke out against televisions, excessive radio programming, and "entertainment" or "artistic" (as opposed to educational) films. Many lobbied for prison uniforms for all inmates or at least the most dangerous ones, together with prohibitions on jewelry (including watches) and using one's own bedding. A few proposals suggested that prisoners pay for medical care or cultural activities; one advocated forced treatment for drug addicts. Some inspectors and party workers criticized the use of sporting and cultural events, which according to Sverdlovsk party officials "more often serve as a way of entertaining [the prisoners], not as a way of reeducating [them]."[120] A few even criticized unrestricted access to colony libraries (which contained pernicious influences such as detective and spy novels and even foreign publications) and to newspapers and magazines. Many advocated the creation in each colony of cell blocks (often referred to by their old name of strengthened-regimen barracks or BURs) with a harsher regimen, only hard physical labor, and lowered rations, where prisoners could be placed by the administration for a set period of time for violating the regimen. Multiple inspection teams recommended that recidivists who did not yield to correctional measures be sent to special-regimen colonies in the Far North for a number of years on hard labor.

Working conditions and wages were also attacked. Nearly all reports suggested that workday credits be abolished for good. Inspectors assigned to Novosibirsk were appalled that some prisoners were earning more than 1,000 rubles per month.[121] Moreover, they charged, it was offensive that criminals with multiple offenses were provided a well-equipped workshop and engaged in the specialized production of radio components when many free citizens were engaged in manual labor. Citing the chief engineer for the colony who charged that such work "was completely not conducive to labor reeducation," the inspectors argued that recidivists such as these should be given only hard physical labor.[122] This idea found echo in other reports. The inspection committee for Iaroslavl Province, for example, said that recidivists engaged in specialized rather than hard labor "do not feel the seriousness of the punishment determined for them."[123] Not surprisingly, some proposed to restore hard labor (*katorga*) for repeat and dangerous offenders; others insisted on a maximum wage for inmates. Many reports found it unnatural that prisoners worked only as many hours as free laborers, with some proposing nine-, ten-, or even twelve-hour days. On a similar note, one proposed making prisoners work two unpaid hours each day improving the colony (since they would no longer be standing in line at the store or preparing their own food). The inspection report from Kalinin Province complained that prisoners were being driven to work even though it was only 3 kilometers away.[124] Some proposals focused on making the vast majority of invalids work. The idea of instituting a penalty ration for those not fulfilling their work norms and especially refusing to work (including by self-mutilation) found widespread support in the reports. Some proposed stricter limits on deconvoying prisoners, calling for it to be available, for example, to only first-time criminals in for minor crimes or to only 10 percent of prisoners in a particular institution.

Not all suggestions contained in these reports attacked the perceived excesses and privileges enjoyed by inmates. Several proposed mandatory education up to seven or ten grades, some called for more societal involvement in the colonies, others for more production zones in the colonies to eliminate the need for contract work, and a few noted the need to make Gulag officials more responsible for reeducation. A couple proposed new forms of encouragement such as the title of "Outstanding Member of the Subdivision" that could be used to inspire prisoners to work hard and follow the regimen regulations. Others suggested greater scientific inquiry into methods of reeducation. It is clear, therefore, that some commitment to reeducation through nonpenal measures remained. In fact, there was one notable exception to the hundreds of reports calling for harsher conditions: the party organization of the Komi Autonomous Soviet Socialist Republic proposed the retention of lightened regimen and living outside the zone as part of a true "progressive" system by which all prisoners would be transferred from harsher to lighter regimens as they became "corrected" and approached release back to society.[125] The overall tenor of the 1960 reports to the Central Committee, however, ran contrary to these suggestions. The "progressive" system was rejected and reeducation was to occur not on the basis of trust and leniency, but through strict obedience and relatively harsh living and working conditions. Criminals were to be constantly reminded, the reports underlined, that they were, in fact, being punished for crimes against society.

The 1961 Statute on Prisons and Corrective-Labor Colonies

These reports and the "camp is not a resort" campaign as a whole culminated in the 3 April 1961 decree of the Central Committee and Council of Ministers "On Measures for Improving the Activity of Corrective-Labor Colonies of the Ministries of Internal Affairs of the Union Republics," which accompanied a new model Statute on Prisons and Corrective-Labor Colonies, the third such statute since Stalin's death. The order noted that the Gulag was not fulfilling its mission of reeducating convicts and preparing them to return to "an honest working life." Penal administrators, it continued, failed to account for changing demographics in the Gulag: more than half of all inmates had multiple convictions or were incarcerated for serious crimes and this contingent was prone to committing additional crimes in the camps and to breaking all manner of regimen regulations by gambling, drinking, abusing narcotics, and so forth. Furthermore, echoing a common complaint from both the Stalin and early Khrushchev periods, the existing regimen types in the Gulag could hardly be distinguished one from another, resulting in different types of prisoners being held in virtually identical conditions. And those conditions, which offered "various sorts of unjustified privileges" and "excesses in cultural and living conditions" did not serve the goals "of punishment and the reeducation of prisoners." It is notable that the aim of punishment in a retributive sense is stated so explicitly. Without doubt, the end of the policy of liberalism had arrived.

After reaffirming that the central mission of the Gulag was to prepare prisoners to be "useful members of Soviet society," the 1961 model statute introduced a number of reforms that corresponded closely to the recommendations found in the December 1960 reports. The difference between it and the 1958 statute it replaced was evident already in the introductory section: the 1958 admonition to treat prisoners humanely and fairly and to reward those who entered "the path to correction" was simply omitted in the 1961 edition, as was the explicit prohibition against measures that brought "physical suffering or the debasement of human dignity."[126] These principles were maintained, as other documents attest, but their glaring omission in the statute, the governing document for places of confinement, is telling of the new emphasis on retribution and a harsh regimen.[127] The section on regimen, however, spelled out in detail the most critical of the 1961 reforms. First, the 1961 statute replaced the 1958 statement on what the regimen was supposed to accomplish ("creation of the best possible conditions for correction and reeducation of prisoners") with the declaration that the regimen is supposed "*to not only punish,* but also cultivate in the prisoners discipline, a need for labor, and conscious obedience to the rules of socialist society."[128] In this manner retributive punishment was heralded and enhanced control based on strict regulations replaced leniency as the primary mode of reeducation. Delving into greater specifics, instead of lightened, standard, and strict-regimen types, the 1961 statute provided for standard (for first-time prisoners convicted of minor crimes); strengthened (for first-timers guilty of serious crimes); strict (for those with prior convictions); and special regimens (for "especially dangerous recidivists" and prisoners with commuted death sentences).[129] Thus, one additional regimen type was added to allow for greater differentiation while lightened regimen was eliminated.[130] More importantly, the 1961 statute rejected the "progressive" system of detention by decreeing that prisoners were not allowed to be transferred from one colony to another based on behavior.[131] Moreover, whereas the 1958 statute allowed for various regimens to exist within one colony to facilitate application of the "progressive" system, the 1961 statute discontinued this practice. The 1961 statute also reintroduced into colony operations the cell block, where unruly inmates could be held in prison-like conditions, and the use of lowered rations as punishment for regimen infractions.[132] Commercial dining halls and public kitchens for prisoner use were abolished, as were the practices of providing shortened workdays before holidays and days off and of granting vacations to well-behaved inmates. Finally, money transfers to prisoners and possession of valuables were forbidden, rules governing deconvoying were made more stringent, films for prisoners were to be strictly reeducational in nature, penalty rations for infractions were introduced, and the standard ration was reduced from around 3,000 calories to 2,413.[133]

The regulations governing each regimen type further exhibit the new emphasis on enacting retribution and creating a strict set of internal regulations. As opposed to one visit per month and unlimited correspondence, package, and store privileges as set forth for standard regimen in 1958, the 1961 statute provided for one public visit every two months, one conjugal visit with a close relative every three months, only one package (to weigh no more than 5 kilograms) every two months, and store purchases from earned wages of no more than 10 rubles per month.[134] These restrictions became more stringent for prisoners in strengthened, strict, and special regimens. Those on strengthened regimen, for example, were given only one public visit every three months, one conjugal visit every six months, one package every three months, and they could only use 7 rubles per month in the store.[135] For strict regimen the conditions were one public visit every four months, one conjugal visit every year, no packages, only 5 rubles per month at the store, and curtailed correspondence rights—only two outgoing letters per month. Last, special-regimen prisoners were restricted to one public visit every six months, no conjugal visits, no packages, 3 rubles per month in the store, and only one outgoing letter per month. Moreover, special-regimen colonies were to be located far from population centers and their prisoners would be held in cells, wear special (striped) clothing, and engage in hard physical labor.

Soon after the model statute was released, the Supreme Soviets of each union republic passed their own versions that differed only very slightly from the original. During the rewriting of legal codes and statutes Soviet judicial officials often expressed concern that republican law codes should be similar to each other yet not exactly the same. Too much similarity would undermine the supposedly federal nature of the Soviet state, yet too much variance could undermine the feeling of socialist unity that was supposed to prevail in Soviet governance. Brezhnev found efforts to bring harmony to these conflicting goals somewhat amusing. In a 3 December 1961 meeting of the Presidium of the Supreme Soviet, which he chaired, he first joked that different climates explained the differences in criminal codes, then, when told that the Russian code allowed up to five years' incarceration for fraud [obman] whereas the Georgian code capped the penalty at six months, he quipped: "That means that our fraud is better than Georgian fraud."[136]

Minor differences among the new republican statutes can be seen in a few examples. The lone substantive difference between the model statute and the Estonian statute, for instance, was that the latter required special clothing not just for especially dangerous recidivists, but also for those held in prison and in strengthened-regimen colonies.[137] The Lithuanian statute included additional detail on parole eligibility and the injunction that "all prisoners are required to work."[138] The Russian statute, meanwhile, set a minimum of 1.75 square meters of living space per prisoner, a specific omitted in the model statute (but a notable decrease from the 2.0 square meters mandated previously by the Gulag).[139] Accompanying the statutes were more detailed sets of instructions clarifying some of the general principles set forth in the statutes. The Lithuanian instructions advised Gulag officials "to not allow prisoners to lead a parasitic way of life." They also allowed for a minimum of 1.5 square meters of space, mandated uniforms for all prisoners and shaved heads for all male inmates, and permitted Gulag officials to mandate unpaid labor for improving and cleaning penal institutions.[140] The desired result of the 1961 model statute and resultant republican statutes is clear: no more lightened regimen, no more living outside the zone, no more ten-day vacations from work, no more indiscriminate deconvoying, no more endless streams of care packages, no more, in the words of Igor Karpets, director of the Soviet Union's chief criminology institute, "babying the zeks [prisoners]."[141]

Farewell to Springtime in the Tundra?

Shortly after the Central Committee approved the 1961 statute governing the Soviet Union's places of confinement, the Supreme Soviet on 5 May 1961 passed a law that complemented the turn away from leniency for criminals.[142] Counterfeiting and grand theft or embezzlement of especially large sums were made capital crimes (joining treason, espionage, diversion, terrorism, banditry, and aggravated premeditated murder), as was a new crime covering "actions that disorganize the work of corrective-labor institutions." Although seemingly amorphous, this was clarified to mean attacking guards, administrators, or fellow prisoners who had "stood on the path to correction," or actively belonging to a gang that did the same. Mishutin from the Procuracy requested that the "disorganization" clause be applied to prisoners who refused to work, boasted tattoos with anti-Soviet content, and otherwise caused trouble for the camp administration; this request resulted in an amendment passed on 6 April 1963 that allowed the crime of "disorganization" to be applied to those who maliciously violated the colony regimen, lived a parasitic way of life, and bore anti-Soviet tattoos.[143] In expanding the list of crimes for which the death penalty could be applied, the 5 March 1961 decree signified not only exasperation with the continued phenomenon of serious crime but also reduced belief in the correctional power of the country's penal institutions. Significantly in this regard, the decree also denied the possibility of parole to those who committed new crimes while on parole, especially dangerous recidivists and those convicted of especially heinous crimes such as banditry, counterfeiting, currency speculation, large-scale embezzlement, aggravated premeditated murder, the rape of a minor, bribery, and state crimes. It also provided the possibility for judges to add two to five years of exile to deprivation of freedom sentences for a variety of state crimes. Brezhnev, as chairman of the Presidium of the Supreme Soviet, reported receiving numerous letters from citizens commending this law.[144]

The 1961 statute on colonies and prisons was also followed by additional laws aimed at increasing punishments for social deviants. After languishing for years, the antiparasite campaign was revived, culminating in new laws in the Soviet Union's largest republics in May and June 1961 that punished those who "are avoiding socially useful work and are leading an antisocial parasitic way of life."[145] According to Supreme Soviet discussions, such measures, based on the principle of "he who does not work shall not eat," had the effect of scaring a lot of people into employment.[146] Later in 1961 and in 1962 the Supreme Soviet continued to increase penalties for a variety of crimes, including foreign currency speculation, attempted murder of a policeman, aggravated rape, and bribery.[147] Although, as Harold Berman argues, this trend toward harsher penalties for social deviants and criminals was significant, it did not fully undermine the legal reforms of the 1950s, protected as they were by "a vast structure of procedures and rights."[148]

A similar conclusion may be drawn regarding penal policy. The 1961 statute and subsequent legislation certainly demarcated a clear shift in the penal policy of the Soviet Union. While not abandoning the goal of reeducation, the statute placed great emphasis on the reforming power of a repressive regimen and affirmed that prisons and corrective-labor colonies were places not just of correction but of retribution. Significantly, while providing for strict separation between first-timers and recidivists (and between those convicted of minor and more serious crimes), regimen conditions for virtually every category of prisoners became harsher. Thus, whereas the MVD's campaign to eliminate inmate privileges had focused primarily on gangsters and other hardened criminals, the new statute, drawing on public anger, subjected even minor criminals to harsh new regulations. Moreover, the progressive system of incarceration, which called for prisoners to be moved up or down the regimen scale depending on their behavior, was mostly abolished in favor of holding inmates in the same institution for the duration of their sentence. The very worst prisoners could still be transferred for a time to prison due to persistent regimen violations and prisoners exhibiting good behavior could be granted a few extra privileges, but this provided little transition to conditions approximating freedom as called for by "progressive" penology. Just as the 1954 and 1958 statutes denoted a significant shift away from the late Stalinist Gulag, so too did the 1961 statute demarcate a sharp break with certain policies of the 1950s. Yet this does not mean that the reforms of the 1950s were wholly undone by the counterreforms of the early 1960s. As the next chapter will detail, many of the reforms of the 1950s remained intact, a few of the more onerous provisions of the 1961 statute were reversed in the following years, and Gulag administrators were often lax in applying the new strictures called for by the statute. Ultimately, the transformations of the mid-1950s had altered the penal system to such an extent that a return to the conditions of the early 1950s was neither possible, nor desired.

As she endured the new regimen created by the 1961 statute, Irina Verblovskaia noted the inescapable irony that as the "Thaw" was progressing on the outside, the camp regimen was becoming harsher.[149] Indeed, the "camp is not a resort" campaign of the late 1950s and early 1960s coincided with the buildup to the Twenty-Second Party Congress, which infused into Soviet society a new optimism for the future. Yet this belief in the perfectibility of man and society, embodied by Khrushchev's speech to the Third Writers' Congress in 1959 and the stunning prediction of communism by 1980, was accompanied by great impatience with those who stood in the way of such dreams.[150] As voiced by an oversight commission member from Moscow Province in 1959, "we won't be taking any thieves, bandits, or robbers forward with us to the future communist system."[151] This duality of enthusiasm and impatience may have even been chosen around 1960 as a ruling technique; as Meade, drawing on Émile Durkheim, notes, "the attitude of hostility toward the lawbreaker has the unique advantage of uniting all members of the community in the emotional solidarity of aggression."[152] While this intolerance for social deviants was building, the Gulag was in the process of eliminating its criminal gangs and cracking down on lawlessness in the camps. Notably, when these two campaigns coalesced in the 1961 statute, which declared the value of retribution in terms of deterrence and the correctional influence of a harsh regimen, the control mechanisms designed for the worst offenders were extended to the entire inmate population. Thus, even those deemed most reformable—first-time prisoners convicted of minor crimes—ended up with harsher living conditions than those enjoyed by many violent recidivists in the 1950s.

Significantly, and perhaps most surprisingly, the MVD was a voice of moderation during the campaign against privileges and in its aftermath, with the political elite, the press, many penologists, the Procuracy, and the general public all taking harder stances toward lawbreakers. The organs of repression in the Khrushchev era, led by both economic and reeducational concerns, emerge paradoxically as less repressive than society at large. Thus, while Verblovskaia likened the liberalization of the Gulag in the mid-1950s to springtime in the tundra, with flowers on the surface but impenetrable permafrost beneath, it seems that the frozen tundra was not simply an entrenched Gulag bureaucracy, as she implies, but Soviet society in general.[153] De-Stalinization for them meant, among other things, consumer goods, prefabricated housing, and a freer cultural and intellectual climate, but they never accepted the new attitude of leniency toward law-breakers. Even as the Soviet public rejected the arbitrary repression of Stalin's rule, they supported his tough approach toward lawbreakers. For ordinary Soviet citizens, "liberalism" toward criminals only meant more crime on the streets, more embezzlement at the workplace, and more corruption in positions of power. Thus, while the MVD worked to retain the emphasis on reeducation, they ultimately lost out to a range of constituencies who retained the tough-on-crime psychological legacy of Stalinism.

Perhaps not surprisingly, the "camp-as-resort" trope outlived the counterre-form campaign of the late 1950s, especially among former Gulag administrators. During the debate surrounding the 1962 publication of Solzhenitsyn's *One Day in the Life of Ivan Denisovich*, for instance, A. G. Panchuk, a retired Gulag offi-cial, attacked the author in a letter to the editor: "Well, what did you expect? Perhaps you thought, Solzhenitsyn, that a camp is a sanatorium or something of the kind? Having committed a grave crime against the state, you would like to stay warm, to be well fed and decently clothed, not to work, and to serve your term in that fashion?"[154] This questioning is significant because Panchuk was responding not to an account of the late-1950s Gulag, the target of the "camp is not a resort" campaign, but to Solzhenitsyn's portrayal of the late-Stalinist Gu-lag. Thus, this new concept of the camp-as-resort was applied retroactively to justify the harshness of the prior regime. Indeed, even after the fall of the Soviet Union, in justifying his service as camp commander of Ozerlag under both Stalin and Khrushchev, Sergei Kuzmich Evstigneev repeated a similar senti-ment. Referencing a famous resort for children of the Pioneer Organization of the Soviet Union, he defended his actions as camp commander with the simple argument: "the corrective-labor camp is not 'Artek.'"[155]

A KHRUSHCHEVIAN SYNTHESIS

The Birth of the Late Soviet Penal System

> So long as prisons and madhouses exist someone must be shut up
> in them. If not you, I. If not I, some third person. Wait till in the
> distant future prisons and madhouses no longer exist, and there will
> be neither bars on the windows nor hospital gowns. Of course, that
> time will come sooner or later.

—Anton Chekhov, "Ward No. 6"

On 22 May 1962, Vasilii Aleksandrovich Samsonov, head of the Procuracy's department for oversight over places of confinement, drafted a futuristic vision of the Soviet correctional system. Looking toward the advent of communism in 1980, the target year set by Khrushchev at the Twenty-Second Party Congress, Samsonov envisioned certain concrete steps that would need to take place first by 1970, then by 1980, for communism to be achieved in the penal sphere. In the first period, according to this plan, crime would be largely rooted out of Soviet society due to rapid growth in the material prosperity, cultural level, and political consciousness of the Soviet citizenry. Minor crimes would be increasingly dealt with through noncustodial forms of correction, thus eliminating the need for standard- and eventually strengthened-regimen colonies. Prisons would also be liquidated, leaving only investigatory isolators (pretrial detention facilities), and those inmates who had been sentenced to prison would be sent to strict- or special-regimen colonies. Here, persuasion would serve as the primary form of reeducation, but "more severe measures of coercion" would also be used on some prisoners. Significantly, this work would be administered by pedagogues, legal professionals, psychologists, and medics, all properly prepared with college education and the interpersonal skills needed to work with hardened criminals. They, in turn, would be supported by strengthened oversight commissions and sponsoring organizations, in addition to local party and labor union associations.

In Samsonov's second period, from 1970–80, the strict- and special-regimen colonies would slowly disappear, with no new inmates arriving and the remaining inmates being reeducated and reintroduced to society through a period of exile. A few designated places of confinement would unfortunately remain because, as Samsonov reminds, as long as capitalist countries existed they would continue to plant spies and saboteurs among the honest workers of the Soviet Union. But with this lone exception, crime in Soviet society would no longer exist by 1980. Those found guilty of certain "excesses" from this point forward would not be considered criminals but would only be censored by comrades' courts and perhaps kept for a short period of time in special barracks attached to their workplace which would be administered by local social organizations. Long-term incarceration controlled by a central agency such as the Ministry of Internal Affairs (MVD) would simply not be needed. Perhaps in an attempt to excuse himself from such wild optimism, Samsonov concluded the report by recommending scientific investigation into how precisely the penal system and the crime that fed it would wither away into oblivion. It appears, however, that this plan for eliminating the Soviet Gulag was simply filed away in the archive, never to be seen again until 2008 when a graduate student from the United States discovered it. Like countless other hopelessly optimistic projections from the Khrushchev period, Samsonov's dream remained just that.[1]

The early to mid-1960s was certainly an era of idealism in the Soviet Union, fueled by rising standards of living, increased productivity, new scientific discoveries, and technological advances. As expressed by journalist Vladimir Pozner, "there was magic in the air . . . an uplifting optimism, even a certainty, that things were going to be absolutely wonderful. . . . Travelling across the country, I was struck again and again by the upbeat atmosphere I encountered. . . . This was genuine euphoria on a national scale."[2] Yet this euphoria ultimately did not translate into the penal sphere. Contrary to Samsonov's vision (and Andrey Ragin's dream in the Chekhov short story quoted in the epigraph), prisons were not closed; colonies of various regimen levels persisted; a new corps of hyperqualified personnel was not recruited; and crime remained a perpetual and serious thorn in the side of the communist vision. The Gulag did not fade away into oblivion, but remained a testament to the failure of Soviet socialism in achieving a more harmonious society. Communism would not be built in the lifetime of Samsonov and his contemporaries, and just administering socialism consumed all their attention.

Indeed, apart from this lone document, the Gulag administrations, now decentralized to the fifteen union republics, together with their oversight bodies, remained firmly engrossed in present problems. The most pressing of these was putting into practice the new regulations from the 1961 model statute governing the camps and colonies of the penal system, a process complicated by a growing inmate population that strained resources. The Gulag also remained deeply committed to economic production, both as a means of self-sustainability and as a method of reeducation. And the aim of reeducation took new twists in the early 1960s, perhaps most intriguingly with the revitalization of self-governing institutions and with the introduction of a campaign aimed at prompting inmates to confess to crimes for which they had not been prosecuted. Last, the Gulag near the end of Khrushchev's reign introduced a new type of minimum-security penal institution and a new form of early release. Taken in total, these changes reflect the continued negotiation among the three competing aims of the Gulag: economics, reeducation, and security. Moreover, they aimed at stabilizing and professionalizing the Gulag both institutionally and culturally, thus putting setting the stage for the less innovative years of the Brezhnev era.

The Decentralized Gulag

In discussing the Gulag of the 1960s it is important to remember that the Gulag technically no longer existed, at least at the All-Union level. Disbanded in January 1960, the MVD of the Soviet Union and its Gulag administration had passed on its administrative functions to the MVDs of the fifteen union republics. In 1962 the republican MVDs were renamed Ministries for the Protection of Public Order (MOOP), although for simplicity's sake they will continue to be referred to as MVDs in this chapter. Ultimately, this decentralization and its associated name change did not last. In 1966 Brezhnev created an All-Union MOOP, and in 1968 he changed the name back to MVD.

As outlined in chapter 1, this decentralization of the penal sector began already in 1956; thus, by 1960 the republican MVDs were prepared to assume their new responsibilities in the penal sphere. The largest and most important of these republican ministries, the Russian MVD, was commanded by Nikolai Pavlovich Stakhanov, who rose through the ranks of the MVD's border guard division until his promotion to minister in 1955. The liquidation of the All-Union MVD in 1960, however, vastly increased his responsibilities as much of the All-Union coordinating and policy-setting functions were shifted to the Russian MVD. Telling in this regard is the increase in his headquarters staff by 1,380 in January 1960. Ultimately, Stakhanov in the early 1960s was beset by problems in the police force and the MVD's internal guards division, not to mention by complications arising from the "camp is not a resort" campaign in the penal sphere.[3] Indeed, after just a year and a half Stakhanov was sacked and replaced by Vadim Stepanovich Tikunov, a lawyer who rose through the ranks of the party bureaucracy until being appointed deputy head of the Committee of State Security (KGB) in 1959, then Russia's minister of internal affairs in July 1961.[4]

Thus, it fell to Tikunov, an outsider like Nikolai Pavlovich Dudorov, to manage the Soviet penal system in the late Khrushchev era, and especially to implement the 1961 Statute on Prisons and Corrective-Labor Colonies.[5]

Complicating this task, however, was a large increase in the inmate population. When the All-Union MVD was disbanded in 1960 in the midst of the 1959 case reviews, the inmate population stood at a low point of 582,717.[6] A year later, with the case reviews completed, there were only 543,981 inmates in the camps and colonies of the Gulag.[7] Very quickly, however, the police and court apparatuses, operating in the tough-on-crime atmosphere of the early 1960s, replaced the low-level offenders who had been released, resulting in a rapid repopulation of the Gulag.[8] Already on 1 January 1962 the Gulag held 764,756 inmates, and by 1 January 1963 that number had reached 877,592.[9] The expanded use of parole and a continued trend of shorter average sentences (from 3.3 years in 1960 to 2.9 years in 1962) then brought about a moderate reduction in the inmate population, which declined to 815,785 on 1 January 1964 and then 731,722 the following year.[10]

Part of the population growth of 1961–62 was anticipated by Gulag authorities, but the actual increase proved larger than anticipated, resulting as in the late 1950s in overcrowded prisons and colonies. The prison population, comprised mostly of pretrial detainees, exploded to 204,667 as of 1 January 1962, severely straining the network of both local and regional prisons.[11] The Estonian colony population more than doubled, from 1,550 in late 1960 to over 3,500 in 1963 and 1964; meanwhile the prison population in the republic rose from just under 500 to a high point of 1,638 at the beginning of 1962.[12] As the Ukrainian MVD complained, "as a result of an increase in repression," the republican inmate population rose from 37,948 in early 1960 to 127,741 in late 1962. By contrast, even before the case reviews there were only 73,400 inmates. As a result of the rapid increase, 46 new colonies had to be rapidly constructed in Ukraine, with many prisoners living in tents for months at a time while more permanent facilities could be constructed.[13] Thus, implementation of the 1961 statute came at a time when the penal system was experiencing a rapid increase in inmate population, together with the overcrowding and haphazard physical plant expansion that went along with it.

Implementing the 1961 Statute

With the statute passed, the first task of implementation was to redefine colonies according to the newly defined regime types and move inmates to the appropriate institutions based on their sentences. Re-sorting prisoners according to new or existing regulations was a constant feature of the Khrushchev era, and in fact just prior to the passage of the 1961 statute the Gulag had carried out such a process, resulting in the transfer of over 25,000 inmates and the reconvoying of another 1,582.[14] With the new changes, much of this work had to be performed all over again. In Sverdlovsk, camp administrators waited until December 1961, after the primary work season had concluded, to begin re-sorting its inmates.[15] Other provinces and republics acted in a more timely manner. The Kazakh MVD reported that it finished sorting its inmates in January 1962, after having transferred 40 percent of them to new institutions.[16] In Ukraine only 11,000 inmates (about 20 percent) had to be re-sorted, and this work was completed by the end of 1961.[17]

With the sorting complete and tens of thousands of new inmates populating the Gulag starting in 1962, one effect of the new regimen regulations became clear. Whereas before the 1961 statute a majority of inmates were held in lightened- or standard-regimen institutions, this was reversed after the re-sorting of 1961.[18] By mid-1963, only 24.8 percent of inmates were on normal regimen, while 28.4 percent were on strengthened regimen, 40.3 were on strict regimen, and 3.1 percent were on special regimen.[19] And lightened-regimen institutions, of course, no longer existed. Thus, the retributive intent of the statute was clearly accomplished, with nearly half of all inmates being subject to the harsher regulations governing life in strict- and special-regimen institutions.

Another notable difference achieved through the 1961 statute and the ensuing prisoner sorting was that courts and Gulag officials from this point forward adhered much more closely to the new regulations governing which inmates were to be held in which regimen types. While some incidents of inmates being held in facilities of the wrong regimen type continued to be uncovered by procurators and other inspectors, especially in women's colonies, they were far less frequent than in the 1950s (not to mention the Stalin era), when regulations were routinely ignored.[20] This speaks to the successful attempt in the early to mid-1960s to impose greater order and control on the penal system. Given the difficulty in achieving meaningful reeducation and the reduced economic profile of the Gulag, Gulag managers relied increasingly on order as a sign of accomplishment and professionalism. As noted in chapter 2 this effort began in the 1950s, but it really achieved critical mass with the passage of the 1961 statute.

Indeed, the new focus on control was evident in other areas of penal life. In conjunction with the 1961 statute the Gulag created two new positions in the colonies: deputy colony commander for regimen and operational work, and an orderly assistant to the commander. These officials would coordinate the maintenance of order and discipline in the colony and ensure that the regimen was being strictly followed.[21] As the Central Committee insisted in mid-1960, the

MVD was to "bring such order to the camps and colonies as to completely eliminate the possibility of committing crimes and infractions of socialist legality."[22] Camp workers were instructed that the new regimen had to be enforced
to its smallest detail, with automatic and predictable consequences for every
infraction.[23] MVD chief Stakhanov asked oversight commissions to inspect their
assigned colonies and prisons to check compliance with the new statute, admonishing them that "all excesses in daily life in places of confinement need to be
liquidated."[24] Alongside articles on production and reeducation in the monthly
journal *K novoi zhizni* (*Toward a New Life*), Gulag workers starting in April 1961
were fed a steady stream of articles on imposing strict discipline and removing
the liberal excesses of the 1950s.[25] As one such article in early 1962 declared, prisoners "are not children"; they should not be rewarded with "needless privileges
and excesses" for being sentenced to incarceration.[26]

This new emphasis on strict adherence to the 1961 statute was certainly
noted by the inmates. As Anatoly Marchenko noted, his thorough orientation
upon arrival at Dubravlag in 1961 gave him the distinct impression that "everything was taken into account, every single movement regulated."[27] And at least
according one metric this campaign was effective: the number of prosecuted
crimes in correctional-labor facilities in Russia steadily declined from 3,637 in
1961 to 1,970 in 1964.[28] While these data cannot be wholly accepted at face value,
as they certainly underreport the level of crime in the Gulag, inspectors and
memoirists alike confirm that crime continued to decline in the 1960s. As voiced
by a prisoner in Kazakhstan, the MVD after the 1961 statute had passed "introduced order (*vveli rezhim*)."[29]

Unsurprisingly, this new "order" was despised by the prisoners, especially the
nearly 50 percent placed on strict and special regimens according to the new
regulations. The Estonian MVD reported a sharp spike in complaints from prisoners about the new regimen restrictions.[30] And the most common complaint,
reflecting the biggest change in everyday life, was the reduction in rations, due
primarily to the new regulations governing purchases and packages. One inmate
wrote to *Novyi Mir* (*New World*) that now inmates were "doomed not to correction but to physical destruction by means of hunger, calculated deprivation, and
suffering in the camps of the USSR."[31] Danylo Shumuk noted that due to the
new attitudes and restrictions "the conditions in the camp, as well as the quality of
the food we received, continued to deteriorate."[32] One prisoner in 1962 complained to Khrushchev himself of the harsh conditions in the special-regimen
colonies, claiming that instead of being reformed, prisoners were becoming invalids. "This form of reeducation," he concluded, "can only be called destruction."[33]
Helene Celmina found that even in the hospital the rations were insufficient, and
prisoners straight from Vladimir Prison, she recalled, "looked as though they had

been dug from a grave. Their faces were emaciated, unnaturally grayish and pale with sunken eyes."[34] Another inmate complained to the Supreme Soviet that his colony commander had placed everyone on penalty rations (although a procurator noted that only those who failed to fulfill their norms were so penalized).[35] The Belorussian MVD, taking the principle of penalty rations to an extreme, began distributing only 450 grams of bread per day, plus hot water, to those who did not fulfill their production norms.[36]

Beyond the reduction in rations, the effect of the new regulations was clear in other ways. At Dubravlag the camp administration announced the new statute with allusions to the "Man behind Bars" article that appeared in the 27 August 1960 edition of *Sovetskaia Rossiia* (*Soviet Russia*), explaining to the prisoners that society demanded the changes.[37] Striped uniforms were introduced, which some prisoners claimed "strongly oppressed them."[38] Prisoners complained of there being only envelopes and soap in the camp stores for months at a time.[39] Others complained of the new restrictions regulating the number of letters one could receive and limiting correspondence to family members alone.[40] Televisions were removed from barracks and placed in the clubs under strict control of the administration.[41] No longer did colonies show films just for entertainment; they were to have a specific political message and were to be accompanied by a discussion to ensure that message was correctly understood.[42] The slogan "films are for workers" was also disseminated among Gulag staff to characterize a new policy of showing movies only to conscientious inmate laborers.[43] Tellingly, the justification given by one camp official for the new regulations was simply "You're not on holiday now."[44]

But even with the "holiday" of the mid-1950s over, conditions for the average prisoner after 1961 did not rival those of Stalin's camps. As will be shown, the Gulag remained committed to correctionalism, which, even though it was now to be based partially on a strict regimen, also meant the continuation of a number of cultural and educational programs enjoyed by the prisoners (along with political lectures that were generally despised). As the political department of the Russian Gulag reminded its workers on the pages of *K novoi zhizni*, prisoners should have access not just to strict discipline and labor, but to sporting events, artistic opportunities, and reading clubs. Referring to the recently concluded "camp is not a resort" campaign, readers were reminded that "some articles have appeared in our press that cast doubt on the necessity of such activities for prisoners." These doubts, however, were misplaced. Everyone, even prisoners, needs these activities and influences: they need to be inspired by art and beauty and lifted up through social engagement.[45]

Indeed, such extracurricular activities were not completely curtailed in the wake of the 1961 statute. Marchenko recalled that sporting events and competitions continued after 1961, as did concerts put on by prisoners.[46] In Estonia, one colony put on a summer games for its prisoners in 1962, complete with volleyball, basketball, shot put, high jump, races of varying distances, weight lifting, tug-of-war, and others.[47] Iu. P. Iakimenko recalled caring for flowers around the barracks.[48] Even in the mid-1960s barracks were whitewashed twice a year and Marchenko reported that "the thing that amazes the visiting stranger from outside most in the camps is that the compound is full of flowers and greenery."[49] Moreover, he admitted that there was ample time for prisoners to play dominoes or chess, to read, or simply to converse.[50] The eight-hour workday, despite calls by some during the campaign of 1960–61 to increase the labor commitment of prisoners, was retained, giving prisoners time in the evenings for relaxation. This is confirmed both by Vladimir Osipov and Shumuk, who reported working "quite conscientiously" during the early 1960s and having ample free time for reading and writing.[51] Gulag administrators and guards were still instructed to address inmates politely by their last name or simply as "citizen prisoner."[52] Even Aleksandr Solzhenitsyn, attending a commission to revise the corrective labor code in the 1960s, could hardly protest the length of the workday or the provision for visitation rights. "Indeed," he mused, "the arrangements for visits seem quite generous to me, and I barely restrain myself from praising them."[53] Conditions in correctional-labor facilities also remained much better than Stalin-era camps because despite the increased focus on creating a harsher regimen, there was no concomitant rise in violence. As V. F. Abramkin notes, murders and even rumors of murders became rare: "A completely different spirit reigned."[54] This was noted by Leonid Sitko as well, who recorded that the criminals and politicals lived peaceably and guards displayed a reluctance to fire even on an escaping prisoner.[55]

Living conditions for prisoners also remained better than during the 1940s and early 1950s because many Gulag officials failed to completely enforce the 1961 statute. Many camp officials engaged in foot-dragging in implementing the statute, even after repeated warnings from higher Gulag officials and from procurators. A report composed for a Ukrainian MVD Collegium meeting on 9 February 1962 noted that Colony No. 49 in Odessa Province still had such a light regimen that "prisoners don't feel at all that they are being punished."[56] An unannounced inspection by an oversight commission in Perm Province found "cases of inexplicable liberalism," such as allowing extra packages for poorly behaved inmates, and appointing large-scale embezzlers to "materially responsible positions."[57] One colony in 1962 reportedly sent its inmates into the woods on a hunting party, with firearms provided by the colony guards.[58] Another allowed its prisoners to wear their own clothes, rather than the new uniforms mandated by the statute.[59]

The most vocal complaints of Gulag administrators being too "liberal" with inmates came from procurators, for whom "socialist legality" now meant full compliance with the 1961 statute.[60] A Sverdlovsk procurator in late 1961 was incensed, for instance, to find that the local strict-regimen colony had a soccer pitch, a boxing ring, a plethora of musical instruments, drapes, a well-stocked store that kept the prisoners supplied with such luxuries as sugar, an excess of packages and visits, and even a stool with the image of the Virgin Mary carved into it.[61] Another in 1962 took a colony commander to task for giving one prisoner the right to spend more money in the colony store than allowed by the new statute because of his "excellent bed-making" and for allowing a second prisoner extra privileges simply for good schoolwork and participation in cultural activities, even though he had a recent history of using drugs, possessing other forbidden items, and trying to smuggle alcohol into the colony.[62] A colony in 1963 was found by procurators to have a store stocked with such luxuries as cheese, cookies, candies, sour cream, and sausage where prisoners were spending more money than allowed by the statute.[63] Inmates in prisons and special-regimen colonies continued to be given light labor, such as sewing or producing cardboard boxes, instead of the hard labor called for by the new statute.[64] Some regional MVD offices refused for a time to abolish their lightened-regimen colonies (a few even created new ones after the statute was issued), while others maintained the practice of allowing certain prisoners to live outside the zone.[65] Astonishingly, some standard- and even strengthened-regimen colonies, especially in Ukraine, as late as January 1963 had only unarmed guards to monitor the prisoners.[66]

There are a few reasons why camp officials were hesitant to strictly enforce the new standards of the 1961 statute. First, even with the accompanying instructions, it was not always clear what was allowed by the statute and what was now prohibited, or at least discouraged. This is evident in a 1961 article in *K novoi zhizni*. It called for an end to "excesses" in the cultural life of prisoners but noted many misunderstandings. One colony commander had removed chess and checkers sets, but this decision was reversed by his superiors. Another continued to hold sporting events, which appeared to hold to "the old line of amusing the prisoners," but the author of the article defended the practice in this instance because it was a colony for young men, for whom "sport has a great educational significance." In a third example the author lauded a switch from a local Komsomol youth performing concerts for the prisoners to the same youth instead helping the prisoners with their own artistic development.[67] Clearly there was no consensus on how strict the colony regimen was supposed to be.

A second important factor that mitigated against strict implementation of the 1961 statute by local Gulag officials was the pressure of keeping prisoners both under control and productive, the two issues (along with outright corruption) that most often led to reprimands or dismissals. As Gresham Sykes notes in his groundbreaking sociological study of prison culture, guards and low-level administrators are usually forced to compromise with inmates in order to keep the institution functioning smoothly, especially during periods of institutional reform; they are, in effect, "under strong pressure to compromise with their captives, for it is a paradox that they can insure their dominance only by allowing it to be corrupted."[68] And this pressure, Sykes notes, becomes even more intense when officials are dependent on prisoner labor for their job security. Such security and especially economic concerns help explain why in many instances local Gulag commanders were supported by their MVD bosses.

A good illustration of the production-order nexus is the matter of deconvoying prisoners, which the 1961 statute severely curtailed. Colony and camp commanders continued to display, in the words of procurators assigned with monitoring fulfillment of the new statute, a "liberal attitude toward deconvoying prisoners." Indeed, the number of deconvoyed prisoners in the USSR as a whole rose from 44,407 on 1 April 1962 to 66,613 on 1 October 1962.[69] Large numbers of inmates were granted deconvoyed status without regard to their character or the nature of their convictions.[70] And this was not just the decision of local Gulag commanders. The Ukrainian MVD already in late 1961, using Anton Semenovich Makarenko's "principle of trust" as justification, sent well-behaved inmates into the fields to help bring in the corn harvest.[71] And as Tikunov himself reported to the Supreme Soviet in 1964, the statute was too strict concerning deconvoying. This especially interfered with the logging camps, which housed primarily inmates on strengthened and strict regimens, but which needed "a large contingent of prisoners who have the right to movement without convoy."[72] In other words, ignoring the statute's restrictions on deconvoying had the full support of Tikunov himself.

But Tikunov's criticism of the statute was not limited to deconvoying. Although most internal reports from 1962–63 credited the 1961 statute with improving discipline among prisoners, thus creating better conditions for labor and reeducation, Tikunov and other high-ranking officials thought the statute had gone too far in terms of harsher living conditions.[73] Tikunov complained that prisoners according to the statute received excessively low wages. After the 50 percent coefficient was administered (inmate wages were set at half the wages of free workers), the average monthly wage for inmates in Russia stood at 30.70 rubles in 1963. Of this, 13.52 was withheld to pay for food, 3.06 for clothing, and 0.22 for income taxes. When garnishments for child support or restitution for crimes committed were added in, many prisoners had little to no take-home pay for saving or purchases. This led many prisoners to refuse to work, which had a negative influence on their reeducation.[74] Even Solzhenitsyn, who met with Tikunov himself to plead for improved conditions for prisoners, reported that Tikunov favored restoring a number of privileges that the 1961 statute had removed, such as allowing more money to be spent at the stores, more packages, unlimited correspondence rights, and self-service kitchens for prisoners.[75] By 1965 Tikunov was advocating even greater reforms, such as a seven-hour work-day for inmates and prisoner wages equal to those of free workers.[76]

Other republican ministers of internal affairs sided with Tikunov's appeals to step back from the harshness of the 1961 statute. They supported his proposal to give prisoners a minimum of 10 percent of their wages to spend, save, or send home to their families as they saw fit.[77] Similarly, the Ukrainian MVD in 1963 asked the Ukrainian Council of Ministers to petition the All-Union Council of Ministers to allow prisoners on special regimen who were fulfilling their work norms on heavy labor to make purchases from the store according to the level provided to strict-regimen prisoners. At only 2,413 calories of guaranteed rations and no supplemental nutrition, the complaint reads, the prisoners were physically deteriorating.[78] And the Kazakh MVD chief in 1962 proposed more radical changes: restoring to Gulag administrators the right to change a prisoner's regimen type, reintroducing lightened-regimen colonies, and allowing select prisoners to live outside the colony zones.[79]

MVD leadership in Moscow also reacted strongly against a plan to move all penal institutions out of Moscow and the surrounding Moscow Province. Such an order was given in November 1960 by the Russian Bureau of the Central Committee, even though the MVD was already transferring large numbers of inmates from Moscow to other provinces and republics.[80] In line with the "camp is not a resort" campaign, the idea was to send criminals out of the capital, which was viewed as a privileged space within the Soviet Union. Plans to implement this decree ran into stiff resistance from the MVD, however, which argued that it was not cost-effective to send inmates to other provinces, and that it inhibited the work of reeducation. And ultimately the MVD triumphed. In 1961 the decree was modified first to allow first-time female convicts to remain in the province and then to allow all first-time criminals convicted of minor crimes to remain in the city and province.[81] Then later that year the MVD received permission to continue sending first-time offenders convicted of serious crimes to the Pavlovskaia colony in Moscow Province.[82] Tikunov in the midst of this struggle even proposed constructing new colonies to increase the prisoner population in the province to over 9,000 instead of 5,650.[83]

Further evidence of the Gulag's reticence to implement the full measure of harshness called for by the "camp is not a resort" campaign is the continued and even increased use of parole. Although abuse of parole was one of the cornerstones of the "camp is not a resort" campaign, parole continued apace and then dramatically increased in the early to mid-1960s. As inspecting procurators often charged, local commanders continued to use parole to rid themselves of their worst inmates. An October 1961 inspection of penal facilities in the Komi Autonomous Soviet Socialist Republic, for instance, revealed that some inmates were being paroled without having served the requisite time; local administrators were composing glaringly false character statements; and penal officials were serving as court justices for parole proceedings, thus assuring all requests would be granted. As a result, malicious offenders were being released into society, where many of them quickly committed new and often violent crimes.[84] Like the continued large-scale use of deconvoying, parole was actively supported by central Gulag administrators who were struggling to cope with an expanding inmate population immediately after the number of colonies was slashed in the wake of the 1959 releases. From 1962 to 1964, around a quarter of a million inmates annually were paroled. And the percentage of inmates nominated for parole that were approved by the courts rose from around 90 percent to 95 percent in the early 1960s.[85]

The political department of the Gulag, while at first striving to maintain balance between the task of reeducation and the new demands of harsh punishment brought about by the 1961 statute, by 1963 was also beginning to question the statute's intent. *K novoi zhizni* in early 1963 published an article by a detachment commander who, rather than condemn the inmates as betrayers of the socialist project, wrote that "the most important thing is to be able to find out the paths to people's hearts and discover the good that is still in them." Strictness was still necessary on occasion, but it "should be used only when it is needed." Moreover, he continued, "I am deeply convinced that a friendly attitude from the educator (*vospitatel'*) will be met with the same from the prisoners."[86] A similar attitude was expressed months later in an article in the same publication by Iu. Feofanov. Attacking both those who created "sanatoriums" and those who, in reaction, created institutions of punishment and revenge, Feofanov advocated a middle ground based on strict yet humane laws and regulations.[87] But the most poignant symbol of the political department's rejection of the premise of the 1961 statute came in April 1964, when on the first page of *K novoi zhizni* it published Khrushchev's famous quote delivered to the Third Writers' Congress in 1959: "We believe that there are no uncorrectable people. . . . In our conditions one must approach people sympathetically, believe in people, see our end goal—the struggle for communism. One must educate and reeducate people."[88]

This attack on the principle of retribution was supported by penologists, who in the wake of the 1961 statute began to once again soften the theory behind the necessity of a strict regimen. G. A. Tumanov of the Higher School of the MVD argued that a harsh regimen, rather than serving as a primary form of reeducation as posited in the "camp is not a resort" campaign, only created the conditions under which reeducation could occur.[89] Taking a more critical tone, N. A. Beliaev in 1963 criticized the new lack of "progressive" steps of increasingly lightened regimen conditions as prisoners moved toward release.[90] Even the Procuracy, initially a stalwart supporter of the 1961 statute, started to take a more moderate position. It ended the Belorussian MVD's practice of harsh penalty rations.[91] And it eventually came to support things like increased rations and wages for prison inmates and more products available for purchase for all prisoners.[92]

This softening of attitudes toward Gulag inmates was on display in the press as well, which began in late 1962 to publish articles signaling that the campaign against inmate privileges had ended. The first of these, which provided a generally sympathetic view of the life of prisoners in a strict-regimen colony, made clear that the favored trope of the camp-as-resort no longer applied to the correctional-labor institutions of the Soviet Union: "It must be said that the prisoners are not deprived of sleep and that they have their daily 2,413 calories, but whoever speaks of 'vacation homes' (*doma otdykha*) obviously does not understand the meaning of deprivation of freedom, compulsory and hard labor, strict routine, constant surveillance and the impossibility of ever being alone."[93] Authors still had to tread carefully with readers, who retained a sharp sense of social justice; they often declared, for instance, that the worst criminals deserved no mercy. Moreover, although there is a return in these articles to the theme of reeducation not through the harshness of the regimen but by means of vocational training, didactic films, and heartfelt persuasion, limits were imposed on how far this could go: "One must be neither sentimental with prisoners nor heartless. Tender emotion and absolute distrust do not bear fruit here."[94] Thus a compromise was struck between the liberalism of the mid-1950s and the strictness of the early 1960s.

This compromise was reflected not just in the press or in the actions of local penal officers, but in official policy as well. Although some of Tikunov's proposals—a guaranteed minimum take-home pay prominent among them—were rejected by the Central Committee, a few steps were, in fact, taken to lighten the harshness of the 1961 statute, especially in regard to the diet of special-regimen prisoners. On 13 September 1962 the Russian Council of Ministers, responding to an independent scientific study that found that 4,000 calories were necessary for lumberjacks, ordered that special-regimen prisoners in logging camps could spend up to 3 rubles per month at the camp stores.[95] Then on 6 April 1963 the Supreme Soviet decreed that convicts engaged in dangerous or hard physical labor should receive an additional hot breakfast, to be served at the worksite.[96] These steps were decidedly incremental, but that was the point. Although advocating further reform himself, Tikunov made clear the party line to Solzhenitsyn in a private meeting in the early 1960s: "It's easy to wreck discipline, difficult to impose it."[97] Khrushchev and his criminal justice policymakers had learned this lesson from the mid-1950s and so by the 1960s were prone to err on the side of caution when it came to loosening the restrictions of the 1961 statute.

One Day in the Life of Ivan Denisovich in the Camps

Solzhenitsyn's presence on judicial commissions and in Tikunov's office was not coincidental. With backing from Khrushchev himself, who by 1962 was moving away from his harsh statements during the tough-on-crime campaign of 1960–61, Solzhenitsyn in November 1962 published his instantly famous *One Day in the Life of Ivan Denisovich* in *Novyi Mir*. Widely debated in Soviet society, including by former prisoners and camp officials, the fictional account of the Soviet Union's most famous political prisoner was nominated for a Lenin Prize and alternately lauded and pilloried in the Soviet press. For some it was a necessary acknowledgment of the arbitrary violence meted out by the Stalin regime; for others it painted too sympathetic a picture of prisoners who, even if they were improperly imprisoned, still displayed a sort of hopelessness and despondence unworthy of Soviet citizens.[98] Not surprisingly, Solzhenitsyn's novella was also hotly debated among current inmates and Gulag administrators. Coming in the immediate wake of the "camp is not a resort" campaign of the late 1950s and early 1960s, *One Day* again posed the question of how Soviet penal institutions should be organized and how Soviet society should relate to lawbreakers.

Prisoners incarcerated for crimes against the Soviet state at Dubravlag were especially interested in Solzhenitsyn's account of life in a Stalin-era camp and debated its value at great length. As Aleksei Grigorevich Murzhenko recalled, "even we, prisoners in the zone, could not understand how such a story was allowed in the press." Astonishment at the deepening of the "camp theme" in the press aside, inmates disagreed on the story's usefulness. Some thought it was potentially harmful, as it told only half-truths about the Stalin-era camps, avoiding direct discussions of brutality, starvation, and death. This would lead people to think that Stalin's camps were not so bad, and that the penal facilities of the 1960s must therefore be just fine. The majority of inmates, however, according to Murzhenko, were excited about the story. Only through such a forum could the country's citizenry, especially its youth, learn about the evils of Stalin's repressive apparatus.[99]

Gulag officials also debated the merits and lessons of the novel. One official at Dubravlag confiscated a copy of the story that inmate Eduard Kuznetsov received in a package, thinking it too inflammatory for state criminals to read, but others at the same camp point who subscribed to *Novyi Mir* did not have theirs taken away.[100] Not surprisingly, given the MVD pushback against the harsh statute of 1961, many within the apparatus found *One Day* instructive and a useful tool for demonstrating the relative humanity of their penal system. At a 1963 conference for Gulag workers in Ukraine, Minister Ivan Kharitonovich Golovchenko of the Ukrainian MVD reminded his subordinates that they had all read *One Day* and that they needed to be careful to not "create the same conditions, the same attitude toward prisoners." As opposed to the guards depicted in the story, they needed to be good educators, steer clear of disciplinary infractions, and remember that "insults and debasement of human dignity [in relation to the prisoners] are not permissible." Those who worked in the old style "of 1937," Golovchenko concluded, "need to be removed immediately, they are dangerous, we do not need them." Such people, he concluded, are "not of our time."[101] For Golovchenko, therefore, *One Day* was a prescient reminder that reeducation and humaneness had to be the defining traits of the post-Stalin Gulag. In the wake of the antiliberalism campaign, which attacked the idea that humaneness was reeducational, this was a strong statement in support of the post-Stalin reforms.

The political department of the Russian Gulag also came out in staunch support of Solzhenitsyn's story, as evidenced by a glowing review of *One Day* in *K novoi zhizni*. Written by A. Ermolaev, a retired MVD colonel, the review emphasized that the prisoners in the story are portrayed as honest, hardworking, and mostly innocent of the crimes for which they are incarcerated. Ivan Denisovich himself is described as "alive, human, he feels close to us." He is "a simple Russian person, a peasant and a soldier, [who] finds the moral power to overcome the violence and arbitrary rule that is thrust upon him." And the camp officials, by contrast, are rightly depicted as "self-loving and power-loving" overlords who ruled with iron fists. In concluding the review, Ermolaev reminds his readers that such camps really existed and that those responsible for them had been justly punished. "We do not have the right to forget," he continued, "that in the period of the cult of personality many honest, Soviet people, devoted to the Motherland, were destroyed." But now in the light of de-Stalinization everything was different: "Now there are none in the corrective-labor institutions serving time without a court order, there are no prisoners for political crimes, there are no Shukhovs [Ivan Denisovich's surname]."[102] Still, Ermolaev warned, the story served as a timely reminder that everyone in the Gulag ranks had to strictly follow the law. This review fit squarely within Khrushchev's initial de-Stalinization narrative of the Cult of Personality as an era of lawlessness. But it was also a clear attack on the antiliberalism campaign that threatened to restore some elements of Stalinist penal practices. Ultimately, while low-ranking Gulag officials disagreed over how to handle the appearance of *One Day* in the living quarters of the prisoners, top-ranking administrators saw it as a pedagogical tool and a rebuke to those trying to introduce harsher living and working conditions into the country's penal facilities.

The Correctional Economy of the Late Khrushchev Era

While implementing and eventually reforming the 1961 statute and using *One Day* as a tool to push back against those who desired increased punishment for lawbreakers, Gulag administrators were persistently occupied in the 1960s by economic and fiscal concern. A primary piece of evidence that demonstrates the continued importance of economic production is the persistence of corrective-labor camps in the logging industry. According to the 1956 Gulag reform plan, these were supposed to be abolished because their large size inhibited reeducation and fostered lawlessness both among inmates and administrators. But lack of funding for the construction of new corrective-labor colonies, together with the persistent need for lumber in the Soviet economy, prevented this from happening in the late 1950s. This tension between the new vision for the Gulag and the necessity of mass-producing lumber persisted into the 1960s.

Indeed, the case review commissions of 1959, which reduced the inmate population by nearly half, presented a prime opportunity to liquidate the camps and transfer their remaining inmates to existing colonies. With 590,990 inmates in the colonies alone in mid-1959 and 582,717 inmates total at the beginning of 1959, it seems clear that the camps could have been eliminated had this been an overriding concern.[103] Yet the production-minded Council of Ministers warned in late 1959 that the logging plan would not be fulfilled because of this massive outflow of prisoners from the logging camps and requested for an additional 65,000–70,000 inmates to be sent to the camps to replenish this labor force. Ultimately, however, the Central Committee declined this request, and instead had the Council of Ministers issue a 1 October 1960 decree ordering the MVD to shutter the logging camps by the end of 1962.[104] The MVD thus ceased all transfers to the logging camps in 1960, hoping, it seems, that the camps would eventually be depopulated and closed as their inmates' terms expired.[105] At the same time, however, it also shuttered a large number of colonies rather than filling them with existing camp inmates. Both the MVD leadership and the Council of Ministers, therefore, remained only partially committed to eliminating the camps. Not surprisingly, with the rise of the inmate population in 1961–62 and the already reduced number of colonies, the MVD was unable to close the camps as scheduled. In 1961 it obtained approval yet again to allow the continued existence of the logging camps, and ultimately the camps persisted into the Brezhnev era.[106] Indeed, in 1964, around a quarter of all working inmates were located in the logging camps, and their output that year amounted to 19,576,000 cubic meters of lumber.[107] Ultimately, this commitment to large-scale production that so exemplified the Stalinist Gulag was never fully extinguished in the Khrushchev era.

Another indicator of the Gulag's continued commitment to economics was a concerted push in the early to mid-1960s to provide each colony with its own production facility, thus eliminating the need to contract out inmate labor to other agencies. This was an existing aim of the 1956 reform plan that remained unfulfilled in the late 1950s due to lack of funding. With the pressure of over-crowding temporarily alleviated in the wake of the 1959 case reviews, the Gulag launched a new effort to make existing colonies economically independent. As Solzhenitsyn discovered in his meetings with justice officials in the 1960s, Tikunov's "main concern [was] to create in every [colony] an industrial base of its own. The Minister reckons that by increasing the number of interesting jobs he can cut out escape attempts."[108]

Yet while security may have played some role in the cutback on contract work—inmates in transit to and at offsite worksites were certainly more likely to attempt escape than those kept in the colonies—other explanations predominated. First, production zones attached to colonies allowed the MVD to exert full control over the production process. Contract disputes with economic agencies consumed much attention of the Gulag bureaucracy, with economic agencies often working at cross-purposes in relation to the Gulag. Moreover, contract work proved to be expensive. It required a larger contingent of guards. And it was also expensive because time in transit was considered part of the eight-hour workday by the Gulag but not by the contracting agency. This therefore cut into inmate wages, which the Gulag used to fund its operations. Inmates at the Nyrobskii Corrective-Labor Camp (Nyroblag) in the early 1960s, for instance, put in an average of only 6 hours 32 minutes of paid work due to the lengthy transport time to and from the worksite.[109] Finally, production zones were viewed as desirable because they offered better opportunities for reeducation than did contract labor. They allowed inmates to work closely with Gulag staff, and the work itself tended to be skilled rather than hard manual labor.

Notably, the effort to build new production zones in corrective-labor colonies was supported by the Russian Bureau of the Central Committee. On 13 September 1961 it admonished the Gulag to provide each colony with the materials and equipment necessary for creating its own productive base, and to endeavor to harmonize the output of each colony with the production profile of the surrounding region. More importantly, this decree called for a list of production sites to be turned over to the Gulag to be prepared by 1 November 1961 and for 3.5 million rubles and a laundry list of heavy equipment to be allocated from the Russian Council of Ministers reserve funds to create new colonies around these sites.[110] Furthermore, the State Planning Agency (Gosplan) was ordered to allocate to colonies their own distinct lines in economic budgets and plans, and to create a reserve fund for the construction of new colonies.[111] The following year the Council of Ministers, responding to a request by MVD officials, allowed the Gulag to reinvest 30 percent of its income from production-related activities into expanding colony production zones.[112] Thus, in addition to approving the MVD's economic restructuring, the Central Committee and Council of Ministers allocated significant resources to achieving this goal.

In the ensuing years various parts of the Soviet penal system reported their success with the in-house production program. Already by early 1962 the Ukrainian MVD had constructed 40,000 square meters of production space, enough to employ 40,500 inmates. As a result, only 11 of its 89 colonies operated on a contract basis.[113] The Lithuanian Gulag reported in early 1963 that it had nearly completed its transition from contract work to production facilities in the colonies and that the results were clear: although the economic plan for 1962 was 75 percent higher than in 1961, it was nonetheless fulfilled. But just as importantly, "attitudes toward labor have changed, and discipline has improved among the vast majority of prisoners."[114] Similarly, an inspection of Belorussian colonies in 1964 revealed that all had their own production zones specializing in furniture assembly, sewing, and metalworking, among others, and that nearly all prisoners were actively engaged in this work.[115]

Yet the turn away from contract labor proved stubbornly difficult. Not only did the contract logging camps remain, the rising inmate population of 1961–63 meant that new colonies had to be rapidly opened. This often meant that time and funding prevented the construction of production zones; indeed, of the first thirty-nine colonies newly opened after the inmate population began to increase, twenty-one were contract colonies.[116] By late 1964, therefore, only 54.2 percent of prisoners in Russia were held in colonies with their own production zones. Another 26.4 percent were held in contract colonies, and 19.4 percent were in the logging camps. By job profile, 23.4 percent of inmates were engaged in construction, 17.9 percent in woodworking, 17.5 percent in metalworking, 13.6 percent in logging, 10 percent in light industry (sewing, shoe production, etc.), 4.3 percent in the production of construction materials, 4.3 percent in agriculture, and 9 percent in other types of work.[117] Hard, unskilled, manual labor performed on a contract basis, therefore, continued to engage roughly half of all inmates.

It is striking how each colony in the post-Stalin Gulag operated as its own little business. With the centralized planning of the Stalin era now largely absent, each institution was responsible for creating a production zone or finding economic enterprises who would accept prisoners as contract laborers and concluding official contracts with them. Those with production zones had the additional responsibility of drumming up orders for their products, locating supplies, and even obtaining credit for capital improvements. Local authorities had to track production, productivity, average prisoner wages and other indicators. But most importantly, they had to be conscious of income and expenses. There was a bottom line that had to be met, a profit to be earned or at least a loss to be controlled.

Indeed, alongside the only partially successful move away from contract labor, the Gulag in the 1960s continued the late-1950s campaign to reduce its budget subsidy. Indeed, the new primary mechanism for achieving subsidy reduction was the creation of production zones, which better allowed Gulag administrators to control income and expenses. One colony in 1964, for instance, reported that it had taken out an 800,000-ruble loan in order to restructure and expand their production zone, and they were now working without subsidy.[118] Commander Matveev, who helped launch the antisubsidy campaign in the 1950s, reported that his colony had a profit of 340,000 rubles in 1962 and 100,000 in 1963.[119] On a larger scale, the Kazakh Gulag reported that in 1962 it had a surplus thanks to the many new production zones it had created for its inmates.[120] Similarly, the Ukrainian Gulag reported that while in 1960 its colonies received a subsidy of 5.7 million rubles, in 1962 they earned a profit of 11.7 million rubles, largely due to the expansion of production facilities. These funds were then used to cover expenses at the prisons and juvenile colonies, but in 1964 the Gulag reported that the prisons and juvenile colonies too were covering their own expenses and returning a profit.[121]

Despite continued focus on production and fiscal concerns, the early 1960s witnessed much more attention to the reeducational value of labor. As before, this rehabilitative effect of labor proved difficult to quantify whereas the level of plan fulfillment was much more tangible. It comes as little surprise, therefore, that Ivan Ovchinnikov, incarcerated in a logging camp in the mid-to-late 1960s, observed that "the lone indicator of the worthiness of a prisoner was his fulfillment percentage at work."[122] Yet other pieces of evidence point to a firmer belief in the usefulness of work in corrections, despite the retributional rhetoric of the "camp is not a resort" campaign. Indeed, the Central Committee in mid-1960, during the height of this counterreform movement, posed the challenge of

focusing on the reeducational side of labor rather than production: "In providing work for prisoners the Ministry of Internal Affairs is guided, by and large,
by the interests of fulfilling production and financial plans. At the same time
the amount of attention paid to labor as the primary means for reeducating
people is completely insufficient."[123] As the deputy head of the Russian Gulag reminded in 1961, production is not "a goal in and of itself." Rather, it is "the primary part of the reeducational process."[124]

This message of labor first and foremost as a correctional device was consistently reinforced for Gulag workers on the pages of *K novoi zhizni* in the early to
mid-1960s. One article by the deputy commander of a new colony described the
transformation that occurred as his inmates, at first without work, were provided
contract employment in a local factory. As they became engaged in this specialized work, "there happened unseen that inner restructuring of consciousness that
only labor can bring." Regimen infractions began to disappear, more inmates
began to enroll in vocational courses and school classes, "but most importantly,"
the deputy commander reminded, "people have been noticeably changed."[125]
Another story about one convict Tsapalkin highlighted the importance of allowing prisoners to work according to their chosen specialty. Tsapalkin is presented
as a mechanic by training who kept asking to be assigned to a job in which he
could use his qualifications, but this was never provided. Unable to fulfill meaningful (for him) labor, he became despondent and bitter. Eventually he reached
his breaking point, unleashing a tirade of profanity on the colony administration,
which, instead of helping him, simply put him on strict regimen. The end result,
according to the journal editors, was that the administration lost the trust not just
of Tsapalkin, but of many other inmates. The moral here is clear: without specialized labor that interested the inmates, they were likely to become not good
Soviet citizens but regimen breakers and recidivists.[126] This story is notable for
its rejection of one of the aims of the "camp is not a resort" campaign: to place
inmates on hard labor rather than specialized work.

Not all specialized labor was created equally, of course, and at times the Gulag
struggled to find meaningful specialized labor for its inmates. V. V. Birkin, inmate of Vorkutlag and Dubravlag from 1958–62, worked six different jobs in his
relatively short time in the camps, including logging, mining gravel, fixing water
pipes, and sewing (at a recently constructed production zone equipped with
new sewing machines).[127] One can reasonably wonder if constantly changing
jobs had the intended reeducational effect on inmates. And in fact, a persistent
complaint of the 1960s, heard from both inmates and inspectors of the penal
system, was that male prisoners were learning specialized sewing skills, when
they would obviously not be employed in sewing after release.[128] Moreover, the

variety of products now produced by the Gulag actually came under criticism by MVD head Tikunov, who in 1963 questioned the need for the Gulag to produce 32 different kinds of tables, 29 kinds of cabinets, and 12 varieties of couches.[129]

Despite these challenges, emphasis on specialized labor contributed to a large expansion of vocational training programs in the Gulag in the 1960s. In the 13 September 1961 decree of the Russian Bureau of the Central Committee, the Ministry of Secondary and Higher Education was called to provide 1,500 specialists to the Gulag for this effort, and additional vocational training for prisoners was to be provided by the Main Administration of Vocational Education attached to the Russian Council of Ministers.[130] Working toward the goal of providing each inmate with specialized vocational credentials if he did not already have them, numerous opportunities for vocational education were created over the following years. Statistics for 1964 show that 138 professional schools, 500 vocational workshops, and over 1,000 vocational rooms operated in the penal facilities of the Soviet Union. In the first nine months of that year, 109,020 passed vocational training courses, including 36,347 in construction, 43,263 in metalworking, and 12,159 in various agricultural specialties.[131]

Problems persisted, of course. Funding was not always available for equipment, textbooks, and instructors. One colony on Sakhalin, for instance, wanted to organize a tractor-driver vocational training course but lacked the funds. A solution was found, however, when the commander proposed that the prisoners help pay for it and those interested agreed to contribute 10 rubles each as tuition.[132] Vocational training was also inhibited because prisoners were forbidden to take time off work for specialized study. In 1962, for instance, the Russian Council of Ministers lobbied the All-Union Council of Ministers on behalf of the Russian MVD to allow it to remove one hundred prisoners from production for two months to conduct an intensive training course designed to turn them into pedagogues for the Gulag's vocational training program. Gosplan and the Ministry of Finance both responded that such training should take place without exempting the chosen prisoners from their daily labor, and this position ultimately won the debate.[133] Thus, vocational training could only be provided if it did not interfere with the eight-hour workday.

The mixed success with implementing vocational training courses illuminates the difficulty inherent in managing the various aims of the Gulag. Providing specialized training and specialized work was clearly the goal, but resources and circumstances often prevented its fulfillment. Hard, unskilled labor still played a large role in the broader Soviet economy, after all, so one cannot expect that the Gulag, of all institutions, would be able to sever its ties to it. In fact, the Gulag of the 1960s was most concerned not with the nature of work, but with the percentage of inmates who were performing paid labor. Indeed, this metric came to be nearly as important as plan fulfillment percentage because it provided a measurable indicator for reeducation through labor. One could not measure the psychological effect of labor on individual prisoners, but one could ensure that they were all working and assume that labor's inherently edifying qualities would take effect. As voiced at a Gulag conference in Ukraine in 1961, "now our task consists of taking all measures to employ the prisoners, otherwise we will not be able to solve the matter of reeducating them. If a prisoner sits without work, he will find himself some other kind of entertainment."[134]

As before, however, the Gulag found it very difficult to get all of its inmates working. Whereas in the third quarter of 1960, in the wake of the 1959 case reviews, 76.4 percent of prisoners were reported to have paid work, already by the first quarter of 1961 that figure had dropped to 69.2 percent as the Gulag population rapidly expanded.[135] By 1964, still only 74 percent of prisoners were on paid labor, with another 9.5 percent of inmates employed in the camp service.[136] The biggest challenge facing the Gulag when it came to providing paid work was the large number of invalids in the penal system. By 1 October 1963 only 6.5 percent of able-bodied inmates were not working, and the percentage of prisoners systematically refusing to work had decreased from 1.9 at the end of 1960 to just 0.6 in the second quarter of 1963.[137] Yet as of late 1964 there were 43,897 invalids, very few of whom had work.[138]

As with most statistics, these paid-work statistics must be viewed skeptically. As the deputy head of the Russian Gulag frankly admitted in the pages of *K novoi zhizni* in 1961, production figures were often marred by upward distortions (*pripiski*) and fraud (*ochkovtiratel'stvo*).[139] As the percentage of inmates on paid labor became increasingly important as a performance metric, local administrators gained more and more incentive to cheat the system, as they had traditionally done with plan fulfillment figures, among other data. Perhaps surprisingly, this disturbed not just higher authorities, but many inmates too. Some in Kherson, for instance, complained of being regularly taken to just "hang out in the mine."[140] The administration could thus count them as working, but with no work to actually perform their productivity plummeted along with their wages. And with scarce wages, of course, they could not make purchases at the store or send money home. Thus, the inmates themselves, while not caring about plan fulfillment or the supposed reeducational value of labor, attached great importance to the tangible monetary fruits of labor and complained when this was not provided. Indeed, it is not surprising in this regard to find some prisoners in the 1960s voluntarily working hours of overtime each day (which was technically illegal, one might add) in order to increase their take-home pay.[141]

Despite increased attention on the reeducational value of labor, ultimately the concerns of the Gulag administration aligned most closely with those of the prisoners from Kherson. As the Ukrainian MVD reminded colony commanders in Kiev Province in 1963, the most important reporting number was production: "This is the primary indicator of your activity and we will ask you seriously about that indicator." Second and third in the hierarchy of reporting, according to the Ukrainian MVD, were the employment of prisoners and the fiscal state of the colony. Other reporting figures, such as regimen infractions and parole numbers, were still important and were becoming more important in the 1960s, but at the end of the day the economic state of each penal institution remained paramount. Similarly, at a Ukrainian MVD Collegium meeting in 1964, Ukrainian MVD head Ivan Golovchenko put a subordinate on the spot, threatening, "You, and tell comrade Karagodnikov too, if you break the first-quarter plan, without even asking I'm going to give you both a reprimand. . . . If you don't fulfill [the plan], then the [Council of Ministers] and [Central Committee] will call us to account. We are transferring this responsibility to you." In Lithuania, a colony commander had his salary reduced by half because he did not fulfill his plan targets. Later, when sufficient progress had been made toward rectifying the situation, his full salary was restored.[142] Even with increased concern for law and order in the wake of the 1961 statute, production clearly still mattered in the Gulag.

Engineering Human Souls: New and Renewed Forms of Reeducation

The same impulses that drove the Gulag to focus on vocational training and specialized labor in the 1960s also produced increasing concern with other forms of reeducation, even as the "camp is not a resort" campaign was in full swing. Although a certain measure of penality was to be reintroduced into penal operations, the ultimate goal remained the correction and reeducation of criminals. As *K novoi zhizni* made clear, "the prisoner is not in a sanatorium but in a place for serving punishment. . . . Hatred for everything reprehensible in the criminal and love for the good that remains in him are fully compatible here."[143]

This principle is highlighted in an article about colony commander Ivan Zakharovich Legkoi that appeared in *K novoi zhizni* in the immediate aftermath of the 1961 statute. Legkoi had no time for reeducation, caring only for the amount of lumber his inmates produced. He ruled through fear, sending brigades who did not fulfill their norms to the penalty isolator, refusing to excuse prisoners from work for illness, and otherwise terrorizing the inmates. Yet in the end, the plan for the previous year was only fulfilled by 35 percent, implying that the inmates were being made worse, not better, by Legkoi's actions. The message of this (quite possibly invented) story was clear: reeducation remained the ultimate goal of the Soviet penal system, and it could only be achieved if prisoners were treated respectfully.[144] These principles were reaffirmed in 1963 by the Ukrainian MVD head Golovchenko, who reminded his subordinates that "the most important task in building communism is the education (*vospitanie*) of people in the spirit of communist morality, the formation of a new person."[145]

The central philosophical underpinning of the reeducational drive of the 1960s was a renewed emphasis on an individualized approach to corrections. As the Central Committee admonished in mid-1960, the MVD was "to organize the work of reeducating prisoners on the basis of a differentiated approach and deep study of the character of each prisoner."[146] This order was rooted in long-standing Soviet penal philosophy but also in new sociological research into crime and its prevention, exemplified most prominently by the publication of A. B. Sakharov's landmark 1961 monograph *On the Character of the Prisoner and the Reasons for Crime in the USSR*. This and other works of the early 1960s renewed emphasis on psychological factors both in defining criminals and treating them.[147] As law professor M. A. Efimov instructed penal officials, it was not enough to understand an inmate, his crime, and his relations with other prisoners. It was not enough to observe him, to read his mail, to find about him from family, friends, and informers, or even to converse with him. One needed to study and understand his psychology. To this end Efimov made two suggestions. First, design and carry out experiments on him, that is, place him in certain (artificially constructed) situations to gauge his reactions. Second, have him compose an autobiographical sketch and then mine it for clues about his temperament, level of culture, interests, life story, and so forth. Only by this highly individualized approach to knowing each convict can one hope to make the psychological connections necessary for reeducation.[148] In the words of another professor at the same conference, "studying the character (*lichnost'*) [of the prisoner] is directed toward the goal of finding out to what degree the prisoner is infected with a criminal psychology, what are its origins, and what in the prisoner is healthy and on which one can rely in reeducational work."[149]

A. Kovalev, professor of pedagogy, expressed this new sentiment in an article directed at Gulag workers: "The educator (*vospitatel'*) should be a psychologist, an engineer of human souls."[150] Although this construction, "engineer of human souls," was a stock phrase from the Stalin era, Kovalev endowed it with new meaning that drew on the most recent psychological research.[151] This was done by delineating three broad psychological types that inhabited the correctional facilities of the Soviet Union. The first group was comprised of those with "egotistical desires and an egotistical character." These eschewed labor in order to live a lazy and "beautiful" life. The second group included those with "significant and stubborn criminal infection." These were habitual criminals, often drunkards, who would usually return to crime after release even if they had behaved admirably in the colonies. The third group were generally healthy, psychologically speaking, but were morally weak. They were often drawn to crime through the influence of others or perhaps through alcohol, but were not prone to crime themselves. Other articles on the psychology of prisoners followed in the pages of *K novoi zhizni* over the next several years, as the Gulag attempted to integrate the best social science research into its correctional program.[152] One in 1964, for instance, included a complex flowchart detailing how to determine the character traits of prisoners.[153] And even colony administrators began to use the same language, with one deputy head of a colony writing in a letter to the editor that "the most important thing for us is the remaking (*peredelka*) of the consciousness of lawbreakers."[154]

In addition to redefining corrections to include much closer attention to prisoners' psychological traits, the early to mid-1960s also witnessed the first serious studies of recidivism in the Soviet Union as the Gulag and academic criminologists attempted to quantify the level of correctional success in the penal institutions. Recidivism had long been acknowledged as a problem, especially in relation to the criminal gangs of the Gulag, but it had never been the object of study. Statistics on recidivism rates and analyses of the reasons behind recidivism are all but absent both in the criminological literature and in Gulag reports prior to 1960. But beginning this year, Gulag facilities were asked to track their recidivism rates for recently released prisoners. A pamphlet published by the political department of the Russian penal administration noted that of those released from Sverdlovsk facilities from 1961 to 1963, only 2.6 percent had committed new crimes. This number was held up as an example, but even it contained the caveat that any recidivism is too much.[155]

Another study on recidivism, this one conducted by faculty of the Sverdlovsk Law Institute, analyzed the characteristics of two thousand recidivists in local facilities. The causes of recidivism, they found, were quite varied, but all the recidivists demonstrated damaged psyches that made crime acceptable. Some justified crime as the only way out of a particular situation. Many were addicted to drugs and alcohol, which prevented them from holding a job and caused them to commit crimes. Some of these, with nothing to live for in normal society, even broke the law in order to return to the colonies. Others similarly wanted to live a "parasitic way of life" and would rather languish in penal facilities than work. Many recidivists were "infected with the poison of criminal romanticism," thinking that they, the criminals, possessed special traits that the general population did not. Some recidivists were angry or prone to self-mutilation. Most had a low cultural level and all shared the common trait of blaming others for their situation.[156]

Another study of recidivism was conducted V. I. Pinchuk, a Leningrad law professor. He found that most "especially dangerous recidivists" in Leningrad Province were adolescents during the war and in the immediate aftermath, and had begun in this period to commit small-scale crimes. Most committed their second crime within a year of being released for their first, and three-quarters of them were released through workday credits during the 1950s and then reincarcerated. Poor education was a final uniting feature of this group.[157]

Studies of recidivism in the 1960s also began to assign blame for the continued problem. An analysis of releases in Kherson in the first quarter of 1964 found that of 769 released inmates, 160 had within months returned to lives of crime. The work situation there was judged difficult, and many of the inmates had not lived in that city before.[158] Primary responsibility was therefore laid on local oversight commissions and procurators, who were not doing enough to ensure a smooth transition to a stable, law-abiding life. More common, however, were studies that blamed the penal facilities for releasing inmates before they had been fully corrected. A group of Gulag workers in Cheliabinsk Province, for instance, conducted a study of recidivism in their province in late 1963 and found that many inmates were being released, including on parole, "with firm antisocial views and habits." In other words, the colonies were not fulfilling their mission to reeducate convicts; they were taking too lax an attitude toward correction. As a result, one-fifth of all inmates released in 1962–63 were living a "parasitic way of life."[159]

In order to more fully effect the correction of their inmates and thereby prevent recidivism, colony administrators, especially detachment heads, were instructed to keep in touch with their former inmates both to aid in their transition to life outside the colony and, through their correspondence, to aid in the reeducation of those still incarcerated.[160] One example of how this was to work was provided in a *K novoi zhizni* article detailing the actions of detachment head P. Iatskevich. Half a year before one of his inmates is released Iatskevich figures out where he would live and work. Upon release he admonishes the prisoner on the rights and obligations of the Soviet citizen and then helps take care of any registration problems that arise in the first days of freedom. After that he maintains contact with the released inmate, using letters as reeducational devices in the colonies. When one former inmate breaks off contact, Iatskevich makes inquiries and finds out that he is living a parasitic life. But a sharply worded letter from Iatskevich restores his desire to live an honest life and he begins to work again.[161]

In addition to conducting and paying attention to studies on the causes of recidivism, the Gulag also attempted in the 1960s to make its staff more professional. Raising the professional and educational qualifications of Gulag personnel, along with finding workers who were cultured, obedient, and not prone to drunkenness, debauchery, or corruption were immediate goals of the post-Stalin era, but ones that proved difficult to achieve. Conditions for Gulag workers in the 1960s, after all, remained primitive in many locations, despite the shift from distant camps to regional colonies. A colony chief from Ukraine lamented that his guards were "living in the dirt" alongside the inmates. A resultant inspection found malnourished guards enduring winters without heating, and getting sick in epidemic proportions.[162] Another official complained in the pages of *K novoi zhizni* that their children for several years did not have a school to attend.[163] A third lamented the extremely limited supplies and services for Gulag workers in the logging camps when compared to logging camps for free workers.[164] As Marchenko explained after talking to one of the guards, from "the way he talks it is clear that his three years are as much a prison sentence to him as the con's years inside."[165] Recruiting qualified people to serve in the Gulag, in other words, continued to be very difficult. As a deputy minister of the Russian MVD complained, personnel departments in the Gulag were hiring virtually anyone, even those with past histories of alcoholism and crime.[166]

Indeed, in 1960 a study group commissioned by the Russian Bureau of the Central Committee and led by MVD chief Stakhanov found that little improvement in the quality of Gulag personnel had been made since 1956. Critically, given their daily interactions with the inmates, about half of the Gulag's 4,092 detachment heads did not have a completed secondary education, supposedly the minimum requirement for the job.[167] How could they reeducate the inmates if they themselves were uneducated? In some places the educational levels of Gulag staff were abysmally low. An inspection into the Novosibirsk corrective-labor colonies in 1960, for instance, found that only 4 out of 171 internal guards had a full secondary education.[168] A simultaneous inspection of Iaroslavl Province was even worse with only 4 out of 424 internal guards possessing a full secondary education.[169] As the author of that report, Procurator General for Russia Illarion Fedorovich Osipenko noted, "it is clear that such personnel are not capable of ensuring the fulfillment of the primary task of correcting and reeducating prisoners."

Other reports likewise pointed to problems in the ranks of Gulag workers.[170] The Central Committee in the first half of 1960, for instance, received over six thousand letters regarding incorrect actions taken by Gulag administrators. These detailed beatings, drunkenness, poor organization of work, insufficient attention to medical care, and various other complaints.[171] Indeed, the official reason given for sacking Stakhanov (along with a top deputy) in 1961 was the lamentable state of discipline among the MVD's internal troops, including in the Gulag. Drunkenness, hooliganism, disrespect for authority, and suicide were rampant in the ranks, yet little was being done to correct the problem.[172] As a Gulag political worker pointed out, many detachment heads showed up to work with hangovers, in dirty and unkempt clothing, unshaven, and ready to harshly punish prisoners who stepped out of line.[173] Similarly, a cartoon in the November 1963 edition of *K novoi zhizni* showed a drunk being hauled away by policemen above a caption explaining that in one correctional-labor institution, twenty-seven staff members in just six months had been detained for drunkenness.[174] As Sergei Dovlatov explained, "generally, administration office workers started resembling the [prisoners] after a month. Even contracted engineers fell into using camp argot. Not to speak of the soldiers." In other words, "almost any prisoner would have been suited to the role of a guard. Almost any guard deserved a prison term."[175]

In response to the low educational levels and corruption among Gulag personnel, the Russian Bureau of the Central Committee in 1960 ordered provincial party apparatuses to send prepared communists, Komsomol members, and demobilized soldiers to work in their corrective-labor institutions.[176] Over the next several months, 200 new guard officers were brought in from the military academies.[177] In the same period, 583 detachment heads were replaced and in mid-1961 the MVD reported that 74.3 percent of all detachment heads had a secondary education.[178] Continued efforts to raise the qualifications of detachment heads meant that over 90 percent had at least a secondary education by 1963.[179] As the head of the Russian Gulag reminded in early 1964, penal workers needed to set the example of a cultured life, a life of education and order and cleanliness, and a life free from swearing and rule-breaking: "All this will arouse in the prisoners the feeling of collectivism, organization, frugality, and the habits of cultured behavior, and in the end will facilitate their reeducation."[180]

Notably, in the 1960s, the Gulag made a concerted effort to include all staff members and guards of penal institutions in the reeducation of the inmates. Tikunov in early 1964, for instance, admonished production personnel in the Gulag to continue to perfect the use of labor in a reeducational capacity. The most important task for the year, he remarked, was to reduce recidivism by improving "the effectiveness of corrective-labor influence on the convicts."[181] The 1960s also witnessed the creation of "councils of reeducators." Comprised of administrators, staff, and guards from various parts of the colony, they were supposed to meet regularly to discuss the coordination and improvement of reeducational efforts.[182]

Without question, however, the detachment heads, the penal officials with the closest daily interactions with the prisoners, were supposed to take the lead in the reeducational effort. Regional best-practices conferences for detachment heads were held in December 1960 in both Leningrad and Irkutsk, and efforts were made to reduce the number of inmates in each detachment to around one hundred, as called for in the 1961 statute.[183] The Lithuanian MVD academy created new courses for new detachment heads, which focused particularly on pedagogy and psychology, and began to cycle existing detachment heads through them as well.[184] *K novoi zhizni* sent out experienced pedagogues to monitor detachment commanders and then share their insights in the pages of the journal. One such article focused on one Comrade Tatarinov in Tula Province, who is presented as the model detachment head. He knows his prisoners intimately, on a deep, psychological basis, and he experiments with a variety of methods to achieve their reeducation.[185] As part of this effort detachment leaders were admonished to be much more vigilant in keeping records on the behaviors and attitudes of their inmates. And apparently this emphasis paid off, at least in some respects. The Supreme Soviet in 1964 began noticing a "significant improvement" in the character statements they received concerning inmates being considered for pardon.[186]

In addition to recruiting more qualified personnel to improve correctional work and stressing the importance of detachments and detachment heads in the reeducational process, the Gulag took additional steps to strengthen the work of reeducation among its inmates. The educational system for inmates was further expanded.[187] In May 1963 the Russian MVD mandated an eight-grade education for prisoners, replacing the existing six-grade education, giving penal facilities two years to implement this decision.[188] USSR-wide statistics at the time of Khrushchev's ouster reveal a network of 400 eight-grade schools, 175 primary schools, 330 middle schools, more than 400 "consultation points," and 212,534 students.[189] Socialist competitions among Gulag brigades were also revised starting in 1960 so as to take not just production but reeducation and regime considerations into account.[190] Subsequent inspections made clear that production figures continued to dominate decisions as to which brigades earned the title of "Brigade of Highly Productive Labor and Model Behavior," but at least they were no longer the only criteria.[191]

Another reform designed to strengthen reeducation of inmates was implemented in 1961, when informal political discussions with prisoners were replaced by more formal, weekly political exercises in groups of around thirty-five inmates, which were often led by the detachment head.[192] The political department of the Russian Gulag began to disseminate these exercises through *K novoi zhizni;* thus, not only were the meeting times made more regular, the content was also more tightly controlled.[193] That does not mean, however, that they were better received. Political prisoners, usually far more educated than the administrators trying to lead the discussion, often mocked the discussions taking place.[194] Religious and political prisoners were also prone to absenteeism even though the exercises were mandatory, accepting whatever punishment the administration decided to mete out.[195] Osipov, for instance, had his right to the camp store and his visitation rights taken away, and another inmate in his camp point was sent to the penalty isolator for fifteen days.[196]

Already mentioned in relation to deconvoying, the idea of placing trust in inmates also continued to be emphasized in the 1960s. The biggest area where this principle can be viewed is the increasing size and importance of the self-governing organizations that were reinstated in the 1950s. Although not allowed in special-regimen colonies, where inmates were locked in solitary confinement, the self-governing organizations in most colonies came to play a more important and more visible role than in the 1950s. New statutes governing these self-governing organizations passed in the various republics in early 1962, and these called for the expansion of the numbers of inmate groups in each institution.[197] One of the most important changes was that, in contrast to the 1950s, activists in the 1960s were not supposed to be given special privileges. Crucially in this regard, they were to be engaged in the primary production of the colony rather than released from labor due to their social activity.[198] In other words, activity in the organizations was supposed to be based on sincere desire for self-betterment, not for the attainment of exclusive privileges.

The second major change to self-governing organizations was the introduction of the section of internal order (initially called the section of social order), an inmate policing organization marked by the red armbands worn by its members.[199] Such a section was first organized on an experimental basis in a Kazakh penal facility in 1956, then formally approved and regulated by statute in late 1959.[200] By the early 1960s it was one of the standard sections organized throughout the Gulag. Because of the power and authority gained by members of this section, it was usually the largest of the self-governing organizations in each penal institution. A cartoon in the August 1961 edition of *K Novoi Zhizni* depicted the role of the new section of internal order by displaying a member, complete with armband, proudly having caught three regimen violators: a drug addict, a gambler, and a drunkard. With the three apprehended violators dangling from the dots of the three exclamation points, the large-font caption made the message clear: "To violators of discipline, parasites, shame!!!"[201] Given such power to expose illegal activity and bring punishment to fellow inmates, power that was prone to abuse, it is not surprising that the section of internal order was often viewed quite negatively by other inmates.

Various corners of the Gulag tried different techniques for improving the work of the self-governing organizations and increasing their size. One colony created a series of classes for activists in which they learned how to do their duties better.[202] In Ukraine they created youth sections to better engage young convicts in the life of the colonies.[203] A Chuvash colony created ten wall newspapers, one for each detachment and each with its own editorial staff.[204] And these efforts apparently paid dividends in the number of inmates engaged in self-governing organizations. Viatlag in late 1962 had 27 activist councils with 447 members and 108 detachment-level activist councils with 867 members. In addition, it engaged 631 inmates in labor sections, 320 in education sections, 443 in sanitation sections, 314 in dining sections, 647 in cultural sections, 525 in physical culture sections, and 2,335 in internal order sections. A total of 6,529 prisoners were thus involved in helping the administration manage the camp.[205] The Ukrainian MVD in early 1962 reported that 35 percent of its inmates were enrolled in self-governing institutions, but by 1964 it was up to 41 percent.[206]

A model example of how self-governing institutions were supposed to work, at least according to the political department of the Russian Gulag, was depicted in an article by a colony boss in the January 1962 edition of *K novoi zhizni*. He reported that because the activists had gained the respect (*avtoritet'*) of the other inmates, they now had 80 percent of all prisoners engaged in the self-governing institutions. They were involved in making parole determinations, they kept the colony clean, they ensured the school was running smoothly, they raised the productivity and quality of labor, and through their influence the number of regimen infractions had dropped dramatically. Work refusals and drug use had become a thing of the past, and because the inmates were so well behaved the colony was able to control costs by curtailing the use of overtime shifts for guards.[207] The opposite example was provided a few months later. The administration of one unnamed colony was not engaged in individualized reeducational work among the inmates and did not support the self-governing organizations, preferring instead to falsify infraction statistics to give the appearance of a well-run colony. In fact, most inmates refused to work and committed many regimes infractions. And when the self-governing organizations attempted to rectify the situation, a mob of inmates attacked the activists, resulting in the death of the chairman of the council of the collective, and the wounding of two members of the section of internal order.[208] When used improperly, this article warned, self-governing institutions could backfire, resulting in the breakdown of discipline and reeducation.

Indeed, the activist organizations became the fault line for conflict between the inmates and the administration and among the inmates themselves. In order to be considered "on the path to the correction," and thus eligible for parole, one usually had to join one of the self-governing councils or sections. And although no extra privileges were supposed to be granted to activists, often it was only the activists who enjoyed the full measure of privileges—packages, visits by family members, purchases at the colony store—that the 1961 statute laid forth for all inmates.[209] Those who refused to become activists, in turn, often resented the privileges and powers gained by their fellow prisoners. Marchenko's memoir expressed a common viewpoint concerning the activists: "Everyone knows that the council of a [detachment] or camp collective is nothing but a willing instrument, a bludgeon in the hands of the authorities." Moreover, he added, it was staffed largely by Nazi collaborators.[210] Osipov reported that in Dubravlag many prisoners refused to interact in any way with the activists.[211]

Calling them a variety of names—"reds," after the red armbands of the section of internal order, kozly (literally "male goat," a highly offensive term that implied both collaboration with the authorities and passive homosexuality), and bitches (another pejorative for collaborator)—many hardened inmates were prone to band together to intimidate or assault activists, especially those in the section of internal order.[212] Reports of such attacks litter the Gulag and Procuracy archives. In January 1961 at Colony No. 1 in Ukraine's Stalin Province, for instance, a group of forty inmates armed themselves with sticks and bricks and attacked a group of activists. When the latter fled into a barrack, the troublemakers lit the barrack on fire and prevented the activists from leaving. Eventually armed guards were able to restore order, but not before three activists were killed in the fire.[213] Similarly, on New Year's Day in 1961, several activists in Colony No. 3 in Lithuania were severely beaten in a mass disturbance where prisoners protested poor treatment by the guards and administrators.[214] Riots and disturbances in Colony No. 2 in Lithuania in July and September 1962 were blamed on rude behavior and beatings by the section of internal order, which was facilitated by the administration granting them too much administrative power.[215]

But in many institutions the activists were able to assert their authority without retribution from their fellow inmates. As F. A. Serebrovym, incarcerated in Magadan Province, recalled, the activists ruled the camp fearlessly, and in fact were instrumental in curbing much of the theft and other crimes committed by prisoners. As a result the colony became a much more harmonious and well-ordered place. Moreover, inmates were anxious to join the activist ranks because this greatly increased their chances of parole.[216] As expressed in Sergei Dovlatov's semifictionalized memoir of his time as a camp guard, prisoner Mishchuk "knew that with an effort he could get his sentence cut in half. Mishchuk became a model worker, an activist, a reader of the newspaper Toward an Early Release. And, most important, he signed up for the Section of Internal Order, the SIO. Now he walked between barracks wearing a red armband."[217] Even some political prisoners, thinking to improve matters, tried their hand at running the self-governing organizations.[218] As voiced by one of these upon joining the ranks of activists, "No one has suffered because I became a brigade leader and a member of the 'council of activists.' On the contrary, I'm trying to make things better for everyone."[219] Vladimir Gridin too joined the activist council along with his peers, if only to prevent less savory characters from occupying these important positions.[220]

The experience of Mark Gol'dman and a few of his fellow political prisoners, however, demonstrates that such attempts often ended in disillusionment. They decided to join the activist council in an effort to help preserve the human dignity of the prisoners while insisting that the inmates perform honest labor. In just three months, however, after attempts by the camp administration to make the council members do things it did not want to do—nothing specific is mentioned but it likely involved requests to approve punishments for and publicly censor regimen-violating prisoners—Gol'dman and his friends left the council. Concluding that the administrators and the system they propped up were "uncorrectable," the disgruntled ex-activists announced and carried out a seven-day hunger strike.[221] This account is confirmed by Gol'dman's friend, Lev Krasnopevtsev, who served as the chairman of that activist council and later recollected that the council to the administration was a game, an attempt to reconcile the irreconcilable antagonism "between the prisoner and the jailer."[222]

The final and perhaps most fascinating method for reeducating inmates in the early to mid-1960s was a concerted attempt to shame prisoners both into good behavior and, more intriguingly, into confessions. Rooted in the new psychological criminology, this effort aimed at cleansing the conscience of offenders, thereby giving them a clean slate on which to start their new lives. The first such appeal, which appeared in *K novoi zhizni* in April 1961, encouraged inmates to confess past crimes that the police had not solved.[223] Then the May 1962 issue of *K novoi zhizni* included a "Letter from an Old Mother" to be read to prisoners, in which the author, A. Zaitseva, spoke of losing three brave sons in the Great Patriotic War. In regard to the prisoners, she then remarked how "shameful, hurtful it is to me to see those young and healthy guys who don't want to do anything useful, but, on the contrary, rob from people. Is this not shame and sorrow for their parents?"[224] These twin motivators—the Great Patriotic War and family—would become central parts of the ensuing campaign.[225]

A few months later *K novoi zhizni* published an account by a camp administrator from Cheliabinsk Province about how they had been publishing stories of ordinary people being harmed by crime in their local camp newspaper. Entitled "To Freedom with a Clean Conscience," this article series reportedly had such an effect on some prisoners that they began confessing to crimes and offering to make restitution. The convict Zotov, for example, reportedly declared, "I am ashamed of my vile act. I stole money from a student, deprived him of his stipend. . . . I ask the administration to take twelve rubles from my personal account and sent it to the victim." Prisoner Volkov similarly wrote: "I not only brought harm to citizen V. T. Fonovaia, who lay in the hospital for two weeks because of me, but also brought harm to society. After all, the hospital bill was paid by the labor union. I ask the administration to found out how much the union paid and recover this loss from my account." In response to this report from Cheliabinsk, the political department of the Russian Gulag discussed and approved this new avenue for reeducational work.[226]

Named "to freedom with a clean conscience" after the series of articles from Cheliabinsk, the shaming campaign continued in earnest in Ukraine with a letter by well-known Ukrainian hero of socialist labor, Nadezhda Grigor'evna Zaglada. Entitled "Don't Live for Personal Gain" it was published first in the internal newspaper of the Ukrainian MVD, *Trudovaia zhizn'* (*Working Life*), then in *K novoi zhizni* in late 1962.[227] Zaglada admonished prisoners to search out their consciences, to behave honorably in the colonies, and to return to freedom ready to participate in the construction of communism. The letter was followed by visits from Zaglada to several colonies in Ukraine where she shared her personal experiences (including being robbed), and, addressing them as a mother, admonished the inmates to "say goodbye once and for all to your dirty habits that have taught you a riotous (*razgul'naia*), vicious (*porochnaia*) life. Honestly atone for your guilt."[228] Other heroes of socialist labor were also brought in to reinforce the campaign, teaching the value of labor and the happiness of living a honorable life. In the words of Evgeniia Alekseevna Doliniuk, another motherly figure, "Only through labor, conscientious labor, can you earn the right to life among the honest Soviet citizens."[229]

The "to freedom with a clean conscience" campaign quickly spread to the other republics, even without the sponsorship of an All-Union MVD to coordinate such policy. Whether due to pressure from party organs or out of a sincere desire to implement best practices in their own republics, MVD administrators began following the example of Cheliabinsk and Ukraine.[230] *K novoi zhizni* in 1963–64 periodically reminded its readers to continue actively persuading prisoners to confess past crimes, and that such confessions should be immediately sent to the police for investigation. Moreover, judges were encouraged to be lenient in assigning punishment owing to the voluntary nature of the confession.[231]

The effect of these efforts, at least according to the official narrative, was overwhelming. Touched by the message of honesty, hundreds of prisoners around Ukraine began confessing to unsolved crimes in the first months of the campaign, with many of them asking for a garnishment of their wages to compensate for the damage they had done.[232] And the pace of confessions did not slacken over the ensuing years. By 1963, the Ukrainian Gulag was obtaining several hundred confessions per month.[233] One inmate in particular confessed to a string of twenty-two thefts in the mid-1950s; in his sentencing for these crimes, the procurator and judges took his confession in account and he was not given an additional sentence to deprivation of freedom.[234] The campaign likewise bore fruit in other republics into the mid-1960s. Lithuania reported that 60 prisoners in 1963 confessed to 139 unsolved crimes, named 14 partners in crime, and related the details of 5 unsolved crimes committed by others.[235] Likewise, the Russian MVD reported that 4,336 prisoners in 1964 confessed to 7,410 crimes that had not been solved by the police.[236]

While the "to freedom with a clean conscience" campaign does not appear in the few extant memoirs from the 1960s, a similar program of reeducation through shame targeted political prisoners. Often using the promise of pardon, Gulag officials attempted to convince politicals to confess and forsake their sins against the Soviet Union. As noted by MVD academic N. Romanenko, the promise of pardon can be "a good reeducational tool" in that it promised immediate release from confinement.[237] But political prisoners in their memoirs express a dim view of such efforts to blackmail them into confessing guilt when they felt that no crime had been committed. Marchenko, returning to his camp after a stint in Vladimir Prison, was taken aback by the new line of questioning taken by his detachment head: ""Do you repent, are you sorry for what you did?"[238] Likewise, Osipov was disgusted when a former political prisoner that he knew was recruited by the camp administration soon after his release to talk with the prisoners and convince them to "disarm."[239] Even Ivan Prokof'evich Sharapov had to endure two fruitless rounds of questioning along the lines of repentance for his crime before being informed that his sentence had been cut (thanks to personal contacts) and he was being released.[240]

Reintroducing the Progressive System: Colony-Settlements and "Chemistry"

The culminating and arguably most important reforms of the Soviet penal system in the late Khrushchev era were the creation of a network of light-regime penal institutions called colony-settlements and the introduction of a new form of early conditional release called "chemistry." Although, as noted previously, the Central Committee was initially conservative in modifying the 1961 Statute on Prisons and Corrective-Labor Colonies, these changes directly attacked two of the central pillars of the "camp is not a resort" counterreform movement: more restricted use of parole and a rejection of the "progressive" system of confinement. Inmates would once again be shown "liberalism" by being transferred to states of partial freedom as reward for good behavior. Like most programs in the Gulag, however, these reforms were not based purely on the idea of reeducation. As the Lithuanian MVD felt prompted to clarify in defense of reeducation, "chemistry" and colony-settlements were created "not only in response to the economic interests of the Soviet state."[241] In fact, it was precisely the pressures of economics and overpopulated penal facilities which made this return to "progressive" penal policy a reality.

On 30 May 1963 the Soviet Central Committee approved a new penal institution called the colony-settlement.[242] This idea apparently originated with the Kazakh MVD, which proposed it to the Kazakh Central Committee in mid-1962.[243] It thereafter gained the support of the Kazakh Procuracy and Supreme Soviet, and ultimately Tikunov, who presented a polished version of the idea to the Soviet Central Committee in April 1963. The idea was to provide a lighter form of punishment for those not eligible for parole because of the seriousness of their crime but who had demonstrated reeducation through good behavior. As Tikunov put it, "there is no need to hold them in standard correctional-labor facilities any longer."[244] While part of the rationale was a return to a progressive system of punishment that rewarded inmates for good behavior and better prepared them for release, there were other motivations as well. It acted as an important release valve for the approximately 150,000 inmates not eligible for parole. And, as Tikunov also reminded the Central Committee, the colony-settlements could help with the economic development of sparsely populated areas.[245] With this in mind it is not surprising that the idea originated in Kazakhstan, which at the time was struggling to keep civilians in the Virgin Lands regions. Well-behaved inmates and their families presented a potential, albeit partial, solution to their labor-shortage problems.

According to the new regulations, transfer to colony-settlements was possible for those on standard or strengthened regimen, provided they had demonstrated good behavior, a conscientious attitude toward work, and participation in the social and cultural life of the colony. Inmates not eligible for parole could be transferred by court decree to colony-settlements after serving two-thirds of their sentence and at least five years, whereas those eligible for parole could be transferred after serving half of their sentence and at least three years. The colony-settlements themselves differed significantly from regular colonies in that they had no cells, no guards, and no restrictions on clothing, visits, correspondence, packages, or the use of money. Inmates would receive normal wages (with some money garnished for administrative expenses), but would work seven-hour days and have freedom of movement in the immediate vicinity of the colony. Furthermore, with approval from the administration inmates could build their own homes, grow their own gardens, and even send for their families to live with them.[246] This institution, similar to the lightened-regimen colonies of the 1950s, allowed the MVD to use its limited guard manpower more efficiently. But it also signified desire to help inmates adjust to conditions of partial freedom before their ultimate release back into society and a restored faith in the reformability of the worst offenders by means of leniency and trust. As *Izvestiia* confidently declared in its announcement of the new institution, "the Soviet corrective-labor system offers even the most inveterate criminal the opportunity to stand on his feet."[247]

Over the next year each republic passed their own decree ordering the MVDs to create these colony-settlements. The first ones established were an agricultural colony-settlement in Kazakhstan and six logging colony-settlements in Russia.[248] Initial inspections of these institutions were generally positive. Production plans were being overfulfilled; regimen infractions were few; inmates were healthily engaged in cultural, education, and political work; many had been reunited with their families in the settlements; and they "expressed gratitude for the conditions that have been created and assured us that through honest labor and model behavior they will justify the trust shown to them."[249] A similar report can be found for Ukraine, which organized its first colony-settlement in early 1964. Located at a state farm, it initially housed two hundred inmates but an expansion would soon bring that number to six hundred. Because this colony-settlement was located near an existing free settlement, it had a school, a library, a club, a hospital, a dining hall, a bath house, and several stores in close proximity. The prisoners were starting to build homes for their families, and they all promised to behave.[250]

The first report of a colony-settlement in *K novoi zhizni* related the experience of a state farm in the Virgin Lands region that was converted into a colony-settlement. There were initially some problems: a few invalids were sent who could not perform farm labor, and some inmates quickly turned to drunkenness. Violators of the regimen were discussed in group meetings, and those who refused to confess and repent were sent back to the regular colonies. But this act of expulsion had the effect of creating a strong collective among those that remained. And this, combined with the positive influence of their families, created a healthy reeducational atmosphere. Even without the presence of guards the inmates were well behaved and hardworking. As voiced by inmate A. Bogomolov, "For more than six years I lived under guard. I never thought that they would allow me to live in the conditions of a colony and work without convoy. I am proud of the trust placed in me and bring all my strength to justify it."[251] A few months later *K novoi zhizni* published six photographs from a colony-settlement that were to be used to help inmates work toward being transferred to these new institutions. They show prisoners happily working, receiving mail, putting money in the bank or using it to buy presents for their families. But most poignantly, one photograph depicts an inmate enjoying time with his wife and young daughter, who is kissing him on the cheek. The message here is unmistakable: life in the colony-settlement was just like life outside the Gulag.[252]

Problems were not wholly absent, however. Some inmates had to be transferred back to their colonies after multiple regimen violations, and some colony-settlement administrators were found to have weak control over their prisoners. A few colony commanders attempted to send their worst inmates to the colony-settlements in order to be rid of them, while holding on to their better-behaved and productive inmates.[253] One colony-settlement commander in Arkhangel'sk Province violated regulations by allowing thirty-two of his prisoners to live outside the zone; several took advantage of this lack of oversight by drinking heavily and wandering through the nearby town. Ten of these were subsequently returned to their former institutions.[254] An article in the March 1964 edition of *K novoi zhizni* depicted a colony-settlement that had not been properly prepared before receiving its inmates, meaning there was a serious shortage of housing. As a result, the prisoners for months were not allowed to invite their families to live with them, resulting in great unhappiness.[255] And late in 1964 the Gulag lamented the presence of "loose women and speculators" in some colony-settlements. It also noted continued problems with drunkenness and various labor violations, such as tardiness and unexcused absences from work. Even the presence of women's councils, comprised of the wives of colony-settlers, though beneficial, was not fully successful in keeping the men in line.[256]

Despite these problems, the colony-settlement program continued to expand throughout 1964 and 1965. By 1 January 1965 there were 35 colony-settlements in the Soviet Union: 22 in Russia, 3 in Uzbekistan, 1 each in 10 other republics, and none in Belorussia, Lithuania, or Armenia. Together they held 11,106 convicts, of which 74.7 percent were not eligible for parole. Continued inspections by the Procuracy showed that in general the new institutions were successful, with only 150 being sent back to their colonies in 1964 and another 57 being convicted of new crimes while in the colony-settlements.[257] Over the course of 1965 the network of colony-settlements continued to expand, with 33 such institutions holding 11,000 inmates in Russia alone on 1 October 1965.[258]

On 20 March 1964 the Supreme Soviet passed another decree that signified restored commitment to "progressive" principles and a more lenient attitude toward convicts, although it was also (and likely primarily) motivated by economic concerns. The decree instituted a new form of parole that allowed "conditional release from deprivation of freedom" for well-behaved and able-bodied prisoners after serving only a very short portion of their term (after only one year of incarceration for terms of up to five years, two years for sentences of five to ten years, and five years for longer terms). Significantly, in light of the "to freedom with a clean conscience" campaign, the freed inmate was to have "demonstrated the desire to redeem his guilt through honest work." Upon release, which was proposed by the colony or camp administration and then approved by a court, the inmates were given all the rights enjoyed by free citizens, but they were required to live and work at a designated construction site (chemical plants, oil refineries, and related factories are specifically mentioned) and could not leave the administrative region in which they were located without explicit police approval. While in the conditional stage of this release, the ex-cons were to be treated like ordinary workers, and they could even, as with the colony-settlements, invite their family to live with them. But if they committed a new crime or otherwise caused trouble they were to be returned to the colony or camp from which they were freed with no credit toward their sentence for their time at the construction site. For those who remained well-behaved until the expiration of their original sentence, they were then free to leave with all citizens' rights restored.[259]

Because chemical plants were mentioned first in the decree in the list of approved construction sites, the chemical industry being an era of heavy investment in the late Khrushchev era, this new form of parole quickly became known as "chemistry" by the inmates of the Gulag. And as the name implies, this was primarily a tool used by the Central Committee to provide a labor force for remote construction sites. Rather than send prisoners, as Stalin did in the 1930s to industrialize the margins of the USSR, Khrushchev decided to release the prisoners first, but still hold them tied to the geographic region where they were needed. In essence, it was a form of exile that sought to take advantage of the higher productivity of nonincarcerated laborers, while also lowering the cost of their maintenance. And like regular parole, it quickly came to be used by penal administrators as a tool to manage the population of each penal institution. Thus, in addition to fulfilling a reeducational function with the possibility of very early release from incarceration, "chemistry" was important both for the national economy and as a release valve for overcrowded penal institutions.

The multifunctionality of "chemistry" made it a very popular form of early release. Within months of the decree the Supreme Soviet allowed parolees of this type to be sent to the Virgin Lands regions in Kazakhstan, thereby increasing the number of prisoners that could be released.[260] Enterprises from various ministries began submitting requests for ex-prisoners. And Gulag administrators quickly moved to relieve overcrowding and, when possible, to get rid of troublemakers while retaining their best workers.[261] Already in September 1964 the Gulag had to warn its workers that the decree was not an amnesty and that the character of prisoners must be taken into account when deciding whom to parole to construction sites. It further instructed that detachment heads and inmate activists should be involved in these decisions as they know the prisoners best.[262] And the courts, in turn, rejected 2,660 inmates put up for "chemistry" in the first seven months of the decree's life.[263]

The eagerness of Gulag bosses to partially empty their institutions was not the only problem that plagued "chemistry." Hundreds of ex-prisoners were quickly sent back to their penal institutions after committing new crimes, and hundreds more fled their new places of residence. Many arrived at the construction site only to find no or very poor housing for them. The Procuracy, for instance, alleged that only 2,860 of the first 34,730 released to construction sites were provided adequate housing upon arrival.[264] Construction managers were occasionally firing the new workers before their term had expired, or using them on projects not authorized by the 20 March 1964 decree.[265] Moreover, the political department of the Gulag complained of the tendency of gas industry managers in Tiumen Province to designate certain construction sites for inmates only, rather than integrating them into existing collectives, which would ostensibly aid in their further reeducation.[266] Here, though, one can certainly understand the point of view of the economic agencies, who were seeking to prevent the transmission of criminal activity into their free workforce.

Despite these challenges, the "chemistry" decree proved even more popular than the colony-settlements, which were only available to those on standard and strengthened regimens. There was demand for the labor and there was a ready supply as well. Already by 1 December 1964, 52,924 inmates had been conditionally released to construction sites. Indeed, in 1964 as a whole, "chemistry" accounted for 12.9 percent of all prisoners released from the Gulag.[267] By the end of 1965, more than 92,000 inmates had been released by this decree.[268]

Colony-settlements and "chemistry" demonstrate a clear institutional refutation of the retributive counterreform movement of the late 1950s and early 1960s. "Liberalism" and the progressive system of confinement, two features of the initial post-Stalin era that were rejected in the "camp is not a resort" campaign, both returned with strong support from the criminal justice establishment and from the top leadership of the USSR. Moreover, these reforms highlight the fluid nature of reform in the Khrushchev era. From 1953 to 1964 the Soviet Union struggled to define the mission and methods of Soviet penal facilities. Juggling the competing aims of corrections, economics, and security in an atmosphere of political instability, scarce resources, and impatience for the future proved conducive to wide swings in policy. Thus, even as Khrushchev attempted to distance the Soviet Union from the repressive legacy of Stalinism, forging a new and stable equilibrium in the penal sector proved difficult. As it turns out, however, the final reforms of 1963–64 were the very ones that ended the era of penal experimentation and achieved relative equilibrium.

Indeed, the outcome of penal experimentation of the Khrushchev era may be seen dialectically as a synthesis between the initial thesis of liberalism as a means of correction and the subsequent antithesis of retribution and harsh regimen conditions. The counter-counterreforms of the mid-1960s—increased rations, heightened use of parole and deconvoying, greater focus on various reeducational programs, colony-settlements, and "chemistry"—forged this synthesis of the two competing post-Stalin narratives and decisively rejected the Stalinist vision of punishment as retribution and labor power. And it was this synthesis, embodied by a partial commitment to "progressive" principles, which remained the guiding philosophy for the duration of the Soviet Union.

Conclusions

KHRUSHCHEV'S REFORMS AND THE LATE (AND POST-)SOVIET GULAG

Prison 'reform' is virtually contemporary with the prison itself: it constitutes, as it were, its programme.

—Michel Foucault, *Discipline and Punish*

In the final analysis, how does one assess Nikita Sergeevich Khrushchev's reforms in the penal sphere? According to the most optimistic of the regime's aims, as expressed in Vasilii Aleksandrovich Samsonov's 1962 report on the future withering away of the Soviet penal system (detailed at the beginning of chapter 5), the reforms ultimately failed. Soviet society in the 1960s and 1970s was riddled with crime—people committed murders and assaults, they stole from one another, they drove while intoxicated, they brewed moonshine, they embezzled money or property from their workplace, and they violated the law in a variety of other ways.[1] And despite efforts to promote noncustodial sanctioning in places of imprisonment, ultimately the Soviets were unwilling to reject state-mandated incarceration as the backbone of the penal system. Yet even though this audacious dream, reminiscent of early Soviet criminology, was once again possible thanks to the post-Stalin Gulag reforms, it is ultimately not the best measuring stick for assessing these reforms.

According to many of the more realistic aims expressed by Khrushchev and other top Soviet officials from 1953 to 1956, the penal reforms of the Khrushchev era achieved remarkable success. Quantitatively, the Gulag was much smaller in 1964 than it was in 1953, and the number of political prisoners in the system had declined sharply. Millions of people removed from society during the Stalin years, together with hundreds of thousands more required to administer and guard them, were released. Despite scarce resources in an age of pervasive reforms, most of the large corrective-labor camps were eliminated in favor of smaller colonies, complete with onsite worksites. Inmates in 1964 were more often imprisoned in their home provinces, rather than being shipped to distant locations such as Kolyma, Vorkuta, and Karaganda. Prisoners enjoyed better living and working conditions in the mid-1960s than they did in the early 1950s, and they had been granted a number of rights not previously enjoyed. Mortality and sickness rates declined, as did the level of violence in the system. The three competing aims of the penal system had been rebalanced, with Khrushchev's Gulag placing much greater emphasis on reeducation than its predecessor. And various oversight bodies, especially the Procuracy, ensured that Gulag workers were held accountable for their actions.

The Gulag, in other words, had taken crucial steps toward correcting the problems with the Stalinist camps identified by Presidium members in their February 1954 meeting (as detailed in chapter 1). By 1964 the Gulag devoted far less energy to "construction," and more "to the correction of people," than it did in the last years of Stalin's life. Although economic concerns continued to play an important role in penal facility operations, no longer did central economic planners treat the Gulag simply as "a source of labor power." There were fewer inmates incarcerated for petty crimes, which prevented them from being "ruined" by the penal experience. The transition to colonies with their own productive bases fulfilled to some extent Khrushchev's desire for a "return to Dzerzhinskii's system of factories and workshops." The Gulag had, to a great extent, been "rebuilt anew."[2] According to Khrushchev and his peers along with the Gulag administration itself, therefore, the reformation of the penal system in the post-Stalin era was a rejection of Stalinism. As Gulag political worker A. Ermolaev declared in his review of Aleksandr Solzhenitsyn's One Day in the Life of Ivan Denisovich, that terrible era of lawlessness had been decisively rejected.

A number of historians, however, have dismissed the de-Stalinization of the Gulag as fleeting and ultimately inconsequential. Solzhenitsyn, speaking of the post-Stalin reforms, famously quipped, "Rulers change, the Archipelago remains."[3] Robert Conquest, who wrote extensively on the Gulag and all things repressive under the Soviet Union, argued that "however one looks at it, the penal and police systems were reformed in the Khrushchev period. Equally, however one looks at it, they did not undergo essential change, did not become truly liberal."[4] More recently, Anne Applebaum, in her Pulitzer Prize-winning history of the Gulag, speaks of "half-baked reforms, new privileges which were quickly removed, and public discussions which were immediately hushed up." By the mid-1960s, she asserts, "it was clear that the neo-Stalinists had triumphed."[5]

Certain pieces of evidence seem to support these contentions. The Gulag still imprisoned a high percentage of the Soviet population in relation to other countries (although the United States would eventually surpass it in this regard). Political prisoners, sentenced by an at times orchestrated justice system, still inhabited the Soviet Gulag of the 1960s and would continue to do so until the fall of communism.[6] The basic organization of camps and colonies remained relatively unchanged (barracks, barbed wire, guards). Production by means of inmate labor remained a serious if not overriding concern for camp administrators. Corruption was never fully stamped out, and guards and inmates alike at times engaged in beatings, rape, and other forms of violence. Ethnic rivalries and a very limited amount of gang affiliation among prisoner groups remained. The Gulag staff was only minimally professionalized. Finally, new efforts at reeducation failed to significantly lower the recidivism rate. In other words, the reforming programs of the 1950s were left partially unfulfilled. Yet this should not be surprising. The very fact that the Soviet penal system remained a penal system ensured a high degree of continuity in policy and practice. In fact, one wonders what Solzhenitsyn, Conquest, and others would have proposed as an alternative to the system they condemned. What, in fact, did Conquest mean by a "truly liberal" penal system?

Criminologists globally in the postwar era promoted a variety of penal measures that avoided incarceration or that placed inmates in "open" institutions, and the Soviets were very much engaged in such efforts.[7] Yet no country, in the East or West, was able to displace incarceration as the backbone of their penal system. From Western Europe to the United States to apartheid South Africa, prisons and their equivalents remained the punishment of choice. And these were not "liberal" institutions, but ones in which compulsory labor, corruption, beatings, and prisoner-on-prisoner violence abounded. Moreover, they were often places of severely curtailed rights and arbitrary rule. Some commentators from the period poignantly noted that prison systems in the West were in essence "totalitarian" islands in otherwise free societies. As N. A. Polanski argued in relation to the U.S. prison system, "the maximum security prison represents a social system in which an attempt is made to create and maintain total or almost total social control. The detailed regulations extending into every area of the individual's life, the constant surveillance, the concentration of power into the hands of a ruling few, the wide gulf between the rulers and the ruled—all are elements of what we would usually call a totalitarian regime."[8] This is not to defend the atrocities committed by and in the Gulag under Stalin and to a lesser extent under Khrushchev, which Solzhenitsyn masterfully exposes, but to remind that some of what he describes is endemic to prisons in general, not to Soviet institutions in particular. When the worst problems are corrected, therefore, one should not be surprised to still find oppression, corruption, confusion of aims, and disparities between rhetoric and reality, for such are the realities of virtually every system of incarceration.

The problem with the assessments of Solzhenitsyn, Conquest, and Applebaum, in other words, is that they judge the Gulag of the 1950s and 1960s against an undefined and ultimately unrealistic standard of what a penal system should look like. In this light it bears noting that comparisons with the Stalinist Gulag persist even now. The partner of a prisoner held in a corrective colony in Mordovia, when asked about conditions there in 2004 remarked, "read Solzhenitsyn's *Gulag Archipelago*; it's just the same today—nothing has changed."[9] And even the current minister of justice, Aleksandr Konovalov, while discussing a proposed set of reforms to the Russian penal system in 2011, complained that Russian prisons "are terribly archaic—they resemble the Gulag or even pre-revolutionary penal servitude."[10] It seems likely, therefore, that the image of the Stalinist Gulag persisting into the Khrushchev era and beyond is used by Solzhenitsyn, Conquest, Applebaum, and others not as an objective basis for comparison, but rather as a symbol to discredit the entire Soviet experiment (and post-Soviet regime).

In the final analysis, therefore, when assessing the Khrushchev era it is important that one not base one's judgments on the regime's failure to live up to its own ideologically driven fantasies for the future, or on some ill-informed conception of how Western prison systems operate. It is certainly true that Khrushchev failed to fully implement his de-Stalinization program in the penal sphere. But in fact the reforms of the Khrushchev period *did* have an important lasting effect on the Soviet penal system. Whereas most of Khrushchev's reforms in agriculture (the meat and milk campaign in particular, along with the push for corn), administration (the party reforms of the early 1960s and the councils of the national economy), and even the legal sphere (campaigns against hooliganism, speculation, and corruption), not to mention the partial and temporary relaxation of censorship that gave the "Thaw" its name, were short-lived and largely ineffective, the reform of the Gulag constituted an important instance of substantive and permanent transformation. This certainly holds true in terms of the Gulag's permanent reduction in size, but it also applies to the reorientation of Gulag aims and the resultant improved conditions experienced by its inmates. Most crucially, although certain inmate privileges were reduced or eliminated in the early 1960s at the culmination of the "camp is not a resort" campaign, many of the most important prisoner-friendly reforms of the 1950s, such as parole and the eight-hour workday, remained. Despite certain continuities, therefore, the Gulag did not return to a state of unchecked (and even abetted) violence, grueling labor, and oppressive living conditions—the defining features of the Stalinist penal system. De-Stalinization in the penal sphere was a real and enduring legacy of the Khrushchev era.

Khrushchev's Reforms beyond Khrushchev

On 14 October 1964 Khrushchev was formally removed from power by Leonid Brezhnev and a number of other high-level conspirators. His hold on power had been tenuous since 1960, with his increasingly erratic governing style and "harebrained scheming" ultimately alienating even his staunch supporters. Yet the forced retirement of Khrushchev did not have nearly the same effect as the death of Stalin nearly twelve years previously. The ensuing succession struggle was muted, there was no "secret speech," and the post-1964 reforms were mostly focused, in the words of Khrushchev's successors, on undoing various "hasty decisions and actions divorced from reality."[11] Lacking among the general population too was the great sense of dread and anticipation that accompanied Stalin's death.

In the Gulag, the reaction to the transfer of power among prisoners and guards alike was also devoid of the passion that defined the announcement of Stalin's death. As Leonid Sitko recorded in his memoir, "We didn't mourn: everyone had for a long time been sick of him."[12] But if there was no mourning, neither was there much celebrating. Anatoly Marchenko recalled some cheering when Khrushchev's portraits were removed from the camp, and in fact a few inmates successfully applied for pardon for their crime of cursing Khrushchev. According to Valdimir Osipov, for example, one who was released had been convicted of writing "communism without Khrushchev" on the wall of his house. Upon Khrushchev's removal, this no longer presented any offense.[13] Part of the reason for the muted reaction to Khrushchev's ouster was that, unlike eleven years previously, no one in the penal system expected dramatic change. And indeed, change was not forthcoming.[14] Documents from the Gulag from late 1964 and 1965 reflect a desire to perfect certain programs, to reform around the edges, but not to change the system wholesale.

In 1969 the Supreme Soviet passed the "Principles of Corrective-Labor Law," a project in the making since the mid-1950s, which was followed by new corrective-labor codes in the fifteen union republics.[15] These codes not only replaced the corrective-labor statute of 1961, they served as the legal replacement of the old 1933 penal code, and as such were published in the national press rather than being issued only as top secret documents as were the three statutes of the Khrushchev era. The new codes reflected the synthesis achieved as a result of the initial reforms of the mid-1950s, the counterreform movement of the late 1950s and early 1960s, and the subsequent steps taken to weaken the harshest elements of the 1961 statute.[16] They solidified in legal form, in other words, the reforms of the Khrushchev era.

While the few dissident memoirists of the Brezhnev period do not write favorably of their time in corrective-labor colonies and prisons—they were not just prisoners, after all, but prisoners of conscience—there is a marked difference between their certainly unpleasant yet somewhat mundane experiences and the intense trials endured by inmates of the Stalinist Gulag.[17] Marchenko's famous assertion in his 1969 memoir *My Testimony* that "today's Soviet camps for political prisoners are just as horrific as in Stalin's time" simply does not stand up to careful scrutiny.[18]

Significantly, the correctional reforms of the Khrushchev era also outlasted the Soviet Union itself; the penal system of the post-1991 Russian Federation is readily discernible as the remnant of its Soviet predecessor. Though shorn of Marxist-Leninist ideology and transferred to the Ministry of Justice in 1998 (in a move reminiscent of the short-lived 1953 move to the same ministry), its physical plant has hardly changed. Visitors and new inmates are confronted with the same drab collection of buildings that foreigners witnessed in the 1950s (complete with fading Soviet slogans admonishing prisoners to high productivity), a result of perpetual underfunding by higher authorities.[19] Penal facilities remain under the same system of classification, consisting primarily of corrective-labor colonies with the same standard, strict, and special regimen types solidified in the Khrushchev era, along with the colony-settlements that originated in 1963 and a few prisons.[20] The philosophy of incarceration as a means of retribution, isolation, and reeducation likewise remains constant.[21]

The post-Soviet penal system since the fall of communism has also exhibited very similar reformist impulses to those witnessed in the Khrushchev era. As Laura Piacentini explains, in the 1990s "new legislation was introduced that aimed at making regimes more humane; the rights of prisoners have been safeguarded; and legal and judicial reform has accelerated so that conditions are brought into line with international standards."[22] Such reforms are also evident in other post-Soviet republics eager to throw off the legacy of Soviet repression.[23] Yet there is also more recent evidence of a counterreform effort designed to make imprisonment harsher.[24] In another parallel, just as in the period following the 1953 amnesty, prison officials in the post-Soviet world struggle with persistent overcrowding caused by a high conviction rate, with the total inmate population rising from around 760,000 (including remand prisoners) in 1992 to a post-Soviet peak of over 1 million prisoners in June 2000; to cope with this problem administrators, like their predecessors in the 1950s, resorted to a series of amnesties over the following years, which has somewhat successfully held the inmate population to well under a million in the recent decade.[25] Moreover, one of the primary challenges that penal officials face is the same question posed by those of the 1950s and 1960s: how to provide work for each inmate.[26] It is interesting here that prison labor in the logging industry of Perm Province, the last remnant of the Gulag camps in the Khrushchev era, persists even today.[27] Despite a monumental change in the political regime in 1991, much within Russian prisons today can be traced to the Soviet era and to the pivotal Khrushchev years in particular. This is the ultimate legacy of Khrushchev's Gulag.

Notes

INTRODUCTION

1. The demise of the thieves-in-law criminal network, which played a dominant role in camp life in the Stalin era, will be discussed in greater detail in chapter 2. A. G. Murzhenko, *Obraz schastlivogo cheloveka Pis'ma iz lageria osobogo rezhima* (London: Overseas Publications Interchange, 1985), 66–100. This and most other Russian-language memoirs are provided online by the Sakharov Center at http://www.sakharov-center.ru /projects/bases/gulag.html. All translations from archival and memoir material are mine. With exception for well-known names (ex. Beria), this book follows the Library of Congress transliteration system.

2. Anatoly Marchenko, *My Testimony,* trans. Michel Scammell (New York: E. P. Dutton, 1969), 3.

3. Aleksandr Isaevich Solzhenitsyn, *The Gulag Archipelago 1918–1956: An Experiment in Literary Investigation,* 3 vols., trans. Thomas P. Whitney (New York: Harper and Row, 1974–78), 3:484.

4. B. F. Sporov, "Pis'mena tiuremnykh sten: povest'," *Nash sovremennik,* no. 10 (1993): 90.

5. Oleg Khlevniuk, *The History of the Gulag: From Collectivization to the Great Terror,* trans. Vadim A. Staklo (New Haven, CT: Yale University Press, 2004); Galina M. Ivanova, *Labor Camp Socialism: The Gulag in the Soviet Totalitarian System,* trans. Carol Flath (Armonk, NY: M. E. Sharpe, 2000); Ivanova, *Istoriia GULAGa, 1918–1958: sotsial'no-ekonomicheskii i politico-pravovoi aspekty* (Moscow: Nauka, 2006); and Anne Applebaum, *Gulag: A History* (New York: Doubleday, 2003). On this see also Golfo Alexopoulos, "The Destructive-Labor Camps: Rethinking Solzhenitsyn's Play on Words," *Kritika: Explorations in Russian and Eurasian History* 16, no. 3 (Summer 2015): 499–526.

6. Among others see S. Dil'manov and E. Kuznetsova, *Karlag* (Almaty: 21 Vek, 1997); N. A. Morozov, *Gulag v Komi krae, 1929–1956* (Syktyvkar: Syktyvkarskii Universitet, 1997); David J. Nordlander, "Capital of the Gulag: Magadan in the Early Stalin Era, 1929–1941" (PhD diss., University of North Carolina, Chapel Hill, 1997); Viktor A. Berdinskikh, *Viatlag: Istoriia odnogo lageria* (Moscow: Agraf, 2001); Christopher S. Joyce, "The Gulag, 1930–1960: Karelia and the Soviet System of Forced Labor" (PhD diss., University of Birmingham, 2001); Steven Barnes, *Death and Redemption: The Gulag and the Shaping of Soviet Society* (Princeton, NJ: Princeton University Press, 2011); Simon Ertz, *Zwangsarbeit im stalinistischen Lagersystem: Eine Untersuchung der Methoden, Strategien und Ziele ihrer Ausnutzung am Beispiel Norilsk, 1935–1953* (Berlin: Duncker & Humblot, 2006); and Alan Barenberg, *Gulag Town, Company Town: Forced Labor and Its Legacy in Vorkuta* (New Haven, CT: Yale University Press, 2014).

7. Wilson Bell, "Sex, Pregnancy, and Power in the Late Stalinist Gulag," *Journal of the History of Sexuality* 24, no. 2 (May 2015): 198–224; Dan Healey, "Lives in the Balance: Weak and Disabled Prisoners and the Biopolitics of the Gulag," *Kritika: Explorations in Russian and Eurasian History* 16, no. 3 (Summer 2015): 527–56; Golfo Alexopoulos, "Amnesty 1945: The Revolving Door of Stalin's Gulag," *Slavic Review* 64, no. 2 (Summer 2005): 274–306; Alexopoulos, "Exiting the Gulag after War: Women, Invalids, and the Family," *Jarbücher für Geschichte Osteuropas* 57, no. 4 (2009): 563–79; Asif Siddiqi,

"Specialists in the Gulag: State and Terror in Stalin's *Sharashka*," *Kritika: Explorations in Russian and Eurasian History* 16, no. 3 (Summer 2015): 557–88; Maria Glamarini, "Defending the Rights of Gulag Prisoners: The Story of the Political Red Cross, 1918–38," *Russian Review* 71, no. 1 (January 2012), 6–29; and Paul R. Gregory and Valery Lazarev, eds., *The Economics of Forced Labor: The Soviet Gulag* (Stanford, CA: Hoover Institution Press, 2003).

8. See, for example, Steven A. Barnes, " 'In a Manner Befitting Soviet Citizens': An Uprising in the Post-Stalin Gulag," *Slavic Review* 64, no. 4 (Winter 2005): 823–50; Barenberg, *Gulag Town*, 120–60; Marta Craveri, "Krisis Gulaga: Kengirskoe vosstanie 1954 goda v dokumentakh MVD," *Cahiers du monde russe* 36, no. 3 (1995): 319–44; Craveri, "The Strikes in Norilsk and Vorkuta Camps, and Their Role in the Breakdown of the Stalinist Forced Labour System," in *Free and Unfree Labour: The Debate Continues*, ed. Tom Brass and Marcel van der Linden (New York: Peter Lang, 1997), 364–78; and Andrea Graziosi, "The Great Strikes of 1953 in Soviet Labor Camps in the Accounts of Their Participants: A Review," *Cahiers du monde russe* 33, no. 4 (1993): 419–45.

9. See, among others, Nanci Adler, *The Gulag Survivor: Beyond the Soviet System* (New Brunswick, NJ: Transaction Publishers, 2002); Adler, *Keeping Faith with the Party: Communist Believers Return from the Gulag* (Bloomington: Indiana University Press, 2012); Miriam Dobson, *Khrushchev's Cold Summer: Gulag Returnees, Crime, and the Fate of Reform after Stalin* (Ithaca, NY: Cornell University Press, 2009); Orlando Figes, *The Whisperers: Private Life in Stalin's Russia* (New York: Metropolitan Books, 2007); Stephen F. Cohen, *The Victims Return: Survivors of the Gulag after Stalin* (Exeter, NH: Publishing Works, 2010); Amir Weiner, "The Empires Pay a Visit: Gulag Returnees, East European Rebellions, and Soviet Frontier Politics," *Journal of Modern History* 78, no. 2 (June 2006): 333–76; Marc Elie, "Les politiques à l'égard des libérés du Goulag: amnistiés et réhabilités dans la region de Novosibirsk, 1953–1960," *Cahiers du Monde russe* 47, nos. 1–2 (2006): 327–48; and Marc Elie and Jeffrey S. Hardy, " 'Letting the Beasts out of the Cage': Parole in the Post-Stalin Gulag, 1953–1973," *Europe-Asia Studies* 67, no. 4 (June 2015): 579–605.

10. Barenberg, *Gulag Town*, 161–230; Mirjam Sprau, "Entstalinisierun verortet: Die Lagerauflösung an der Kolyma," *Jarbücher für Geschichte Osteuropas* 57, no. 4 (2009): 535–62.

11. Marc Elie, "Khrushchev's Gulag: The Soviet Penitentiary System after Stalin's Death, 1953–1964," in *The Thaw: Soviet Society and Culture during the 1950s and 1960s*, ed. Denis Kozlov and Eleonor Gilburd (Toronto: University of Toronto Press, 2013), 109–42.

12. Moshe Lewin, *The Soviet Century* (London: Verso, 2005), 168.

13. See, for instance, Harold J. Berman, "The Dilemma of Soviet Law Reform," *Harvard Law Review* 76, no. 5 (March 1963): 929–51.

14. Gresham Sykes, *The Society of Captives: A Study of Maximum Security Prison* (Princeton, NJ: Princeton University Press, 1958), 63.

15. William Taubman, *Khrushchev: The Man and His Era* (New York: W. W. Norton, 2004), 270–89.

16. Credit is due to Stephen Kotkin for this insight.

17. "Ot Tsentral'nogo Komiteta Kommunisticheskoi Partii Sovetskogo Soiuza, Soveta Ministrov Soiuza SSR i Prezidiuma Verkhovnogo Soveta SSSR," *Pravda*, 6 March 1953, 1.

18. RGASPI, f. 82, op. 2, d. 441, l. 101. For this and subsequent references to archival material from the former Soviet Union, the following standard abbreviations are used: f. stands for collection (*fond*), op. stands for register (*opis*), d. stands for folder (*delo*), and l. stands for pages (*list*). Multiple pages and folders are represented by ll. and dd.

19. For more on the postwar era and how the problems of late Stalinism carried into the Khrushchev era see, among others, Elena Zubkova, *Russia after the War: Hopes, Illusions, and Disappointment, 1945–1957*, trans. Hugh Ragsdale (Armonk, NY: M. E. Sharpe,

1998); Donald Filtzer, *Soviet Workers and De-Stalinization: The Consolidation of the Modern System of Soviet Production Relations, 1953–1964* (Cambridge: Cambridge University Press, 1992); Melanie Ilic and Jeremy Smith, eds., *Soviet State and Society under Nikita Khrushchev* (London: Routledge, 2009); Jeremy Smith and Melanie Ilic, eds., *Khrushchev in the Kremlin: Policy and Government in the Soviet Union, 1956–64* (London: Routledge, 2010); Polly A. Jones, ed., *The Dilemmas of De-Stalinization: Negotiating Cultural and Social Change in the Khrushchev Era* (London: Routledge, 2006); and Juliane Fürst, *Stalin's Last Generation: Soviet Post-War Youth and the Emergence of Mature Socialism* (Oxford: Oxford University Press, 2010).

20. Seweryn Bialer, *Stalin's Successors: Leadership, Stability, and Change in the Soviet Union* (Cambridge: Cambridge University Press, 1980), 66.

21. For more on this see Yoram Gorlizki and Oleg Khlevniuk, *Cold Peace: Stalin and the Soviet Ruling Circle, 1945–1953* (Oxford: Oxford University Press, 2004).

22. Elena Zubkova, "The Rivalry with Malenkov," in *Nikita Khrushchev*, ed. William Taubman, Sergei Khrushchev, and Abbott Gleason (New Haven, CT: Yale University Press, 2000), 67–84.

23. Sergei Khrushchev, "The Military-Industrial Complex," in Taubman et al., *Nikita Khrushchev*, 244–45.

24. This approach, "to evaluate the Gulag phenomenon as a whole and set it in international context," was set forth as an ideal by John Keep in 1999, but thus far little toward this end has been accomplished. John Keep, "Comments on Wheatcroft," *Europe-Asia Studies* 51, no. 6 (September 1999): 1091. One partial effort to place the Gulag in comparative context, albeit with a very broad scope, is Kate Brown, "Out of Solitary Confinement: The History of the Gulag," *Kritika: Explorations in Russian and Eurasian History* 8, no. 1 (2007): 67–103.

25. Michel Foucault, *Discipline and Punish: The Birth of the Prison*, trans. Alan Sheridan (New York: Pantheon Books, 1977), 169; John Brewer, *The Sinews of Power: War, Money, and the English State, 1688–1783* (Cambridge, MA: Harvard University Press, 1990); Clive Emsley, *Crime, Police, and Penal Policy: European Experiences, 1750–1940* (Oxford: Oxford University Press, 2013).

26. See, for instance, Ronald R. Thomas, *Detective Fiction and the Rise of Forensic Science* (Cambridge: Cambridge University Press, 2003). On the tsarist criminal justice system see, among others, Joan Neuberger, *Hooliganism: Crime, Culture, and Power in St. Petersburg, 1900–1914* (Berkeley: University of California Press, 1993); Bruce F. Adams, *The Politics of Punishment: Prison Reform in Russia, 1863–1917* (DeKalb: Northern Illinois Press, 1996); Abby M. Schrader, *Languages of the Lash: Corporal Punishment and Identity in Imperial Russia* (DeKalb: Northern Illinois University Press, 2002); Jane Burbank, *Russian Peasants Go to Court: Legal Culture in the Countryside, 1905–1917* (Bloomington: Indiana University Press, 2004); Jonathan W. Daly, "Criminal Punishment and Europeanization in Late Imperial Russia," *Jahrbücher für Geschichte Osteuropas* 47, no. 3 (2000): 341–62; and Zygmunt Bialkowski, "The Transformation of Academic Criminal Jurisprudence into Criminology in Late Imperial Russia" (PhD diss., University of California, Berkeley, 2008).

27. Cesare Lombroso, *Criminal Man*, trans. Mary Gibson and Nicole Hahn Rafter (Durham, NC: Duke University Press, 2006); and Emile Durkheim, *The Division of Labor in Society*, trans. George Simpson (New York: Free Press, 1933), 291–341. For more on theories of crime in this era see C. Bernaldo de Quirós, *Modern Theories of Criminality*, trans. Alfonso de Salvio (Boston, MA: Little, Brown, 1912).

28. Robert K. Merton, "Social Structure and Anomie," *American Sociological Review* 3, no. 5 (October 1938): 672–82.

29. Edwin H. Sutherland, *Principles of Criminology*, 4th ed. (Chicago: Lippincott, 1947).

30. See, for instance, *Second United Nations Congress on the Prevention of Crime and the Treatment of Offenders* (New York: United Nations, Department of Economic and Social Affairs, 1960), 8–16, 31, 38.

31. See, among others, Negley K. Teeters, *The Cradle of the Penitentiary: The Walnut Street Jail at Philadelphia, 1773–1835* (Philadelphia, PA: Pennsylvania Prison Society, 1955); Georg Rusche and Otto Kirchheimer, *Punishment and Social Structure* (New York: Columbia University Press, 1939); David J. Rothman, *The Discovery of the Asylum: Social Order and Disorder in the New Republic* (Boston, MA: Little, Brown, 1971); Foucault, *Discipline and Punish*; Dario Melossi and Massimo Pavarini, *The Prison and the Factory: Origins of the Penitentiary System*, trans. Glynis Cousin (New York: Macmillan, 1981); Patricia O'Brien, *The Promise of Punishment: Prisons in Nineteenth-Century France* (Princeton, NJ: Princeton University Press, 1982); and Norval Morris and David J. Rothman, eds., *The Oxford History of the Prison: The Practice of Punishment in Western Society* (Oxford: Oxford University Press, 1995).

32. See, for instance, Anand A. Yang, "Disciplining 'Natives': Prison and Prisoners in Early Nineteenth-Century India," *South Asia* 10, no. 2 (1987): 29–45; Peter Zinoman, *The Colonial Bastille: A History of Imprisonment in Vietnam, 1862–1940* (Berkeley: University of California Press, 2001); Frank Dikötter, *Crime, Punishment and the Prison in Modern China* (New York: Columbia University Press, 2002); Daniel V. Botsman, *Punishment and Power in the Making of Modern Japan* (Princeton, NJ: Princeton University Press, 2005); Carlos Aguirre, *The Criminals of Lima and Their Worlds: The Prison Experience, 1850–1935* (Durham, NC: Duke University Press, 2005); Terance D. Miethe and Hong Lu, eds., *Punishment: A Comparative Historical Perspective* (Cambridge: Cambridge University Press, 2005); Barry S. Godfrey and Graeme Dunstall, eds., *Crime and Empire, 1840–1940: Criminal Justice in Local and Global Context* (Devon, UK: Willan Publishing, 2005); Frank Dikötter and Ian Brown, eds., *Cultures of Confinement: A History of the Prison in Africa, Asia, and Latin America* (Ithaca, NY: Cornell University Press, 2007); and Mary Gibson, "Global Perspectives on the Birth of the Prison, *American Historical Review* 116, no. 4 (October 2011): 1040–63.

33. David J. Rothman, *Conscience and Convenience: The Asylum and Its Alternatives in Progressive America* (Boston, MA: Little, Brown, 1980); William James Forsythe, *Penal Discipline, Reformatory Projects, and the English Prison Commission, 1895–1939* (Exeter, UK: University of Exeter Press, 1990); and Jonathan Simon, *Poor Discipline: Parole and the Social Control of the Underclass, 1890–1990* (Chicago: University of Chicago Press, 1993), chaps. 1–2.

34. Charles Bright, *The Powers That Punish: Prison and Politics in the Era of the "Big House," 1920–1955* (Ann Arbor: University of Michigan Press, 1996); James B. Jacobs, *Statesville: The Penitentiary in Mass Society* (Chicago: University of Chicago Press, 1977), 28–31; and Volker Janssen, "Convict Labor, Civic Welfare: Rehabilitation in California's Prisons, 1941–1971" (PhD diss., University of California, San Diego, 2005), 25–44.

35. Richard F. Wetzell, *Inventing the Criminal: A History of German Criminology, 1880–1945* (Chapel Hill: University of North Carolina Press, 2000); Nikolas Wachsmann, *Hitler's Prisons: Legal Terror in Nazi Germany* (New Haven, CT: Yale University Press, 2004); Giulio Battaglini, "The Fascist Reform of the Penal Law in Italy," *Journal of Criminal Law and Criminology* 24, no. 1 (May–June 1933): 278–89; Edward M. Wise, "Introduction," in *The Italian Penal Code*, trans. Edward M. Wise (Littleton, CO: Fred B. Rothman, 1978); and Tiago Pires Marques, *Crime and the Fascist State, 1850–1940* (London: Pickering & Chatto, 2013).

36. See, for instance, Mark Benney, *The Truth about English Prisons* (London: Fact, 1938); and Herman Franke, *The Emancipation of Prisoners: A Socio-Historical Analysis of the Dutch Prison Experience* (Edinburgh: Edinburgh University Press, 1995), 211–43.

37. Iain R. Smith and Andreas Stucki, "The Colonial Development of Concentration Camps (1868–1902)," *Journal of Imperial and Commonwealth History* 39, no. 3 (September 2011): 417–37; Zygmunt Baumann, "A Century of Camps?," in *The Baumann Reader,* ed. P. Beilharz (Oxford: Oxford University Press, 2001), 266–80; Alex J. Bellamy, *Massacres and Morality: Mass Atrocities in an Age of Civilian Immunity* (Oxford: Oxford University Press, 2012), 75–78; Vejas Gabriel Liulevicius, *War Land on the Eastern Front: Culture, National Identity and German Occupation in World War I* (Cambridge: Cambridge University Press, 2000); and Alon Rachamimov, *POWs and the Great War: Captivity on the Eastern Front* (Oxford: Berg, 2002).

38. Nikolaus Wachsmann, *KL: A History of the Nazi Concentration Camp* (New York: Farrar, Straus and Giroux, 2015), 6–9.

39. Janssen, "Convict Labor," 38–41; Blake McKelvey, *American Prisons: A History of Good Intentions* (Montclair, NJ: Patterson Smith, 1977), 307–8.

40. John C. Burke, ed., "Correctional Camps: Report of a Panel Discussion," in *Proceedings of the Eighty-Fifth Annual Congress of Correction* (New York: American Correctional Association), 65–67.

41. Patricia O'Brien, "The Prison on the Continent: Europe, 1865–1965," in *The Oxford History of the Prison: The Practice of Punishment in Western Society,* ed. Norval Morris and David J. Rothman (New York: Oxford University Press, 1998), 194–95.

42. For more on this see Jeffrey S. Hardy, "The Gulag and the Penitentiary Reappraised: Post-War Penal Convergence in the United States and Soviet Union, 1950–1965," in *The Soviet Union and the United States: Rivals of the Twentieth Century,* ed. Eva-Maria Stolberg (Frankfurt: Peter Lang, 2013), 169–94.

43. On the expansion of policing under Stalin especially see Paul Hagenloh, *Stalin's Police: Public Order and Mass Repression, 1926–1941* (Washington, DC: Woodrow Wilson Center Press and John Hopkins University Press, 2009); and David R. Shearer, *Policing Stalin's Socialism: Repression and Social Order in the Soviet Union, 1924–1953* (New Haven, CT: Yale University Press, 2009).

44. As David Granick in his study of Soviet businessmen remarked, "It seems a fair generalization that all Soviet managers are, ipso facto, criminals according to Soviet law." David Granick, *The Red Executive: A Study of the Organization Man in Soviet Industry* (New York: Doubleday, 1960), 43. For more on the black market in the post-Stalin era see Gregory Grossman, "The 'Second Economy' of the USSR," *Problems of Communism* 26 (September–October 1977): 25–40; and Valery Chalidze, *Criminal Russia,* trans. P. S. Falla (New York: Random House, 1977), 68–97, 146–96.

45. Walter D. Connor, *Deviance in Soviet Society: Crime, Delinquency, and Alcoholism* (New York: Columbia University Press, 1972).

46. Louise Shelley, "Soviet Criminology: Its Birth and Demise, 1917–1936" (PhD diss., University of Pennsylvania, 1977); Peter H. Solomon, "Soviet Penal Policy, 1917–1934: A Reinterpretation," *Slavic Review* 39, no. 2 (June 1980): 195–217; Peter H. Solomon, *Soviet Criminologists and Criminal Policy: Specialists in Policy-Making* (New York: Columbia University Press, 1978); and Sharon A. Kowalsky, *Deviant Women: Female Crime and Criminology in Revolutionary Russia, 1880–1930* (DeKalb: Northern Illinois University Press, 2009).

47. The best expression of this ideal is perhaps Jean-Antoine-Nicolas Condorcet, *Esquisse d'un tableau historique des progrès de l'esprit humain* (Paris: Agasse, 1795).

48. Even into the 1960s and beyond these were called "remnants of the past" or the "remnants of capitalism" by Soviet criminologists. See, for instance, A. S. Shliapochnikov, "V. I. Lenin i kommunisticheskaia partiia o zadache bor'by s prestupnost'iu," in *Problemy iskoreneniia prestupnosti,* ed. V. N. Kudriavtsev (Moscow: Iuridicheskaia literatura, 1965), 20; A. A. Gertsenzon, *Vvedenie v sovetskuiu kriminologiiu* (Moscow:

Iuridicheskaia literatura, 1965), 122–23; and M. D. Shargorodskii and N. A. Beliaev, eds., *Sovetskoe ugolovnoe pravo: chast' obshchaia* (Saint Petersburg: Izdatel'stvo leningradskogo universiteta, 1960), 213–14.

49. Dobson, *Khrushchev's Cold Summer,* 156–85; Brian LaPierre, *Hooligans in Khrushchev's Russia: Defining, Policing, and Producing Deviance During the Thaw* (Madison: University of Wisconsin Press, 2012), 97.

50. A. S. Makarenko, *Pedagicheskaia poema* (Moscow: Populiarnaia literatura, 1931); Oleg Kharkhordin, *The Collective and the Individual in Russia: A Study of Practices* (Berkeley: University of California Press, 1999), 90–97.

51. On the visits of the 1920s and 1930s see Michael David-Fox, *Showcasing the Great Experiment: Cultural Diplomacy and Western Visitors to Soviet Russia, 1921–1941* (Oxford: Oxford University Press, 2011), chap. 3; Paul Hollander, *Political Pilgrims: Travels of Western Intellectuals to the Soviet Union, China, and Cuba, 1928–1978* (Oxford: Oxford University Press, 1981), 142–56; and Lenka Von Koerber, *Soviet Russia Fights Crime* (New York: E. P. Dutton, 1935). On propaganda efforts see the first Soviet sound film, Nikolai Ekk's *Putevka v zhizn'* (Moscow: Mezhrabpomfilm, 1931); Nikolai Pogodin, "Aristocrats," *Four Soviet Plays,* ed. Ben Blake, trans. Anthony Wixley (New York: International Publishers, 1937); and Maxim Gorky, L. Auerbach, and S. G. Firin, eds., *Belomor: An Account of the Construction of the New Canal between the White Sea and the Baltic Sea* (New York: Harrison Smith and Robert Haas, 1935).

52. A. Ia. Vyshinskii, "Predislovie," in *Ot tiurem k vospitatel'nym uchrezhdeniiam,* ed. A. Ia. Vyshinskii (Moscow: Gosudarstvennoe Izdatel'stvo Sovetskoe Zakonodatel'stvo, 1934), 5–15.

53. For scholarly accounts of the continued devotion to reeducation throughout Stalin's reign see Barnes, *Death and Redemption,* 57–68; Julie S. Draskoczy, *Belomor: Criminality and Creativity in Stalin's Gulag* (Boston, MA: Academic Studies Press, 2014); and Wilson Bell, "One Day in the Life of Educator Khrushchev: Labour and *Kulturnost'* in the Gulag Newspapers," *Canadian Slavonic Papers* 46, nos. 3–4 (September–December 2004): 289–313.

54. As one British commentator lamented in 1960, "The lessons of the nineteenth century have not been learned by all of us, and the Prison Commissioners have to struggle against loudly advocated punitive policies as well as against general public apathy, in its efforts to rehabilitate criminals." D. L. Howard, *The English Prisons: Their Past and Their Future* (London: Methuen, 1960), 127.

55. The precise name of this entity was altered several times between 1930 and 1960, but it continued to be referred to in official documents by its original acronym.

56. Nghia M. Vo, *The Bamboo Gulag: Political Imprisonment in Communist Vietnam* (London: McFarland, 2004); Chol-Hwan Kang and Pierre Rigoulot, *Aquariums of Pyongyang: Ten Years in a North Korean Gulag* (New York: Basic Books, 2001); Ruth Wilson Gilmore, *Golden Gulag: Prisons, Surplus, Crisis, and Opposition in Globalizing California* (Berkeley: University of California Press, 2007); Caroline Elkins, *Britain's Gulag: The Brutal End of Empire in Kenya* (London: Jonathan Cape, 2005); Mark Dow, *American Gulag: Inside U.S. Immigration Prisons* (Berkeley: University of California Press, 2004); and Anne Applebaum, "Amnesty's Amnesia," *Washington Post,* 8 June 2005, A21.

57. See, for instance, Robert Conquest, *The Great Terror: A Reassessment* (New York: Oxford University Press, 1990); Ivanova, *Labor Camp Socialism;* Ivanova, *Istoriia GULAGa, 1918–1958;* and Applebaum, *Gulag.*

58. This was a primary point of attack for anti-Soviet exposés of the Cold War era. David J. Dallin and Boris I. Nikolaevsky, *Forced Labor in Soviet Russia* (New Haven, CT: Yale University Press, 1947); Stanislaw Swianiewicz, *Forced Labour and Economic Development: An Inquiry into the Experience of Soviet Industrialization* (London: Oxford University Press, 1965); Steven Rosefielde, "An Assessment of the Sources and Uses of Gulag

Forced Labour, 1929–56," *Soviet Studies* 33, no. 1 (January 1981): 51; Solzhenitsyn, *Gulag Archipelago,* 2:578; and John L. Scherer and Michael Jakobson, "The Collectivisation of Agriculture and the Soviet Prison Camp System," *Europe-Asia Studies* 45, no. 3 (May 1993): 533–46. Some researchers have even found that people were imprisoned in direct response to plan targets, although the available evidence suggests that this was an exception rather than the rule. James R. Harris, "The Growth of the Gulag: Forced Labor in the Urals Region, 1929–1931," *Russian Review* 56, no. 2 (April 1997): 279.

59. As Barnes argues, "one must consider that the Gulag was in fact a penal institution first, and a productive institution second." Barnes, *Death and Redemption,* 39.

60. Indeed, as in so many other regimes, the Soviet penal system both mimicked and served as a laboratory for the construction of the broader society. As Foucault noted, the modern prison served as a "primal model for the reconstruction of the social body." Foucault, *Discipline and Punish,* 169. On this see also Melossi and Pavarini, *Prison and the Factory.* The weaker version of this argument, that prisons reflected broader society rather than serving as its model, can be found applied to the Soviet case, for instance in Laura Piacentini, *Surviving Russian Prisons: Punishment, Economy and Politics in Transition* (Cullomton, UK: Willan, 2004), 31.

61. Relying on memoir accounts and demographic data, Steven Rosefielde in 1981 wrote that "from 1934–1950 Gulag workers on average constituted more than 20% of the non-agricultural labour force, diminishing thereafter." Rosefielde, "Assessment of the Sources and Uses," 76. Even Steven Wheatcroft, who gave much lower estimates, provided a maximum figure of 4–5 million in the Gulag in 1939. Steven Wheatcroft, "On Assessing the Size of Forced Concentration Camp Labour in the Soviet Union, 1929–1956," *Soviet Studies* 33, no. 2 (April 1981): 286. This debate over the size of the Gulag continued until more reliable figures were provided in the late 1980s and early 1990s.

62. The tsarist penal system expanded rapidly after 1905, increasing from some 85,000 inmates in 1900 to 177,000 in 1914. The Soviet penal system, by contrast, averaged 190,000 in 1930. Michael Jakobson, *Origins of the Gulag: The Soviet Prison Camp System, 1917–1934* (Lexington: University Press of Kentucky, 1993), 10; Khlevniuk, *History of the Gulag,* 307.

63. J. Arch Getty, Gabor T. Rittersporn, and Viktor N. Zemskov, "Victims of the Soviet Penal System in the Pre-War Years: A First Approach on the Basis of Archival Evidence," *American Historical Review* 98, no. 4 (October 1993): 1048–49.

64. GARF, f. R-9414, op. 1, d. 1427, l. 141.

65. Ibid.

66. Patrick A. Langan, John V. Fundis, Lawrence A. Greenfeld, and Victoria W. Schneider, *Historical Statistics on Prisons in State and Federal Institutions, Yearend 1925–86* (Washington, DC: U.S. Department of Justice, 1988), 8–10.

67. Gavin Berman and Aliyah Dar, *Prison Population Statistics* (London: House of Commons Library, 2013), 20; Hanns von Hofer, Tapio Lappi-Seppälä, and Lars Westfelt, *Nordic Criminal Statistics, 1950–2010* (Stockholm: Kriminologiska institutionen, Stockholm University, 2012), 68.

68. Article 58 was found in the Criminal Code of the Russian Soviet Federative Socialist Republic. Other union republics in the Soviet Union had their own criminal codes with differently numbered articles covering counterrevolutionary crimes.

69. V. P. Kozlov, ed., *Istoriia stalinskogo GULAGa: konets 20-kh—pervaia polovina 50-kh godov,* 7 vols. (Moscow: Rosspen, 2004), 4:91.

70. On 1 January 1953 Gulag records show 539,483 counterrevolutionary inmates out of a total of 2,472,247. GARF, f. R-9414, op. 1, d. 1398, l. 1.

71. For more on political prisoners outside the Soviet Union see Barton Ingraham, *Political Crime in Europe: A Comparative Study of France, Germany, and England* (Berkeley:

University of California Press, 1979); and Padraic Kenney, "'I Felt a Kind of Pleasure in Seeing Them Treat Us Brutally': The Emergence of the Political Prisoner, 1865–1910," *Comparative Studies in Society and History* 54, no. 4 (October 2012): 863–89.

72. Petr Dmitriev, *"Soldat Berii": vospominaniia lagernogo okhranika* (Leningrad: Chas pik, 1991), 7.

73. By far the most outlandish estimate belonged to the usually reliable Avraham Shifrin, who reported to his readers that "more than 60 000 000 innocent human beings have perished in these camps." Avraham Shifrin, *The First Guidebook to Prisons and Concentration Camps of the Soviet Union*, 2nd ed. (New York: Bantam Books, 1982), 366.

74. Khlevniuk, *History of the Gulag*, 327; Kozlov, *Istoriia stalinskogo GULAGa*, 4:492.

75. Khlevniuk, *History of the Gulag*, 198.

76. Edwin Bacon, *The Gulag at War: Stalin's Forced Labour System in the Light of the Archives* (New York: New York University Press, 1994), 149; Kozlov, *Istoriia stalinskogo GULAGa*, 4:512.

77. Official statistics show 0.92 percent for 1951 and 0.84 percent for 1952. GARF, f. R-9414, op. 1, d. 2883, l. 111. This is confirmed by memoirists such as Solzhenitsyn, who noted that the increased rations of the early 1950s in comparison with the lean years of the 1940s gave prisoners enough energy to organize revolts.

78. Simon Ertz, "Lagernaia sistema v 1930-e–1950-e gg.: evoliutiia struktury i printsipov upravleniia," in *Gulag: ekonomiki prinuditel'nogo truda*, ed. Leonid Borodkin, Paul Gregory, and Oleg V. Khlevniuk (Moscow: Rosspen, 2005), 90–128.

79. GARF, f. R-9414, op. 1, d. 112, ll. 15–16.

80. All provinces and republics within the Soviet Union had their own division of corrective-labor camps and colonies, although for smaller regions these were categorized as departments (*otdel*) rather than divisions (*upravlenie*).

81. GARF, f. R-9414, op. 1, d. 112, l. 80.

82. ERAF, f. 17sm, op. 4, d. 150, l. 8.

83. Exceptions to this general organizational scheme were abundant. Some camp branches were small and were therefore not broken down into camp points. Some camp points were broken down even further into smaller subunits, often called camp companies (*podkomandirovka*). There were also occasional independent camp points that reported directly to the camp rather than a camp branch, and independent camp divisions that reported directly to the Gulag rather than a particular camp.

84. GARF, f. R-8131, op. 32, d. 4967, l. 238.

85. GARF, f. R-9414, op. 1, d. 112, l. 29.

86. A small minority of prisoners in any given year resided in more primitive accommodations, primarily tents and dugouts, usually due to the newness of their facility coupled with immediate pressure to produce not barracks but coal or railroad track or lumber. For a good first-account of this see Fyodor Vasilevich Mochulsky, *Gulag Boss: A Soviet Memoir*, trans. Deborah Kaple (Oxford: Oxford University Press, 2010), 32–36.

87. For representative schemas of camp branch layouts see, for instance, GARF, f. R-9414, op. 1a, d. 280, l. 8; and GARF, f. R-9414, op. 1a, d. 282, l. 6.

88. GARF, f. R-9414, op. 1, d. 1427, l. 140.

89. See, for instance, Evgeniia Ginzburg's account of her two years in prison in the late 1930s or Iu. I. Ivanov's remarks on his prison stay in the early 1960s. Eugenia Semyonovna Ginzburg, *Journey into the Whirlwind*, trans. Paul Stevenson and Max Hayward (New York: Harcourt, 1967), 193–266; and [Iu. E. Ivanov], "Gorod Vladimir," in *Samizdat veka*, ed. Anatolii Strelianyi, Genrikh Sapgir, Vladimir Bakhtin, and Nikita Ordynskii (Moscow: Itogi veka, 1999), 55–62.

90. This idea was even enshrined in the 1936 constitution. V. I. Lenin, *Polnoe sobranie sochinenii*, 5th ed. (Moscow: Izdatel'stvo politicheskoi literatury, 1963), 33:94.

91. As the American Correctional Association declared in 1954, "unless we can contrive to solve the prison labor problem we must abandon the idea that we are operating institutions of correction and reform and that adult prisoners can be released from such institution better and not worse than when they entered." American Correctional Association, *Manual of Correctional Standards* (Washington, DC: American Correctional Association, 1954), 273. See also Edwin H. Sutherland and Donald R. Cressey, *Principles of Criminology,* 6th ed. (Chicago: J. B. Lippincott, 1960), 514–22.

92. Jack Schaller, "Work and Imprisonment: An Overview of the Changing Role of Prison Labor in American Prisons," *Prison Journal* 62, no. 2 (October 1982): 3–4.

93. Khlevniuk, *History of the Gulag,* 213.

94. Barnes, *Death and Redemption,* 41–43.

95. Ibid., 71–78.

96. In his provocative book *Death and Redemption,* Barnes argues that labor in the rehabilitative sense, in fact, continued to outweigh plan fulfillment, or that the two sides of labor cannot be properly disentangled. See, for instance, p. 134.

97. Solzhenitsyn, *Gulag Archipelago,* 2:198.

98. Alan Barenberg, "Prisoners without Borders: *Zazonniki* and the Transformation of Vorkuta after Stalin," *Jahrbücher für Geschichte Osteuropas* 57, no. 4 (2009): 525.

99. For more on this see Wilson T. Bell, "Was the Gulag an Archipelago? De-Convoyed Prisoners and Porous Borders in the Camps of Western Siberia," *Russian Review* 72, no. 1 (January 2013): 116–41.

100. Joachim J. Savelsberg, "Knowledge, Domination and Criminal Punishment Revisited: Incorporating State Socialism," *Punishment & Society* 1, no. 1 (July 1999): 45–70.

101. Fouacult, *Discipline and Punish,* 234.

102. Khlevniuk, *History of the Gulag,* 53.

103. Ibid., 170–72.

104. As Yoram Gorlizki argues, however, "campaignism" in criminal justice in the late Stalin era was more muted than in the 1930s. Yoram Gorlizki, "Rules, Incentives and Soviet Campaign Justice after World War II," *Europe-Asia Studies* 51, no. 7 (November 1999): 1245–65.

105. Aleksei Tikhonov, "The End of the Gulag," in *The Economics of Forced Labor: The Soviet Gulag,* ed. Paul R. Gregory and Valery Lazarev (Stanford, CA: Hoover Institution Press, 2003), 67–73.

106. Alexopoulos, "Amnesty 1945," 274–306.

107. Peter H. Solomon Jr., *Soviet Criminal Justice under Stalin* (Cambridge: Cambridge University Press, 1996), 409–13; Gorlizki, "Rules, Incentives and Soviet Campaign Justice," 1249–61.

108. Ivanova, *Labor Camp Socialism,* 53–55; and Barnes, *Death and Redemption,* 164–85.

109. Leonid Borodkin and Simon Ertz, "Forced Labour and the Need for Motivation: Wages and Bonuses in the Stalinist Camp System," *Comparative Economic Studies* 47, no. 2 (June 2005), 418–36; and Simon Ertz, "Trading Effort for Freedom: Workday Credits in the Stalinist Camp System," *Comparative Economic Studies* 47, no. 2 (June 2005): 476–91.

110. Barnes, *Death and Redemption,* 199–200.

111. As Seweryn Bialer argued, the post-Stalin succession acted "as a catalyst for pressures and tendencies which already exist within the polity and society but which previously had limited opportunity for expression and realization." Seweryn Bialer, *Stalin's Successors: Leadership, Stability, and Change in the Soviet Union* (Cambridge: Cambridge University Press, 1980), 66.

1. RESTRUCTURING THE PENAL EMPIRE

1. Viacheslav Mikhailovich Molotov, *Molotov Remembers: Inside Kremlin Politics* (Chicago: Ivan R. Dee, 1993), 347.

2. Cited in Elena Zubkova, *Russia after the War: Hopes, Illusions, and Disappointment, 1945–1957,* trans. Hugh Ragsdale (Armonk, NY: M. E. Sharpe, 1998), 152.

3. Yoram Gorlizki and Oleg Khlevniuk, *Cold Peace: Stalin and the Soviet Ruling Circle, 1945–1953* (Oxford: Oxford University Press, 2004), 141.

4. Ibid., 170–71; Zubkova, *Russia after the War,* 148–54.

5. Vera S. Dunham, *In Stalin's Time: Middleclass Values in Soviet Fiction* (Durham, NC: Duke University Press, 1990), 15–20.

6. Mark B. Smith, *Property of Communists: The Urban Housing Program from Stalin to Khrushchev* (DeKalb: Northern Illinois University Press, 2010), 179–83.

7. A. P. Butkovsky, "The Fate of a Sailor," in *Voices from the Gulag,* ed. Aleksandr Solzhenitsyn (Evanston, IL: Northwestern University Press, 2011), 198.

8. Semen Badash, *Kolyma ty moia, Kolyma . . . dokumental'naia povest'* (New York: Effect, 1986), 68.

9. M. B. Rabinovich. *Vospominaniia dolgoi zhizni* (Saint Petersburg: Evropeiskii dom, 1998), 340.

10. John Noble, *I Was a Slave in Russia: An American Tells His Story* (New York: Devin-Adair, 1958), 141.

11. Eugenia Ginzburg, *Within the Whirlwind,* trans. Ian Boland (London: Collins and Harvill Press, 1981), 359.

12. Incredibly, Margaret Werner reported receiving three days off work. Karl Tobien, *Dancing under the Red Star* (Colorado Springs, CO: Waterbrook, 2006), 256–57.

13. Michael Solomon, *Magadan* (Princeton, NJ: Vertex, 1971), 168–69.

14. Karlo Štajner, *Seven Thousand Days in Siberia,* trans. Joel Agee (New York: Farrar, Straus and Giroux, 1988), 359. Some memoirists, including Solzhenitsyn, however, relate that only after Beria's arrest did local administrators and guards begin to change their behavior and act with uncertainty, "of which the prisoners were keenly aware." Aleksandr Isaevich Solzhenitsyn, *The Gulag Archipelago 1918–1956: An Experiment in Literary Investigation,* 3 vols., trans. Thomas P. Whitney (New York: Harper and Row, 1974–78), 3:281.

15. Marta Craveri and Oleg Khlevniuk, "Krizis ekonomiki MVD (konets 1940-kh–1950-e gody)," *Cahiers du Monde russe* 36, nos. 1–2 (1995): 182–83; Galina M. Ivanova, *Labor Camp Socialism: The Gulag in the Soviet Totalitarian System,* trans. Carol Flath (Armonk, NY: M. E. Sharpe, 2000), 66; Anne Applebaum, *Gulag: A History* (New York: Doubleday, 2003), 471–75; and I. D. Batsaev, *Osobennosti promyshlennogo osvoeniia severovostoka Rossii v period massovykh politicheskikh repressyi (1932–1953),* Dalstroi (Magadan: SVKNII DVO RAN, 2002), 184.

16. Steven Barnes, *Death and Redemption: The Gulag and the Shaping of Soviet Society* (Princeton, NJ: Princeton University Press, 2011), 202–3.

17. Cited in Vladislav M. Zubok, *Failed Empire: The Soviet Union in the Cold War from Stalin to Gorbachev* (Chapel Hill: University of North Carolina Press, 2008), 96. Note that unless otherwise specified the term Presidium in this book refers to the Presidium of the Central Committee of the Communist Party, which until 1952 was known as the Politburo.

18. Cited in Zubkova, *Russia after the War,* 178.

19. Some have argued that Malenkov's personality was ill-suited for seizing power, thereby leaving the door open for Beria's initiative. Amy Knight, *Beria: Stalin's First Lieutenant* (Princeton, NJ: Princeton University Press, 1993), 182. This is confirmed by Molo-

tov, who characterized Malenkov as "an excellent executive" who nevertheless remained "silent on critical issues." Molotov, *Molotov Remembers,* 337.

20. Knight, *Beria,* 183–94.

21. For this argument see, for example, William Taubman, *Khrushchev: The Man and His Era* (New York: W. W. Norton, 2004), 245; and Applebaum, *Gulag,* 480.

22. Not surprisingly, Khrushchev himself levied this charge at his former associate. Roy A. Medvedev and Zhores A. Medvedev, *Khrushchev: The Years in Power* (New York: W. W. Norton, 1975), 9–10.

23. Seweryn Bialer, *Stalin's Successors: Leadership, Stability, and Change in the Soviet Union* (Cambridge: Cambridge University Press, 1980), 66; Taubman, *Khrushchev,* 245.

24. O. Khlevniuk, "Beriia: predely istoricheskoi 'reabilitatsii'," *Svobodnaia Mysl'* 2 (1995): 110.

25. Knight, *Beria,* 184. As an interesting side note, Gulag memoirist Joseph Scholmer recalled that a few inmates at Vorkuta who had known Beria personally referred to him as Stalin's Fouchet, the French Revolution figure renowned for nonideological political opportunism and betrayal. Joseph Scholmer, *Vorkuta* (New York: Holt, 1955), 195.

26. A. I. Kokurin and N. V. Petrov, eds., *GULAG: glavnoe upravlenie lagerei, 1917–1960* (Moscow: Mezhdunarodnyi fond "Demokratiia," 2000), 786–88.

27. Yoram Gorlizki, "Anti-Ministerialism and the USSR Ministry of Justice, 1953–1956: A Study in Organizational Decline," *Europe-Asia Studies* 48, no. 8 (December 1996): 1291–92.

28. Kokurin and Petrov, *GULAG,* 788–91.

29. This ill-advised track through swamp and permafrost was never completed. Kokurin and Petrov, *GULAG,* 789.

30. For more on the problems in the late Stalinist Gulag economy see Marta Craveri and Oleg V. Khlevniuk, "Krisis ekonomiki MVD (Konets 1940kh–1950e gody)," *Cahiers du monde russe et soviétique* 36, nos. 1–2 (1995): 179–90; and—James Heinzen, "Corruption in the Gulag: Dilemmas of Officials and Prisoners," *Comparative Economic Studies* 47, no. 2 (June 2005): 456–75.

31. "Ob amnistii: ukaz Prezidiuma Verkhovnogo Soveta SSSR ot 27 marta 1953," *Pravda,* 28 March 1953, 1.

32. Golfo Alexopoulos, "Amnesty 1945: The Revolving Door of Stalin's Gulag," *Slavic Review* 64, no. 2 (Summer 2005): 276–77; I. L. Marogulova, "Pravovaia priroda amnistii i pomilovaniia," *Sovetskoe gosudarstvo i pravo,* no. 5 (1991): 67.

33. Alexopoulos, "Amnesty 1945," 279.

34. Ibid., 284.

35. It is surely not coincidental, given the rapid preparation for the 1953 amnesty, that it freed the same percentage of prisoners from largely the same convict groups as did Stalin's amnesty of 1945. Ibid., 302.

36. RGANI, f. 5, op. 30, d. 36, l. 9.

37. Andrei Artizov, ed., *Reabilitatsiia—kak eto bylo: dokumenty Prezidiuma TSK KPSS i drugie materialy,* 3 vols. (Moscow: Mezhdunarodnyi fond "Demokratiia," 2000–2004), 1:15–18.

38. Beyond these general provisions, many of the details of the amnesty were worked out by the Ministry of Justice over the following months as camp workers and procurators submitted literally hundreds of questions regarding the criminal record of individual prisoners. See, for example, the decision of 22 April 1953, which clarified that those convicted of embezzling more than 50,000 rubles were not to be amnestied, regardless of whether they were prosecuted under the 7 August 1932 or 4 June 1947 law. GARF, f. R-9401, op. 1a, d. 521, ll. 29–30.

39. Nanci Adler, *The Gulag Survivor: Beyond the Soviet System* (New Brunswick, NJ: Transaction Publishers, 2002), 78; GARF, f. R-9414, op. 1, d. 1398, l. 1. Before archival documentation became available, estimates of the scope of the amnesty were as high as 8 million out of a supposed labor camp population of 12 million. Robert Conquest, *The Great Terror: A Reassessment* (New York: Oxford University Press, 1990), 478.

40. A good summary of the post-amnesty crime wave and the public's reaction to it can be found in Miriam Dobson, *Khrushchev's Cold Summer: Gulag Returnees, Crime, and the Fate of Reform after Stalin* (Ithaca, NY: Cornell University Press, 2009), 37–43.

41. GARF, f. R-9414, op. 1, d. 202, l. 29.

42. Miriam Dobson, "'Show the Bandit-Enemies No Mercy!': Amnesty, Criminality and Public Response in 1953," in *The Dilemmas of De-Stalinization: Negotiating Cultural and Social Change in the Khrushchev Era,* ed. Polly A. Jones (London: Routledge, 2006), 26.

43. See GARF, f. R-7523, op. 58, dd. 130–32; Adler, *Gulag Survivor,* 81.

44. GARF, f. R-7523, op. 58, d. 132, l. 45.

45. GARF, f. R-7523, op. 58, d. 132, l. 34. Another reportedly proclaimed upon the announcement of the amnesty, "Now, with the announcement of the amnesty, we need to work ten times better and become honest citizens of our country. I am thankful to our Soviet Government and Communist Party for their concern for us." GAMO, f. R-23, op. 1, d. 4695, l. 32. It is difficult, of course, to ascertain the sincerity of this and similar statements given to camp officials when prompted to comment on their amnesty. Some, no doubt, said whatever they thought would keep them out of further trouble. But it would be far too cynical to believe that it was all nonsense; many of those released undoubtedly felt a sense of duty and obligation toward the state that freed them before their full sentence had been served.

46. GAMO, f. R-23, op. 1, d. 3153, l. 112.

47. GAMO, f. R-23, op. 1, d. 4695, l. 35.

48. GAMO, f. R-23, op. 1, d. 3153, l. 113.

49. Solzhenitsyn, *Gulag Archipelago,* 2:431.

50. GARF, f. R-9414, op. 1, d. 747, l. 154. Another 44,211 Dal'stroi inmates had their sentences halved. GARF, f. R-9414, op. 1, d. 820, l. 31.

51. GAMO, f. R-23, op. 1, d. 4682, l. 49.

52. GAMO, f. R-23, op. 1, d. 4690, ll. 102, 121–22. Indeed, Mitrakov had to specifically ask to have Dal'stroi's production targets reduced, citing a loss of 12,642 workers out of 59,874 engaged in mining. GAMO, f. R-23, op. 1, d. 4694, ll. 45–46.

53. GAMO, f. R-23, op. 1, d. 4689, l. 200.

54. This problem was also present at the Norilskskii Corrective-Labor Camp. Its commander attempted to delay the departure of amnestied prisoners, claiming that they were needed for railway construction. GARF, f. 9414, op. 1, d. 729, l. 12.

55. GAMO, f. R-23, op. 1, d. 4686, l. 180.

56. Barnes, *Death and Redemption,* 206–8; Alan Barenberg, *Gulag Town, Company Town: Forced Labor and Its Legacy in Vorkuta* (New Haven, CT: Yale University Press, 2014), 123–26.

57. GARF, f. R-9414, op. 1, d. 135, ll. 85–86.

58. Kokurin and Petrov, *GULAG,* 367.

59. V. P. Kozlov, ed., *Istoriia stalinskogo GULAGa: konets 20-kh—pervaia polovina 50-kh godov,* 7 vols. (Moscow: Rosspen, 2004), 2:488; GARF, f. R-9414, op. 1, d. 118, ll. 227a–232.

60. GARF, f. R-9414, op. 1, d. 118, ll. 227a–232. As always, the Gulag felt compelled to modestly overfulfill the plan.

61. On this transfer see Kokurin and Petrov, *GULAG,* 372–73; Kozlov, *Istoriia stalinskogo GULAGa,* 2:460–61.

62. Kokurin and Petrov, *GULAG,* 791–93.

63. GARF, f. R-9492, op. 2, d. 147, ll. 21–24.

64. Kozlov, *Istoriia stalinskogo GULAGa,* 1:589–94.

65. Peter H. Solomon Jr., *Soviet Criminal Justice under Stalin* (Cambridge: Cambridge University Press, 1996), 406–8.

66. Serious crimes were defined here as counterrevolutionary crimes, banditry, murder, theft committed in a gang, robbery, or a second instance of hooliganism or theft. RGASPI, f. 82, op. 2, d. 905, ll. 80–93.

67. Adler, *Gulag Survivor,* 80.

68. The Doctors' Plot was an imagined conspiracy of Jewish doctors in the early 1950s to murder high-ranking Soviet officials, including Stalin himself. Hundreds were arrested, and Soviet media began a campaign against Soviet Jews allegedly acting in harmony with Western intelligence services, but Stalin's death brought a swift end to the investigation. For more on this see Jonathan Brent and Vladimir P. Naumov, *Stalin's Last Crime: The Plot against the Jewish Doctors, 1948–1953* (New York: HarperCollins, 2003).

69. Ibid., 78–79; Artizov, *Reabilitatsiia,* 1:43–45.

70. Viktor N. Zemskov, "GULAG (istoriko-sotsiologicheskii aspect)," *Sotsialogicheskie issledovania,* no. 6 (1991): 14; A. I. Kokurin and A. I. Pozharov, "'Novy kurs' L. P. Berii," *Istoricheskii arkhiv,* no. 4 (1996): 135.

71. Leon Lipson, "Socialist Legality: The Road Uphill," in *Russia under Khrushchev,* ed. Abraham Brumberg (New York: Praeger, 1962), 445.

72. "Sovetskaia sotsialisticheskaia zakonnost' neprikosnovenna," *Pravda,* 7 April 1953, 1.

73. Dobson, *Khrushchev's Cold Summer,* 25.

74. Knight, *Beria,* 217–24.

75. Kozlov, *Istoriia stalinskogo GULAGa,* 1:598; Artizov, *Reabilitatsiia,* 1:69–70.

76. Kozlov, *Istoriia stalinskogo GULAGa,* 1:599.

77. As this extrajudicial body could only sentence people to up to eight years in the camps, it was deemed unnecessary to review those cases previous to 1945 as the prisoners by 1953 should already have been released. Even without the 1937–44 period, this was a daunting task of reviewing 133,668 cases. Artizov, *Reabilitatsiia,* 1:72–74.

78. RGANI, f. 5, op. 30, d. 36, ll. 75–76.

79. GARF, f. R-5446, op. 87, d. 1247, ll. 48–51.

80. Harold J. Berman, *Justice in the U.S.S.R: An Interpretation of Soviet Law,* rev. ed. (Cambridge, MA: Harvard University Press, 1963), 67.

81. Artizov, *Reabilitatsiia,* 1:65–66; Barenberg, *Gulag Town, Company Town,* 140–43.

82. GARF, f. R-9401, op. 1a, d. 513, ll. 110–11.

83. Barnes, *Death and Redemption,* 79–106.

84. See, for instance, the Standard Minimum Rules for the Treatment of Prisoners, which were adopted by the First United Nations Congress on the Prevention of Crime and the Treatment of Offenders in 1955 and then approved by the Economic and Social Council of the United Nations in 1957. *First United Nations Congress on the Prevention of Crime and the Treatment of Offenders* (New York: United Nations, Department of Economic and Social Affairs, 1956), 67.

85. TsDAVO, f. 8, op. 1, d. 78, l. 134.

86. Gorlizki, "Anti-Ministerialism," 1292.

87. TsDAVO, f. 8, op. 1, d. 78, l. 138.

88. TsDAVO, f. 8, op. 1, d. 81, ll. 2–7, 29–34, 42–50, 90–101.

89. Kokurin and Petrov, *GULAG,* 372–73. The actual transfer occurred on 15 February 1954.

90. Instead of suggesting a return of the Gulag to the MVD, Liamin suggested that it be separated from the MIu and placed directly under the Council of Ministers. This

proposal was apparently ignored, but it is likely that his letter contributed to the decision to remove the Gulag from the MIu. Kozlov, *Istoriia stalinskogo GULAG,* 2:460–61.

91. Ibid., 2:457.

92. Ibid., 2:458.

93. GARF, f. R-9414, op. 1, d. 202, l. 26.

94. Gorlizki, "Anti-Ministerialism," 1282–98.

95. GARF, f. R-9414, op. 1, d. 203, l. 5.

96. GARF, f. R-9401, op. 1a, d. 524, l. 226.

97. Kozlov, *Istoriia stalinskogo GULAGa,* 2:483.

98. To be more specific, there were thirty-five of the larger administrations (*upravleniia*) of corrective-labor camps and colonies and fifty-five of the smaller departments (*otdely*) of corrective-labor colonies. Kokurin and Petrov, *GULAG,* 374.

99. Kozlov, *Istoriia stalinskogo GULAGa,* 2:484–85.

100. Kokurin and Petrov, *GULAG,* 376–77.

101. A. I. Kokurin and N. V. Petrov, eds., *Lubianka: VChK-OGPU-NKVD-NKGB-MGB-MVD-KGB, 1917–1960* (Moscow: Mezhdunarodnyi fond "Demokratiia," 1997), 148–49.

102. A. A., Fursenko, ed., *Prezidium TsK KPSS 1954–1964,* 3 vols. (Moscow: Rosspen, 2003–6), 1:22. As Ivanova describes it, the Gulag under Stalin was comprised largely of "sewage from the state security organs." Ivanova, *Labor Camp Socialism,* 142.

103. Fursenko, *Presidium TsK KPSS,* 1:21.

104. Ibid.

105. Ibid., 1:22–23.

106. Kokurin and Petrov, *GULAG,* 797; A. I. Kokurin and N. V. Petrov, eds., *Lubianka: VChK-OGPU-NKVD-NKGB-MGB-MVD-KGB, 1917–1960* (Moscow: Mezhdunarodnyi fond "Demokratiia," 1997), 146.

107. For the pertinent section from the 12 March 1954 edict see Kozlov, *Istoriia stalinskogo GULAGa,* 2:469.

108. Ibid., 2:484–94.

109. Ibid., 2:492.

110. For the 10 July 1954 statute see Kokurin and Petrov, GULAG, 151–62, or Kozlov, *Istoriia stalinskogo GULAGa,* 498–508. A draft of the accompanying decree can be found at Kozlov, *Istoriia stalinskogo GULAGa,* 2:492–94.

111. Kokurin and Petrov, *GULAG,* 151.

112. LYA, f. V-141, op. 2, d. 184, l. 68.

113. ERAF, f. 77sm, op. 1, d. 252, l. 152; ERAF, f. 17sm, op. 4, d. 184, l. 123.

114. Fursenko, *Prezidium TsK KPSS,* 1:119–20, 905 (n.5).

115. Harold J. Berman, "Soviet Law Reform: Dateline Moscow 1957," *Yale Law Journal* 66, no. 8 (July 1957): 1203; Kozlov, *Istoriia stalinskogo GULAGa,* 7:602. There was significant internal discussion on what constituted "petty" in the lead-up to this law. See, for instance, GARF, f. R-7523, op. 75, d. 642, ll. 1–69.

116. P. C. Romashkin, *Amnistiia i polimovanie v SSSR* (Moscow: Gosudarstvennoe izdatel'stvo iuridicheskoi literatury, 1959), 77.

117. Berman, "Soviet Law Reform," 1203.

118. GAMO, f. R-23, op. 1, d. 188, l. 231.

119. Kozlov, *Istoriia stalinskogo GULAGa,* 1:620.

120. GARF, f. R-7523, op. 75, d. 598, l. 5.

121. GARF, f. R-9414, op. 1, d. 1398, l. 43.

122. Ibid.; GARF, f. R-7523, op. 88, d. 1184, l. 116.

123. See, for instance, TsDAGO, f. 1, op. 82, d. 158, ll. 145–46.

124. GARF, f. R-7523, op. 88, d. 1184, l. 116.

125. Kozlov, *Istoriia stalinskogo GULAGa*, 2:158.

126. GARF, f. A-385, op. 26, d. 93, ll. 1–5.

127. Marc Elie and Jeffrey S. Hardy, "'Letting the Beasts out of the Cage': Parole in the Post-Stalin Gulag, 1953–1973," *Europe-Asia Studies* 67, no. 4 (June 2015), 583.

128. Ibid., 583–89.

129. See, for instance, GARF, f. R-7523, op. 75, d. 7, ll. 92–96.

130. By March 1955 an agreement on this matter still had not been reached. GARF, f. R-7523, op. 75, d. 598, l. 10.

131. GARF, f. R-7523, op. 75, d. 45, ll. 1–7.

132. GARF, f. R-7523, op. 75, d. 45, l. 13.

133. GARF, f. R-7523, op. 83, d. 1184, ll. 112, 114.

134. GARF, f. R-9414, op. 1, d. 1398, l. 43.

135. Ibid.

136. GARF, f. R-9414, op. 1, d. 323, l. 12.

137. Kokurin and Petrov, *GULAG*, 170.

138. GARF, f. R-7523, op. 107, d. 229, l. 1; GARF, f. R-7523, op. 72, d. 606, ll. 191–203; and GARF, f. R-7523, op. 72, d. 619, ll. 60–70.

139. Fursenko, *Prezidium TsK KPSS*, 2:167.

140. Artizov, *Reabilitatsiia*, 1:259–60.

141. Ibid., 2:172, 184–85.

142. GARF, f. R-9414, op. 1, d. 323, l. 12.

143. See, for example, Artizov, *Reabilitatsiia*, 1:19–23, 74–75, for reports relating to these cases.

144. Ibid., 1:103–5.

145. Ibid., 1:213.

146. Ibid., 2:71.

147. Ibid., 1:144; GARF, f. R-9414, op. 1, d. 1398, l. 10.

148. Adler, *Gulag Survivor*, 98.

149. GARF, f. R-7523, op. 85, d. 251, ll. 16–18.

150. Małgorzata Giżejewska, *Kołyma 1944–1956: we wspomnieniach Polskich więźnów* (Warsaw: Instytut Studiów Politycznych Polskiej Akademii Nauk, 2000), 297.

151. Orlando Figes, *The Whisperers: Private Life in Stalin's Russia* (New York: Metropolitan Books, 2007), 553.

152. Kai T. Erikson, *Wayward Puritans: A Study in the Sociology of Deviance* (New York: Wiley, 1966), 16.

153. GARF, f. R-9414, op. 1, d. 202, l. 17; GARF, f. R-9414, op. 1, d. 252, ll. 10–12.

154. Kokurin and Petrov, *GULAG*, 375, 399.

155. One was created in Pavlodar, for instance, where 7,000 prisoners in 1955 began construction on a new combine factory together with housing for its future workers. GARF, f. R-5446, op. 88, d. 657, ll. 45–46.

156. Kokurin and Petrov, *GULAG*, 693.

157. GARF, f. R-5446, op. 88, d. 915, l. 94.

158. Barenberg, *Gulag Town, Company Town*, 186.

159. GARF, f. R-5446, op. 88, d. 915, ll. 48–49.

160. GARF, f. R-5446, op. 88, d. 915, ll. 9–10, 30–32. This impulse continues today. The Russian government in the post-Soviet era, for instance, has investigated the possibility of turning Butyrka Prison, located in the heart of Moscow, into a commercial development. But this is not a uniquely Russian phenomenon. Elected officials in the state of Utah finally succeeded after years of trying to relocate the state penitentiary out of a Salt Lake City suburb in order to turn the site into a lucrative mixed-use development. Nabi Abdullaev, "For Sale: 18th-Century Butyrskaya Prison," *Moscow Times*, 21 July 2001, 1;

Matt Canham, "Legislature OKs Prison Move to Salt Lake City," *Salt Lake Tribune,* 19 August 2015.

161. Nikita Sergeevich Khrushchev, *Khrushchev Remembers,* trans. and ed. Strobe Talbott (Boston: Little, Brown, 1970), 338.

162. Fursenko, *Prezidium TsK KPSS,* 1:77.

163. Vladimir Nekrasov, *Trinadtsat 'zheleznykh' narkomov: istoriia NKVD—MVD ot A. I. Rykova do N. A. Shchelokova, 1917–1982* (Moscow: Versty, 1995), 284.

164. Ibid., 286–87.

165. Fursenko, *Prezidium TsK KPSS,* 1:94.

166. RGANI, f. 5, op. 32, d. 39, l. 10.

167. RGANI, f. 5, op. 32, d. 39, l. 9.

168. RGANI, f. 5, op. 32, d. 39, l. 24. Others included his deputy ministers S. A. Vasil'ev, T. A. Strokach, K. P. Cherniaev, and his new head of police M. V. Barsukov.

169. Taubman, *Khrushchev,* 276.

170. Khrushchev, *Khrushchev Remembers,* 343.

171. Fursenko, *Prezidium TsK KPSS,* 1:94.

172. Polly Jones, *Myth, Memory, Trauma: Rethinking the Stalinist Past in the Soviet Union, 1953–70* (New Haven, CT: Yale University Press), 23.

173. Taubman, *Khrushchev,* 276.

174. N. S. Khrushchev, *Doklad na zakrytom zasedanii XX s'ezda KPSS* (Moscow: Gospolitizdat, 1959).

175. Fursenko, *Prezidium TsK KPSS,* 2:210.

176. Ibid., 2:939 (n.4); Artizov, *Reabilitatsiia,* 29–31; GARF, f. R-7523, op. 107, d. 160, ll. 1–2; and GARF, f. R-7523, op. 72, d. 606, ll. 142–64.

177. Fursenko, *Prezidium TsK KPSS,* 1:930 (n.5).

178. Artizov, *Reabilitatsiia,* 2:168.

179. For an account of one of the commissions at the Karagandinskii Corrective-Labor Camp (Karlag) see Barnes, *Death and Redemption,* 235–37.

180. GARF, f. R-9414, op. 1, d. 1427, l. 11; Artizov, *Reabilitatsiia,* 2:193. It appears that the majority of those released returned peacefully to society. In Ukraine, for example, "the MVD noted that most integrated peacefully into workplaces, and some even excelled at work on the collective farms." Amir Weiner, "The Empires Pay a Visit: Gulag Returnees, East European Rebellions, and Soviet Frontier Politics," *Journal of Modern History* 78, no. 2 (June 2006), 338.

181. Alla Tumanov, *Where We Buried the Sun: One Woman's Gulag Story,* trans. Gust Olson (Edmonton: NuWest Press, 1999), 233.

182. GDA SBU, f. 6, d. 43533fp, ll. 16–259.

183. Kokurin and Petrov, *GULAG,* 164–81.

184. This proposal had actually been included in the 1954 statute, but the Ministry of Finance had quickly obtained a reversal of the order through a Council of Ministers decree on 30 September 1954 and the Gulag continued to operate on a self-financing basis (along with an annual subsidy from the government to cover losses). GARF, f. R-9401, op. 2, d. 264, l. 310.

185. Artizov, *Reabilitatsiia,* 2:87–89. This letter is discussed in Ivanova, *Labor Camp Socialism,* 67–68; and Applebaum, *Gulag,* 510.

186. RGANI, f. 89, op. 16, d. 1, ll. 86–88.

187. Fursenko, *Prezidium TsK KPSS,* 2:456–62; Kokurin and Petrov, *GULAG,* 187–92.

188. Kokurin and Petrov, *GULAG,* 186.

189. GARF, f. R-9414, op. 3, d. 88, l. 96.

190. GARF, f. R-9414, op. 1, d. 255, ll. 44–51. Just days previously six camps, including the Sibirskii Corrective-Labor Camp (Siblag) and Dubravlag, had been transferred to the Russian MVD. GARF, f. R-9401, op. 2, d. 480, l. 14.

191. Fursenko, *Prezidium TsK KPSS,* 1:123.

192. GARF, f. R-9414, op. 1, d. 255, l. 42.

193. GARF, f. R-9414, op. 1, d. 257, l. 66.

194. Kokurin and Petrov, *GULAG,* 794.

195. GARF, f. R-9414, op. 1, d. 257, l. 24. This is confirmed by another report which declared that forestry camp administration "strives to ensure that the plan is fulfilled, and takes no interest in questions concerning people's living conditions." GARF, f. R-9414, op. 1, d. 257, l. 39.

196. See GARF, f. R-9414, op. 1, d. 255, l. 31.

197. GARF, f. R-9414, op. 1, d. 253, l. 151. See also GARF, f. 7523, op. 72, d. 629, l. 220 for an order transferring the coal mine of Karlag to the Kazakh Ministry of Coal Industry.

198. At times, though, particularly in his secret speech, Khrushchev used the term revolutionary legality. In his mind, apparently, these terms were synonymous. Dobson, *Khrushchev's Cold Summer,* 81.

199. GARF, f. R-9414, op. 3, d. 131, l. 149.

200. See GARF, f. R-9414, op. 1, dd. 196–99, 307, 316.

201. GARF, f. R-9414, op. 1, d. 318, l. 95.

202. GARF, f. R-9414, op. 1, d. 311, l. 175; GARF, f. R-9414, op. 1, d. 312, ll. 66–67.

203. GARF, f. R-9414, op. 1, d. 318, l. 134; Kokurin and Petrov, *GULAG,* 207.

204. GARF, f. R-9414, op. 1, d. 318, l. 96.

205. GARF, f. R-9414, op. 1, d. 319, ll. 163–64.

206. GARF, f. R-9414, op. 1, d. 278, ll. 6–7; GARF, f. R-9414, op. 1, d. 318, l. 133; GARF, f. R-9414, op. 1, d. 1427, ll. 132–33 Most of the remaining camps at this point were engaged in producing lumber for the Ministry of Forestry.

207. See GARF, f. R-9414, op. 1, d. 305; GARF, f. R-9414, op. 1, d. 319, ll. 114–15.

208. GARF, f. R-9414, op. 1, d. 1427, l. 132.

209. GARF, f. R-9414, op. 1, d. 318, ll. 96–97.

210. GARF, f. R-9414, op. 1, d. 319, l. 117.

211. Kokurin and Petrov, *GULAG,* 169.

212. GARF, f. R-9414, op. 1, d. 283, l. 140.

213. See, for example, GARF, f. R-9414, op. 1, d. 311, ll. 36–37, which singles out Ukraine and Lithuania; and GARF, f. R-9414, op. 1, d. 312, l. 71.

214. ERAF, f. 17sm, op. 4, d. 212, l. 241.

215. GARF, f. R-9401, op. 2, d. 505, l. 302; GARF, f. R-9414, op. 1, d. 312, l. 166. This latter figure still represented approximately 12 percent of all convictions during 1959.

216. RGANI, f. 13, op. 1, d. 914, ll. 125–26.

217. Romashkin, *Amnistiia i polimovanie,* 78–79.

218. GARF, f. R-9414, op. 1, dd. 282, 286–87.

219. RGANI, f. 5, op. 30, d. 277, l. 1.

220. GARF, f. R-9414, op. 1, d. 323, l. 12.

221. GARF, f. R-9414, op. 1, d. 1427, ll. 11, 33.

222. GARF, f. R-7523, op. 77, d. 71, ll. 64–66.

223. For more on this see GARF, f. A-385, op. 26, d. 172; and RGANI, f. 13, op. 1, d. 240, ll. 80–157.

224. RGANI, f. 13, op. 1, d. 240, ll. 17–18.

225. RGANI, f. 13, op. 1, d. 768, l. 32.

226. GARF, f. R-7523, op. 108, d. 37, l. 2.

227. Valerii Rodos, *Ia syn palacha: vospominanie* (Moscow: Chastnyi arkhiv, 2008), 178–82.

228. In the end he was sent in internal exile to Kazakhstan, where he died of alcoholism on 19 March 1962. Fursenko, *Prezidium TsK KPSS,* 1:438–39, 1074.

229. GARF, f. R-9414, op. 1, d. 1398, l. 1; GARF, f. R-9414, op. 1, d. 1427, ll. 11, 132; GARF, f. R-9492, op. 6, d. 290, l. 3.

230. For population figures for the Soviet Union at large see E. M. Andreev, L. E. Darskii, and T. L. Kharkova, *Naselenie Sovetskogo Soiuza, 1922–1991* (Moscow: Nauka, 1993), 70.

231. Khrushchev's Gulag by 1960, however, does not fit the definition of "mass imprisonment" provided by leading criminologist David Garland, who defines it as a relatively high rate of imprisonment combined with "the systematic imprisonment of whole groups of the population," rather than just "the incarceration of individual offenders." Although certain categories of crime in the Soviet Union under Khrushchev would not be recognized as such in the West, there was no substantial imprisonment of "whole groups" of Soviet peoples after the releases of the 1950s. David Garland, "The Meaning of Mass Imprisonment," *Punishment and Society* 3, no. 1: 6.

232. RGANI, f. 13, op. 2, d. 383, l. 19.

233. See, for example, V. V. Birkin, "Deti 'Khrushchevskoi ottepeli,'" in *Pravda cherez gody: stat'i, vospominaniia, dokumenty,* vol. 3 (Donetsk: Region, 1999), 127; and V. M. Gridin, *My, kotorykh ne bylo . . . : vospominaniia o GULAGe v stukhakh i proze* (Odessa: Astroprint, 1996), 6.

234. GARF, f. R-9414, op. 1, d. 1398, ll. 1–10; GARF, f. R-9414, op. 1, d. 1427, ll. 11–12, 133. For more on the antihooligan campaign see Brian LaPierre, "Making Hooliganism on a Mass Scale: The Campaign against Petty Hooliganism in the Soviet Union, 1956–1964." *Cahiers du monde russe* 47, nos. 1–2 (January–June 2006): 349–75; and Brian LaPierre, *Hooligans in Khrushchev's Russia: Defining, Policing, and Producing Deviance During the Thaw* (Madison: University of Wisconsin Press, 2012).

235. Kokurin and Petrov, *GULAG,* 438; GARF, f. R-9414, op. 1, d. 1427, l. 135.

236. GARF, f. R-9492, op. 6, d. 259, l. 78.

237. Kokurin and Petrov, *GULAG,* 164.

238. GARF, f. R-9414, op. 1, d. 1427, ll. 10, 134.

239. He was initially placed in charge of planning the 1967 International and Universal Exposition, which was to be held in Moscow until the Soviets canceled their sponsorship in 1962 (allowing Montreal to host it). Dudorov was given a minor post as the head of the Administration of the Production of Construction Materials for Moscow city executive committee, where he worked for ten years before retiring. Nekrasov, *Trinadtsat 'zheleznykh' narkomov,* 321.

2. REORIENTING THE AIMS OF IMPRISONMENT

1. ERAF, f. 17sm, op. 4, d. 173, l. 255.

2. GARF, f. R-8131, op. 32, d. 4961, l. 10.

3. In both the Stalin and post-Stalin era, most reports on the state of the Gulag as a whole or a particular subunit within the Gulag were broken down into three primary categories: the regimen (*rezhim*), production, and reeducation.

4. On the aims of the early Soviet penal system see Michael Jakobson, *Origins of the Gulag: The Soviet Prison Camp System, 1917–1934* (Lexington: University Press of Kentucky, 1993).

5. As noted American criminologist Donald Cressey in 1961 remarked, prisons are devoted "to keeping inmates, using inmates, and serving inmates." Donald R. Cressey, ed., *The Prison: Studies in Institutional Organization and Change* (New York: Holt, Rinehart

and Winston, 1961), 5. Further discussion of these interacting themes in other settings may be found, for instance, in Gresham Sykes, *The Society of Captives: A Study of Maximum Security Prison* (Princeton, NJ: Princeton University Press, 1958); D. L. Howard, *The English Prisons: Their Past and Their Future* (London: Methuen, 1960); and S. E. Idada, "The Aims and Philosophy of Imprisonment," in *The Prison System in Nigeria,* ed. T. O. Elias (Lagos: University of Lagos Press, 1968), 151–67.

6. Here I refer to general or indirect deterrence rather than specific deterrence; the former refers to the deterrent effect sentencing and punishing has on the general population whereas the latter denotes prevention of future crime by the offender.

7. Peter H. Solomon Jr., *Soviet Criminal Justice under Stalin* (Cambridge: Cambridge University Press, 1996), 227; David R. Shearer, *Policing Stalin's Socialism: Repression and Social Order in the Soviet Union, 1924–1953* (New Haven, CT: Yale University Press, 2009), 423.

8. David Garland, *Punishment and Modern Society: A Study in Social Theory* (Chicago: University of Chicago Press, 1990), 19.

9. For contemporary examples see, for instance, Albert Konrad Herling, *The Soviet Slave Empire* (New York: Wilfred Funk, 1951); Charles A. Orr, ed., *Stalin's Slave Camps: An Indictment of Modern Slavery* (Boston, MA: Beacon Press, 1952); Roger N. Baldwin, ed., *A New Slavery: Forced Labor: The Communist Betrayal of Human Rights* ([New York]: Oceana, 1953); and Bertram D. Wolfe, "Note on the Soviet Slave Labor Reform of 1954–55," *Russian Review* 15, no. 1 (January 1956): 57–59.

10. Aleksandr Isaevich Solzhenitsyn, *The Gulag Archipelago 1918–1956: An Experiment in Literary Investigation,* 3 vols., trans. Thomas P. Whitney (New York: Harper and Row, 1974–78), 2:594.

11. The same was true of the MVD's special settlements for repressed *kulaks.* Lynne Viola, *The Unknown Gulag: The Lost World of Stalin's Special Settlements* (Oxford: Oxford University Press, 2007), 91.

12. As Adam Hochchild found in his discussion with a former camp official, "from the colonel's words you would not have known that it was a prison. Instead, he talked almost entirely about [the camp's] role in the Soviet economy." Adam Hochschild, *The Unquiet Ghosts: Russians Remember Stalin* (Boston, MA: First Mariner Books, 1994), 65.

13. Jakobson, *Origins of the Gulag,* 53–69.

14. Viola, *Unknown Gulag,* 57, 190.

15. Oleg Khlevniuk "The Economy of the OGPU, NKVD, and MVD of the USSR, 1930–1953," in *The Economics of Forced Labor: The Soviet Gulag,* ed. Paul R. Gregory and Valery Lazarev (Stanford, CA: Hoover Institution Press, 2003), 52.

16. Steven Barnes, *Death and Redemption: The Gulag and the Shaping of Soviet Society* (Princeton, NJ: Princeton University Press, 2011), 167–72; and Alan Barenberg, *Gulag Town, Company Town: Forced Labor and Its Legacy in Vorkuta* (New Haven, CT: Yale University Press, 2014), 98–104.

17. James Heinzen, "Corruption in the Gulag: Dilemmas of Officials and Prisoners," *Comparative Economic Studies* 47, no. 2 (June 2005): 456–75.

18. Negley K. Teeters, *World Penal Systems: A Survey* (Philadelphia: Pennsylvania Prison Society, 1944), 207.

19. For more on this see Jeffrey S. Hardy, "The Gulag and the Penitentiary Reappraised: Post-War Penal Convergence in the United States and Soviet Union, 1950–1965," in *The Soviet Union and the United States: Rivals of the Twentieth Century,* ed. Eva-Maria Stolberg (Frankfurt: Peter Lang, 2013), 169–94.

20. A. I. Kokurin and N. V. Petrov, eds., *GULAG: glavnoe upravlenie lagerei, 1917–1960* (Moscow: Mezhdunarodnyi fond "Demokratiia," 2000), 667.

21. GARF, f. R-9401, op. 1a, d. 510, ll. 333–35.

22. GARF, f. R-9492, op. 5, d. 160, l. 167.

23. See, for instance, GARF, f. R-9492, op. 1, d. 282; GARF, f. R-9492, op. 5, dd. 160, 186; TsDAVO, f. 8, op. 1, d. 73, ll. 91, 96; and TsDAVO, f. 8, op. 1, d. 78, l. 111.

24. GARF, f. R-9492, op. 1, d. 282, ll. 10–11.

25. TsDAVO, f. 8, op. 1, d. 78, ll. 183–84.

26. Igor Denisovich Batsaev, *Osobennosti promyshlennogo osvoeniia severo-vostoka Rossii v period massovykh politicheskikh repressyi (1932–1953), Dal'stroi* (Magadan: SVK-NII DVO RAN, 2002), 180.

27. Khlevniuk, "Economy of the OGPU," 65.

28. GARF, f. R-9414, op. 1, d. 202, ll. 11–12.

29. Ibid.

30. GARF, f. R-9414, op. 1, d. 202, l. 80.

31. GAMO, f. R-23, op. 1, d. 5192, l. 37.

32. GAMO, f. R-23, op. 1, d. 5206, l. 38.

33. GARF, f. R-7523, op. 107, d. 136, ll. 28–29.

34. GARF, f. R-7523, op. 107, d. 124, l. 7.

35. Solzhenitsyn, *Gulag Archipelago*, 2:201.

36. GARF, f. R-9401, op. 2, d. 480, l. 270.

37. Simon Ertz, "Trading Effort for Freedom: Workday Credits in the Stalinist Camp System," *Comparative Economic Studies* 47, no. 2 (June 2005): 484–89; Marc Elie and Jeffrey S. Hardy, " 'Letting the Beasts out of the Cage': Parole in the Post-Stalin Gulag, 1953–1973," *Europe-Asia Studies* 67, no. 4 (June 2015): 583–86.

38. GARF, f. R-5446, op. 88, d. 925, ll. 8–20.

39. GARF, f. R-9492, op. 6, d. 117, l. 27. In Estonia and perhaps other republics the practice continued in truncated form until 1960. ERAF, f. 17sm, op. 4, d. 230, l. 102.

40. GAMO, f. R-137, op. 16, d. 58, l. 6.

41. I. V. Ovchinnikov, *Ispoved' kulatskogo syna* (Moscow: Desnitsa, 2000), 309.

42. See, for instance, Jakobson, *Origins of the Gulag*, 142; and Kokurin and Petrov, *GULAG*, 62–64.

43. Solzhenitsyn, *Gulag Archipelago*, 2:587.

44. GARF, f. R-9414, op. 1, d. 311, l. 11.

45. See, for instance, Patricia O'Brian, "The Prison on the Continent: Europe, 1865–1965," in *The Oxford History of the Prison: The Practice of Punishment in Western Society,* ed. Norval Morris and David J. Rothman (New York: Oxford University Press, 1998), 182–84; Carlos Aguirre, *The Criminals of Lima and Their Worlds* (Durham, NC: Duke University Press, 2005), 155–63; Sykes, *Society of Captives*, 26.

46. Efforts to place the Gulag on the state budget would continue through the mid-1960s. GARF, f. R-7523, op. 109, d. 413, l. 31.

47. GARF, f. R-9414, op. 1, d. 311, ll. 108–19.

48. GARF, f. R-9414, op. 1, d. 311, l. 193.

49. ERAF, f. 17sm, op. 4, d. 203, l. 129.

50. GARF, f. R-9414, op. 1, d. 311, l. 185; Kokurin and Petrov, *GULAG*, 211.

51. GARF, f. R-9414, op. 1, d. 311, ll. 29–30. Larger camp points were also suggested with the goal of making the remaining camps more economical. See GARF, f. R-9414, op. 1, d. 312, l. 102–3.

52. GARF, f. R-9414, op. 1, d. 309, l. 173; GARF f. R-9414, op. 1, d. 318, l. 98.

53. GARF, f. R-9414, op. 1, d. 311, l. 114.

54. Oleg Khlevniuk, *The History of the Gulag: From Collectivization to the Great Terror,* trans. Vadim A. Staklo (New Haven, CT: Yale University Press, 2004), 62, 177.

55. A. A., Fursenko, ed., *Prezidium TsK KPSS 1954–1964,* 3 vols. (Moscow: Rosspen, 2003–6), 2:236.

56. GARF, f. R-9414, op. 1, d. 312, l. 5.

57. GARF, f. R-9414, op. 1, d. 311, l. 17.

58. In April 1958 Dudorov reported that 35–40 percent of prison inmates were working. GARF, f. R-9414, op. 1, d. 311, l. 10.

59. GARF, f. R-9414, op. 1, d. 312, l. 97.

60. GARF, f. R-9414, op. 1, d. 311, l. 26.

61. GARF, f. R-9414, op. 1, d. 162, l. 162.

62. See, for example, GARF, f. R-9414, op. 1, d. 318, l. 52.

63. GARF, f. R-9414, op. 1, d. 311, l. 39.

64. ERAF, f. 17sm, op. 4, d. 206, l. 55; ERAF, f. 17sm, op. 4, d. 213, l. 8. The range among the fifteen republics for 1958 was 0 to 1,619 rubles, with Russia at 1,158 rubles per prisoner.

65. ERAF, f. 17sm, op. 4, d. 176, l. 18; ERAF, f. 17sm, op. 4, d. 203, l. 129.

66. ERAF, f. 17sm, op. 4, d. 217, l. 23; ERAF, f. 77sm, op. 1, d. 382, l. 2.

67. RGANI, f. 13, op. 1, d. 264, l. 9; RGANI, f. 13, op. 1, d. 764, l. 130; RGANI, f. 13, op. 1, d. 768, l. 10.

68. Vladimir Voinovich, *Moscow 2042,* trans. Richard Lourie (San Diego, CA: Harcourt, Brace, Jovanovich, 1987), 314.

69. Solzhenitsyn, *Gulag Archipelago,* 2:468.

70. Maxim Gorky, L. Auerbach, and S. G. Firin, eds., *Belomor: An Account of the Construction of the New Canal between the White Sea and the Baltic Sea* (New York: Harrison Smith and Robert Haas, 1935); originally published in Russian as M. Gor'kii, L. Averbakh, and S. Firin, eds., *Belomorsko-Baltiiskii Kanal imini Stalina: istoriia stroitel'stva* (Moscow: Istoriia Fabrik i Zavodov, 1934).

71. Barnes, *Death and Redemption,* 58.

72. GARF, f. R-9492, op. 5, d. 194, ll. 184–87.

73. See, for instance, GARF, f. R-9414, op. 1, d. 378, ll. 147–48; GARF, f. R-9414, op. 1, d. 1631, ll. 2–4; GARF, f. R-9414, op. 1, d. 1665, ll. 163–66; and GARF, f. R-9414, op. 1, d. 1666, l. 15.

74. ERAF, f. 17sm, op. 4, d. 129, l. 81.

75. *First United Nations Congress on the Prevention of Crime and the Treatment of Offenders* (New York: United Nations, Department of Economic and Social Affairs, 1956), 67.

76. Herman Franke, *The Emancipation of Prisoners: A Socio-Historical Analysis of the Dutch Prison Experience* (Edinburgh: Edinburgh University Press, 1995), 244–75.

77. Michel Foucault, *Discipline and Punish: The Birth of the Prison,* trans. Alan Sheridan (New York: Pantheon Books, 1977), 264–68.

78. Nanci Adler, *The Gulag Survivor: Beyond the Soviet System* (New Brunswick, NJ: Transaction Publishers, 2002), 83–84.

79. Fursenko, *Prezidium Tsk KPSS,* 1:21.

80. ERAF, f. 77sm, op. 1, d. 231, l. 141.

81. Kokurin and Petrov, *GULAG,* 694.

82. GARF, f. R-9414, op. 3, d. 81, ll. 5–28; GARF, f. R-9414, op. 3, d. 87, ll. 46–49.

83. GARF, f. R-9414, op. 1, d. 311, l. 9.

84. Petr Dmitriev, *"Soldat Berii": vospominaniia lagernogo okhranika* (Leningrad: Chas pik, 1991), 36, 40.

85. Ibid., 137.

86. Among countless other examples see GDA MVS, f. 6, op. 2, d. 237, l. 24.

87. GARF, f. R-9492, op. 5, d. 160, l. 176.

88. GARF, f. R-9492, op. 5, d. 161, ll. 146–47.

89. For typical examples see GARF, f. R-9401, op. 1a, d. 542, l. 195; GARF, f. R-9492, op. 5, d. 160, ll. 176–77; and GARF, f. R-8131, op. 32, d. 3033, l. 109.

90. GDA MVS, f. 6, op. 2, d. 206, l. 137.

91. GARF, f. A-461, op. 13, d. 33, l. 23.

92. GARF, f. A-461, op. 11, d. 581, l. 7.

93. Rygor Klimovich, *Konets Gorlaga* (Minsk: Nasha Niva, 1999), 334.

94. A. E. Kropochkin, "Memoirs of Former Prisoner SL-208," in *Voices from the Gulag*, ed. Aleksandr Solzhenitsyn (Evanston, IL: Northwestern University Press, 2011), 399.

95. M. S. Goldman, "'. . . Ne etomu menia desiat' let v komsomole uchili . . .'" *Karta*, 1997, nos. 17–18: 51.

96. Cursing and general rudeness between inmates and guards is fairly standard in most prison systems. See, among many other examples, Ted Conover, *Newjack: Guarding Sing Sing* (New York: Random House, 2000).

97. GDA MVS, f. 6, op. 2, d. 417, l. 7.

98. GARF, f. R-8131, op. 32, d. 6880, l. 17.

99. GARF, f. R-8131, op. 32, d. 5598, l. 8.

100. P. M. Losev, *Material'no-bytovoe i meditsinskoe obespechenie zakliuchennykh* (Moscow: Vysshaia shkola MVD SSSR, 1957), 5–7, 14–15.

101. Tsvi I. Preigerzon, *Dnevnik vospominanii byvshego lagernika (1949–1955)*, trans. I. B. Mints (Moscow: Vozvrashchenie, 2005), 249.

102. Małgorzata Giżejewska, *Kołyma 1944–1956: we wspomnieniach Polskich więźnów* (Warsaw: Instytut Studiów Politycznych Polskiej Akademii Nauk, 2000), 108. See also Goldman, "'. . . Ne etomu,'" 52.

103. Among an endless stream of reports detailing poor living conditions, a Procuracy investigation of the Severo-Pechorskskii Corrective-Labor Camp (Sevpechlag) from 1953 gives a sense of some of the problems: insufficient beds, beddings, and dishes; few medical personnel; hundreds of prisoners living in dirty tents in subfreezing temperatures; female inmates being transferred in the middle of winter to barracks that lacked doors, window panes and operable stoves; and rotten food and an absence of fresh vegetables, meat, and dairy that led to scurvy and other diseases. GARF, f. R-8131, op. 32, d. 3757, ll. 10–12.

104. Karl Tobien, *Dancing under the Red Star* (Colorado Springs, CO: Waterbrook, 2006), 258.

105. The commercial dining hall system began as a trial in mid-1954 and was thereafter expanded. GARF, f. R-9401, op. 1a, d. 543, l. 30.

106. GARF, f. R-9401, op. 1a, d. 531, l. 168.

107. GARF, f. R-9401, op. 1a, d. 542, l. 326.

108. GARF, f. R-9414, op, 1, d. 2883, ll. 111, 251.

109. GARF, f. R-9401, op. 1a, d. 542, l. 358.

110. Goldman, "'. . . Ne etomu,'" 52.

111. Alan Barenberg, "Prisoners without Borders: *Zazonniki* and the Transformation of Vorkuta after Stalin," *Jahrbücher für Geschichte Osteuropas* 57, no. 4 (2009): 521–23.

112. GARF, f. R-9401, op. 1a, d. 542, l. 249.

113. This is confirmed, for example, by a procurator sent to Magadan in 1954 to help oversee Dal'stroi and Sevvostlag, who noted a marked improvement in living conditions after 1956. I. V. Pantiukhin, *Stolitsa kolymskogo kraia: zapiski Magadanskogo prokurora* (Petrozavodsk: Molodezhnaia gazeta, 1995), 184.

114. Ol'ga Biriuzova, "Ia liubliu tebia, zhizn'," *Detektiv i politka* 5, no. 15 (1991): 324.

115. Karlo Štajner, *Seven Thousand Days in Siberia*, trans. Joel Agee (New York: Farrar, Straus and Giroux, 1988), 359–60.

116. Preigerzon, *Dnevnik vospominanii*, 263–64, 274.

117. Vladimir Fedorovich Abramkin and Valentina Fedorovna Chesnakova, eds., *Tiuremnyi mir glazami politzakliuchennykh, 1940–1980-e gg* (Moscow: Sodeistvie, 1998), 13.

118. Giżejewska, *Kołyma 1944–1956*, 108.

119. GARF, f. R-8131, op. 32, d. 6128, l. 82.

120. See, among many others, Robert Conquest, *The Great Terror: A Reassessment* (New York: Oxford University Press, 1990), 320–40; Anne Applebaum, *Gulag: A History* (New York: Doubleday, 2003), xv; Khlevnyuk, "Economy of the OGPU, NKVD, and MVD," 57; Valery Lazarev, "Conclusions," in Gregory and Lazarev, *Economics of Forced Labor*, 189.

121. Galina M. Ivanova, *Istoriia GULAGa, 1918–1958: sotsial'no-ekonomicheskii i politico-pravovoi aspekty* (Moscow: Nauka, 2006), 389. The Soviet Union never did ratify Convention No. 105, adopted by the International Labor Organization in 1957, which prohibited forced labor "as a punishment for holding or expressing political views or views ideologically opposed to the established political, social or economic system." *List of Ratifications by Convention and by Country* (Geneva: International Labour Office, 1994), 140–41.

122. *First United Nations Congress*, 67 (emphasis mine).

123. RGANI, f. 5, op. 30, d. 712, ll. 73–74.

124. RGANI, f. 13, op. 1, d. 764, l. 152.

125. Solzhenitsyn, *Gulag Archipelago*, 2:194–95.

126. Kokurin and Petrov, *GULAG*, 188.

127. ERAF, f. 17sm, op. 4, d. 184, l. 11.

128. Kokurin and Petrov, *GULAG*, 211.

129. GARF, f. R-9414, op. 1, d. 318, l. 99.

130. Kokurin and Petrov, *GULAG*, 211. As a ranking member of the Gulag leadership explained during a January 1958 conference, using prisoners to assemble envelopes was not appropriate. GARF, f. R-9414, op. 1, d. 312, l. 12.

131. RGANI, f. 13, op. 1, d. 264, l. 9.

132. RGANI, f. 13, op. 1, d. 764, l. 105.

133. Nadezhda Ulanovskaia and Maiia Ulanovskaia, *Istoriia odnoi sem'i* (Moscow: Vest'-VIMO, 1994), 347.

134. ERAF, f. 17sm, op. 4, d. 203, ll. 182–83.

135. GARF, f. R-5446, op. 90, d. 466, ll. 49–50.

136. GDA MVS, f. 6, op. 2, d. 393, l. 17. See also P. D. Borodin, ed., *O tvorcheskom primenenii pedagogicheskogo naslediia A. S. Makarenko v rabote s zakliuchennymi* (Moscow: Izdanie polittotdela GUMZ MVD RSFSR, 1960), 11.

137. Fursenko, *Prezidium TsK KPSS*, 2:236.

138. The Gulag's internal newspapers in 1959 had a combined circulation of one hundred thousand. GARF, f. R-9414, op. 1, d. 318, l. 144.

139. ERAF, f. 17sm, op. 4, d. 184, l. 15.

140. M. M. Molostov, *Revisionism—58* (Phoenix: Atheneum, 1991), 579.

141. Solzhenitsyn, *Gulag Archipelago*, 3:487.

142. N. I. Krivoshein, "Dan' pamiati, ili, 'Smotri, zhidenka primorili,'" *Zvedza*, no. 4 (2003): 135.

143. Solzhenitsyn paints a picture of an innovative, even overbearing political and cultural section in the early 1930s that was soon snuffed by the cold necessity of plan fulfillment. In the postwar period the flame of political and cultural work would occasionally flicker, but there were no serious efforts to maintain a constant push in this direction. Solzhenitsyn, *Gulag Archipelago*, 2:470–76, 491–92.

144. By 1959 the Gulag contained 1,456 libraries with over 2.3 million books. GARF, f. R-9414, op. 1, d. 318, l. 144. True, some colonies, including several in Kazakhstan, were found to be completely devoid of books while others in non-Russian republics only had books in Russian. But the renewed effort to provide sanctioned reading material for Gulag inmates confirms that the education and political indoctrination of convicts had become a serious concern. GARF, f. R-9414, op. 1, d. 311, l. 52.

145. Igor' Baryshnikov, "Sbornik—zarodysh zhurnala," in *Zhurnaly v pogonakh*, ed. O. L. Ivanova (Moscow: Ob'edinennaia redaktsiia MVD Rossii, 2001), 299.

146. Krivoshein, "Dan' pamiati," 135.

147. ERAF, f. 17sm, op. 4, d. 184, l. 16; ERAF, f. 77sm, op. 1, d. 295, l. 73.

148. For the widespread presence of football (soccer) in the 1930s-era Gulag see Wilson Bell, "The Gulag and Soviet Society in Western Siberia, 1929–1953" (PhD diss., University of Toronto, 2011), 90; M. I. Rybal'chenko, "Chempion na katorga," in *Dorogi za koliuchuiu provoloku*, ed. V. M. Gridin (Odessa: Astroprint, 1996), 85–106; and Nikolai Petrovich Starostin, *Futbol skvoz' gody* (Moscow: Sovetskaia Rossiia, 1989), 61–81. I am grateful to Steven Maddox for these references and look forward to future publications from him on this subject.

149. Goldman, "'. . . Ne etomu,'" 52. See also ERAF, f. 17sm, op. 4, d. 184, l. 16; and ERAF, f. 77sm, op. 1, d. 293, l. 7.

150. Preigerzon, *Dnevnik vospominanii*, 187.

151. Nerijus Adomaitis, "Basketball Helped Lithuanians Survive the Gulag," *Reuters*, 24 August 2011, available at http://www.reuters.com/article/2011/08/24/us-lithuania -gulag-basketball-idUSTRE77N5N820110824.

152. GARF, f. R-9414, op. 1, 255, l. 80. On the Stalin-era educational system see Barnes, *Death and Redemption*, 58–59.

153. Kokurin and Petrov, *GULAG*, 213.

154. Camp commanders sought especially as activist council members norm-fulfilling prisoners who enjoyed authority (*avtoritet*') among their fellow inmates and who had the skills and desire for social work. ERAF, f. 77sm, op. 1, d. 273, l. 120; ERAF, f. 77sm, op. 1, d. 295, l. 70.

155. Cited in Samuel Kucherov, *The Organs of Soviet Administration and Justice: Their History and Operation* (Leiden: E. J. Brill, 1970), 169. For more on these institutions of social justice see Brian LaPierre, *Hooligans in Khrushchev's Russia: Defining, Policing, and Producing Deviance During the Thaw* (Madison: University of Wisconsin Press, 2012), 132–67; Oleg Kharkhordin, *The Collective and the Individual in Russia: A Study of Practices* (Berkeley: University of California Press, 1999); Yoram Gorlizki, "Delegalization in Russia: Soviet Comrades' Courts in Retrospect," *American Journal of Comparative Law* 46, no. 3 (Summer 1998): 403–25; Gordon B. Smith, *Reforming the Russian Legal System* (Cambridge: Cambridge University Press, 1996), 59–62; and Deborah A. Field, *Private Life and Communist Morality in Khrushchev's Russia* (New York: Peter Lang, 2007), 30–32.

156. J. E. Baker, *The Right to Participate: Inmate Involvement in Prison Administration* (Metuchen, NJ: Scarecrow Press, 1974).

157. For the statute governing the new comrades' courts see GARF, f. R-9414, op. 3, d. 92, ll. 88–89.

158. See, for instance, ERAF, f. 77sm, op. 1, d. 295, l. 70; and ERAF, f. 17sm, op. 4, d. 203, l. 197.

159. GARF, f. R-9414, op. 1, d. 310, l. 56.

160. See, for example, ERAF, f. 17sm, op. 4, d. 184, l. 14; ERAF, f. 77sm, op. 1, d. 184, l. 13; ERAF, f. 77sm, op. 1, d. 273, ll. 11, 199; and ERAF, f. 77sm, op. 1, d. 295, l. 71.

161. ERAF, f. 77sm, op. 1, d. 273, ll. 9–10.

162. ERAF, f. 77sm, op. 1, d. 273, l. 13. Most of these were released, however, over the course of the ensuing year and by the end of 1955 only around 10 percent of prisoners were considered activists.

163. Solzhenitsyn, *Gulag Archipelago*, 3:487.

164. ERAF, f. 77sm, op. 1, d. 323, p. 37. The abbreviation p. here stands for order (*prikaz*), which is used in lieau of page numbers in this file.

165. RGANI, f. 13, op. 1, d. 768, l. 13.

166. Borodin, *O tvorcheskom primenenii*, 7.

167. For more on the detachments see Kharkhordin, *Collective and the Individual*, 300–305.

168. I. L. Averbakh, *Ot prestupleniia k trudu* (Moscow: Sovetskoe zakonodatel'stvo, 1936), 141–42.

169. GARF, f. R-7523, op. 75, d. 14, l. 84.

170. Kokurin and Petrov, *GULAG*, 209.

171. GARF, f. R-9414, op. 1, d. 313, l. 291.

172. GARF, f. R-9414, op. 1, d. 823, l. 156.

173. This conference is notable because it included a significant number of low-level administrators such as detachment commanders and heads of camp points. As one camp point head remarked, "as long as I've worked in the camps, this is the first time the MVD has convened such a conference for lower-ranked workers." GARF, f. R-9414, op. 1, d. 313, 45.

174. GARF, f. R-9414, op. 1, d. 1778, l. 3.

175. GARF, f. R-9414, op. 1, d. 319, l. 5.

176. ERAF, f. 17sm, op. 4, d. 203, l. 130.

177. N. I. Krivoshein, "Blazhennyi Avgustin," *Zvezda*, no. 7 (2001): 174.

178. GARF, f. R-9414, op. 1, d. 311, l. 5.

179. Kokurin and Petrov, *GULAG*, 457.

180. Howard, *English Prisons*, 141.

181. Sykes, *Society of Captives*, 18, 21.

182. *First United Nations Congress*, 67.

183. In the first half of 1952, the Gulag prosecuted just over 8,000 inmates for crimes committed in the camps, a sizable reduction from the over 23,000 prosecuted in 1945 when the inmate population was much lower. The campaign was also credited with reducing the number of (officially reported) murders from 2,011 in 1951 to 1,284 in 1952. V. P. Kozlov, ed., *Istoriia stalinskogo GULAGa: konets 20-kh—pervaia polovina 50-kh godov*, 7 vols. (Moscow: Rosspen, 2004), 6:188, 286, 684n.309.

184. GARF, f. R-9414, op. 1, d. 318, l. 137.

185. See GAMO, f. R-23, op. 1, d. 5210, ll. 12–13; and GAMO, f. R-23, op. 1, d. 5611, ll. 14–15.

186. GARF, f. R-9414, op. 1, d. 318, l. 137.

187. Solzhenitsyn, *Gulag Archipelago*, 3:243; GARF f. R-8131, op. 32, dd. 3769–70.

188. G. M. Temin, *V teni zakona: bol' o perezhitom* (Saint Petersburg: Liki Rossii, 1995), 63.

189. GARF, f. R-7523, op. 107, d. 136, ll. 15–19.

190. GARF f. R-9414, op. 1, d. 283, l. 284.

191. Fursenko, *Prezidium TsK KPSS*, 2:457.

192. O. B. Borovskii, "'Levsha' ponevole," in *Pechal'naia pristan'*, ed. I. L. Kuznetsov (Syktyvkar: Komi knizhnoe izdatel'stvo, 1991), 298.

193. ERAF, f. 17sm, op. 4, d. 184, l. 19; ERAF, f. 17sm, op. 4, d. 188, l. 142.

194. Štajner, *Seven Thousand Days*, 359.

195. Danylo Shumuk, *Life Sentence: Memoirs of a Ukrainian Political Prisoner*, trans. Ivan Jaworsky and Halya Kowalska (Edmonton: Canadian Institute of Ukrainian Studies, University of Alberta, 1984), 343.

196. GARF, f. R-7523, op. 75, d. 14, ll. 71–85. This is confirmed by another prisoner, who charged that the thieves forced the other prisoners to give them half their wages and that the administration and wardens were complicit in propping up the thieves. GARF, f. R-7523, op. 75, d. 45, ll. 9–11.

197. GARF, f. R-7523, op. 107, d. 124, ll. 58–62.

198. GARF, f. R-9414, op. 1, d. 318, l. 137.

199. Kokurin and Petrov, *GULAG,* 167; GARF, f. R-9414, op. 3, d. 134, l. 31.

200. For more on the practice of deconvoying under Stalin see Barenberg, "Prisoners without Borders," and Wilson T. Bell, "Was the Gulag an Archipelago? De-Convoyed Prisoners and Porous Borders in the Camps of Western Siberia," *Russian Review* 72, no. 1 (January 2013): 116–41.

201. Fursenko, *Prezidium TsK KPSS,* 2:235.

202. GARF, f. R-7523, op. 107, d. 136, l. 24.

203. Fursenko, *Prezidium TsK KPSS,* 2:457.

204. Kokurin and Petrov, *GULAG,* 192. The process of consolidating political prisoners began already in 1956 as the case review commissions were performing their labor. Temin, *V teni zakona,* 85.

205. Kokurin and Petrov, *GULAG,* 193; GARF, f. R-9414, op. 1, d. 318, l. 137.

206. GARF, f. R-8131, op. 32, d. 6748, l. 11. In 1972 most political prisoners were transferred to correctional institutions in Perm Province. Leona Toker, *Return from the Archipelago: Narratives of Gulag Survivors* (Bloomington: Indiana University Press, 2000), 25.

207. GARF, f. R-9414, op. 1, d. 309, l. 67.

208. GARF, f. R-9414, op. 1A, dd. 603–6.

209. This can be found in GARF, f. R-9414, op. 4, d. 202, ll. 1–40. According to an acquaintance of his, however, his work was criticized and ultimately rejected for analyzing at length a phenomenon that was no longer supposed to exist. Baryshnikov, "Sbornik," 301.

210. GARF, f. R-9414, op. 1, d. 310, l. 12.

211. GARF, f. R-9414, op. 1, d. 317, ll. 199–200.

212. GARF, f. R-9414, op. 1, d. 662, ll. 107–9.

213. GARF, f. R-9414, op. 1, d. 257, l. 37.

214. GARF, f. R-8131, op. 32, d. 4955, l. 16.

215. Kokurin and Petrov, *GULAG,* 210.

216. GARF, f. R-9414, op. 1, d. 286, l. 38.

217. Sergei Dovlatov, *The Zone: A Prison Camp Guard's Story,* trans. Anne Frydman (New York: Alfred A. Knopf, 1985), 19.

218. See, for example, ERAF, f. 17sm, op. 4, d. 232, l. 52; ERAF, f. 77sm, op. 1, d. 350, l. 150.

219. GARF f. R-9413, op. 1, d. 225, ll. 135–38.

220. GARF, f. R-9414, op. 4, d. 202, l. 45.

221. Baryshnikov, "Sbornik," 299; GARF f. R-9413, op. 1, d. 225, l. 194.

222. GARF f. R-9413, op. 1, d. 225, ll. 195–96.

223. GARF f. R-5446, op. 91, d. 264, ll. 40–41.

224. GARF, f. R-9414, op. 4, d. 202, ll. 41–130.

225. Baryshnikov, "Sbornik," 299.

226. GARF, f. R-9414, op. 1, d. 310, l. 90. Indeed, the most prominent gang of Stalin's Gulag, the *vory v zakone* (thieves-in-law), was effectively dismantled in the late 1950s, although it later reappeared in the Soviet penal apparatus in the 1980s. Federico Varese, "The Society of the *Vory-v-Zakone,* 1930s–1950s," *Cahiers du monde russe* 39, no. 4 (1998): 531; Varese, *The Russian Mafia* (Oxford: Oxford University Press, 2001); and Marc Elie, "Banditen und Juristen im Tauwetter GULag: Reform, kriminelle Gegenkultur und kirminologische Expertise," *Jahrbücher für Geschichte Osteuropas* 57, no. 4 (2009): 492–512.

227. See, for instance, Anatoly Marchenko, *My Testimony,* trans. Michel Scammell (New York: E. P. Dutton, 1969), 339–48; and Andrei Amalrik, *Notes of a Revolutionary,* trans. Guy Daniels (New York: Alfred A. Knopf, 1982), 160–62.

228. GARF, f. R-9414, op. 1, d. 318, l. 137; GARF, f. R-9414, op. 1, d. 235, l. 138; GARF, f. R-9414, op. 1, d. 319, l. 169; RGANI, f. 13, op. 1, d. 764, l. 139.

229. GARF, f. R-9414, op. 1, d. 319, l. 36; GARF, f. R-9414, op. 3, d. 143, ll. 44–45.

230. As Oleg Khlevniuk points out, Procuracy reports are important because the organization competed with the MVD for power within the Soviet criminal justice establishment. Khlevniuk, *History of the Gulag,* 7.

231. For a reporting form used to quantify "political-educational" work in the correctional-labor institutions in 1956 see GARF, f. R-9414, op. 3, d. 93, ll. 118–19.

232. A. Dalakishvili, "Tri voprosa," *K novoi zhizni,* no. 9 (September 1961): 36.

233. ERAF, f. 77sm, op. 1, d. 261, ll. 137, 182; GARF, f. A-461, op. 11, d. 771, l. 52.

234. See, for example, ERAF, f. 17sm, op. 4, d. 173, l. 140; ERAF, f. 17sm, op. 4, d. 176, l. 6.

235. Barnes, *Death and Redemption,* 134.

236. RGANI, f. 13, op. 1, d. 872, l. 179.

237. RGANI, f. 13, op. 1, d. 764, l. 130.

238. RGANI, f. 13, op. 1, d. 764, l. 132.

239. Richard H. McCleery, "The Governmental Process and Informal Social Control," in Cressey, *Prison,* 184.

240. Batsaev, *Osobennosti,* 182. See also Adler, *Gulag Survivor,* 93.

3. OVERSIGHT AND ASSISTANCE

1. GARF, f. A-461, op. 13, d. 36, ll. 1–2. Such accusations, modeled on similar petitions found in the Soviet press, were also prominent outside the penal system. Gleb Tsipursky, "'As a Citizen, I Cannot Ignore These Facts': Soviet Whistleblowing and State Response, 1955–1961," *Jahrbücher für Geschichte Osteuropas* 58, no. 1 (2010): 57.

2. For more on this incident see GARF, f. A-461, op. 13, d. 36, as well as somewhat embellished retellings by Anatoly Marchenko and Valentyn Moroz, who years later served as prisoners in Dubravlag: Anatoly Marchenko, *My Testimony,* trans. Michel Scammell (New York: E. P. Dutton, 1969), 56–57; and Valentyn Moroz, *Boomerang: The Works of Valentyn Moroz,* ed. Yaroslav Bihun (Baltimore, MD: Smoloskyp, 1974), 7–8.

3. The Russian word *kontrol* does not translate perfectly into English, but connotes regulation, inspection, and monitoring rather than control in the strict sense. The Workers' and Peasants' Inspectorate (Rabkrin), State Control Commission, Party Control Commission, Secret Police, Procuracy, and the Communist Party itself were the more prominent of the Soviet Union's institutions of control.

4. See Oleg Khlevniuk, *The History of the Gulag: From Collectivization to the Great Terror,* trans. Vadim A. Staklo (New Haven, CT: Yale University Press, 2004), 108, 248.

5. For more on the Soviet Procuracy see George Ginsburgs, "The Soviet Procuracy and Forty Years of Socialist Legality," *American Slavic and East European Review* 18, no. 1 (February 1959): 34–62; Glenn G. Morgan, *Soviet Administrative Legality: The Role of the Attorney General's Office* (Stanford, CA: Stanford University Press, 1962); Gordon B. Smith, *The Soviet Procuracy and the Supervision of Administration* (Alphen aan den Rijn, The Netherlands: Sijthoff & Noordhoff, 1978); Aleksandr G. Zviagintsev and Iurii G. Orlov, *Prigovorennye vremenem: rossiiskie i sovetskie prokurory, XX vek., 1937–1953* (Moscow: Rosspen, 2001); and Zviagintsev and Orlov, *Zalozhniki vozhdei: rossiistie i sovetskie prokurory XX vek, 1954–1992* (Moscow: Rosspen, 2006).

6. This charge was included in the first statute on procuratorial oversight, issued 28 May 1922. M. P. Maliarov, *Prokurorskii nadzor v SSSR* (Moscow: Iuridicheskaia literatura, 1969), 305. In the 1930s the right of procurators to oversee places of confinement was confirmed in the Corrective-Labor Code. Peter H. Solomon Jr., *Soviet Criminal*

Justice under Stalin (Cambridge: Cambridge University Press, 1996), 175; D. N. Pritt, "The Russian Legal System," in *Twelve Studies in Soviet Russia,* ed. Margaret I. Cole (London: Victor Gollancz, 1933), 162.

7. Recent works on the Stalinist Gulag, while at times using procurators' reports to describe the terrible living conditions suffered by prisoners, have all but ignored the Procuracy's oversight role. See, for instance, Anne Applebaum, *Gulag: A History* (New York: Doubleday, 2003), 197, 203, 211; and Khlevniuk, *History of the Gulag,* 248.

8. Petr Dmitriev, *"Soldat Berii": vospominaniia lagernogo okhranika* (Leningrad: Chas pik, 1991), 140; E. G. Shirvindt and B. S. Utevskii, *Sovetskoe ispravitel'no-trudovoe pravo* (Moscow: Gosiurizdat, 1957), 4–6.

9. GARF, f. R-8131, op. 32, d. 3760, ll. 54, 93–94.

10. R. A. Rudenko, "Zadachi dalneishego ukrepleniia sotsialisticheskoi zakonnosti v svete reshenii XX s'ezda KPSS," *Sovetskoe gosudarstvo i prava,* no. 4 (1956): 19. For a brief overview of how the legal educational program was strengthened under Khrushchev see Darrell P. Hammer, "Legal Education in the USSR," *Soviet Studies* 9, no. 1 (July 1957): 20–27.

11. Moshe Lewin, *The Soviet Century* (London: Verso, 2005), 115. This is supported by an interview conducted with a former Gulag guard officer as part of the Harvard Project on the Soviet Social System. See *Harvard Project on the Soviet Social System,* Schedule B, Vol. 1, Case 136 (Interviewer S. H.), Part II: 4–5 (Widener Library, Harvard University). Still, as Applebaum is keen to remind, the very presence of procurators' reports on dire conditions in the Gulag makes clear that Gulag bosses and their superiors knew the camps were every bit as bad as Varlam Shalamov and Aleksandr Solzhenitsyn later made them out to be. Applebaum, *Gulag,* 279.

12. GARF, f. R-8131, op. 32, d. 2229, l. 30.

13. GARF, f. R-8131, op. 28, d. 1378, l. 18.

14. GARF, f. R-8131, op. 32, d. 3024, ll. 1–4.

15. Yoram Gorlizki, "Anti-Ministerialism and the USSR Ministry of Justice, 1953–1956: A Study in Organizational Decline," *Europe-Asia Studies* 48, no. 8 (December 1996): 1284.

16. Rudenko was appointed procurator general on 30 June 1953, just days after Beria's arrest. He would remain in this post for the next twenty-seven years. Zviagintsev and Orlov, *Zalozhniki vozhdei,* 38–39.

17. See, for instance, GARF, f. R-8131, op. 32, dd. 2234, 3287–88.

18. GARF, f. R-8131, op. 32, d. 2229, ll. 60, 115–17, 129–30.

19. GARF, f. R-8131, op. 32, d. 3284, ll. 56–59.

20. GARF, f. R-8131, op. 32, d. 3760, l. 118.

21. The primary reporting categories for inspections were to be: (1) General details, including demographic data; (2) Regimen information, including isolation and guarding; (3) Organization of labor; (4) Living conditions; (5) Disciplinary practice; (6) Political reeducational work; (7) Struggle against crime; and (8) Relations with (and especially abuse of) prisoners. GARF, f. R-8131, op. 32, d. 3285, ll. 74–76. The categories of inspection by 1958 remained largely the same, although new sections were added to cover parole and complaints. See GARF, R-8131, op. 32, d. 6126, ll. 261–62.

22. GARF, f. R-8313, op. 32, d. 4968, l. 229.

23. GARF, f. R-8131, op. 32, d. 3024, ll. 79–80; and GARF, f. R-8131, op. 32, d. 3287, ll. 34–37. This process of shifting control to local procuracies had actually begun in early 1953, before Stalin's death, when the procurator general placed colonies and camp points located far from the republican or provincial capital (where the camp procuracies were usually located) under the procuratorial oversight of local city or regional procurators. This order affected 180 local procurator's offices. GARF, f. R-8131, op. 32, d. 2229, ll. 30–44.

24. See I. V. Pantiukhin, *Stolitsa kolymskogo kraia: zapiski Magadanskogo prokurora* (Petrozavodsk: Molodezhnaia gazeta, 1995), 83–85.

25. GARF, f. R-8131, op. 32, d. 3768, ll. 218–19.

26. GARF, f. A-461, op. 13, d. 35, ll. 1–3; GARF, f. A-461, op. 13, d. 40, ll. 1, 4; GARF, f. A-461, op. 13, d. 38, ll. 12–13.

27. GARF, f. R-8131, op. 32, d. 4966, ll. 1–17.

28. GARF, f. R-8131, op. 32, d. 5497, ll. 2, 9; GARF, f. R-8131, op. 32, d. 6129, ll. 6, 9.

29. GARF, f. R-8131, op. 32, d. 2235, ll. 130–35. For the 1933 statute see V. G. Lebedinskii and D. I. Orlov, eds., *Sovetskaia prokuratura v vazhneishikh dokumentakh* (Moscow: Gosudarstvennoe izdatel'stvo iuridicheskoi literatury, 1956), 403–6.

30. GARF, f. R-8131, op. 32, d. 3026, ll. 5–69.

31. I. N. Shiriaev and G. A. Metelkina, *Sovetskaia prokuratura: sbornik dokumentov* (Moscow: Iuridicheskaia literatura, 1981), 141.

32. Ibid., 145; TsDAGO, f. 1, op. 24, d. 5418, l. 11.

33. GARF, f. A-461, op. 13, d. 33, l. 3.

34. Shiriaev and Metelkina, *Sovetskaia prokuratura,* 145–46.

35. Note that this remark was made not in the "secret speech," but in Khrushchev's report to the full Congress. N. S. Khrushchev, *Report of the Central Committee of the Communist Party of the Soviet Union to the 20th Party Congress* (Moscow: Foreign Languages Publishing House, 1956), 113.

36. Nanci Adler, *The Gulag Survivor: Beyond the Soviet System* (New Brunswick, NJ: Transaction Publishers, 2002), 91.

37. GARF, f. R-7523, op. 85, d. 240a, l. 26; GARF, f. R-9492, op. 5, d. 165, ll. 73–74.

38. GARF, f. A-461, op. 13, d. 11, l. 18.

39. GARF, f. A-461, op. 13, d. 40, ll. 2–3.

40. GARF, f. A-461, op. 13, d. 40, l. 2.

41. GARF, f. A-461, op. 12, d. 31, l. 126.

42. GARF, f. R-8131, op. 32, d. 4454, ll. 92–93.

43. GARF, f. R-7523, op. 75, d. 7, l. 93.

44. See, for example, GARF, f. A-461, op. 13, d. 53, l. 1.

45. See, for example, GARF, f. A-461, op. 13, d. 40, ll. 5–7; GARF, f. A-461, op. 13, d. 41, l. 9; GARF, f. A-461, op. 13, d. 53, ll. 1, 29–30.

46. GARF, f. A-461, op. 13, d. 40, ll. 5–6.

47. [Iu. E. Ivanov], "Gorod Vladimir," in *Samizdat veka,* ed. Anatolii Strelianyi, Genrikh Sapgir, Vladimir Bakhtin, and Nikita Ordynskii (Moscow: Itogi veka, 1999), 60.

48. GARF, f. A-461, op. 13, d. 33, l. 31.

49. See, for example, GARF, f. R-8131, op. 32, d. 4454, l. 100.

50. Marchenko, *My Testimony,* 239; RGANI, f. 13, op. 1, d. 764, l. 150.

51. GARF, f. R-8131, op. 32, d. 4968, l. 229.

52. GARF, f. R-8131, op. 32, d. 4573, ll. 31–35. See, for example, GARF, f. R-8131, op. 32, d. 5597, l. 29; GARF, f. R-8131, op. 32, d. 4964, ll. 125–26.

53. Pantiukhin, *Stolitsa kolymskogo kraia,* 85–87.

54. GARF, f. R-8131, op. 32, d. 3767, l. 13.

55. A. N. Kuzin, *Malyi srok: vospominaniia v forme esse so svobodnym siuzhetom* (Moscow: Rudomino, 1994), 82.

56. GARF, f. R-8131, op. 32, d. 6725, ll. 235–36.

57. GARF, f. R-9492, op. 5, d. 196, l. 188.

58. GARF, f. R-8131, op. 32, d. 6395, l. 282.

59. See RGANI, f. 13, op. 1, d. 240, ll. 80–157, for the 1959 case review commissions, for example, each one of which included a local procurator.

60. Pantiukhin, *Stolitsa kolymskogo kraia,* 133.

61. Such a tendency is common to most bureaucracies, regardless of political system. For a similar case of prison officials resisting new monitoring from outside in 1970s Massachusetts see Kelsey Kauffman, *Prison Officers and Their World* (Cambridge, MA: Harvard University Press), 6–14.

62. See, for example, comments by the head of the Irkutsk MVD at a 15 December 1955 conference on improving the work of procurators. GARF, f. R-8131, op. 32, d. 4454, ll. 340–41.

63. GARF, f. A-461, op. 13, d. 5, l. 34.

64. GARF, f. R-8131, op. 32, d. 6128, l. 5.

65. GARF, f. R-8131, op. 32, d. 6128, l. 9.

66. GARF, f. A-461, op. 11, d. 767, l. 78.

67. GARF, f. R-8131, op. 32, d. 6122, l. 80.

68. GAMO, f. R-23, op. 1, d. 5611, ll. 26–29.

69. GARF, f. R-8131, op. 32, d. 5492, ll. 14–15.

70. GARF, f. R-8131, op. 32, d. 2229, ll. 218–19.

71. GARF, f. R-8131, op. 32, d. 2229, l. 223.

72. TsDAGO, f. 1, op. 82, d. 158, ll. 145–46.

73. GARF, f. R-8131, op. 32, d. 6390, l. 98.

74. Pantiukhin, *Stolitsa kolymskogo kraia,* 45.

75. Ibid., 44.

76. GARF, f. R-7523, op. 107, d. 124, l. 16. This was apparently an old camp saying that was repeated by camp officials under Stalin. See, for instance, A. E. Kropochkin, "Memoirs of Former Prisoner SL-208," in *Voices from the Gulag,* ed. Aleksandr Solzhenitsyn (Evanston, IL: Northwestern University Press, 2011), 369.

77. GARF, f. A-461, op. 13, d. 5, l. 37.

78. GARF, f. A-461, op. 13, d. d, l. 35.

79. GARF, f. A-461, op. 13, d. 5, ll. 24–25.

80. GARF, f. R-8131, op. 32, d. 4955, ll. 13–14.

81. See, for example, GARF, f. R-8131, op. 32, d. 4957, ll. 29, 89, 144, 270–72; GARF, f. R-8131, op. 32, d. 5492, ll.16–17.

82. GARF, f. R-8131, op. 32, d. 4454, l. 93.

83. GARF, f. A-461, op. 13, d. 31, l. 369.

84. GARF, f. R-8131, op. 32, d. 6121, ll. 21–29.

85. Peter H. Solomon, "Soviet Politicians and Criminal Prosecutions: The Logic of Intervention," in *Cracks in the Monolith: Party Power in the Brezhnev Era,* ed. James R. Millar (Armonk, NY: M. E. Sharpe, 1992), 13.

86. See, for example, GARF, f. R-8131, op. 32, d. 3025, ll. 1–12, 46–47, 140–51; GARF, f. R-8131, op. 32, d. 3030, ll. 45–256.

87. GARF, f. R-8131, op. 32, d. 3030, ll. 257–71; GARF, f. R-8131, op. 32, d. 3030, ll. 272–76.

88. GARF, f. R-8131, op. 32, d. 3033, ll. 16–17.

89. Pantiukhin, *Stolitsa kolymskogo kraia,* 97.

90. GARF, f. R-8131, op. 32, d. 3769, l. 43.

91. Pantiukhin, *Stolitsa kolymskogo kraia,* 87–88.

92. For early examples, see GARF, f. 9492, op. 5, d. 165, ll. 73–5; GARF, f. R-8131, op. 32, d. 3767, l. 20; and GARF, f. R-8131, op. 32, d. 4000, ll. 42–44.

93. GARF, f. R-8131, op. 32, d. 4955, l. 13.

94. GARF, f. A-461, op. 13, d. 5, l. 18.

95. See, for instance, GARF, f. A-461, op. 13, d. 7, ll. 10–11; GARF, f. A-461, op. 13, d. 53, l. 14; GARF, f. R-8131, op. 32, d. 4968, l. 43; GARF, f. R-8131, op. 32, d. 5497, l. 215; and GARF, f. R-8131, op. 32, d. 6120, l. 45.

96. GARF, f. R-8131, op. 32, d. 5064, ll. 29–30.

97. GARF, f. A-461, op. 11, d. 1185, l. 21.

98. GARF, f. R-8131, op. 32, d. 5492, l. 3.

99. GARF, f. R-9401, op. 2, d. 506, l. 189.

100. Danylo Shumuk's account of both the late Stalinist Gulag and Khrushchev's penal system, for instance, is notable in its absence of any reference to serious abuses by the administration or prisoner-on-prisoner violence in the 1960s, whereas such was common in the earlier period. Danylo Shumuk, *Life Sentence: Memoirs of a Ukrainian Political Prisoner,* trans. Ivan Jaworsky and Halya Kowalska (Edmonton: Canadian Institute of Ukrainian Studies, University of Alberta, 1984), 341–56. Similarly, Vladimir Bukovsky's account of Gulag life in a criminal camp in the late 1960s reports only isolated instances of violence and punishment for guards who beat or humiliated prisoners. Vladimir Bukovsky, *To Build a Castle: My Life as a Dissenter,* trans. Michael Scammell (New York: Viking Press, 1979), 314, 325.

101. GARF, f. A-461, op. 13, d. 33, l. 9.

102. GARF, f. R-8131, op. 32, d. 4955, l. 2.

103. GARF, f. R-8131, op. 32, d. 4965, l. 141.

104. GARF, f. R-8131, op. 32, d. 6120, l. 98.

105. GARF, f. A-461, op. 11, d. 978, l. 90.

106. GARF, f. R-8131, op. 32, d. 6122, l. 14.

107. GARF, f. R-8131, op. 32, d. 6122, ll. 51–52.

108. GARF, f. R-8131, op. 32, d. 5598, l. 64.

109. GARF, f. R-8131, op. 32, d. 5063, l. 68. For similar cases see GARF, f. R-8131, op. 32, d. 5598, ll. 2–4; and GARF, f. R-8131, op. 32, d. 6120, l. 98.

110. GARF, f. R-8131, op. 32, d. 5598, ll. 2–4.

111. In the Khrushchev period these regulations were set forth in statutes governing places of confinement that were issued in 1954, 1958, and 1961. See A. I. Kokurin and N. V. Petrov, eds., *GULAG: glavnoe upravlenie lagerei, 1917–1960* (Moscow: Mezhdunarodnyi fond "Demokratiia," 2000), 151–62, 195–207; and RGANI, f. 13, op. 1, d. 295, ll. 53–72.

112. TsDAGO, f. 1, op. 24, d. 5507, ll. 129–34.

113. TsDAGO, f. 1, op. 24, d. 5507, l. 135.

114. GARF, f. A-461, op. 11, d. 978, ll. 88–89.

115. GARF, f. R-8131, op. 32, d. 7036, l. 49.

116. Leon Boim, "Ombudmanship in the Soviet Union," *American Journal of Comparative Law* 22, no. 3 (Summer 1974): 510–12.

117. G. M. Temin, *V teni zakona: bol' o perezhitom* (Saint Petersburg: Liki Rossii, 1995), 93–96.

118. GARF, f. A-461, op. 11, d. 1362, l. 22.

119. Harold J. Berman, *Justice in the U.S.S.R: An Interpretation of Soviet Law,* rev. ed. (Cambridge, MA: Harvard University Press, 1963), 285–98.

120. See Robert Conquest, *Industrial Workers in the USSR* (London: Bodley Head, 1967); Melanie Ilic, "What Did Women Want? Khrushchev and the Revival of the *Zhensovety,*" in *Soviet State and Society under Nikita Khrushchev,* ed. Melanie Ilic and Jeremy Smith, 104–21; and Junbae Jo, "Dismantling Stalin's Fortress: Soviet Trade Unions in the Khrushchev Era," in Ilic and Smith, *Soviet State and Society,* 122–21.

121. TsDAVO, f. 288, op. 9, d. 2198, l. 157.

122. On the comrades' courts see Yoram Gorlizki, "Delegalization in Russia: Soviet Comrades' Courts in Retrospect," *American Journal of Comparative Law* 46, no. 3 (Summer 1998): 403–25. On the antiparasite campaign see Marianne Armstrong, "The Campaign against Parasites," in *Soviet Policy-Making: Studies of Communism in Transition,*

ed. Peter H. Juviler and Henry W. Morton (New York: Praeger, 1967), 163–82; and Sheila Fitzpatrick, "Social Parasites: How Tramps, Idle Youth, and Busy Entrepreneurs Impeded the Soviet March to Communism," *Cahiers du Monde russe* 47, nos. 1–2 (January–June 2006): 377–408. On the ability to free prisoners into the care of families or social collectives see Miriam Dobson, *Khrushchev's Cold Summer: Gulag Returnees, Crime, and the Fate of Reform after Stalin* (Ithaca, NY: Cornell University Press, 2009), 161–64.

123. Harold J. Berman, "The Dilemma of Soviet Law Reform," *Harvard Law Review* 76, no. 5 (March 1963): 950.

124. GARF, f. A-461, op. 11, d. 1180, l. 25; TsDAGO, f. 1, op. 24, d. 5224, l. 7.

125. GARF, f. A-385, op. 26, d. 93, l. 3.

126. GARF, f. R-9414, op. 3, d. 88, l. 176; Kokurin and Petrov, *GULAG,* 175.

127. GARF, f. R-9401, op. 2, d. 481, l. 432.

128. Kokurin and Petrov, *GULAG,* 191.

129. ERAF, f. 17sm, op. 4, d. 197, ll. 29–30, 48, 118.

130. GARF, f. R-9414, op. 1A, d. 348e, l. 35.

131. GARF, f. R-9414, op. 1A, d. 348e, ll. 35–36; ERAF, f. 17sm, op. 4, d. 212, l. 273.

132. A. A., Fursenko, ed., *Prezidium TsK KPSS 1954–1964,* 3 vols. (Moscow: Rosspen, 2003–6), 1:195.

133. V. N. Kalinin, Iu. B. Utevskii, and A. M. Iakovlev, *Sovetskie ispravitel'no-trudovye uchrezhdeniia* (Moscow: Gosizdat, 1960), 10.

134. ERAF, f. 17sm, op. 4, d. 234, l. 294. Notably, this reform did not pass in Russia until 1965. GARF, f. A-385, op. 26, d. 273, l. 11.

135. GARF, f. A-461, op. 11, d. 1360, l. 26.

136. See, for example, Fursenko, *Prezidium TsK KPSS,* 1:213; RGANI, f. 13, op. 1, d. 682, l. 93.

137. LYA, f. V-141, op. 2, d. 212, l. 138.

138. GARF, f. A-461, op. 11, d. 421, l. 4.

139. GDA MVS, f. 3, op. 1, d. 203, l. 276.

140. ERAF, f. 17sm, op. 4, d. 216, l. 18.

141. GARF, f. A-461, op. 11, d. 770, l. 15.

142. Kokurin and Petrov, *GULAG,* 213.

143. GDA MVS, f. 3, op. 1, d. 203, ll. 274, 276. In Lithuania by 1959 there were 12 for the 4 prisons and 8 corrective-labor colonies. LYA, f. V-141, op. 2, d. 225, l. 195.

144. GARF, f. A-461, op. 11, d. 1360, l. 22.

145. GARF, f. A-461, op. 11, d. 585, l. 8.

146. GARF, f. R-8131, op. 32, d. 6566, l. 13; GARF, f. A-461, op. 11, d. 576, l. 12.

147. GARF, f. A-461, op. 11, d. 581, l. 29.

148. ERAF, f. 17sm, op. 4, d. 234, l. 294.

149. GARF, f. R-8131, op. 32, d. 6567, l. 40.

150. GDA MVS, f. 3, op. 1, d. 224, ll. 87–88.

151. GDA MVS, f. 3, op. 1, d. 262, ll. 71, 82–83.

152. GDA MVS, f. 6, op. 2, d. 413, ll. 175–77.

153. See, for example, ERAF, f. 17sm, op. 4, d. 234, l. 90; ERAF, f. 17s, op. 4, d. 203, ll. 129–30; ERAF, f. 77sm, op. 1, d. 350, l. 12; GARF, f. A-461, op. 11, d. 578, l. 7; GARF, f. A-461, op. 1, d. 601, l. 21; GARF, f. A-461, op. 1, d. 765, l. 6.

154. TsDAGO, f. 1, op. 24, d. 4948, l. 6; GARF, f. A-385, op. 26, d. 221, l. 10; GARF, f. A-461, op. 11, d. 1360, l. 27.

155. GDA MVS, f. 6, op. 2, d. 413, ll. 184–85.

156. ERAF, f. 17sm, op. 4, d. 251, ll. 2.

157. GARF, f. A-461, op. 11, d. 1183, l. 50.

158. GARF, f. R-7523, op. 109, d. 285, l. 34.

159. GARF, f. A-385, op. 26, d. 221, l. 10.

160. GARF, f. A-461, op. 11, d. 1360, l. 25.

161. GARF, f. A-461, op. 11, d. 577, l. 17.

162. F. A. Tomasevich, *Prokurorskii nadzor za sobliudeniem zakonnosti v mestakh lisheniia svobody* (Saratov: Privolzhskoe knizhnoe izdatel'stvo, 1966), 47–48.

163. See, for example, GDA MVS, f. 6, op. 2, d. 413, ll. 185; GARF, f. R-8131, op. 32, d. 6588, l. 89; and GARF, f. A-461, op. 11, d. 1186, l. 3.

164. Such was the conclusion of a report on Russian oversight commissions in 1964, which criticized the tendency to rubber-stamp (*shtampovat'*) such requests. GARF, f. A-461, op. 11, d. 1360, l. 25.

165. GARF, f. A-385, op. 26, d. 221, ll. 34–35.

166. I. Apeter, "Ispravitel'no-trudovaia politika epokhi vstupleniia v sotsializm," in *Ot tiurem k vospitatel'nym uchrezhdeniiam,* 445.

167. Lynne Viola, *The Best Sons of the Fatherland: Workers in the Vanguard of Soviet Collectivization* (New York: Oxford University Press, 1987), 23, 173; Sheila Fitzpatrick, *Stalin's Peasants: Resistance and Survival in the Russian Village after Collectivization* (New York: Oxford University Press, 1994), 227; Petr E. Shelest, *Da ne sudimy budete: dnevnikovye zapisi, vospominaniia chlena Politburo TsK KPSS* (Moscow: Edition q, 1995), 118.

168. GARF, f. R-9414, op. 1, d. 309, l. 143.

169. See Fursenko, *Prezidium TsK KPSS,* 1:207–21.

170. GARF, f. R-8131, op. 32, d. 6566, l. 13; GDA MVS, f. 3, op. 1, d. 222, l. 259. By late 1959 there were 120 sponsoring organizations and 97 colonies in Ukraine, but while some colonies had multiple sponsors, others had none. GDA MVS, f. 3, op. 1, d. 205, l. 230, 234.

171. ERAF, f. 17sm, op. 4, d. 234, l. 295.

172. GARF, f. R-9414, op. 1, d. 319, l. 144. For the lauded Cheliabinsk example see Leonid Eliseev, "Retsidiva ne budet!," *Izvestiia,* 14 October 1959, 6; and A. Salmin and A. Kuznetsov, "Shefskaia rabota kollektivov trudiashchikhsia v ispravitel'no-trudovykh uchrezhdeniiakh," in *Vtoroe rozhdenie,* ed. G. A. Usachev (Cheliabinsk: Cheliabinsk knizhnoe izdatel'stvo, 1960), 3–14.

173. GARF, f. R-9414, op. 1, d. 319, l. 147.

174. GARF, f. R-9414, op. 1, d. 319, l. 145; GDA MVS, f. 3, op. 1, d. 262, l. 82; and GDA MVS, f. 6, op. 2, d. 413, l. 201.

175. GDA MVS, f. 3, op. 1, d. 205, ll. 230, 234.

176. GDA MVS, f. 3, op. 1, d. 224, ll. 87–88.

177. GDA MVS, f. 6, op. 2, d. 395, l. 18.

178. GARF, f. R-8131, op. 32, d. 6567, ll. 39–40.

179. ERAF, f. 77sm, op. 1, d. 405, ll. 70–71.

180. GARF, f. A-461, op. 11, d. 581, l. 30.

181. GARF, f. A-461, op. 11, d. 1379, l. 50.

182. Ibid.

183. GARF, f. A-461, op. 11, d. 1376, l. 7.

184. GDA MVS, f. 6, op. 2, d. 393, l. 77.

185. GARF, f. R-8131, op. 32, d. 6128, l. 4.

186. GDA MVS, f. 6, op. 2, d. 393, l. 117.

187. GDA MVS, f. 3, op. 1, d. 203, ll. 274, 279; GDA MVS, f. 3, op. 1, d. 262, ll. 71, 81.

188. GARF, f. R-7523, op. 109, d. 413, l. 17.

189. GDA MVS, f. 6, op. 2, d. 395, l. 17.

190. GDA MVS, f. 6, op. 2, d. 413, ll. 49–50

191. GARF, f. A-461, op. 11, d. 1373, l. 25.

192. The same appreciation for assistance without oversight seemed to be the case for many collective farms in relation to their urban sponsors in the 1930s. Viola, *Best Sons of the Fatherland,* 157–58.

193. The special camp courts, which had been created on 30 December 1944 both to relieve regular courts of cases involving crimes committed in the camps and to maintain as much as possible a veil of secrecy over Gulag operations, were disbanded by a Supreme Soviet decree on 29 April 1954. GARF, f. R-9401, op. 1a, d. 531, l. 385. For more on these courts see Galina M. Ivanova, *Istoriia GULAGa, 1918–1958: sotsial'no-ekonomicheskii i politico-pravovoi aspekty* (Moscow: Nauka, 2006), 422–23.

194. TsDAGO, f. 1, op. 24, d. 4948, l. 6.

195. GARF, f. R-7523, op. 75, d. 775, ll. 1, 17.

196. GARF, f. R-9401, op. 2, d. 506, ll. 218–19.

197. See, for example, GARF, f. A-385, op. 126, d. 195, ll. 4–7; GARF, f. A-461, op. 11, d. 765, l. 9; and M. A. Efimov, *Dokazatel'stva ispravleniia i perevospitaniia zakliuchennogo i ikh otsenka* (Moscow: Politotdel MZ MOOP RSFSR, 1964), 9.

198. GARF, f. R-7523, op. 77, d. 102, ll. 96–98. This power was reaffirmed in June 1961. GARF, f. R-7523, op. 77, d. 1041, ll. 1, 5.

199. See, among many examples, GDA MVS, f. 3, op. 1, d. 262, l. 77, and LYA, f. V-141, op. 2, d. 225, l. 186.

200. Russian minister of internal affairs Nikolai Pavlovich Stakhanov unsuccessfully fought this reform. GARF, f. A-385, op. 126, d. 148, ll. 11–12.

201. GARF, f. R-9414, op. 1, d. 310, l. 99. This structure was challenged in 1955 by the Iakutsk party committee, which complained to the Central Committee that Gulag party officials in the republic were not acting in harmony with the local party and that this had a negative effect on "the interests of production." They proposed that the separate Gulag party structure should be liquidated, a suggestion resisted, of course, by the head of the Gulag political department L. Lukoianov. Lukoianov defended the necessity of a separate structure while maintaining that local party members should coordinate their work with communists in the camp political departments. In the end the Central Committee sided with the Lukoianov and dismissed the Iakutsk complaint. RGANI, f. 5, op. 32, d. 30, ll. 31–34.

202. A. Brovkin, "Glavnoe vnimanie—nereshennym zadacham," *K novoi zhizni,* no. 1 (January 1961): 7.

203. V. Buivolov, "Zalog uspekha—v opore na obshchestvennost'," *K novoi zhizni,* no. 1 (January 1961): 11.

204. V. Lev, "V tsekhakh bol'shikh zavodov," *K novoi zhizni,* no. 1 (January 1962): 31.

205. Komsomol members also served on the 1959 case review board. See, for example, LYA, f. V-145/1, op. 1, d. 92, ll. 1–6.

206. GARF, f. R-9401, op. 2, d. 506, l. 238.

207. GARF, f.A-461, op. 11, d. 585, l. 8.

208. GARF, f. R-9414, op. 3, d. 114, l. 301.

209. Ibid.

210. See, for example, Ann Livschiz, "De-Stalinizing Soviet Childhood: The Quest for Moral Rebirth, 1953–58," in *The Dilemmas of De-Stalinization: Negotiating Cultural and Social Change in the Khrushchev Era,* ed. Polly A. Jones (London: Routledge, 2006), 117–34; Juliane Fürst, "The Arrival of Spring?," in Jones, *Dilemmas of De-Stalinization,* 135–53; and Emily Lygo, "The Need for New Voices: Writers' Union Policy towards Young Writers 1953–64," in Jones, *Dilemmas of De-Stalinization,* 193–208.

211. GDA MVS, f. 3, op. 1, d. d. 262, l. 89. The increasing presence and unruly nature of youth in the camps is confirmed by Marchenko, *My Testimony,* 320.

212. Brovkin, "Glavnoe vnimanie," 8.

213. GDA MVS, f. 3, op. 1, d. 222, l. 259.

214. GDA MVS, f. 6, op. 2, d. 413, ll. 5–6.

215. GDA MVS, f. 6, op. 2, d. 413, ll. 41–44; V. Kovrizhnykh, "Pod kontrolem aktivistov," *K novoi zhizni,* no. 6 (June 1964): 49.

216. B. Belousov, "Eto delo i nashe, profsoiuznoe," *K novoi zhizni,* no. 3 (March 1961): 16–17; G. Borisov, "V storone ot zhizni," *K novoi zhizni,* no. 6 (June 1964): 50–51.

217. See, for example, GARF, f. R-9414, op. 3, d. 114, l. 302; and GARF, f. R-9401, op. 2, d. 505, l. 313.

218. GDA MVS, f. 3, op. 1, d. 299, l. 23.

219. See, for example, GARF, f. R-9414, op. 6, d. 99, l. 4; TsDAGO, f. 1, op. 24, d. 4948, l. 17.

220. GARF, f. A-461, op. 11, d. 581, l. 30; GARF, f. R-8131, op. 11, d. 6120, l. 78.

221. GARF, f. R-8131, op. 11, d. 6394, l. 89.

222. GDA MVS, f. 6, op. 2, d. 413, l. 8.

223. *K novoi zhizni,* no. 8 (August 1961): 43.

224. GARF, f. R-8131, op. 11, d. 6567, l. 40.

225. *K novoi zhizni,* no. 11 (November 1961): 79.

226. TsDAGO, f. 1, op. 24, d. 5785, ll. 88, 90.

227. N. Bagaev, "Na obshchestvennykh nachalakh," *K novoi zhizni,* no. 1 (January 1962): 6.

228. See, for example, RGANI, f. 13, op. 1, d. 872, ll. 89–183.

229. For some of their reports see TsDAGO, f. 1, op. 24, d. 4306.

230. The U.S. penal system has long struggled with violence, perpetrated by both guards and prisoners. See, for example, Kauffman, *Prison Officers,* 118–64; Lee Bowker, *Prison Victimization* (New York: Elsevier, 1980); Michael Braswell, Steven Dillingham, and Reid Montgomery Jr., eds., *Prison Violence in America* (Cincinnati, OH: Anderson Publishing, 1985); Ray A. March, *Alabama Bound: Forty-Five Years inside a Prison System* (Tuscaloosa: University of Alabama Press, 1978). Even the United Kingdom, with a robust system of oversight, has not in recent years been able to overcome "the culture of casual cruelty in prisons in England and Wales, because they have been thwarted by serious failures of political will, an engrained political refusal to tackle the problems of overcrowding and an apparently intractable culture of casual cruelty." Diana Medlicott, "Preventing Torture and Casual Cruelty in Prisons through Independent Monitoring," in *The Violence of Incarceration,* ed. Phil Scraton and Jude McCulloch (New York: Routledge, 2009), 259.

231. *Manual of Correctional Standards* (New York: American Prison Association, 1954); *Manual of Correctional Standards* (New York: American Correctional Association, 1966).

232. See, for instance, the case of the Louisiana State Penitentiary at Angola, which underwent significant reforms in the mid-1950s after extensive press coverage of a severe case of inmate self-mutilation. Mark T. Carleton, *Politics and Punishment: The History of the Louisiana State Penal System* (Baton Rouge: Louisiana State University Press, 1971), 137–59.

4. UNDOING THE REFORMS

1. V. M. Gridin, *My, kotorykh ne bylo . . . : vospominaniia o GULAGe v stukhakh i proze* (Odessa: Astroprint, 1996), 47–48. Iu. I. Dodonov likewise remarked that, especially after his time in jail and transit prisons, the corrective-labor camp "seemed like freedom to me." Iu. I. Dodonov, *Vstretimsia na barrikadakh* (Murom: Memorial, 1996), 22.

2. For more on this see Jeffrey S. Hardy, "Gulag Tourism: Khrushchev's 'Show' Prisons in the Cold War Context, 1954–1959," *Russian Review* 71, no. 1 (January 2012): 49–78.

3. Stephen F. Cohen, "The Friends and Foes of Change: Reformism and Conservatism in the Soviet Union," in *The Soviet Union since Stalin,* ed. Stephen F. Cohen and Alexander Rabinowitch (Bloomington: Indiana University Press, 1980), 17.

4. Marc Elie, "Khrushchev's Gulag: The Soviet Penitentiary System after Stalin's Death, 1953–1964," in *The Thaw: Soviet Society and Culture during the 1950s and 1960s,* ed. Denis Kozlov and Eleonor Gilburd (Toronto: University of Toronto Press, 2013), 125. Elie sees this shift occurring largely because of the crime wave that accompanied the mass releases of 1959–60, but the evidence presented here suggests the official stance toward inmates was beginning to change already before the 1959 case reviews had begun.

5. Miriam Dobson, *Khrushchev's Cold Summer: Gulag Returnees, Crime, and the Fate of Reform after Stalin* (Ithaca, NY: Cornell University Press, 2009), 15, 238–39. The enthusiasm/impatience duality was also noted at the time by contemporary observers of Soviet law and society. See, for example, Harold J. Berman, "The Dilemma of Soviet Law Reform," *Harvard Law Review* 76, 5 (1963): 945–47.

6. Brian LaPierre, *Hooligans in Khrushchev's Russia: Defining, Policing, and Producing Deviance During the Thaw* (Madison: University of Wisconsin Press, 2012), 171.

7. Eugenia Semyonovna Ginzburg, *Journey into the Whirlwind,* trans. Paul Stevenson and Max Hayward (New York: Harcourt, 1967), 406.

8. MEMO, f. 2, op. 2, d. 66, l. 195.

9. Michael Solomon, *Magadan* (Princeton, NJ: Vertex, 1971), 224.

10. Henri Dusart, "Visite à un 'camp de correction par le travail,'" *Le Populaire,* 4 June 1956, 2.

11. L. Rostovtsev and I. Brinner, eds., *K chestnomu trudu* (Tbilisi: Politotdel ITU MVD Gruzinskogo SSR, 1959).

12. The similar expression of "coddling" prisoners has likewise been a long-standing reductionist argument against penal reform in the United States and elsewhere. In discussing prison reform in 1950s Louisiana, for instance, Mark Carleton writes that "in order to comfort those who suspected their regime of convict-coddling, assurances were given that inmates were 'not treated with kid gloves' and did not 'live off the fat of the land.'" Mark T. Carleton, *Politics and Punishment: The History of the Louisiana State Penal System* (Baton Rouge: Louisiana State University Press, 1971), 168. See also, among many others, *Task Force Report: Correction* (Washington, DC: U.S. Government Printing Office, 1967), 16; Bert Useem and Peter Kimball, *States of Siege: U.S. Prison Riots, 1971–1986* (New York: Oxford University Press, 1989), 16; Charles Bright, *The Powers That Punish: Prison and Politics in the Era of the "Big House," 1920–1955* (Ann Arbor: University of Michigan Press, 1996), 204.

13. Aleksandr Isaevich Solzhenitsyn, *The Gulag Archipelago 1918–1956: An Experiment in Literary Investigation,* 3 vols., trans. Thomas P. Whitney (New York: Harper and Row, 1974–78), 3:487–89. A similar argument is made by memoirist Iu. P. , who thought Gulag administrators rejected the reforms of the 1950s because they would have led to fewer prisoners and, in turn, a smaller Gulag bureaucracy. MEMO, f. 2, op. 3, d. 66, l. 258. And Danylo Shumuk remarked, after being reincarcerated following a brief hiatus in freedom in 1958, that "Beria's henchmen were beginning to reassert themselves." Danylo Shumuk, *Life Sentence: Memoirs of a Ukrainian Political Prisoner,* trans. Ivan Jaworsky and Halya Kowalska (Edmonton: Canadian Institute of Ukrainian Studies, University of Alberta, 1984), 329.

14. See, for instance, GDA MVS, f. 3, op. 1, d. 262, ll. 71, 177–78.

15. GARF, f. R-9414, op. 1, d. 1427, ll. 132, 134.

16. GARF, f. R-9414, op. 1, d. 283, l. 205.

17. GARF, f. R-9414, op. 1, d. 287, l. 155.

18. V. A. Poznanskii, ed., *Problemy razvitiia Sovetskogo ispravitel'no-trudovogo zakonodatel'stva* (Saratov: Saratovskii gosudarstvennyi iuridicheskii institut imeni D. I. Kurskogo, 1961), 269–70.

19. Ibid., 252–53.

20. Ibid., 264–65.

21. Solzhenitsyn, *Gulag Archipelago,* 3:488.

22. ERAF, f. 17sm, op. 4, d. 203, ll. 133–34.

23. ERAF, f. 17sm, op. 4, d. 203, ll. 161–83.

24. ERAF, f. 77sm, op. 1, d. 350, ll. 4, 9.

25. LYA, f. V-141, op. 1, d. 335, l. 137.

26. TsDAGO, f. 1, op. 82, d. 181, l. 6.

27. TsDAGO, f. 1, op. 82, d. 181, l. 38.

28. GARF, f. R-9401, op. 2, d. 499, ll. 361–64.

29. GARF, f. R-9401, op. 2, d. 499, l. 363.

30. GARF, f. R-8131, op. 32, d. 4955, ll. 5, 84–267.

31. GARF, f. R-8131, op. 32, d. 4955, ll. 218–19.

32. TsDAGO, f. f. 1, op. 82, d. 181, l. 69.

33. GARF, f. R-9414, op. 3, d. 131, l. 103.

34. GDA MVS, f. 6, op. 2, d. 360, l. 15.

35. A. Mishutin, "Strogo sobliudat' zakonnost," *K novoi zhizni,* no. 6 (June 1961): 3.

36. I. V. Pantiukhin, *Stolitsa kolymskogo kraia: zapiski Magadanskogo prokurora* (Petrozavodsk: Molodezhnaia gazeta, 1995), 69.

37. ERAF, f. 17sm, op. 4, d. 203, l. 134.

38. ERAF, f. 77sm, op. 1, d. 343, l. 150.

39. LYA, f. V-145/18, op. 2, d. 51, l. 82.

40. GARF, f. R-9414, op. 3, d. 131, l. 91.

41. Before 1960 the political department had issued occasional corrections-themed pamphlets under the titles *Sbornik materialov po perevospitaniiu osuzhdennykh* and *Ispravitel'no-trudovye uchrezhdeniia.* Initially, *K novoi zhizni* had a circulation of 5,000, but that was expanded to 8,000 the following year. Igor' Baryshnikov, "Sbornik—zarodysh zhurnala," in *Zhurnaly v pogonakh,* ed. O. L. Ivanova (Moscow: Ob'edinennaia redaktsiia MVD Rossii, 2001), 298–99; Lidiia Grechneva, "Vremeni ne podvlasten," in Ivanova, *Zhurnaly v pogonakh,* 303.

42. Editor's note, *K novoi zhizni,* no. 1 (January 1960): 2.

43. A. Okhrimenko, "Stavka na vzyskanie," *K novoi zhizni,* no. 9 (September 1960): 24–27; V. Barabanov, "Chelovek—prezhde vsego," *K novoi zhizni,* no. 11 (November 1960): 35.

44. GARF, f. R-9414, op. 1, d. 283, l. 119.

45. GARF, f. R-9401, op. 2, d. 506, l. 312.

46. GARF, f. R-9401, op. 2, d. 505, l. 319.

47. I. S. Noi, ed., *Voprosy kodifikatsii sovetskogo ispravitel'no-trudovogo zakonodatel'stva* (Saratov: Saratovskii iuridicheskii institut im. D. I. Kurskogo, 1960), 3–9. This view was also expressed by others at the MVD school. See, for example, the conference address given by Lieutenant Colonel Polibin in 1957. GARF, f. R-9413, op. 1, d. 235, ll. 145–51. The original Lenin citation ("replace prisons with correctional institutions") comes from the Party Program adopted at the Eighth Party Congress in 1919. V. I. Lenin, *Polnoe sobranie sochinenii,* 5th ed. (Moscow: Izdatel'stvo politicheskoi literatury, 1963), 38:408, 431. The phrase was then modified and popularized by A. Ia. Vyshinskii's *Ot tiurem k vospitatel'nym uchrezhdeniiam* (Moscow: Gosudarstvennoe izdatel'stvo sovetskoe zakonodatel'stvo, 1934).

48. See, for example, *Materialy nauchnoi konferentsii, posviashennoi problemam ispravitel'no-trudovogo prava* (Tomsk: Tomskii gosudarstvennyi universitet im. V. V. Kuibysheva, 1961), 25; and V. N. Kalinin, Iu. B. Utevskii, and A. M. Iakovlev, *Sovetskie ispravitel'no-trudovye uchrezhdeniia* (Moscow: Gosizdat, 1960), 11–22.

49. On the repression of criminology under Stalin see Peter Solomon, "Soviet Criminology: Its Demise and Rebirth," in *Crime, Criminology and Public Policy: Essays in Honour of Sir Leon Radzinowicz*, ed. Roger Hood (London: Heinemann, 1974), 571–94; Louise Shelley, "Soviet Criminology: Its Birth and Demise, 1917–1936" (PhD diss., University of Pennsylvania, 1977), 197; and Iu. P. Kasatkin, "Ocherk istorii izucheniia prestupnosti v SSSR," in *Problemy iskoreneniia prestupnosti*, ed. V. N. Kudriavtsev (Moscow: Iuridicheskaia literatura, 1965), 218.

50. RGANI, f. 5, d. 34, l. 70, l. 21.

51. Noi, *Voprosy kodifikatsii*, 13–20. Noi was especially outspoken on and heavily criticized for his writings on the biological roots of crime. Walter D. Connor, *Deviance in Soviet Society: Crime, Delinquency, and Alcoholism* (New York: Columbia University Press, 1972), 183–84.

52. Noi, *Voprosy kodifikatsii*, 23–28, 46. For similar sentiments see also G. A. Usachev, ed., *Vtoroe rozhdenie* (Cheliabinsk: Cheliabinsk knizhnoe izdatel'stvo, 1960).

53. *Materialy nauchnoi konferentsii*, 15–27; for Lenin's use of these terms see, for instance, Lenin, *Polnoe sobranie sochinenii*, 42:139, 43:54.

54. *Materialy nauchnoi konferentsii*, 96–97. This view was also held by N. N. Pashe-Ozerskii. Poznanskii, *Problemy razvitiia*, 259.

55. Poznanskii, *Problemy razvitiia*, 249–50.

56. Ibid., 230–37.

57. Ibid., 259.

58. I. S. Samoshchenko, "Osnovnye puti pravonarushenii v sovetskoi obshchestve," *Pravovedenie*, no. 2 (February 1962): 30–31.

59. N. Struchkov, "V. I. Lenin ob ubezhdenii i prinuzhdenii," *K novoi zhizni*, no. 4 (April 1961): 6.

60. B. S. Utevskii, "Sozdat' ispravitel'no-trudovuiu pedagogiku," in *O tvorcheskom primenenii pedagogicheskogo naslediia A. S. Makarenko v rabote s zakliuchennymi*, ed. P. D. Borodin (Moscow: Izdanie politotdela GUMZ MVD RSFSR, 1960), 97–99.

61. P. Ganin, "Na oshibochnykh positsiiakh," *K novoi zhizni*, 1962, no. 3 (March 1962): 75–77.

62. B. Volkov, "Distsiplina i rezhim," *K novoi zhizni*, no. 4 (April 1961): 40–41.

63. George W. Breslauer, "Khrushchev Reconsidered," in *The Limits of Destalinization in the Soviet Union: Political Rehabilitations in the Soviet Union since Stalin*, ed. Albert P. Van Goudoever, trans. Frans Hijkoop (London: Croom Helm, 1986), 50–59. See also Polly A. Jones, "The Dilemmas of De-Stalinization," in *The Dilemmas of De-Stalinization: Negotiating Cultural and Social Change in the Khrushchev Era*, ed. Polly A. Jones (London: Routledge, 2006), 5–6.

64. The most notorious of these crime waves, as noted in chapter 1, occurred in 1953 following the first and largest of the post-Stalin amnesties. On popular and press reaction to this release, succinctly characterized by the statement, "empathy for the returnees was rare," see Miriam Dobson, "'Show the Bandit-Enemies No Mercy!': Amnesty, Criminality and Public Response in 1953," 29–34; and Amir Weiner, "The Empires Pay a Visit: Gulag Returnees, East European Rebellions, and Soviet Frontier Politics," *Journal of Modern History* 78, no. 2 (June 2006): 333–76.

65. See, for example, GARF f. R-5446, op. 89, d. 1801, ll. 125–56; GARF f. 7523, op. 85, d. 250; and Dobson, *Khrushchev's Cold Summer*, 165–67.

66. Petr E. Shelest, *Da ne sudimy budete: dnevnikovye zapisi, vospominaniia chlena Politburo TsK KPSS* (Moscow: Edition q, 1995), 122.

67. RGANI, f. 5, op. 32, d. 89, ll. 159–62. See also Dobson, *Khrushchev's Cold Summer,* 141–43; and Sheila Fitzpatrick, "Social Parasites: How Tramps, Idle Youth, and Busy Entrepreneurs Impeded the Soviet March to Communism," *Cahiers du Monde russe* 47, nos. 1–2 (January–June 2006): 394–96.

68. Cited in Dobson, *Khrushchev's Cold Summer,* 167.

69. On this see Donald Filtzer, *Soviet Workers and De-Stalinization: The Consolidation of the Modern System of Soviet Production Relations, 1953–1964* (Cambridge: Cambridge University Press, 1992), 32–34.

70. GARF, f. R-7523, op. 108, d. 77, l. 14.

71. GARF, f. R-7523, op. 85, d. 253, ll. 45–73.

72. Dobson, *Khrushchev's Cold Summer,* 168.

73. GARF f. R-7523, op. 108, d. 77, ll. 1–20; Dobson, *Khrushchev's Cold Summer,* 169. See also LaPierre, *Hooligans in Khrushchev's Russia,* 185–88.

74. On the limitation of using letters to gauge public opinion see Dobson, *Khrushchev's Cold Summer,* 10–14.

75. George H. Meade, "The Psychology of Punitive Justice," *American Journal of Sociology* 23, no. 5 (March 1918): 590–92.

76. GARF, f. R-9401, op. 2, d. 505, l. 304. Dudorov opposed and tried to overturn these provisions, arguing that they "arouse in such prisoners the feeling of hopelessness and bitterness." GARF, f. R-7523, op. 108, d. 330, ll. 2–15. Rudenko, Supreme Court Chairman Gorkin, and V. Zolotukhin, deputy head of the department of administrative organs of the Central Committee, all supported the provision and prevented its removal. Dudorov's position is affirmed in a letter from a prisoner to his aunt in early 1959 in which he laments that because of the new law codes, "we will never meet again, I will remain deprived of freedom my entire life." MEMO, f. 2, op. 3, d. 66, l. 276.

77. D. S. Polianskii, "O proektakh Zakonov 'Osnovy ugolovnogo zakonodatel'stva Soiuza SSR i soiuznykh respublikh,' 'Ob ugolovnoi otvetstvennosti za gosudarstvennye prestupleniia' i 'Ob ugolovnoi otvetstvennosti za voinskie prestupleniia,'" *Pravda,* 26 December 1958, 7–8.

78. "Rech' deputata Ia. N. Zarobian," *Izvestiia,* 26 December 1958, 11.

79. "Rech' deputata B. I. Samsonov," *Izvestiia,* 26 December 1958, 12.

80. "Sluzhenie narodu—vysokoe prizvanie Sovetskikh pisatelei: rech' tovarishcha N. S. Khrushcheva na III s'ezde pisatelei 22 May 1959," *Pravda,* 24 May 1959, 2. For more on this see "Novaia zhizn' Konstantina Nogovitsina," *Izvestiia,* 8 September 1962, 6; and Dobson, *Khrushchev's Cold Summer,* 146–50.

81. One must note here that the Khrushchev regime to this point had not moved to abolish the death penalty. In fact, it extended the death penalty, which at Stalin's death in 1953 could only be applied to treason and other high-level political crimes, to cover first-degree murder. Ger P. Van der Berg, "The Soviet Union and the Death Penalty," *Soviet Studies* 35, no. 2 (April 1983): 159.

82. D. Vorontsov, "'Vysokaia gumannost', proiavlennaia k cheloveku,'" *Pravda,* 5 July 1959, 2. Still, it is significant that of the seven letters published, six were attributed to prisoners or former prisoners. Indeed, the MVD internally noted similar reactions among its prisoners. Prisoner Katliaev from Perm Province, for example, is recorded to have said, "We are all thankful to N. S. Khrushchev and in return we will give all our strength to serve out our sentence honestly." GARF, f. R-9401, op. 2, d. 506, ll. 236–38.

83. A. Kanaev, "Oni vernutsia k chestnomu trudu," *Izvestiia,* 18 August 1959, 2.

84. V. Kalinin and N. Struchkov, "Nakazanie i vospitanie," *Izvestiia,* 4 October 1959, 3.

85. Sheinin, "Verit' v cheloveka," *Izvestiia*, 22 January 1960, 6. For more articles proclaiming the reformability of criminals see A. Kanaev, "Cheloveku nado verit'!," *Izvestiia*, 4 June 1959, 4; and Iu. Lukianov, "Esli chelovek ostupilsia," *Izvestiia*, 7 August 1959, 3.

86. Georgii V. Papin, "Put' k domu," *Izvestiia*, 20 March 1960, 6.

87. Similar stories of redemption were also distributed in the late Stalin Gulag, but were hid from public view. See, for instance, Steven Barnes, *Death and Redemption: The Gulag and the Shaping of Soviet Society* (Princeton, NJ: Princeton University Press, 2011), 130–34.

88. V. Monakhov, "Prestupnik i obshchestvo," *Novyi Mir,* no. 8 (August 1960): 181.

89. Ibid., 188.

90. Thomas C. Wolfe, *Governing Soviet Journalism: The Press and the Socialist Person after Stalin* (Bloomington: Indiana University Press, 2005).

91. Kai T. Erikson, *Wayward Puritans: A Study in the Sociology of Deviance* (New York: Wiley, 1966), 12–13.

92. "Vyrodok," *Izvestiia*, 18 July 1958, 4.

93. V. Sukharevich, "Gumannost' po Orlu," *Literaturnaia Gazeta*, 23 July 1960, 6.

94. I. Kasiukov and N. Monchadskaia, "Chelovek za reshetkoi," *Sovetskaia Rossiia,* 27 August 1960, 2–3.

95. "'Chelovek za reshetkoi'—obzor pisem," *Sovetskaia Rossiia,* 17 September 1960, 2–3.

96. RGANI, f. 13, op. 1, d. 784, ll. 38–40.

97. RGANI, f. 13, op. 1, d. 788, ll. 61–75.

98. RGANI, f. 13, op. 1, d. 788, ll. 34–37. Credit is due to Marc Elie for pointing me to this material.

99. V. Babanov, "'Osvobozhden dosrochno . . .' za chto?," *Komsomol'skaia Pravda,* 8 December 1960, 4.

100. G. Lopukhin, "Retsidivist na progulke," *Izvestiia*, 21 June 1961, 3.

101. B. A. Muradian, "'Retsidivist na progulke,'" *Izvestiia*, 11 July 1961, 3.

102. For articles highlighting instances where courts, procurators, and the police were reportedly too lenient with lawbreakers see, for instance, S. Kashurkov, "Volk na parukakh," *Izvestiia*, 17 August 1961, 4; and Iu. Feofanov, "Pora podvesti chertu," *Izvestiia,* 13 January 1962, 4.

103. Elie, "Khrushchev's Gulag," 126. Here he relies on the traditional "conflict model" of understanding the Khrushchev regime. See Stephen F. Cohen, "The Friends and Foes of Change: Reformism and Conservatism in the Soviet Union," in Cohen and Rabinowitch, *Soviet Union since Stalin,* 11–31.

104. Dobson, *Khrushchev's Cold Summer,* 15.

105. Andrei Artizov, ed., *Reabilitatsiia—kak eto bylo: dokumenty Prezidiuma TSK KPSS i drugie materialy,* 3 vols. (Moscow: Mezhdunarodnyi fond "Demokratiia," 2000–2004), 1:88.

106. GARF, f. R-7523, op. 108, d. 23, l. 13.

107. GARF, f. R-7523, op. 108, d. 23, l. 21.

108. GARF, f. R-7523, op. 108, d. 25, ll. 15–16.

109. GARF, f. R-7523, op. 108, d. 37, l. 5.

110. A. A., Fursenko, ed., *Prezidium TsK KPSS 1954–1964,* 3 vols. (Moscow: Rosspen, 2003–6), 1:213.

111. N. S. Khrushchev, "Vruchenie ordena Lenina Moldavskoi SSR," *Pravda,* 15 May 1959, 2–3.

112. Viacheslav Mikhailovich Molotov, *Molotov Remembers: Inside Kremlin Politics* (Chicago: Ivan R. Dee, 1993), 365.

113. Fursenko, *Prezidium Tsk KPSS,* 1:526–29.

114. N. S. Khruhshchev, "Doklad N. S. Khrushcheva," *Pravda,* 18 October 1961, 11.

115. Iurii Aksiutin, "Popular Responses to Khrushchev," in *Nikita Khrushchev,* ed. William Taubman, Sergei Khrushchev, and Abbott Gleason (New Haven, CT: Yale University Press, 2000), 196–200.

116. These meetings were held across the union in September 1960. RGANI, f. 13, op. 1, d. 768, ll. 10–12.

117. For these reports see RGANI, f.13, op. 1, dd. 872–74.

118. RGANI, f.13, op. 1, d. 872, ll. 106–7; RGANI, f.13, op. 1, d. 872, l. 159.

119. RGANI, f. 13, op. 1, d. 872, ll. 106–11.

120. RGANI, f. 13, op. 1, d. 874, l. 45.

121. The average wage for prisoners in Iaroslavl Province, for comparison, was 251 rubles per month, and many free workers did not make 1,000 rubles per month (the average monthly wage in 1955 being 715 rubles). RGANI, f.13, op. 1, d. 872, l. 179; Filtzer, *Soviet Workers and De-Stalinization,* 32, 104, 247–48.

122. RGANI, f. 13, op. 1, d. 872, ll. 108–9.

123. RGANI, f. 13, op. 1, d. 872, l. 178.

124. RGANI, f. 13, op. 1, d. 872, l. 156.

125. RGANI, f. 13, op. 1, d. 873, ll. 94–99.

126. A. I. Kokurin and N. V. Petrov, eds., *GULAG: glavnoe upravlenie lagerei, 1917–1960* (Moscow: Mezhdunarodnyi fond "Demokratiia," 2000), 196.

127. LYA, f. V-141, op. 1, d. 349, l. 7.

128. Kokurin and Petrov, *GULAG,* 197; ERAF, f. 17sm, op. 4, d. 244, l. 66 (emphasis mine).

129. The Central Committee later clarified that political prisoners should be held in strict regimen facilities unless they warranted special regimen. In both cases politicals were to be fully separated from regular criminals. RGANI, f. 13, op. 2, d. 393, l. 16. In December 1960 there were 5,524 prisoners in the Gulag whose death sentences had been commuted to from 10 to 25 years imprisonment. Most of them had been convicted of aggravated murder. RGANI, f. 5, op. 30, d. 341, l. 126.

130. Despite exclusion from the 1958 statute, a few special-regimen colonies (sometimes called special strict colonies) existed in the late 1950s. Curiously, for women the 1961 statute meant a reduction in regimen types from three (lightened, standard, and strict) to only two (standard and strict). ERAF, f. 17sm, op. 4, d. 244, l. 66; Kokurin and Petrov, *GULAG,* 198.

131. ERAF, f. 17sm, op. 4, d. 244, l. 66.

132. ERAF, f. 17sm, op. 4, d. 244, ll. 67, 77. Cell blocks differed from penalty isolators in that prisoners were held for longer periods of time for systematic regimen violations whereas the isolators were for short-term stays for isolated infractions.

133. ERAF, f. 17sm, op. 4, d. 244, ll. 67, 74–77; P. M. Losev, *Material'no-bytovoe i meditsinskoe obespechenie zakliuchennykh* (Moscow: Vysshaia shkola MVD SSSR, 1957), 10. The 1958 statute forbade the possession of money, but not valuables. Kokurin and Petrov, *GULAG,* 198.

134. ERAF, f. 17sm, op. 4, d. 244, l. 68; Kokurin and Petrov, *GULAG,* 198–99. These restrictions could be loosened after a prisoner had served one-third his term on good behavior; he could then spend up to 20 rubles at the camp store, receive one package per month, and enjoy extra visits.

135. ERAF, f. 17sm, op. 4, d. 244, l. 68.

136. GARF, f. R-7523, op. 108, d. 45, ll. 16–17.

137. ERAF, f. 17sm, op. 4, d. 245, l. 122.

138. LYA, f. V-141, op. 1, d. 351, ll. 75, 85.

139. RGANI, f. 13, op. 1, d. 295, l. 68.

140. LYA, f. V-141, op. 1, d. 349, ll. 4–58.

141. Solzhenitsyn, *Gulag Archipelago,* 3:504.

142. "Ob usilenii bor'by s osobo opasnymi prestupleniiami," *Vedomosti Verkhovnogo Soveta Soiuza Sovetskikh Sotsialisticheskikh Respublik,* 11 May 1961, 475–76.

143. GARF, f. R-7523, op. 108, d. 45, l. 35; ERAF, f. 17sm, op. 4, d. 270, l. 25.

144. GARF, f. R-7523, op. 108, d. 44, l. 28.

145. Harold J. Berman, *Justice in the U.S.S.R: An Interpretation of Soviet Law,* rev. ed. (Cambridge, MA: Harvard University Press, 1963), 84.

146. GARF, f. R-7523, op. 108, d. 45, ll. 31–32.

147. Berman, *Justice in the U.S.S.R.,* 85–86; Dobson, *Khrushchev's Cold Summer,* 177.

148. Berman, *Justice in the U.S.S.R.,* 88.

149. I. S. Verblovskaia, "V zhenskoi zone," in *Ozerlag: kak eto bylo,* ed. L. S. Mukhin (Irkutsk: Vostochno-Sibirskoe knizhnoe izdatel'stvo, 1992), 363.

150. Berman, "Dilemma of Soviet Law Reform," 945–47.

151. Cited in Dobson, *Khrushchev's Cold Summer,* 159.

152. Meade, "Psychology of Punitive Justice," 591. This is affirmed by Harold Garfinkel, who avers in his discussion of degradation ceremonies that "moral indignation may reinforce group solidarity." Harold Garfinkel, "Conditions of Successful Degradation Ceremonies," *American Journal of Sociology* 61, no. 5 (March 1956): 421.

153. I. S. Verblovskaia, "Pis'mo byvshei uznitsy," in *Uroki gneva i liubvi: sbornik vospominanii o godakh repressii (20-e–80-e gg.),* ed. T. V. Tigonen (Saint Petersburg: Vyborgskaia storona, 1993), 153.

154. Cited in Denis Kozlov, *The Readers of Novyi Mir: Coming to Terms with the Stalinist Past* (Cambridge, MA: Harvard University Press, 2013), 229.

155. S. K. Evstigneev, "Ia byl soldatom partii," in Mukhin, *Ozerlag,* 11.

5. A KHRUSHCHEVIAN SYNTHESIS

1. GARF, f. R-8131, op. 32, d. 6880, ll. 91–92.

2. Vladimir Pozner, *Parting with Illusions: The Extraordinary Life and Controversial Views of the Soviet Union's Leading Commentator* (New York: Atlantic Monthly Press, 1990), 150. See also John Bushnell, "The 'New Soviet Man' Turns Pessimist," in *The Soviet Union since Stalin,* ed. Stephen F. Cohen and Alexander Rabinowitch (Bloomington: Indiana University Press, 1980), 179–84.

3. Vladimir Nekrasov, *Trinadtsat 'zheleznykh' narkomov: istoriia NKVD—MVD ot A. I. Rykova do N. A. Shchelokova, 1917–1982* (Moscow: Versty, 1995), 324–27.

4. Ibid., 349–50.

5. Tikunov was relieved of his post in 1966 with the resurrection of the All-Union MVD. Thereafter he served as a Soviet diplomat in Romania, Cameroon, and Upper Volta. Ibid., 368.

6. GARF, f. R-9414, op. 1, d. 1427, l. 132. In addition, there were 71,084 in prisons, with 18,849 on prison regimen and the rest in pretrial detention. GARF, f. R-9413, op. 1, d. 269, l. 76.

7. GARF, f. R-7523, op. 95a, d. 110, l. 29. Thanks to Marc Elie for providing this and other inmate population data from the 1960s.

8. Brian LaPierre, *Hooligans in Khrushchev's Russia: Defining, Policing, and Producing Deviance During the Thaw* (Madison: University of Wisconsin Press, 2012), 189–94.

9. GARF, f. R-7523, op. 109, d. 207a, ll. 25–26.

10. GARF, f. R-7523, op. 95a, d. 290, l. 3; GARF, f. R-9492, op. 6, d. 259, l. 78.

11. GARF, f. R-7523, op. 109, d. 207a, ll. 25–26.

12. ERAF, f. 17sm, op. 4, d. 266, l. 1; ERAF, f. 17sm, op. 4, d. 267, ll. 44, 95; ERAF, f. 77sm, op. 1, d. 442, l. 75.

13. The number of colonies in Ukraine expanded from 77 to 105 in 1958–60, then dropped to 81 in the wake of the case reviews before expanding to 127 in early 1963. GDA MVS, f. 3, op. 1, d. 205, l. 230; GDA MVS, f. 3, op. 1, d. 262, ll. 71–72; GDA MVS, f. 6, op. 2, d. 392, l. 143.

14. Eight thousand of these transfers were in Ukraine. RGANI, f. 13, no. 1, d. 768, l. 29; TsDAGO, f. 1, op. 24, d. 5418, l. 3.

15. GARF, f. R-8131, op. 32, d. 6733, l. 4.

16. D. Pankov, "Novoe vkhodit v zhizn'," *K novoi zhizni,* no. 4 (April 1963): 10.

17. GDA MVS, f. 3, op. 1, d. 262, l. 76.

18. As of 15 May 1959, the Russian camps and colonies held 80,352 on lightened regimen, 584,774 on standard regimen, 62,367 on strengthened regimen, and 5,196 on special strengthened regimen. GARF, f. R-9414, op. 1, d. 2668, ll. 53–54.

19. GARF, f. R-7523, op. 109, d. 294, l. 3.

20. GARF, f. R-7523, op. 109, d. 294, ll. 3–4.

21. F. Kuznetsov, "V interesakh rezhima i poriadka," *K novoi zhizni,* 1963, no. 6 (June 1963): 6–7.

22. RGANI, f. 13, op. 1, d. 264, l. 11.

23. B. Volkov, "Distsiplina i rezhim," *K novoi zhizni,* no. 4 (April 1961): 39–41.

24. N. Stakhanov, "Nasha opora," *K novoi zhizni,* no. 4 (April 1961): 15.

25. P. Podymov, "Strogo sobliudat' trebovaniia rezhima," *K novoi zhizni,* no. 9 (September 1961): 25–28; P. Starovoi, "Zakkonost'—v tsentre vnimaniia," *K novoi zhizni,* no. 5 (May 1963): 35.

26. Editors, "Vazhnoe sredstvo perevospitaniia," *K novoi zhizni,* no. 3 (March 1962): 2–5.

27. Anatoly Marchenko, *My Testimony,* trans. Michel Scammell (New York: E. P. Dutton, 1969), 41.

28. GARF, f. R-7523, op. 109, d. 413, l. 13.

29. Vladimir Fedorovich Abramkin and Valentina Fedorovna Chesnakova, eds., *Tiuremnyi mir glazami politzakliuchennykh, 1940–1980-e gg* (Moscow: Sodeistvie, 1998) 13.

30. ERAF, f. 17sm, op. 4, d. 265, ll. 132–35.

31. Cited in Miriam Dobson, *Khrushchev's Cold Summer: Gulag Returnees, Crime, and the Fate of Reform after Stalin* (Ithaca, NY: Cornell University Press, 2009), 223.

32. Danylo Shumuk, *Life Sentence: Memoirs of a Ukrainian Political Prisoner,* trans. Ivan Jaworsky and Halya Kowalska (Edmonton: Canadian Institute of Ukrainian Studies, University of Alberta, 1984), 352. Marchenko and others also complained not just about the quantity but the quality of food. See, for example, Marchenko, *My Testimony,* 39, 47, 105, 215, 224–25.

33. GARF, f. R-8131, op. 28, d. 1720, ll. 9–11.

34. Helene Celmina, *Women in Soviet Prisons* (New York: Paragon House, 1985), 136, 222.

35. GARF, f. R-7523, op. 108, d. 72, l. 1.

36. GARF, f. R-7523, op. 109, d. 285, l. 105.

37. Leonid Sitko, "Dalekoe blizkoe: Dubrovlag pri Khrushcheve," *Novyi Mir,* no. 10 (1997): 154.

38. GARF, f. A-461, op. 11, d. 978, l. 92; ERAF, f. 17sm, op. 4, d. 266, ll. 22–23; Sitko, "Dalekoe blizkoe," 157.

39. Celmina, *Women in Soviet Prisons,* 107.

40. I. S. Verblovskaia, "Pis'mo byvshei uznitsy," in *Uroki gneva i liubvi: sbornik vospominanii o godakh repressii (20-e–80-e gg.),* ed. T. V. Tigonen (Saint Petersburg: Vyborgskaia storona, 1993), 155.

41. ERAF, f. 17sm, op. 4, f. 266, l. 19.

42. B. Vaisman, "Disputy posle kinoseansov," *K novoi zhizni,* no. 4 (April 1962): 66.

43. V. Kurskii, "Po starinki . . . : v podrazdeleniiakh Altaiskogo Kraia medlenno perestraivaiut vospitatel'nuiu rabotu," *K novoi zhizni,* no. 1 (January 1962): 8.

44. Marchenko, *My Testimony,* 210.

45. V. Kolbanovskii, "Psikhologiia lichnosti prestupnika i zadachi ego perevospitaniia," *K novoi zhizni,* no. 10 (October 1961): 45.

46. Marchenko, *My Testimony,* 253–55. Celmina, though, reported no cultural productions in the 1960s, only literary evenings. Celmina, *Women in Soviet Prisons,* 122.

47. ERAF, f. 77sm, op. 1, d. 405, ll. 35, 72.

48. When he tried to grow berries inside the zone, however, he was told that only flowers were permitted. MEMO, f. 2, op. 3, d. 66, ll. 344–45.

49. Celmina, *Women in Soviet Prisons,* 95; Marchenko, *My Testimony,* 325.

50. Marchenko, *My Testimony,* 45.

51. Vladimir Osipov, *Dubravlag: predo monoiu ikona i zapretnaia zona . . .* (Moscow: Nash Sovremennik, 2003), 38–39; Shumuk, *Life Sentence,* 356.

52. LYA, f. V-141, op. 1, d. 349, l. 29.

53. Aleksandr Isaevich Solzhenitsyn, *The Gulag Archipelago 1918–1956: An Experiment in Literary Investigation,* 3 vols., trans. Thomas P. Whitney (New York: Harper and Row, 1974–78), 3:500.

54. Abramkin and Chesnakova, *Tiuremnyi mir,* 71.

55. Sitko, "Dalekoe blizkoe," 158, 163.

56. GDA MVS, f. 3, op. 1, d. 265, l. 153; GDA MVS, f. 3, op. 1, d. 265, l. 154.

57. I. Dubrovskii et al., "Starye bolezni daiut sebia znat'," *K novoi zhizni,* no. 4 (April 1962): 11–13.

58. *K novoi zhizni,* no. 3 (March 1962): 61.

59. GDA MVS, f. 3, op. 1, d. 286, l. 14.

60. See, for example, GARF, f. R-8131, op. 32, d. 6131, l. 8; GARF, f. R-8131, op. 32, d. 6567, ll. 37–39. The Russian Procuracy in 1965 even advocated eliminating standard and strengthened regimens, arguing that they were too lax. GARF, f. A-461, op. 11, d. 1603, l. 17.

61. GARF, f. R-8131, op. 32, d. 6733, ll. 7–8.

62. Ibid.

63. GARF, f. A-461, op. 11, d. 998, l. 101.

64. GARF, f. R-8131, op. 32, d. 7036, l. 11.

65. GARF, f. R-8131, op. 32, d. 7036, ll. 20, 29.

66. GARF, f. R-8131, op. 32, d. 7036, ll. 17–20.

67. Iu. Gavrilov, "Konets 'kinomanii,'" *K novoi zhizni,* no. 12 (1961): 38–39.

68. Gresham Sykes, *The Society of Captives: A Study of Maximum Security Prison* (Princeton, NJ: Princeton University Press, 1958), 58.

69. GARF, f. A-385, op. 26, d. 221, l. 4; GARF, f. R-8131, op. 32, d. 7036, l. 20.

70. GARF, f. A-385, op. 26, d. 221, ll. 4–5; Iu. Maslov and G. Oboznyi, "Bez konvoia," *K novoi zhizni,* no. 9 (September 1964): 29–30.

71. A. Brovkin, "Preduprezhdat' i iskoreniat' prestupnost'," *K novoi zhizni,* no. 1 (January 1962): 17.

72. GARF, f. A-385, op. 26, d. 251, l. 1.

73. See, for instance, GARF, f. A-385, op. 26, d. 221, ll. 1–2; ERAF, f. 4778, op. 27a, d. 1, l. 56.

74. GARF, f. A-385, op. 26, d. 251, l. 2; GARF, f. R-7523, op. 109, d. 294, ll. 8–9.

75. Solzhenitsyn, *Gulag Archipelago,* 3:501.

76. GARF, f. R-7523, op. 109, d. 413, l. 19.

77. GARF, f. R-7523, op. 109, d. 294, ll. 8–9. See also L. Borisov, "Vosstanovit' garantiinyi minimum," *K novoi zhizni,* no. 11 (November 1962): 29. As of late 1964, however, this request had not been granted. GARF, f. R-7523, op. 109, d. 413, l. 18.

78. GDA MVS, f. 3, op. 1, d. 277, l. 251–53.

79. GARF, f. R-8131, op. 32, d. 6880, ll. 126–27.

80. Even with 7 colonies in the city and province, the MVD had to transfer 11,811 prisoners to other provinces in 1958, 16,575 in 1959, and 4,685 in 1960. RGANI, f. 13, op. 1, d. 791, ll. 110, 113–14.

81. RGANI, f. 13, op. 1, d. 271, l. 4; RGANI, f. 13, op. 1, d. 791, l. 108; RGANI, f. 13, op. 1, d. 295, l. 43. The decision was altered primarily because of the cost to found new colonies to house Moscow's prisoners, estimated at 108 million rubles. RGANI, f. 13, op. 1, d. 791, ll. 110–11.

82. RGANI, f. 13, op. 2, d. 126, l. 52.

83. RGANI, f. 13, op. 1, d. 791, l. 119.

84. GARF, f. A-385, op. 26, d. 195, ll. 1–7.

85. GARF, f. R-9492, op. 6, d. 117, l. 27. For more on this see Marc Elie and Jeffrey S. Hardy, "'Letting the Beasts out of the Cage': Parole in the Post-Stalin Gulag, 1953–1973," *Europe-Asia Studies* 67, no. 4 (June 2015): 589–94.

86. A. Alekseev, "Strogost'? Da, no spravedlivaia," *K novoi zhizni,* no. 2 (February 1963): 17–18.

87. Iu. Feofanov, "Nenavist' ili strogost'?," *K novoi zhizni,* no. 7 (July 1963): 45–47.

88. *K novoi zhizni,* no. 4 (April 1964): 2.

89. G. A. Tumanov, *Rezhim lisheniia svobody po sovetskomu ispratel'no-trudovomu pravu* (Moscow: Vysshaia shkola MOOP RSFSR, 1964), 6–7.

90. N. A. Beliaev, *Tseli nakazaniia i sredstva ikh dostizheniia v ispravitel'no-trudovykh uchrezhdeniiakh* (Saint Petersburg: Izdatel'stvo leningradskogo universiteta, 1963), 141–43.

91. GARF, f. R-7523, op. 109, d. 285, l. 105.

92. GARF, f. R-7523, op. 109, d. 413, l. 31. And by 1965 the Procuracy supported the seven-hour workday for inmates along with a minimum guaranteed take-home wage. GARF, f. R-7523, op. 109, d. 413, l. 31.

93. A. Vasinskii, "Nakazanie," *Izvestiia,* 5 September 1962, 5.

94. Ibid.

95. Despite MVD lobbying, by late 1964 this had not been extended to the remaining special-regimen prisoners. GARF, f. A-385, op. 26, d. 251, l. 2; GARF, f. A-461, op. 11, d. 978, ll. 134–35.

96. ERAF, f. 17sm, op. 4, d. 270, ll. 50–54.

97. Unfortunately, no trace of this astonishing meeting could be found in archival documentation. Solzhenitsyn, *Gulag Archipelago,* 3:502.

98. Cited in Denis Kozlov, *The Readers of* Novyi Mir: *Coming to Terms with the Stalinist Past* (Cambridge, MA: Harvard University Press, 2013), 209–38.

99. A. G. Murzhenko, *Obraz schastlivogo cheloveka Pis'ma iz lageria osobogo rezhima* (London: Overseas Publications Interchange, 1985), 99–100.

100. Ibid., 99.

101. GDA MVS, f. 6, op. 2, d. 393, ll. 287–91.

102. A. Ermolaev, "'Odin den' Ivana Denisovicha,'" *K novoi zhizni,* no. 1 (January 1963): 75.

103. GARF, f. R-9414, op. 1, d. 1427, ll. 42, 132.

104. RGANI, f. 13, op. 1, d. 791, l. 111.

105. RGANI, f. 13, op. 1, d. 914, ll. 125–28; RGANI, f. 13, op. 1, d. 768, l. 32.

106. RGANI, f. 13, op. 1, d. 294, l. 19.

107. GARF, f. R-7523, op. 109, d. 413, ll. 14–15, 21–22.

108. Solzhenitsyn, *Gulag Archipelago,* 3:503.

109. GARF, f. R-7523, op. 109, d. 413, l. 24.

110. RGANI, f. 13, op. 1, d. 295, l. 42.

111. RGANI, f. 13, op. 1, d. 295, ll. 43, 46.

112. GARF, f. R-7523, op. 109, d. 413, l. 31.

113. TsDAGO, f. 1, op. 24, d. 5507, l. 3.

114. A. Gailiavichius, "Kazhdoi kolonii—svoe predpriiatie!" *K novoi zhizni,* no. 2 (February 1963): 45–47.

115. GARF, f. R-7523, op. 109, d. 285, l. 104.

116. RGANI, f. 13, op. 1, d. 768, ll. 30–31.

117. GARF, f. R-7523, op. 109, d. 413, ll. 21–22.

118. G. Baryshnikov, "V Bor'be za rentabel'nost," *K novoi zhizni,* no. 2 (February 1964): 50–51.

119. V. Matveev, "Na puti k tseli," *K novoi zhizni,* no. 2 (February 1964): 38.

120. D. Pankov, "Novoe vkhodit v zhizn'," *K novoi zhizni,* no. 4 (April 1963): 11.

121. GDA MVD, f. 3, op. 1, d. 280, ll. 142–43; I. Golynnyi, "Polnost'iu otkazat'sia ot dotatsii," *K novoi zhizni,* 1963, no. 1 (January 1963): 38–39; V. Onishchenko, "Bez dotatsii," *K novoi zhizni,* no. 3 (March 1964): 38–39.

122. I. V. Ovchinnikov, *Ispoved' kulatskogo syna* (Moscow: Desnitsa, 2000), 344.

123. RGANI, f. 13, op. 1, d. 264, l. 9.

124. N. Sorokin, "V bor'be za plan vospityvaiutsia osuzhdennye," *K novoi zhizni,* no. 8 (August 1961): 7.

125. V. Lev, "V tsekhakh bol'shikh zavodov," *K novoi zhizni,* no. 1 (January 1962): 31–33.

126. A. Okhrimenko, "Kogda teriaiut doverie . . . ," *K novoi zhizni,* no. 1 (January 1961): 31–32.

127. V. V. Birkin, "Deti 'Khrushchevskoi ottepeli,'" in *Pravda cherez gody: stat'i, vospominaniia, dokumenty,* vol. 3 (Donetsk: Region, 1999), 125–30.

128. A. Dalakishvili, "Tri voprosa," *K novoi zhizni,* no. 9 (September 1961): 38.

129. V. Tikunov, "Pretvorim v zhizn' resheniia noiabr'skogo plenuma TsK KPSS," *K novoi zhizni,* no. 1 (January 1963): 3.

130. RGANI, f. 13, op. 1, d. 295, ll. 44, 46.

131. GARF, f. R-7523, op. 109, d. 413, l. 29.

132. O. Lavrushenkov, "Platnye kursy mekhanizatorov," *K novoi zhizni,* no. 10 (October 1963): 51.

133. GARF, f. R-5446, op. 96, d. 1220, ll. 7–11.

134. GDA MVS, f. 6, op. 2, d. 360, l. 18.

135. RGANI, f. 13, op. 1, d. 768, ll. 30–31.

136. GARF, f. R-7523, op. 109, d. 413, ll. 14–15.

137. Those who refused work were characterized as recidivist thieves, former vagrants, sectarians, inmates with very short sentences, and those with heavy wage garnishments. GARF, f. R-7523, op. 109, d. 294, ll. 5–8.

138. GARF, f. R-7523, op. 109, d. 413, l. 21.

139. N. Sorokin (deputy head of the Gulag adminstration for Russia), "V bor'be za plan vospityvaiutsia osuzhdennye," *K novoi zhizni,* no. 8 (August 1961): 9. This charge was repeated again the following year: "Ochkovtirateli nakazany," *K novoi zhizni,* no. 6 (June 1962): 16.

140. GARF, f. R-7523, op. 109, d. 413, l. 23. A similar complaint is found in Lithuania. LYA, f. 141, op. 1, d. 374, l. 175.

141. LYA, f. 141, op. 1, d. 394, l. 78; Marchenko, *My Testimony*, 229; Ovchinnikov, *Ispoved' kulatskogo syna*, 342. Others, preferring rest to extra cash, were able to manipulate the brigade system so that each day a few brigade members stayed in the camp while the others produced enough to cover the plan target for the whole brigade. Marchenko, *My Testimony*, 218.

142. LYA, f. 141, op. 1, d. 398, l. 277.

143. A. Mandrugin, "V kazhdom iskat' khoroshee," *K novoi zhizni*, no. 2 (February 1964): 25.

144. N. Ivanov, "Samoupravstvo vmesto vospitaniia," *K novoi zhizni*, 1962, no. 3 (March 1962): 40–42.

145. GDA MVS, f. 6, op. 2, d. 395, l. 306.

146. RGANI, f. 13, op. 1, d. 264, l. 11.

147. A. B. Sakharov, *O lichnosti prestupnika i prichinakh prestupnosti v SSSR* (Moscow: Gosudarstvennoe Izdatel'stvo iuridicheskoi literatury, 1961).

148. M. A. Efimov, "Znachenie, programma, i metodika izucheniia linchnosti zakliuchennogo," in *Metodika izucheniia lichnosti zakliuchennogo i opredelenie naibolee effektivnykh cposobov vospitatel'nogo vozdeistviia na nego s tsel'iu ispravleniia i perevospitaniia* (Sverdlovsk: MOOP RSFSR, 1965), 7–21.

149. Iu. I. Shutov, "Osobennosti izucheniia lichnosti retsidivistov," in *Metodika izucheniia*, 62–63.

150. A. Kovalev, "Psikhologicheskie osnovy individual'nogo podkhoda k zakliuchennym," *K novoi zhizni*, no. 8 (August 1961): 29.

151. For a prime example of the use of this phrase see Andrei Zhdanov's 1934 speech to the Congress of Soviet Writers. A. A. Zhdanov, "Soviet Literature: The Richest in Ideas, the Most Advanced Literature," *Soviet Writers' Congress: The Debate on Socialist Realism and Modernism* (London: Lawrence and Wishart, 1977), 15–26.

152. K. Platonov and A. Seinenskii, "Struktura lichnosti," *K novoi zhizni*, no. 8 (August 1964): 29–32.

153. K. Platonov and A. Seinenskii, "Metody izucheniia lichnosti zakliuchennogo," *K novoi zhizni*, no. 9 (September 1964): 18–21.

154. "Eto ne mozhet ne volnovat': obzor pisem chitatelei," *K novoi zhizni*, no. 2 (February 1963): 24–25.

155. M. A. Efimov, *Dokazatel'stva ispravleniia i perevospitaniia zakliuchennogo i ikh otsenka* (Moscow: Politotdel MZ MOOP RSFSR, 1964), 17.

156. Shutov, "Osobennosti izucheniia lichnosti retsidivistov," 65–70.

157. V. I. Pinchuk, "Nekotorye dannye k kharakteristike osobo opasnykh retsidivistov," *Voprosy preduprezhdeniia prestupnosti* 2 (1965): 27–31.

158. GARF, f. R-7523, op. 109, d. 295, l. 6.

159. I. Goloborod'ko, "Pochemu sovershaiutsia povtornye prestupleniia," *K novoi zhizni*, no. 4 (April 1964): 54–55.

160. Iu. Klushin, "Sud'by osvobodivshikhsia," *K novoi zhizni*, no. 7 (July 1962): 26–27; N. Sukhova, "My otvechaem za kazhdogo osvobodivshegosia," *K novoi zhizni*, no. 10 (October 1962): 10.

161. N. Litovchak, "Zabota ob osvobodivshikhsia," *K novoi zhizni*, no. 4 (April 1963): 47.

162. GDA MVS, f. 3, op. 1, d. 266, ll. 20, 101–9.

163. Iu. Agaev, "Dveri shkoly zakrylis'," *K novoi zhizni*, no. 1 (January 1963): 31.

164. V. Maiorov, "Chto meshaet rabote vospitatelia," *K novoi zhizni*, no. 1 (January 1963): 61.

165. Marchenko, *My Testimony*, 88. Or as one inmate in Sergei Dovlatov's story asked his guard, "Which one of us is in prison? You or me?" Sergei Dovlatov, *The Zone: A Prison Camp Guard's Story*, trans. Anne Frydman (New York: Alfred A. Knopf, 1985), 125.

166. A. Zverev, "Uspekh dela reshaiut liudi," *K novoi zhizni,* no. 8 (August 1962): 2–5.

167. RGANI, f. 13, op. 1, d. 764, l. 140; LYA, f. 141, op. 1, d. 350, l. 192.

168. RGANI, f. 13, op. 1, d. 872, l. 105.

169. RGANI, f. 13, op. 1, d. 872, l. 182.

170. LYA, f. 141, op. 1, d. 362, l. 306.

171. RGANI, f. 13, op. 1, d. 764, ll. 150–52.

172. RGANI, f. 13, no. 1, d. 291, ll. 26–30.

173. V. I. Miasnikov, "Sovershenstvovat' metodiku vospitatel'noi raboty," in *Metodika izucheniia,* 82.

174. *K novoi zhizni,* no. 11 (November 1963): 65.

175. Dovlatov, *Zone,* 47, 141.

176. RGANI, f. 13, op. 1, d. 264, ll. 9–12.

177. RGANI, f. 13, op. 1, d. 768, l. 35.

178. Ibid.

179. N. Gusev, "Nachal'nik otriada," *K novoi zhizni,* no. 4 (April 1963): 5.

180. A. Senatov, "Za kulturu v rabote," *K novoi zhizni,* no. 3 (March 1964): 2–4. See also S. Iapeev, "I na proizvodstve, i v bytu," *K novoi zhizni,* no. 4 (April 1964): 17–18.

181. V. Tikunov, "Bol'shie zadachi novogo goda," *K novoi zhizn,* no. 1 (January 1964): 4.

182. Efimov, *Dokazatel'stva ispravleniia,* 18–19.

183. RGANI, f. 13, op. 1, d. 768, l. 13; N. Karmanov, "Nagruzka ne po silam," *K novoi zhizni,* no. 7 (July 1962): 61. Ovchinnikov, however, reported being in a detachment with six hundred inmates in the mid-1960s. Ovchinnikov, *Ispoved' kulatskogo syna,* 342.

184. A regional conference for detachment heads, including those from Belorussia, was also held in Vilnius in 1963. LYA, f. 141, op. 2, d. 256, ll. 24–25.

185. Ia. Turbovskoi, "Chto my uvideli v otrade tov. Tatarinova," *K novoi zhizni,* no. 1 (January 1961): 47–48.

186. GARF, f. R-7523, op. 109, d. 293, l. 10.

187. RGANI, f. 13, op. 1, d. 768, l. 32; GDA MVS, f. 6, op. 2, d. 393, l. 23; Celmina, *Women in Soviet Prisons,* 123.

188. N. Ivanov, "Pochemu zakliuchennye ne uchatsia," *K novoi zhizni,* no. 11 (November 1963): 24–25.

189. GARF, f. R-7523, op. 109, d. 413, ll. 29–30.

190. RGANI, f. 13, op. 1, d. 768, l. 13.

191. V. Kurskii, "Po starinki . . . : v podrazdeleniiakh Altaiskogo Kraia medlenno perestraivaiut vospitatel'nuiu rabotu," *K novoi zhizni,* no. 1 (January 1962): 7–8.

192. LYA, f. 141, op. 2, d. 256, l. 26; A. Shubin, "Ne besedy, a politicheskie zaniatiia," *K novoi zhizni,* no. 9 (September 1961): 42–46.

193. See, for instance, L. Grigorian and N. Gents, "Kollektivizm—osnova vzaimootnoshenii v sotsialistichekom obshchestve," *K novoi zhizni,* no. 9 (September 1962): 42–45; and N. Chernitskii, " 'Berech' I ukrepliat' sotsialisticheskuiu sobstvennost'—vazhneishaia zadacha grazhdanina SSSR," *K novoi zhizni,* no. 11 (November 1962): 41–44.

194. GDA MVS, f. 6, op. 2, d. 393, l. 22; Marchenko, *My Testimony,* 41, 255–56.

195. GDA MVS, f. 6, op. 2, d. 382, l. 199; Marchenko, *My Testimony,* 258.

196. Osipov, *Dubravlag,* 26.

197. See, for instance, LYA, f. 141, op. 1, d. 363, ll. 132–43.

198. B. Vaisman, "Aktiv rabotaet ne za l'goty i privilegii," *K novoi zhizni,* no. 12 (December 1962): 32–33.

199. Red armbands as a symbol of devotion of Bolshevism had a long history in the Soviet Union, dating back to the Civil War era. In the Khrushchev era they were prominently worn by members of the Voluntary People's Patrols (*druzhinniki*), who performed

essentially the same policing functions outside the Gulag that the section of internal order did inside the Gulag. On this see Oleg Kharkhordin, *The Collective and the Individual in Russia: A Study of Practices* (Berkeley: University of California Press, 1999), 285–91; and LaPierre, *Hooligans in Khrushchev's Russia*, 132–56; and Dobson, *Khrushchev's Cold Summer*, 135–77.

200. GARF, f. R-9414, op. 1, d. 2633, ll. 167–72; GARF, f. R-9414, op. 1, d. 2668, ll. 94–96.

201. *K novoi zhizni*, no. 8 (August 1961): 81.

202. M. Persheev, "Shkola aktiva zakliuchennykh," *K novoi zhizni*, no. 10 (October 1963): 34–36.

203. A. Brovkin, "Preduprezhdat' I iskoreniat' prestupnost'," *K novoi zhizni*, no. 1 (January 1962): 17.

204. I. Razin, "Sila primera," *K novoi zhizni*, no. 12 (December 1962): 62.

205. GARF, f. A-385, op. 26, d. 221, l. 41.

206. GDA MVS, f. 3, d. 1, op. 290, l. 154; A. Brovkin, "Preduprezhdat' I iskoreniat' prestupnost'," *K novoi zhizni*, no. 1 (January 1962): 17.

207. M. Mukhutdinov, "Rastet avtoritet aktivistov," *K novoi zhizni*, no. 1 (January 1962): 29–30. For a similar example see K. Gaipnazarov, "Samodeiatel'nost osuzhdennykh splotila otriad," *K novoi zhizni*, no. 12 (December 1962): 29–30.

208. N. Lipilin, "V otryve ot aktiva," *K novoi zhizni*, no. 3 (March 1962): 26–28.

209. Shumuk, *Life Sentence*, 352.

210. Marchenko, *My Testimony*, 244–46.

211. Osipov, *Dubravlag*, 24.

212. Abramkin and Chesnakova, *Tiuremnyi mir*, 14–15; Osipov, *Dubravlag*, 14; Murzhenko, *Obraz schastlivogo cheloveka*, 91.

213. TsDAGO, f. 1, op. 24, d. 5419, l. 62.

214. LYA, f. 141, op. 2, d. 235, ll. 139–42.

215. LYA, f. 141, op. 1, d. 362, ll. 166–74.

216. Abramkin and Chesnakova, *Tiuremnyi mir*, 73–76.

217. Dovlatov, *Zone*, 16.

218. Marchenko, *My Testimony*, 245.

219. Shumuk, *Life Sentence*, 348.

220. V. M. Gridin, *My, kotorykh ne bylo . . . : vospominaniia o GULAGe v stukhakh i proze* (Odessa: Astroprint, 1996), 109–10.

221. M. S. Gol'dman, "'. . . Ne etomu menia desiat' let v komsomole uchili . . .'" *Karta*, 1997, nos. 17–18: 54–55.

222. L. N. Krasnopevtsev, "'. . . U nas byla svoia tochka zreniia . . . ,'" *Karta*, nos. 17–18 (1997): 67.

223. M. Sudarikov, "Iavka s povinnoi," *K novoi zhizni*, no. 4 (April 1961): 56–57.

224. A. Zaitseva, "Slovo staroi materi," *K novoi zhizni*, no. 5 (May 1962): 75–77.

225. For more on how the war was employed to shame people, especially the youth, into submission in broader Soviet society in the 1960s and 1970s see Nina Tumarkin, *The Living and the Dead: The Rise and Fall of the Cult of World War II in Russia* (New York: Basic Books, 1994).

226. P. Voronov, from Cheliabinsk Province, "Na svobodu—s chestoi sovest'iu," *K novoi zhizni*, no. 9 (September 1962): 13–15.

227. N. Zaglada, "Zhit' ne radi korysti," *K novoi zhizni*, no. 11 (November 1962): 63–65.

228. Voronov, "Na svobodu," 26.

229. *Na svobodu—s chistoi sovest'iu!* (Kiev: Politotdel ITU MOOP Ukrainskoi SSSR, 1963), 41.

230. See, for example, LYA, f. 141, op. 1, d. 387, l. 352.

231. Editors, "Dobrovol'noe priznanie," *K novoi zhizni*, no. 11 (November 1963): 15–16. Not all, however, complied with these instructions. The Lithuanian MVD complained that harsh sentences were sometimes handed down, despite the voluntary nature of the confessions. LYA, f. 141, op. 1, d. 387, l. 352.

232. *Na svobodu3*.

233. GDA MVS, f. 6, op. 2, d. 392, l. 185.

234. GDA MVS, f. 3, op. 1, d. 292, l. 138.

235. LYA, f. 141, op. 1, d. 404, l. 237.

236. GARF, f. R-7523, op. 109, d. 413, l. 17.

237. N. Romanenko, "Vozmozhnost' pomilovaniia—vazhnyi stimul dlia osuzhden-nykh," *K novoi zhizni*, no. 1 (January 1963): 76.

238. Marchenko, *My Testimony*, 213.

239. Osipov, *Dubravlag*, 48–49.

240. I. P. Sharapov, *Odna iz tain KGB* (Moscow: Izdatel'stvo avtora, 1990), 46–47.

241. LYA, f. 141, op. 1, d. 394, l. 2.

242. RGANI, f. 13, op. 2, d. 567, l. 164; RGANI, f. 13, op. 2, d. 173, l. 28.

243. GARF, f. R-8131, op. 32, d. 6880, ll. 127–30.

244. RGANI, f. 13, op. 2, d. 567, l. 165.

245. RGANI, f. 13, op. 2, d. 567, l. 166.

246. RGANI, f. 13, op. 2, d. 174, ll. 38–40.

247. V. Biriukov and F. Kuznetsov, "My verim v sovest'," *Izvestiia*, 22 November 1963, 3.

248. GARF, f. R-7523, op. 109, d. 294, ll. 10–11.

249. GARF, f. R-7523, op. 109, d. 296, ll. 3–6, 15–17.

250. GDA MVS, f. 3, op. 1, d. 292, ll. 101–3.

251. S. Zatolokin, "Pervaia koloniia-poselenie," *K novoi zhizni*, 1963, no. 11 (November 1963): 13–14.

252. "Odin den' v kolonii-poselenii," *K novoi zhizni*, 1964, no. 1 (January 1964): 68–70.

253. GARF, f. R-7523, op. 109, d. 296, ll. 3–6, 15–17.

254. GARF, f. A-461, op. 11, d. 1367, l. 15.

255. A. Sokolov, "Vazhnomu delu—chetkost' i organizovannost'," *K novoi zhizni*, no. 3 (March 1964): 33–34.

256. N. Ablizin, "Chemu uchit opyt kolonii-poselenii," *K novoi zhizni*, no. 12 (December 1964): 57.

257. GARF, f. R-7523, op. 109, d. 413, ll. 1–5.

258. GARF, f. R-7523, op. 109, d. 413, l. 7; GARF, f. A-461, op. 11, d. 1595, l. 26.

259. GARF, f. R-7523, op. 83, d. 1075, ll. 1–4.

260. GARF, f. R-7523, op. 83, d. 1080, ll. 6–7.

261. GARF, f. R-7523, op. 109, d. 409, ll. 123–25.

262. N. Sorokin, "Doverie i trebovatel'nost'," *K novoi zhizni*, no. 9 (September 1964): 5–6.

263. GARF, f. R-7523, op. 109, d. 409, l. 44.

264. GARF, f. A-461, op. 11, d. 1595, ll. 37, 40. One must add, however, that free workers often faced similar circumstances. As Donald Filtzer discovered, "as late as 1965, large chemical plants in the Kuzbass were still unable to provide living quarters for between a quarter and a third of their workers." Donald Filtzer, *Soviet Workers and De-Stalinization: The Consolidation of the Modern System of Soviet Production Relations, 1953–1964* (Cambridge: Cambridge University Press, 1992), 51.

265. GARF, f. R-7523, op. 109, d. 409, ll. 47–49, 82.

266. Sorokin, "Doverie i trebovatel'nost'."

267. GARF f. R-7523, op. 83, d. 1184, l. 116.

268. GARF, f. R-7523, op. 83, d. 1184, l. 137. For more on chemistry see Elie and Hardy, "'Letting the Beasts out of the Cage,'" 597–601.

CONCLUSIONS

1. Valery Chalidze, *Criminal Russia*, trans. P. S. Falla (New York: Random House, 1977); and Louise Shelley, "The Geography of Soviet Criminality," *American Sociological Review* 45, no. 1 (February 1980): 111–22.

2. A. A., Fursenko, ed., *Prezidium TsK KPSS 1954–1964*, 3 vols. (Moscow: Rosspen, 2003–6), 1:21–23.

3. Aleksandr Isaevich Solzhenitsyn, *The Gulag Archipelago 1918–1956: An Experiment in Literary Investigation*, 3 vols., trans. Thomas P. Whitney (New York: Harper and Row, 1974–78), 3:494.

4. Robert Conquest, *The Great Terror: A Reassessment* (New York: Oxford University Press, 1990), 478.

5. Anne Applebaum, *Gulag: A History* (New York: Doubleday, 2003), 510, 533.

6. Robert Hornsby, "The Outer Reaches of Liberalization: Combating Political Dissent in the Khrushchev Era," in *Khrushchev in the Kremlin: Policy and Government in the Soviet Union, 1956–64*, ed. Jeremy Smith and Melanie Ilic (London: Routledge, 2010), 64–71. On the fairly pathetic state of the last corrective-labor colony for political prisoners, Perm 35, see Jean-Pierre Vaudon, "Last Days of the Gulag?" *National Geographic* 177, no. 3 (March 1990): 40–47.

7. See, for instance, *First United Nations Congress on the Prevention of Crime and the Treatment of Offenders* (New York: United Nations, Department of Economic and Social Affairs, 1956), 23–24, 64.

8. N. A. Polanski, "The Prison as an Autocracy," *Journal of Criminal Law and Criminology* 33 (May–June 1942): 16–22. See also Gresham Sykes, *The Society of Captives: A Study of Maximum Security Prison* (Princeton, NJ: Princeton University Press, 1958), xxxi–xxxii.

9. Cited in Judith Pallot, Laura Piacentini, and Dominique Moran, "Patriotic Discourses in Russia's Penal Peripheries: Remembering the Mordovan *Gulag*," *Europe-Asia Studies* 62, no. 1 (2010): 14.

10. Tamara Shkel', "Proshchanie s GULAGom," *Rossiiskaia Gazeta*, 22 September 2011.

11. William Taubman, *Khrushchev: The Man and His Era* (New York: W. W. Norton, 2004), 620.

12. Leonid Sitko, "Dalekoe blizkoe: Dubrovlag pri Khrushcheve," *Novyi Mir*, no. 10 (1997): 164.

13. Anatoly Marchenko, *My Testimony*, trans. Michel Scammell (New York: E. P. Dutton, 1969), 281, 283; Vladimir Osipov, *Dubravlag: predo monoiu ikona i zapretnaia zona . . .* (Moscow: Nash Sovremennik, 2003), 44.

14. Osipov, *Dubravlag*, 42.

15. "Osnovy ispravitel'no-trudovogo zakonodatel'stvo SSSR i soiuznykh respublik," *Pravda*, 12 July 1969, 2–3; M. Evteev and A. Saratovskikh, "Osnovy ispravitel'no-trudovogo zakonodatel'stva i ispravitel'no-trudovye kodeksy," *Sotsialisticheskaia zakonnost'*, no. 7 (1973): 19–23.

16. On this see Walter D. Connor, *Deviance in Soviet Society: Crime, Delinquency, and Alcoholism* (New York: Columbia University Press, 1972), 206–10, 269.

17. See, among others, Vladimir Fedorovich Abramkin and Valentina Fedorovna Chesnakova, eds., *Tiuremnyi mir glazami politzakliuchennykh, 1940–1980-e gg* (Moscow: Sodeistvie, 1998); Andrei Amalrik, *Notes of a Revolutionary*, trans. Guy Daniels (New

York: Alfred A. Knopf, 1982); Edward Kuznetsov, *Prison Diaries*, trans. Howard Spier (New York: Stein and Day, 1975); Vladimir Bukovsky, *To Build a Castle: My Life as a Dissenter*, trans. Michael Scammell (New York: Viking Press, 1979); and Vladimir Pimonov, *Govoriat 'osobo opasnye': sbornik interv'iu* (Moscow: Detektiv-Press, 1999).

18. Marchenko, *My Testimony*, 3.

19. Laura Piacentini, *Surviving Russian Prisons: Punishment, Economy and Politics in Transition* (Cullomton, UK: Willan, 2004), 17–18.

20. As of 2003 there were 749 colonies of adult offenders in Russia, along with 7 prisons. Piacentini, *Surviving Russian Prisons*, 3–4. Estonia has in the post-Soviet era attempted to transition to a cellular prison system, but Lithuania continues to use the Soviet model of corrective-labor colonies of varying regimen type. Jaan Sootak, Rando Antsmäe, and Olavi Israel, "Estonia," in *Imprisonment Today and Tomorrow: International Perspectives on Prisoners' Rights and Prison Conditions*, 2nd ed., ed. Dirk van Zyl Smit and Frieder Dünkel (The Hague: Kluwer Law International, 2001), 238–52; and Viktoras Justickis and Justinas Peckaitis, "Lithuania," in van Zyl Smit and Dünkel, *Imprisonment Today and Tomorrow*, 448–66.

21. Piacentini, *Surviving Russian Prisons*, 54–83.

22. Ibid., xiv.

23. See Sootak et al., "Estonia"; and Justickis and Peckaitis, "Lithuania."

24. See Damien Sharkov, "Russian Parliament Approves 'Sadistic' Prison Reform Law at First Reading," *Newsweek Europe*, 22 October 2015, available at http://europe.newsweek.com/russian-parliament-approves-sadistic-prison-reform-law-first-reading-335270.

25. Roy D. King, "Russian Prisons after Perestroika: End of the Gulag?," *British Journal of Criminology* 34, special issue, "Prisons in Context" (1994): 67; Piacentini, *Surviving Russian Prisons*, 2. For the most current information (a prison population of 642,444 including pretrial detainees as of 1 November 2015) see International Centre for Prison Studies, *World Prison Brief*, available at http://www.prisonstudies.org/country/russian-federation.

26. King, "Russian Prisons," 78.

27. Judith Pallot, "Forced Labour for Forestry: The Twentieth Century History of Colonisation and Settlement in the North of Perm' *Oblast*'," *Europe-Asia Studies* 54, no. 7 (July 2002): 1055–83.

Select Bibliography

ARCHIVAL MATERIAL

ERAF   Eesti Riigiarhiivi Filiaali (Branch of the Estonian State Archive)

     Fond 17sm: Secretariat of the Ministry of Internal Affairs (MVD), Estonian SSR

     Fond 77sm: Department of Corrective-Labor Colonies, MVD, Estonian SSR

     Fond 4778:   Party Committee of the MVD, Estonian SSR

GAMO   Gosudarstvennyi arkhiv Magadanskoi oblasti (State Archive of Magadan Province)

     Fond R-23:   Dal'stroi

GARF   Gosudarstvennyi arkhiv Rossiiskoi Federatsii (State Archive of the Russian Federation)

     Fond A-385:   Supreme Soviet, RSFSR

     Fond A-461:   Procuracy, RSFSR

     Fond R-5446:   Council of Ministers, USSR

     Fond R-7523:   Supreme Soviet, USSR

     Fond R-8131:   Procuracy, USSR

     Fond R-9401:   MVD, USSR

     Fond R-9413:   Prison Department of the MVD, USSR

     Fond R-9414:   Main Administration of Places of Confinement of the MVD, USSR

     Fond R-9474:   Supreme Court, USSR

     Fond R-9492:   Ministry of Justice, USSR

GDA MVS   Galuzevii derzhavnii arkhiv Ministerstva vnutrishnikh sprav Ukrainy (State Archive Branch of the Ministry of Internal Affairs of Ukraine)

     Fond 3:   Secretariat of the MVD, Ukrainian SSR

     Fond 6:   Administration of Corrective-Labor Camps and Colonies, MVD, Ukrainian SSR

GDA SBU   Galuzevii derzhavnii arkhiv Sluzhby bezpeki Ukrainy (State Archive Branch of the Security Service of Ukraine)

     Fond 6:   Investigatory Files

LYA   Lietuvos Ypatingasis Archyvas (Lithuanian Special Archives)

     Fond V-141:   Secretariat of the MVD, Lithuanian SSR

     Fond V-145/1:   Department of Corrective-Labor Colonies, MVD, Lithuanian SSR

     Fond V-148/18:   Corrective-Labor Colony No. 2

MEMO   Arkhiv istorii politicheskikh represii v SSSR (1918–1956), Obshchestvo "Memoriala" (Archive of the History of Political Repressions in the USSR [1918–1956], Memorial Society)

     Fond 2:   Memoirs and Literary Works

RGANI   Rossiiskii gosudarstvennyi arkhiv noveishei istorii (Russian State Ar-
              chive of Contemporary History)
                  Fond 5:   Apparatus of the Central Committee of the
                                    Communist Party (TsK KPSS)
                  Fond 13:   TsK KPSS Bureau for the RSFSR
                  Fond 89:   Communist Party of the Soviet Union on Trial
RGASPI   Rossiiskii gosudarstvennyi arkhivsotsial'no-politicheskoi istorii (Rus-
              sian State Archive of Social-Political History)
                  Fond 82:   Molotov Viacheslav Mikhailovich
TsDAGO   Tsentral'nii derzhavnii arkhiv gromads'kikh ob'ednan' Ukraini (Cen-
              tral State Archive of Public Organizations of Ukraine)
                  Fond 1:   Central Committee of the Communist Party of
                                    Ukraine
TsDAVO   Tsentral'nii derzhavnii arkhiv vishchikh organiv vladi ta upravlinnia
              Ukraini (Central State Archive of Supreme Organs of Power and Gov-
              ernment of Ukraine)
                  Fond 8:   Ministry of Justice, Ukrainian SSR
                  Fond 288:   Procuracy, Ukrainian SSR

PUBLISHED DOCUMENT COLLECTIONS

Artizov, Andrei, ed. *Reabilitatsiia—kak eto bylo: dokumenty Prezidiuma TSK KPSS i drugie
    materialy*. 3 volumes. Moscow: Mezhdunarodnyi fond "Demokratiia," 2000–2004.
Fursenko, A. A., ed. *Prezidium TsK KPSS 1954–1964*. 2 vols. Moscow: Rosspen, 2003–6.
Khrushchev, N. S. *Doklad na zakrytom zasedanii XX s'ezda KPSS*. Moscow: Gospolitizdat,
    1959.
——. *Report of the Central Committee of the Communist Party of the Soviet Union to the
    20th Party Congress*. Moscow: Foreign Languages Publishing House, 1956.
Kokurin, A. I., and N. V. Petrov, eds. *GULAG: glavnoe upravlenie lagerei, 1917–1960*. Mos-
    cow: Mezhdunarodnyi fond "Demokratiia," 2000.
——. *Lubianka: VChK-OGPU-NKVD-NKGB-MGB-MVD-KGB, 1917–1960*. Moscow:
    Mezhdunarodnyi fond "Demokratiia," 1997.
Kozlov, V. P., ed. *Istoriia stalinskogo GULAGa: konets 20-kh—pervaia polovina 50-kh go-
    dov*. 7 vols. Moscow: Rosspen, 2004.
Lebedinskii, V. G., and D. I. Orlov, eds. *Sovetskaia prokuratura v vazhneishikh dokumen-
    takh*. Moscow: Gosudarstvennoe izdatel'stvo iuridicheskoi literatury, 1956.
Lenin, V. I. *Polnoe sobranie sochinenii*. 5th ed. Moscow: Izdatel'stvo politicheskoi liter-
    atury, 1963.
Shiriaev, I. N., and G. A. Metelkina, eds. *Sovetskaia prokuratura: sbornik dokumentov*.
    Moscow: Iuridicheskaia literatura, 1981.

MEMOIRS AND LITERARY WORKS

Amalrik, Andrei. *Notes of a Revolutionary*. Translated by Guy Daniels. New York: Alfred A.
    Knopf, 1982.
Badash, Semen. *Kolyma ty moia, Kolyma . . . dokumental'naia povest'*. New York: Effect, 1986.
Bardach, Janusz, and Kathleen Gleeson. *Surviving Freedom: After the Gulag*. Berkeley:
    University of California Press, 2003.
Biriuzova, Ol'ga. "Ia liubliu tebia, zhizn'." *Detektiv i politka* 5, no. 15 (1991): 303–39.
Birkin, V. V. "Deti 'Khrushchevskoi ottepeli.'" In *Pravda cherez gody: stat'i, vospomina-
    niia, dokumenty*, vol. 3, 124–31. Donetsk: Region, 1999.

Blake, Ben, ed. *Four Soviet Plays*. New York: International Publishers, 1937.

Borovskii, O. B. "'Levsha' ponevole." In *Pechal'naia pristan'*, edited by I. L. Kuznetsov, 281–308. Syktyvkar: Komi knizhnoe izdatel'stvo, 1991.

Bukovsky, Vladimir. *To Build a Castle: My Life as a Dissenter*. Translated by Michael Scammell. New York: Viking Press, 1979.

Celmina, Helene. *Women in Soviet Prisons*. New York: Paragon House, 1985.

Chekhov, Anton. *Ward No. 6 and Other Stories*. Translated by Constance Garnett. New York: Barnes and Noble Classics, 2003.

Chistiakov, Ivan. *Sibirskoi dal'nei storonoi: Dnevnik okhranika BAMa, 1935–1936*. Moscow: CORPUS, 2014.

Dmitriev, Petr. *"Soldat Berii": vospominaniia lagernogo okhranika*. Leningrad: Chas pik, 1991.

Dodonov, Iu. I. *Vstretimsia na barrikadakh*. Murom: Memorial, 1996.

Dovlatov, Sergei. *The Zone: A Prison Camp Guard's Story*. Translated by Anne Frydman. New York: Alfred A. Knopf, 1985.

Ginzburg, Eugenia Semyonovna. *Journey into the Whirlwind*. Translated by Paul Stevenson and Max Hayward. New York: Harcourt, 1967.

——. *Within the Whirlwind*. Translated by Ian Boland. London: Collins and Harvill Press, 1981.

Goldman, M. S. "'. . . Ne etomu menia desiat' let v komsomole uchili . . .'" *Karta*, nos. 17–18 (1997): 46–57.

Gridin, V. M. *My, kotorykh ne bylo . . . : vospominaniia o GULAGe v stukhakh i proze*. Odessa: Astroprint, 1996.

Harvard Project on the Soviet Social System. Schedule B, Vol. 1, Case 136 (Interviewer S. H.). Widener Library, Harvard University.

Hašek, Jaroslav. *The Good Soldier Švejk*. London: Everyman's Library, 1993.

Ivanova, O. L. *Zhurnaly v pogonakh*. Moscow: Ob'edinennaia redaktsiia MVD Rossii, 2001.

Khrushchev, Nikita Sergeevich. *Khrushchev Remembers*. Translated and edited by Strobe Talbott. Boston, MA: Little, Brown, 1970.

Klimovich, Rygor. *Konets Gorlaga*. Minsk: Nasha Niva, 1999.

Krasnopevtsev, L. N. "'. . . U nas byla svoia tochka zreniia . . . ,'" *Karta*, nos. 17–18 (1997): 65–70.

Krivoshein, N. I. "Blazhennyi Avgustin," *Zvezda*, no. 7 (2001): 172–82.

——. "Dan' pamiati, ili, 'Smotri, zhidenka primorili,'" *Zvezda*, no. 4 (2003):129–43.

Kuzin, A. N. *Malyi srok: vospominaniia v forme esse so svobodnym siuzhetom*. Moscow: Rudomino, 1994.

Kuznetsov, Edward. *Prison Diaries*. Translated by Howard Spier. New York: Stein and Day, 1975.

Marchenko, Anatoly. *My Testimony*. Translated by Michel Scammell. New York: E. P. Dutton, 1969.

Michnik, Adam. "Scenes from the Polish Hell." In *The Cultural Gradient: The Transmission of Ideas in Europe, 1789–1991*, edited by Catherine Evtuhov and Stephen Kotkin, 257–76. Lanham, MD: Rowman & Littlefield, 2003.

Mochulsky, Fyodor Vasilevich. *Gulag Boss: A Soviet Memoir*. Translated by Deborah Kaple. Oxford: Oxford University Press, 2010.

Molostov, M. M. *Revisionism—58*. Phoenix: Atheneum, 1991.

Molotov, Viacheslav Mikhailovich. *Molotov Remembers: Inside Kremlin Politics*. Chicago: Ivan R. Dee, 1993.

Moroz, Valentyn. *Boomerang: The Works of Valentyn Moroz*. Edited by Yaroslav Bihun. Baltimore, MD: Smoloskyp, 1974.

Mukhin, L. S., ed. *Ozerlag: kak eto bylo.* Irkutsk: Vostochno-Sibirskoe knizhnoe izdatel'stvo, 1992.

Murzhenko, A. G. *Obraz schastlivogo cheloveka, ili Pis'ma iz lageria osobogo rezhima.* London: Overseas Publications Interchange, 1985.

Noble, John H. *I Was a Slave in Russia: An American Tells His Story.* New York: Devin-Adair, 1958.

Osipov, Vladimir. *Dubravlag: predo monoiu ikona i zapretnaia zona . . .* Moscow: Nash sovremennik, 2003.

Ovchinnikov, I. V. *Ispoved' kulatskogo syna.* Moscow: Desnitsa, 2000.

Pantiukhin, I. V. *Stolitsa kolymskogo kraia: zapiski Magadanskogo prokurora.* Petrozavodsk: Molodezhnaia gazeta, 1995.

Pimonov, Vladimir. *Govoriat 'osobo opasnye': sbornik interv'iu.* Moscow: Detektiv-Press, 1999.

Preigerzon, Tsvi I. *Dnevnik vospominanii byvshego lagernika (1949–1955).* Translated by I. B. Mints. Moscow: Vozvrashchenie, 2005.

Rabinovich, M. B. *Vospominaniia dolgoi zhizni.* Saint Petersburg: Evropeiskii dom, 1998.

Rodos, Valerii. *Ia syn palacha: vospominanie.* Moscow: Chastnyi arkhiv, 2008.

Scholmer, Joseph. *Vorkuta.* New York: Holt, 1955.

Sharapov, I. P. *Odna iz tain KGB.* Moscow: Izdatel'stvo avtora, 1990.

Shelest, Petr E. *Da ne sudimy budete: dnevnikovye zapisi, vospominaniia chlena Politburo TsK KPSS.* Moscow: Edition q, 1995.

Shumuk, Danylo. *Life Sentence: Memoirs of a Ukrainian Political Prisoner.* Translated by Ivan Jaworsky and Halya Kowalska. Edmonton: Canadian Institute of Ukrainian Studies, University of Alberta, 1984.

Sitko, Leonid. "Dalekoe blizkoe: Dubrovlag pri Khrushcheve." *Novyi Mir,* no. 10 (1997): 142–66.

Solomon, Michael. *Magadan.* Princeton, NJ: Vertex, 1971.

Solzhenitsyn, Aleksandr Isaevich. *The Gulag Archipelago 1918–1956: An Experiment in Literary Investigation.* 3 volumes. Translated by Thomas P. Whitney. New York: Harper and Row, 1974–1978.

———. *One Day in the Life of Ivan Denisovich.* Translated by Ralph Parker. New York: E. P. Dutton, 1963.

———, ed. *Voices from the Gulag.* Translated by Kenneth Lantz. Evanston, IL: Northwestern University Press, 2010.

Sporov, B. F. "Pis'mena tiuremnykh sten: povest'," *Nash sovremennik,* no. 10 (1993): 65–91.

Štajner, Karlo. *Seven Thousand Days in Siberia.* Translated by Joel Agee. New York: Farrar, Straus and Giroux, 1988.

Strelianyi, Anatolii, Genrikh Sapgir, Vladimir Bakhtin, and Nikita Ordynskii, eds. *Samizdat veka.* Moscow: Itogi veka, 1999.

Temin, G. M. *V teni zakona: bol' o perezhitom.* Saint Petersburg: Liki Rossii, 1995.

Tobien, Karl. *Dancing under the Red Star.* Colorado Springs: Waterbrook, 2006.

Tumanov, Alla. *Where We Buried the Sun: One Woman's Gulag Story.* Translated by Gust Olson. Edmonton: NuWest Press, 1999.

Ulanovskaia, Nadezhda, and Maiia Ulanovskaia. *Istoriia odnoi sem'i.* Moscow: Vest'-VIMO, 1994.

Verblovskaia, I. S. "Pis'mo byvshei uznitsy." In *Uroki gneva i liubvi: sbornik vospominanii o godakh repressii (20-e–80-e gg.),* edited by T. V. Tigonen, 153–58. Saint Petersburg: Vyborgskaia storona, 1993.

Voinovich, Vladimir. *Moscow 2042.* Translated by Richard Lourie. San Diego, CA: Harcourt, Brace, Jovanovich, 1987.

Index

Abramkin, V. F., 167
Akhmatova, Anna, 39
Altai, 118, 122
amnesty: of 1947, 18, 23; of 1953, 23–25; of 1954, 35–36; of 1955, 37–38; of 1957, 53
Angarlag. *See* Angarskii Corrective-Labor Camp
Angarskii Corrective-Labor Camp, 102
anti-theft laws of 1948, 12, 18, 35
Applebaum, Anne, 2, 202
Arkhangel'sk Province, 197
Armenia, 127
Averbakh, I. L., 84
Azerbaijan, 112

Bakin, P. N., 42
Bakov, I. I., 139
Barenberg, Alan, 2, 17
Barnes, Steven, 2, 20
Bashkiria, 111, 127
Beliaev, N. A., 172
Belorussia, 118, 122, 165, 172, 177
Beria, L. P., 5, 18, 21–23, 25–27
Berman, Harold, 28, 115, 157
Birkin, V. V., 179
Boim, Leon, 114
Breslauer, George, 140
Brezhnev, L. I., 46, 148, 155, 157
Briansk Province, 117–18, 125
Bulganin, N. A., 32
Butkovsky, A. P., 19
Butrimas, Juozas, 82

case reviews, 29, 38–39, 43–44
Celmina, Helene, 165
Central Committee of the Communist Party, 35, 42, 52, 69, 93–94, 128, 150, 164–65; Presidium of, 31–33, 42–44, 47–48, 149–50; Russian Bureau of, 79, 146–47, 170, 176–77, 186–87
Chaunchukotlag. *See* Chaun-Chukotskii Corrective-Labor Camp
Chaun-Chukotskii Corrective-Labor Camp, 111
Cheliabinsk Province, 121, 185, 192–93

"chemistry", 194, 197–200
Chita, 122
Cohen, Stephen, 131
colony-settlements, 194–97
commissions of 1959, 53–54
Committee of State Security, 22, 26, 46
communism, promise of, 9–10, 158, 160–61
Communist Party organizations (local), 40–42, 107, 110, 150–53, 187; in the Gulag, 72–73, 98, 125; involvement in reeducation, 82, 125, 160; involvement in release, 53. *See also* Communist Youth League; oversight commissions
Communist Youth League, 53, 116, 122, 125, 147
comrades' courts. *See* self-governing organizations
Conquest, Robert, 202
corrective-labor colonies, 14–15; construction of, 50–51, 64–65, 163; preference for, 33–34, 45–47
Council of Ministers, 28–30, 51–52, 80, 172, 175–77, 180
courts, 37, 117–18, 123–25, 164
crime inside the Gulag, 58, 73–74, 83–84, 86–92, 105–13, 135, 153, 165. *See also* gangs
crime outside the Gulag, 6–9, 23–24, 52–53, 70, 140–41, 156, 201
criminology, 6–7, 9–10, 138–40, 171–72, 183–85. *See also* humaneness; "progressive" system; reeducation; retribution; "socialist legality"
cultural programs, 47, 69, 81–82, 151, 165

Dagestan, 114
Dal'lag. *See* Dal'nyi Corrective-Labor Camp
Dal'nyi Corrective-Labor Camp, 63
Dal'stroi. *See* Far Northern Construction Trust
deconvoying of prisoners, 88–90, 109–13, 135, 152–54, 169
de-Stalinization, 4, 22, 27, 57, 158–59, 174
detachments (*otriady*), 84–85, 118, 122, 126–27, 137, 185–88, 190–91, 199
Dobson, Miriam, 10, 131, 140, 148
Dolgikh, I. I., 25, 33, 35

CPSIA information can be obtained
at www.ICGtesting.com
Printed in the USA
LVOW12*2155150418

573478LV00005BA/135/P